Banking in China (1890s–1940s)

From the 1890s to the 1940s, French State and entrepreneurial companies were enticed to promote French interests, beyond mere colonial targets, for the sake of economic patriotism. Chinese concessions, not including Hong Kong, were thus inserted into geo-economic moves, and French stakeholders asserted their philosophy of competition and displayed their means of influence and investment. In this book, the author assesses the challenges which confronted French actors in the face of powerful British imperial action overseas, all the more so because German Belgian, Japanese, and then also North-American competitors joined the fray.

The book targets three concessions: Canton/Guangzhou, Tientsin/Tianjin, and Hankeou/Wuhan because of their significance in the emergence of a modern economy in the country. The three main sections of the book explore the position of French stakeholders, mainly businesspeople, merchant houses, bankers, and a few industrialists, in these three port-cities and China overall. The chapters gauge their capital of influence and networking, commercial tools, and banking skills in the face of competition and the hardships of dealing with the changes in economic productive systems or clusters in the various port-cities and their areas, rich with commercial offshoots. Also, several chapters underscore the uncertainties caused by geopolitical and military events in China. For each of the three concessions, commercial and banking systems, the assessments of the successes and limits of the French bankers and merchants are investigated, with the aim of evaluating the reality of French entrepreneurialism and power in the regions prospected by the offshoots of French capitalism.

The book will be an invaluable resource for academics interested in the history of banking and finance, business, entrepreneurship, colonialism and "economic patriotism" in Chinese history, in geo-economics and in connected history.

Hubert Bonin is a researcher in modern economic history at Sciences Po Bordeaux and at the GREThA research centre at Bordeaux University. His fields are banking history, business history, economic history of World War I, business and banking in the French concessions in China, Bordeaux wine history and maritime logistics history.

Banking, Money and International Finance

Frontier Capital Markets and Investment Banking
Principles and Practice from Nigeria
Temitope W. Oshikoya and Kehinde Durosinmi-Etti

French Banking and Entrepreneurialism in China and Hong Kong
From the 1850s to 1980s
Hubert Bonin

Banking, Lending and Real Estate
Claudio Scardovi and Alessia Bezzecchi

The Regulation of Financial Planning in Australia
Current Practice, Issues and Empirical Analysis
Angelique Nadia Sweetman McInnes

Financial Risk Management in Banking
Evidence from Asia Pacific
Shahsuzan Zakaria and Sardar M. N. Islam

The Economics of Financial Cooperatives
Income Distribution, Political Economy and Regulation
Amr Khafagy

Financial Integration in the European Monetary Union
Sławomir Ireneusz Bukowski

Banking in China (1890s–1940s)
Business in the French Concessions
Hubert Bonin

For more information about this the series, please visit www.routledge.com/series/BMIF

Banking in China (1890s–1940s)

Business in the French Concessions

Hubert Bonin

LONDON AND NEW YORK

First published 2020
by Routledge
2 Park Square, Milton Park, Abingdon, Oxon OX14 4RN

and by Routledge
605 Third Avenue, New York, NY 10017

First issued in paperback 2021

Routledge is an imprint of the Taylor & Francis Group, an informa business

© 2020 Hubert Bonin

The right of Hubert Bonin to be identified as author of this work has been asserted by him in accordance with sections 77 and 78 of the Copyright, Designs and Patents Act 1988.

Publisher's Note
The publisher has gone to great lengths to ensure the quality of this reprint but points out that some imperfections in the original copies may be apparent.

British Library Cataloguing-in-Publication Data
A catalogue record for this book is available from the British Library

Library of Congress Cataloging-in-Publication Data
A catalog record for this book has been requested

ISBN 13: 978-1-03-223684-1 (pbk)
ISBN 13: 978-0-367-46657-2 (hbk)

Typeset in Bembo
by Apex CoVantage, LLC

Contents

Acknowledgements   xiv
List of tables   xv
Previous works by the author   xx

PART I
Issues   1

Introduction   3

1   **Launching business offensives in China**   6
     1. Issues of economic patriotism and balance of trade power 6
     2. The emergence of a French banking strategy in China 7
     3. Banque de l'Indochine *as a leverage force in favour
        of economic patriotism 8*

PART II
Years of expansion in French concessions (1900s–1920s)   13

2   **French business and banking in Guangzhou
     port-city (1900s–1920s): from an offshoot
     to embeddedness**   15
     1. The issue of a breakthrough into the Guandgong cluster 16
     *2. The Guangzhou bridgehead (1902–1918): from a
        function of support to a community of business 17*
        A. The emergence of a Guangdong cluster 18
        B. A leveraging force at the service of the silk trade 19
        C. Financing general activities 21

3 Tianjin as a seductive port-city for French business at the start of the twentieth century   26

1. *The institutional background 26*
   A. *Imperialism versus nationalism (1899–1902) 26*
   B. *Some later tensions 28*
   C. *Local authorities relying on* Banque de l'Indochine *28*
2. *The emergence of the Tianjin port-city and business hub 28*
   A. *The issue of currencies 29*
   B. *The take-off of the port-city 29*
   C. *Developing banking business in Tianjin 29*
   D. *The issue of the commercial harbour 31*
3. *Tianjin as a port-city for the French community of interests 32*
   A. *Taking part in a few basic investments 32*
   B. *Religious missions as stakeholders in the local economy 33*
Conclusion: facing competition successfully 33

4 Tianjin as a leverage to internationalised markets and to Chinese connections   36

1. Banque de l'Indochine *confronted with nationalist eruption and political conflicts (1911–1913) 36*
2. *The growing importance of business with foreign houses 37*
   A. *The prosperity of* FOREX *37*
   B. *Financing trading houses 38*
   C. *Even investment banking? 39*
3. Banque de l'Indochine *as a local bank for Chinese in Tianjin 39*
   A. Banque de l'Indochine *embedded in Tianjin 40*
   B. *The comprador's business before World War I 40*
4. *The results of a steadfast banking strategy in Tianjin in the 1910s 42*

5 French trade and banking footholds in Wuhan: challenging British hegemony up the Yangtze (1903–1914)   45

1. *How important was it to be embedded in Wuhan? 46*
2. *Wuhan: towards an "open" economy 46*
3. *Which local resources to feed exchanges? 47*
   A. *Rural resources 47*
   B. *Black tea 48*
4. *Little flows of imports 49*
5. *Competition as elsewhere 49*

**6   Wuhan banking between economic patriotism and
     overall business**   53

  1. Banque de l'Indochine *at the core of French business in
     Wuhan 53*
     A. *A new business community 53*
     B. *Human and financial resources 54*
  2. *A dynamic strategy: the French offensive in the Wuhan region 54*
     A. *Trade finance and commercial banking 55*
     B. *Advances without formal collaterals 55*
     C. *FOREX operations 56*
  3. *Widening the customer base 58*
     A. *Belgian customers 59*
     B. *Native prospects 60*
  4. *Credit to import/export houses 61*
     A. *German trading houses 61*
     B. *British trading houses 61*

**7   *Banque de l'Indochine*'s breakthrough in Wuhan
     (in the 1900s–1910s)**   65

  1. *Privileged French customers 65*
  2. *Hurdles on the path of expansion 67*
     A. *The effects of the general crisis of 1907 67*
     B. *Local worries in the first semester of 1910 67*
     C. *The effects of the Wuchang Uprising (1911) 67*
  3. *Was it worth investing in the Wuhan market? 68*
     A. Banque de l'Indochine *stirring fresh competition 68*
     B. *A sustainable offshoot 69*
  4. *A piece within a large jigsaw puzzle 70*

PART III
**The rebirth of business in the French concessions in
the 1920s**   75

**8   A community of business interests resisting civil war
     in Guangzhou**   77

  1. Banque de l'Indochine *as a gate to the Guangzhou
     marketplace 77*
  2. *Crisis looming over the port-city at the beginning of the
     1920s 81*
     A. *The dire post-war recession 82*
     B. *The effects of civil war and disorder 83*
     C. *Disappointment about Chinese business 84*

9   The rebirth of the Guangzhou port cluster   86

   1. The return of prosperity: a first apex of Guangzhou port-city 86

   2. The Banque de l'Indochine *branch's triumph in silk trade
   banking 88*

   3. New scope for silk trading: a port-city on two international legs 92

   4. Guangzhou as a regional platform 96

   5. Guangzhou and Hong Kong: sister port-cities 97

   6. Assessing the niche strategy of Banque de l'Indochine *97*

   7. Guangzhou harbour and banking into "proto-globalisation" 101

**10 *Banque de l'Indochine* in the Tianjin marketplace
   in the 1920s**   105

   1. Competition as a background 105

   2. Catholic missions reinforcing the French basis 106

   3. Promoting a portfolio of banking skills 107

     A. Entertaining the foreign exchange specialty 107

     B. Commercial banking enhanced 107

     C. Olivier as a close client of Banque de l'Indochine *107*

     D. An internationalised marketplace 109

     E. The comprador business after World War I 109

   4. Big business for French industrialists? 110

   5. The Manchurian French dream from the Tianjin city-port 111

   6. Business despite uncertainties in the 1920s 112

11 The effects of World War I on the Wuhan branch   118

   1. The issue of German business 118

   2. The issue of cash 119

   3. The issue of European war 120

   4. Risks due to regional civil wars 120

   5. Hardships for the Wuhan branch 121

     A. The quasi-paralysis of the Wuhan branch (1917–1920) 122

     B. The branch manager challenged 123

   6. Misfits and disappointment (1916–1920) 125

**12 A turbulent environment for the Wuhan
   marketplace in the 1920s**   127

   1. The Wuhan marketplace: appeal versus tensions 127

     A. Wuhan, a highly attractive marketplace 127

     B. A fragile environment 129

     *C. Business hampered by internal tensions in China
      (until 1925) 129*

D. *Wuhan at the heart of political struggles in 1926* 131

E. *Testing times in Wuhan with the war of the factions
(1927–1929)* 132

2. *Fierce inter-banking competition* 133

13 **The Wuhan branch serving French and foreign companies** 137

1. *The difficult job of rebuilding commercial banking
(1920–1922)* 137

A. *A tough period dealing with the legacy of the war years* 137

B. *Uncertain profitability (1920–1922)* 139

2. *The power of foreign exchange business* 140

3. Banque de l'Indochine *promoting French interests in
Wuhan* 142

A. Banque de l'Indochine *within the French community* 142

B. *A larger French clientele* 143

4. *Discount business thriving* 145

14 **Corporate banking flourishes in Wuhan in the 1920s** 152

1. *Active support for international trade* 152

A. *The key role of advances on bills* 152

B. *A branch with an international outlook* 154

2. *Financing flows of Chinese mining products* 156

3. Banque de l'Indochine *supporting import flows* 157

4. *The pace of growth of the* Banque de l'Indochine *branch* 159

A. *Strengthening and diversification of the client base
(1922–1925)* 159

B. *Enduring a slowdown (1926–1928)* 160

C. *A lacklustre year for French banking in Wuhan in 1929* 162

Conclusion 166

PART IV

Facing crisis and wars in the 1930s 169

15 **French business and banking in the port-city
of Guangzhou in the 1930s** 171

1. *French businessmen and bankers caught in a worrying
environment* 172

A. *Guangzhou gathering momentum as a modernised city* 172

B. *Power struggles in Guangdong* 173

C. *The effects of the Sino-Japanese war* 174

2. New business opportunities 176
  A. Financing the armaments trade 176
  B. Contributing to the modernisation of South China? 179
  C. Financing fresh exports of wolfram ore 179

16 *Banque de l'Indochine* facing the crisis in Guangzhou in
   the 1930s   182
  1. The Guangzhou market hurt by the widespread economic
     crisis 182
  2. The silk business stricken by the crisis 184
  3. Growing competition from Japanese trade houses 189
  4. The import trade shattered 190
  5. The intensification of the crisis 190

17 Positive reactions to the crisis in Guangzhou   194
  1. Competition and risk management 194
  2. Still a profitable branch? 196
  3. Banque de l'Indochine *still more as a bank rooted in
     Guangzhou 197*
  4. Success despite the crisis 200
    A. Facing the demand for change 200
    B. The crisis as a "stress test" for the Banque de l'Indochine
       branch 200
  5. The Banque de l'Indochine's *branch and Guangzhou port-city
     life 201*

18 Classic business at stake in Guangzhou in the 1930s   204
  1. General considerations about Guangzhou exchanges 204
  2. The evolution of American outlets 204
  3. The evolution of the silk trade 209
  4. A new silk connection: Indochina involved 215
  5. FOREX operations as a key activity 217
  6. A diversified niche 218
    A. The dependence on Paris allocations 218
    B. The intermediation of the comprador 220
    C. Diversification at stake 221

19 Tianjin through issues of geopolitics
   (mid-1930s–mid-1940s)   225
  1. A troubled environment for business: Tianjin and Japanese inflows
     (1935–1937) 226

2. *Tianjin business during the Sino-Japanese war*
(1937–1941) 228
A. *Tianjin taking profit from its position 228*
B. *The concessions between autonomy and the Japanese order 230*
C. *Confusion about currencies 232*

20 **Geopolitics versus banking and business in Tianjin**　　　　235
1. *The ultimate apex of a micro-business world 235*
A. *The Mission still a key actor of the French concession 235*
B. *The concession as a conservatoire of French*
entrepreneurship? 236
2. Banque de l'Indochine *as a banking flagship amid foreign and*
Chinese competition 239
3. Banque de l'Indochine *practicing business in Tianjin, between*
hardships and stable clients 242
A. *Banking skills in risk management at stake 242*
B. *Olivier still a close companion 247*
C. *Narrow paths for business 248*
3. *Managing treasuries as a challenge 249*

21 **The Tianjin marketplace struggling against ordeals**
(1939–1945)　　　　252
1. *Free trade at stake 252*
2. *A dwindling marketplace at the start of the 1940s 253*
3. *The French concession through dire ordeals 256*
4. *Tianjin through total war and the Japanese order*
(1941–1945) 257
5. *From storytelling to assessment: Tianjin as a case study 258*

22 **French companies in Wuhan facing competition, crises**
and wars in the 1930s　　　　263
1. *Crises cut off Wuhan's lifeblood 263*
A. *The effects of the global economic crisis on the Wuhan*
market 263
B. *The Wuhan marketplace once again the scene of military*
tensions 264
2. *A need for extreme prudence 267*
3. *Economic patriotism weakened 270*
A. *French interests in decline 270*
B. *A branch with close links to the French community 272*
C. *Olivier, still a special client of the* Banque de l'Indochine
branch 273
D. *The downturn in business in francs 275*

23 **The resilience of the *Banque de l'Indochine* branch
    in Wuhan (1930–1939)**   278
    *1. The erosion of trade in the Wuhan marketplace
    (1930–1936) 278*
    A. A kind of final flourish? 278
    B. The erosion of Wuhan's role in international trade 279
    C. A spirit of initiative to fend off the competition 280
    2. A steady downturn between 1937 and 1939 282
    3. The resilience of the Banque de l'Indochine *branch despite its
    faraway location 283*
    A. A mixed pool of funds 283
    B. A sensible balance between activities 283
    C. A decline in profitability 287
    *4. The end of a chapter of banking and business history
    overseas 287*

PART V
From conclusions to broader issues   295

24 **The Asian scope of French business and banking
    (1890s–1940s)**   297
    1. The emergence of a French banking strategy in China 298
    2. From imperialism to economic patriotism 302
    3. Managing trade between Indochina and China 303

25 **French bankers and economic patriotism
    in the Chinese port-cities (1890s–1930s)**   310
    1. A growing concern: supporting French exports to China 310
    A. Capital goods at stake 311
    B. Armaments at stake 313
    *2. The French government supporting the import of Chinese
    products 315*
    A. Banque de l'Indochine *as the banker for the silk trade 316*
    B. Banque de l'Indochine *as a companion to French trading
    houses 317*
    3. Regaining decisive roles for financing international trade 319
    A. Participating in intercontinental FOREX *and payment flows 320*
    *B. New scope for silk trading: Guangzhou on two international
    legs 320*

26 Was the strategy of economic patriotism successful?
From an imperial bank to an international bank? 324
1. *Internationalised economic patriotism 325*
2. *French communities of interests involved in emerging China 325*
3. *Business in China confronted with alternate history 326*
4. *Portfolios of skills and capital of competence 328*
    A. *Management history at stake 328*
    B. *A capital of cultural connections 329*
5. *Issues of business and connected history 331*

Name index 336
Subject index 339

Acknowledgements

- The first leverage force was to be found in the use of the archives of *Banque de l'Indochine*—kept within the *Banque de l'Indochine* fund at the Historical Archives of *Crédit agricole* SA—because the latter bank absorbed Indosuez Bank in 1996–1997, which itself had succeeded to *Banque de l'Indochine* in 1975. I therefore thank their (past) boss Roger Nougaret (and his assistant Annie Deu-Fillon) for easing our access to such records. Thereafter I met with equal welcoming and efficient services from their successors, Anne Brunterch and then Pascal Pénot, for specialised records to complement my studies.
- A few successive academic research programs endorsed my research programs about China and helped to finance my travels to attend international conferences and workshops about Far Eastern business and banking history—for instance, in Japan, Hong Kong and Tianjin. I could there find stimulation to develop my research and moreover opportunities to broaden my scope and to debate with specialised colleagues.
- These research programs were financed mainly by the Aquitaine Region, committed to sustain specialists working at Bordeaux University in human sciences and thus business and economic history in order to enhance the ranking and reputation of its academic standing.
- Sciences Po Bordeaux and the French State provided me with ten years of a special "excellence bonus" to help me to attend archives centres and conference workshops.
- The archivists of the Archives of Foreign Affairs in Nantes (for the Consulates archives), of *Société générale* and BNP Paribas (for *Comptoir national d'escompte de Paris*), also contributed to my investigations.
- *Crédit agricole SA* financed the translation of five chapters of this book in 2018 (thanks to Pascal Pénot's intermediary).
- The Routledge publisher (and Pickering & Chatto beforehand) had already welcomed three books, the first two in its Banking, Money & International Finance series (*Asian Imperial Banking History*, 2015; *Colonial and Imperial Banking History*, 2016 and 2018) and the third one, *French Banking and Entrepreneurialism in China and Hong Kong: Banking, Money and International Finance (1890s–1990s)* in 2019: this propped up this further offensive in the history of French business abroad, along the methods and prospects of "connected history".

Tables

3.1 Exchanges through Tianjin as assessed by *Banque de l'Indochine* branch in 1903–1906   28

3.2 Overdraft facilities provided by the Paris head office to the Tianjin branch on 10 October 1907   30

4.1 FOREX position of the *Banque de l'Indochine* branch in 1908   38

4.2 Credits from the *Banque de l'Indochine* branch on 10 October 1907   38

4.3 Locking up of funds with the salt gabelle system on 1 April 1911   41

4.4 Returns of the main *Banque de l'Indochine* branches at end of the 1910s   42

5.1 Exports of rural commodities through Wuhan in the first half of 1911   47

5.2 The major trading houses in Wuhan for the export of rural commodities in 1908   48

5.3 The leading commodities exported from Wuhan in 1915   48

5.4 Exports of tea from Wuhan in 1908   49

5.5 Current accounts by banks in Wuhan at the end of June 1907   50

6.1 Amount of overdrafts on unpledged goods from the branch of Wuhan in 1905–1912   56

6.2 Major customers of the *Banque de l'Indochine* branch in Wuhan for advances on bills to be delivered in 1912   57

7.1 Breakdown of credit amounts of advances on bills to be delivered at the *Banque de l'Indochine*'s Wuhan branch in May 1916   66

7.2 Part of *Banque de l'Indochine* in the financing of exports from Wuhan in 1909–1915   69

7.3 Profits and losses of the *Banque de l'Indochine*'s Wuhan branch in 1904–1914   70

7.4 Returns of the major *Banque de l'Indochine* branches in the first semester 1916   71

8.1 Returns of the *Banque de l'Indochine*'s main branches at the turn of the 1920s   81

9.1   Advances on silk balls by the *Banque de l'Indochine's*
      Guangzhou branch in 1926–1930   88
9.2   Status of advances on goods by the *Banque de l'Indochine*
      branch in Guangzhou on 30 May 1923   89
9.3   Amount of silk commercial paper purchased by the *Banque
      de l'Indochine's* Guangzhou branch to each merchant house
      connected to the Lyon market in 1928–1929   90
9.4   Guangzhou exports of raw silk balls in 1926–1929   91
9.5   Guangzhou from a mere China–Europe port-city to a
      trans-Pacific one in 1928–1929   93
9.6   *Banque de l'Indochine's* participation in the financing of
      Guangzhou silk exports in 1925   95
9.7   Position of the *Banque de l'Indochine's* main Chinese branches
      in the first term of 1930   99
9.8   Growth of the *Banque de l'Indochine's* Guangzhou branch in
      1926–1929   100
10.1 A few important French trade houses in Tianjin at the end of
      the 1920s   108
10.2 Situation of the *Banque de l'Indochine* branch of Tianjin on 31
      December 1928   114
10.3 Position of the main Chinese branches of *Banque de
      l'Indochine* during the first term of 1930   115
11.1 Total operations by the *Banque de l'Indochine* Wuhan branch
      in 1914–1917   120
11.2 Dwindling operations at the *Banque de l'Indochine* Wuhan
      branch in 1916–1919   121
11.3 Amortisation of bad debts by the *Banque de l'Indochine*
      branch in Wuhan in 1918   122
11.4 Profits and losses of the *Banque de l'Indochine's* Wuhan branch
      in 1904–1920   124
11.5 Returns of the branch of Wuhan in comparison with the
      major *Banque de l'Indochine* branches at the turn of the 1920s   125
12.1 Port rankings by maritime customs receipts in 1923–1925   128
12.2 Maritime customs receipts in some ports in 1923–1925   128
13.1 Situation of the Wuhan branch of *Banque de l'Indochine* in the
      early 1920s   141
13.2 Purchases of commercial paper on one to four months' sight
      by the Wuhan branch of *Banque de l'Indochine* in 1921–1922   147
13.3 Transactions involving remittances of commercial paper
      ("gold" applications) at the Wuhan branch of *Banque de
      l'Indochine* in 1924–1925   148
13.4 Transactions involving remittances of commercial paper by
      the Wuhan branch of *Banque de l'Indochine* in the mid-1920s   148
13.5 Transactions involving purchases of commercial paper at the
      Wuhan branch of *Banque de l'Indochine* in 1926–1928   148

13.6	Commercial transactions of the Wuhan branch of *Banque de l'Indochine*: negotiated "gold" remittances in 1923–1925	149
14.1	Overseas exports of some regional products from Wuhan in 1928	154
14.2	Imports into Wuhan in 1926–1928	157
14.3	Current loans outstanding by *Banque de l'Indochine* in Wuhan in 1922–1923	159
14.4	Debit accounts of the *Banque de l'Indochine* branch in Wuhan in 1925–1926	160
14.5	Core operations of the Wuhan branch of *Banque de l'Indochine* in 1924–1929	164
14.6	Accounts of the *Banque de l'Indochine* branch in 1924–1929	165
15.1	Vessels having entered and cleared at the Guangzhou port in 1933–1934	172
16.1	Silk trade in Guangzhou in the 1930s	185
16.2	Breakdown of the remittances of bills managed by the *Banque de l'Indochine*'s branch	187
16.3	Silk exports from Guangzhou in 1930–1935	188
16.4	Advances on silk by the *Banque de l'Indochine* branch in Guangzhou in 1927–1935	189
16.5	Amount of negotiations of commercial remittances by the Guangzhou *Banque de l'Indochine* branch in 1932–1936	190
16.6	Financial position of the *Banque de l'Indochine*'s branch in Guangzhou at the end of June 1931	191
17.1	Breakdown of the 16 million in bills of exchange (francs and pounds) negotiated by the *Banque de l'Indochine*'s Guangzhou branch during the first half of 1932	196
17.2	Results from operations by the *Banque de l'Indochine* branch in Guangzhou in the 1930s	198
17.3	Data about specialised operations by the *Banque de l'Indochine* branch in Guangzhou in the 1930s	199
18.1	Hints about Guangzhou trade in 1929–1931	205
18.2	Guangzhou trade: Exports in 1930–1932	205
18.3	Guangzhou trade: Imports in 1930–1932	206
18.4	International trade of the Guangzhou port-city in 1930–1931	206
18.5	Main sellers of remittances in USD in 1930–1934 (companies trading from Guangzhou to the United States and transferring their risk to the *Banque de l'Indochine*)	207
18.6	Main sellers of remittances in FRF (companies trading from Guangzhou to Lyon/Paris and transferring their risk to the *Banque de l'Indochine*) in 1930–1934	210
18.7	Main sellers of remittances in British pounds (companies trading from Guangzhou to the City and transferring their risk to the *Banque de l'Indochine*) in 1930–1934	212
18.8	Advances on goods by the *Banque de l'Indochine* branch in Guangzhou on 17 July 1930	213

18.9   Advances on goods by the *Banque de l'Indochine*'s branch
        (HK$): situation at the end of 1931   213
18.10   Advances granted through the intermediary of the
        comprador in 1932–1933   213
18.11   Silk dispatches from Guangdong during the export campaign
        of 1935/36   216
18.12   FOREX operations completed by the *Banque de l'Indochine*
        branch in Guangzhou in 1930–1934   219
18.13   Results from arbitrage operations by the *Banque de
        l'Indochine*'s Guangzhou branch in the 1930s   220
18.14   Use of resources by the *Banque de l'Indochine*'s branch in
        Guangzhou in 1929–1934   222
19.1   Exports from Tianjin in 1936   226
19.2   Ships reaching Tianjin and Tsingtao harbours in 1937–1938   229
19.3   Banknotes circulated in northern China in March 1938   232
20.1   Sales of electric power in Tianjin in 1937   236
20.2   Breakdown of *Banque de l'Indochine* branch operations on
        bills remitted against documentary credits in 1939   237
20.3   Estimates of the origins of a few imports in Tianjin in 1935   238
20.4   Main trading houses and merchants in Tianjin in
        the mid-1930s   239
20.5   Situation of the *Banque de l'Indochine* branch of Tianjin in
        1939–1941   241
20.6   Interests and commissions earned by the *Banque de l'Indochine*
        branch in Tianjin in 1939–1941   243
20.7   Returns of the *Banque de l'Indochine* branch in Tianjin
        in 1938–1941   244
20.8   Trade completed by *Olivier-Chine*'s branch in Tianjin at the
        end of the 1930s   248
20.9   Treasury operations in currencies by the *Banque de l'Indochine*
        branch in Tianjin in 1938–1941   249
21.1   Evolution of Tianjin trade in 1937–1938   253
21.2   Dwindling operations of *Banque de l'Indochine* in Tianjin in
        1941–1944   259
22.1   Volume of exports handled by Wuhan in the 1930s   267
22.2   France's share of foreign exports from Wuhan in 1931   271
22.3   French market share by volume of exports from Wuhan in
        the second half of 1936   272
22.4   Outstanding advances to client firms from *Banque de
        l'Indochine* in Wuhan in June 1936   275
23.1   Wuhan branch funds in 1929–1934   284
23.2   Funds of the Wuhan branch of *Banque de l'Indochine*
        in 1935–1936   284
23.3   Business of the Wuhan branch of *Banque de l'Indochine* in
        1929–1934   285

23.4 Balance of the discount and arbitrage transactions of the Wuhan branch of *Banque de l'Indochine* in 1929–1934 — 286

23.5 Foreign exchange transactions of *Banque de l'Indochine* in Wuhan in 1935–1939 — 288

23.6 Assets of the Wuhan branch of *Banque de l'Indochine* in the second half of the 1930s — 288

23.7 Profitability of *Banque de l'Indochine*'s Wuhan branch in the first half of the 1930s — 289

23.8 Profits of *Banque de l'Indochine*'s Wuhan branch in 1935–1939 — 290

23.9 Return on capital employed at the Wuhan branch of *Banque de l'Indochine* in 1935–1936 — 291

24.1 Trade between China and Indochina — 303

24.2 International trade of the Guangzhou port-city — 304

24.3 Share of Saigon exports as part of exports to Hong Kong in 1905–1924 — 305

24.4 Rice flows at Hong Kong hub in April–October 1930 — 305

24.5 Rice export from Indochina in 1929–1939 — 306

24.6 Indochina's commercial partners in 1924 — 306

25.1 France's major Asian commercial partners in 1913 — 319

25.2 Exports from Tianjin in 1936 — 319

25.3 Guangzhou from merely a Chinese-European port-city to a trans-Pacific hub in 1928–1929 — 321

Previous works by the author

Hubert Bonin's publications on economic Asian history:

French Banking and Entrepreneurialism in China and Hong Kong, from the 1850s to 1980s, Abingdon, Routledge, 2019, "Banking, Money & International Finance".

Colonial and Imperial Banking History, with Nuno Valerio (eds.), Abingdon, Routledge, 2016, "Banking, Money & International Finance" (reedited, paperback, 2018).

Asian Imperial Banking History, with Nuno Valerio & Kazuhiko Yago (eds.), Abingdon, Pickering & Chatto/Routledge, 2015, "Banking, Money & International Finance".

"Le lotus noir: le combat contre la fraude et la ruse dans les concessions françaises en Chine (années 1890–années 1940)", in Marguerite Figeac-Monthus & Christophe Lastécouères (eds.), *Territoires de l'illicite: Ports et îles. De la fraude au contrôle (XVIe-XXe siècles)*, Paris, Armand Colin, 2012, pp. 203–220, "Recherches".

"French banking in Hong Kong: From the 1860s to the 1950s", in Shizuya Nishimura, Toshio Suzuki & Ranald Michie (eds.), *The Origins of International Banking in Asia: The Nineteenth and Twentieth Centuries*, Oxford, Oxford University Press, 2012, pp. 124–144.

"Les banquiers français en Chine (1860–1950): Shanghai et Hong Kong, relais d'un impérialisme bancaire ou plates-formes d'outre-mers multiformes?", in Laurent Cesari & Denis Varaschin (eds.), *Les relations franco-chinoises au vingtième siècle et leurs antécédents*, Arras, Artois Presses Université, 2003, pp. 157–172.

"Les banquiers français à Shanghai dans les années 1860–1940", in *Le Paris de l'Orient. Présence française à Shanghai, 1849–1946*, Boulogne-sur-Seine, Albert Kahn Museum, 2002, pp. 113–119.

"L'activité des banques françaises dans l'Asie du Pacifique des années 1860 aux années 1940", *Revue française d'histoire d'outre-mer*, 1994, 81(305), pp. 401–425.

La Société générale en Russie (Histoire des activités financières et bancaires de la Société générale en Russie dans les années 1880–1917), Paris, "La collection historique de la Société générale", 1994 (published in French and Russian; reedited in 2005).

"The French banks in the Pacific area (1860–1945)", in Olive Checkland, Shizuya Nishimura & Norio Tamaki (eds.), *Pacific Banking (1859–1959): East Meets West* (proceedings of a Tokyo conference in 1993), London, MacMillan, and New York, St. Martin's Press, 1994, pp. 61–74.

"Le Comptoir national d'escompte de Paris, une banque impériale (1848-1940)", *Revue française d'histoire d'outre-mer*, 1991, 78(293), pp. 477–497.

Part I
Issues

Introduction

This little introduction aims only at specifying the progress of my searches directed towards the relations between the banking place of Paris and the economic area of China and the China Sea, against the backgrounds of the relations with that area of the Pacific Ocean. Indeed, the first chapter of this book is devoted to presenting the key stakes which were considered here.

The prevailing theme for every banking historian has been to ponder the weight of the radiation[1] and of the competitiveness of the Parisian financial and banking marketplace[2] before the advent of the powerful City and of its European competitors, regarding operations in Europe, in North America (before the breakthrough of the New York marketplace, becoming powerful after the World War I), in the colonial sectors, in the activities centred on Central and Eastern Europe (in particular Russia until 1918, then in the states that succeeded the Empire), in Latin America, and finally in Asia, at first in Japan, then more and more so in China and Hong Kong. To study the activity of the French banks in China provides a tool to measure the fighting spirit and talent at the heart of this arena of competition. The overall geopolitics of banking or geo-economics will therefore benefit from such a focused survey.[3]

The second research project is aimed at appreciating the entrepreneurial spirit, the initiatives of banks and companies and the reactivity of French capitalism before new spaces for expansion opened in Asia, in addition to Indochina. China was generally an attractive territory for capitalist and trade penetration in the light of French economic patriotism.[4] Certainly, a few French companies worked in India, but this country became more or less a private British ground. From port-cities like Hong Kong and from foreign concessions, granted and strengthened in the years 1840–1860, decisive opportunities offered themselves to multiform economic imperialism.

This research program is centred on the concessions gained on the basis of abstract and methodological approaches, which had already matured, by studying the portfolio of skills and the relational networks of merchant banks[5] and certain big banks. It was prepared with my participation in several conferences or in workshops of international congresses. It helped me build a toolbox to consider, with acuteness, aspects of the colonial and imperial banks[6] and of the active banks in Asia itself,[7] in general[8] or in Hong Kong,[9] for instance.

Through its three case studies about the French concessions in Guangzhou, Wuhan and Tianjin, my research program took a new step from the overall "imperial" spreading out and from the Asian-wide scope of business to targeted assessments of French economic power in a few offshoot locations acting as gateways to the Chinese import–export markets. The historian's path has to patiently follow these stages to develop his or her investigations step by step, and the Routledge series' welcoming of this new book offers a relevant opportunity to achieve such progress.

These searches have drawn on colleagues' numerous works, cited in the references of chapters, in the course of the book. They also benefited from the enormous files of the archives of the *Banque de l'Indochine*, as kept in the archives of the group *Crédit agricole* and complemented by the files of other banks (*Crédit lyonnais*, also within the archives of *Crédit agricole*; *Comptoir national d'escompte de Paris*, today within the archives of BNP Paribas; *Société générale, Banque de l'union parisienne*, both at the *Société générale* archives) and by those of the archives of the Ministry of Foreign Affairs, in particular for certain consulates.

Thus this book aims to be a fellow traveller with the rich works already published in Japan, in Hong Kong and in the Anglo-American world—whilst waiting for the breakthrough works of Chinese colleagues themselves. The book is focused on only a few concessions (Guangzhou/Canton, Hankeou/Wuhan and Tianjin/Tientsin) because the concession of Kwong Chou Wan/Kouang-Tchéou-Wan/Fort-Boyard depended directly on the Indochina authorities and because the concession of Shanghai deserves a dedicated book of its own,[10] thanks to the huge volume of archives.

Notes

1 Hubert Bonin, "Le rayonnement international des banques françaises (1900–1940): essai d'évaluation", in Maurice Lévy-Leboyer (ed.), *L'économie française dans la compétition internationale*, Paris, Cheff, 2006, pp. 117–143. Hubert Bonin, "The international factors in the development of the French banking system", in Rondo Cameron & Valery Bovykin (eds.), *International Banking & Industrial Finance, 1870–1914*, Oxford, Oxford University Press, 1992. Hubert Bonin, "Europeanized French bankers? (from the 1830s to the 1970s)", *Business History*, Routledge, October–December 2014, volume 56, n°7–8, pp. 1312–1334. Hubert Bonin, "Des banquiers cosmopolites? Le monde de la banque et les diasporas (des années 1730 aux années 1930)", *Diasporas. Histoire & sociétés*, March 2007, n°9, *Chercher fortune*, pp. 11–31.
2 Hubert Bonin, "The challenged competitiveness of the Paris banking and finance markets, 1914–1958", in Youssef Cassis & Éric Bussière (eds.), *London and Paris as International Financial Centres in the Twentieth Century*, Oxford, Oxford University Press, 2005, pp. 183–204.
3 Hubert Bonin, "Banks and geopolitics: Issues of finance connections", in Joseph Mark Munoz (ed.), *Handbook in the Geopolitics of Business*, Cheltenham, UK & Northampton, US, Edward Elgar, 2013, pp. 125–138. Hubert Bonin, "Geo-economics and banking", in Joseph Mark Munoz (ed.), *Advances in Geoeconomics*, Cheltenham, UK & Northampton, US, Edward Elgar, 2017, pp. 217–226. Hubert Bonin, "La géographie historique de la finance", in Claude Dupuy & Stéphanie Lavigne (eds.), *Géographies de la finance mondialisée*, Paris, La Documentation française, "Les Études", 2009, pp. 19–34.

4 Hubert Bonin "French bankers and economic patriotism in the Chinese port-cities (1880s–1930s)", in Melanie Aspey, Peter Hertner, Krzysztof Kaczmar, Jakub Skiba, Dieter Stiefel & Nuno Valerio (eds.), *Foreign Financial Institutions & National Financial Systems. Studies in Banking & Financial History*, Frankfurt, EABH, 2013, pp. 15–54.

5 Hubert Bonin & Carlo Brambilla (eds.), *Investment Banking History: National and Comparative Issues (19th–21st Centuries)*, Brussels, Peter Lang, "Euroclio: Studies & Documents", 2014.

6 Hubert Bonin & Nuno Valerio (eds.), *Colonial & Imperial Banking History*, Abingdon, Routledge, "Banking, Money & International Finance", 2016 (reedited in paperback in 2018).

7 Hubert Bonin, "The French banks in the Pacific area (1860–1945)", in Olive Checkland, Shizuya Nishimura & Norio Tamaki (eds.), *Pacific Banking (1859–1959): East Meets West*, London, Macmillan; New York, St. Martin's Press, 1994, pp. 61–74. Hubert Bonin, "L'activité des banques françaises dans l'Asie du Pacifique, des années 1860 aux années 1940", *Revue française d'histoire d'outre-mer*, 1994, tome 81, n°305, pp. 401–425. Hubert Bonin, Nuno Valerio & Kazuhiko Yago (eds.), *Asian Imperial Banking History*, Abingdon, Routledge, "Banking, Money & International Finance", 2015.

8 Hubert Bonin, "Les banquiers français en Chine (1860–1950): Shanghai et Hong Kong, relais d'un impérialisme bancaire ou plates-formes d'outre-mers multiformes?", in Laurent Cesari & Denis Varaschin (eds.), *Les relations franco-chinoises au vingtième siècle et leurs antécédents*, Arras, Artois Presses Université, 2003, pp. 157–172. Hubert Bonin, "Les banquiers français à Shanghai dans les années 1860–1940", in *Le Paris de l'Orient. Présence française à Shanghai, 1849–1946*, Boulogne-sur-Seine, Musée Albert Kahn, 2002, pp. 113–119.

9 Hubert Bonin, "French banking in Hong Kong: From the 1860s to the 1950s", in Shizuya Nishimura, Toshio Suzuki & Ranald Michie (eds.), *The Origins of International Banking in Asia: The Nineteenth & Twentieth Centuries*, Oxford, Oxford University Press, 2012, pp. 124–144.

10 Antoine Vannière, *Kouang Tchéou-Wan, colonie clandestine. Un territoire à bail français en Chine du Sud, 1898–1946*, Paris, Les Indes savantes, 2020.

1 Launching business offensives in China

In the South-East Asia area and throughout the Chinese commercial flows, the influence of British or Japanese banks has largely prevailed, by scale and strength over the activities of French banks. They have tried nonetheless to loosen the hold of their competitors in order to play some part in the Asian money markets and to follow the development of commercial exchanges, either those locally expanded, those joining the Pacific places or those linking Asia and Europe. Two axes of action can be defined: (1) supporting trade between the Far East and Europe and (2) propping up the half-political/half-financial penetration in China, especially against the United Kingdom, a penetration which ought to strengthen the dimension and range of the Paris financial place. Chinese port-cities have asserted themselves durably as a somewhat emblematic kind of "cosmopolitan" marketplace, as Pierre Singaravélou has analysed in the circumstances in Tianjin.[1]

1. Issues of economic patriotism and balance of trade power

French banks' competitiveness had to be tested in each commercial and money market all along the Chinese coast open to Western traders and bankers, where they could broaden the scope of their portfolio of skills through the acquisition of the specific commercial and financial know-how required for relations with Chinese customers, Asian traders or European firms active there. This process required, of course, consolidating their ability in mastering the specific risks created by extending their reach into such new business areas against a background of overall competition among foreign firms scrambling to get footholds in the North Chinese and Hebei markets.[2]

In 1924, *Banque de l'Indochine* wrote a thick report about the economic prospects for French business in the Hupeh state,[3] which was then rich with 25 million inhabitants. It could therefore be included within the overall offensive relaunched in China after World War I, even if it was lagging far behind in the main areas to which French business and banking were already committed. All in all, in 1923, the total European, Japanese and American population in China reached a total of 325,000—complemented by 120,000 Russian refugees in Harbin. Along with this report, a force of 661 British trade houses were active in the country, struggling with 409 American ones, 244 German ones (with 2,200 German expatriates) and only 242 French houses, with 3,400 expatriates. And the balance of power was clearly not in favour of French interests: France had tackled only 2 per cent of Chinese foreign trade, the same as Germany (coming out of its war defeat), whilst the United States grappled with 6 per cent, Japan 31 per cent and Great Britain 39 per cent, whereas Chinese trade merchants kept 16 per cent in their grip.

The issue of economic patriotism was thus clear: the French concessions had to be used as leverage forces to broaden the scope of French trade, exports and imports, financing. Guangzhou, Tianjin and Wuhan were placed at the core of such offensives—even if the Shanghai marketplace was a crucial gate to the Chinese market, it will not be scrutinised in this book, except through many allusions thanks to its dense relationship with the other regions.

2. The emergence of a French banking strategy in China

In fact, China had not been the main target of French banks active in Asia because they had first to fuel the business fostered by the development of French firms in Indochina, starting from the 1860s to the 1880s after the two-stage conquest of the peninsula. Then the Indochinese commercial business itself opened the doors of the Hong Kong market (for rice exports). But French traders penetrated more and more Chinese markets to get their high-value materials (silk)[4] and to establish some bridgeheads for exports of consumer goods (textiles, machines, etc.), particularly through Hong Kong and the Guangzhou [Canton] coast, where banks accompanied the move with the opening of branches. A second area became the Centre-West area, joined from Haiphong harbour by the newly completed Yunnan railway reaching the region,[5] which French businessmen dreamed of as a key outlet, able to short circuit the British predominance on the Yangze basin,[6] all the more because of the amplification of commercial relations with the East owing to the opening of the Suez canal[7] in 1869.

A "Chinese strategy" took shape therefore in the 1890s among French diplomats[8] and businessmen, and they longed for a powerful banking arm there, able to alleviate the weight of British trading firms and influence in China[9] and in particular the banking hegemony of Hong Kong & Shanghai Bank (HSBC)[10] and of Chartered. Several banks drew schemes of Asian deployment. But a cooperative spirit prevailed in favour of the building of a sole tool able to challenge British leaders and their competitors from Japan (Yokohama Specie Bank,[11] in charge of financing trade abroad) and Germany (*Deutsch-Asiatisch Bank*, linked to *Deutsche Bank*). In fact, several countries lagging behind British influence conceived such a strategy to promote a single banking firm in charge of representing the interests of its country in China and in the surrounding areas: the *Deutsch-Asiatisch Bank*, the Russian–Chinese Bank (with a few French interests) and the *Banque sino-belge* from Brussels were similar parts of such a scheme.

A first stage of the process was animated by a bank created as early as 1848, *Comptoir d'escompte de Paris*, which had defined a strategy consisting altogether of national growth with the support of traders, especially in the import–export places and the ports, in order to stimulate the business fighting spirit immediately after the conclusion of the free trade treaties.[12] It had decided to settle in Shanghai as soon as 1860 and then seeded about ten branches in the Eastern countries in the 1860s: in Yokohama (1867), in Hong Kong, in Calcutta, Bombay, Madras and Pondicherry, and in Cochinchina. *Comptoir d'escompte de Paris* appeared therefore as "the French Bank" in the Orient, all the more when it strengthened its Chinese settlement in 1886/1887 with the opening of branches in Tianjin, Fou Tcheou and Wuhan, as the prospects of trade there seem interesting. But *Comptoir d'escompte de Paris* faced a huge crisis in Paris in 1889 and collapsed, and its successor, *Comptoir national d'escompte de Paris*, focused its activities eastwards on Egypt, India and Australia.

3. *Banque de l'Indochine* as a leverage force in favour of economic patriotism

The French State was thus committed to enticing bankers to extend operations along the Sea of China, demanding that *Banque de l'Indochine*,[13] which had been the issuing and commercial bank of southern and central Indochina (Cochinchine and Annam) since 1875 and also of northern Indochina (Tonkin) from 1888, to change its strategic scope. In November 1897, it balanced the renewal of its issuing concession in Indochina for 30 years against the deployment of the bank in China and in South-East Asia through the opening of branches. *Banque de l'Indochine* had to bear the French flag in key commercial markets, of course with apriority in Hong Kong, Canton and Shanghai but also in northern China. After only *Banque de Paris & des Pays-Bas*, *Crédit industriel & commercial*, *Comptoir d'escompte de Paris* and *Haute Banque* merchant banks had godfathered the creation of *Banque de l'Indochine* in 1875, the other big Paris deposit banks (*Société générale* in 1887 and *Crédit lyonnais* in 1896) joined the equity and the board of *Banque de l'Indochine* and relied on that latter, as their daughter or their sister bank, to represent the French business community in China along a kind of "coopetition".

> They perceive that the Far East French colonies required an autonomous banking institution, altogether the vanguard and the representative of High Finance in Asia, that gathered the large affairs and transmitted them to its Parisian partners, to which it procured a flow of profitable operations, like the credits issued through acceptances or the exchange operations. Multiplying the banking institutions in Asia would contribute to weaken the French position there in front of the British community that knew remarkably how to mix diplomacy and finance and that have founded strong colonial banks like the Hong Kong & Shanghai Bank or the Chartered.[14]

In the meantime, *Comptoir national d'escompte de Paris*—weakened by the resignation of its German and Swiss managers in Asia who had rejoined British or Germans banks there and by its own crash of 1889 and also shaken by the economic, monetary (with the acute depreciation of silver metal) and military (because of the Sino-Japanese war) in the Far East during the first half of the 1890s—decided to close its Yokohama branch in 1893 and those in Tianjin and Fou Tcheou/Fuzhou in 1899. For some time, the whole banking strategy in China had now to be borne by *Banque de l'Indochine*, which inherited the Hong Kong branch of *Comptoir d'escompte de Paris* 1894 and settled in Shanghai in July 1898 (and further in Singapore in 1905).[15]

The geopolitical circumstances stimulated such a move because China had entered a new series of harsh concessions to "the Powers", having to lease more harbours, to dedicate more tax revenues to the Boxers indemnity as pledges to bonds, and even to welcome troops which guaranteed the completion of the agreements—even if Chinese nationalists denounced them as "unequal agreements". The balance of power was indeed not in favour of the Chinese kingdom, and the installation of *Banque de l'Indochine* in northern cities was in fact part of this "imperialist" system linking geopolitical pressure and business penetration,[16] within the strategy of *"impérialisme à la française"* promoting *"la France impériale"*[17] beyond mere colonial deployment.

At the same time, however, French interests in Asia started being promoted by another bank, *Banque russo-chinoise*,[18] which associated in 1896 with some banks from Paris, with two-thirds of the capital subscribed in France and in Belgium, and with other banks from Russia—especially *Banque internationale de Saint-Petersbourg*—in order to get a share in the development of Manchuria and of northern China, stimulated by the opening of the Trans-Siberian and Trans-Manchurian railroad, for the construction of which *Banque russo-chinoise* constituted *Compagnie des chemins de fer de l'Est chinois* in 1896 (Eastern Chinese Railway).

But the purpose was meanwhile somewhat grander as *Banque russo-chinoise* intended to become the spearhead of the penetration of French and Russian interests in the Chinese regions located north of the Yang Ze Kiang. It recovered the Wuhan and Tianjin branches of *Comptoir national d'escompte de Paris* in 1895 and settled in Beijing in order to work more closely and efficiently with the financial authorities, especially for the loans intended to pay the war indemnity to Japan, other loans and treasury advances. It led thus to the negotiation of the financing of the Shansi Railway in 1902–1903 and negotiated its FRF 40 million bonds in the Paris marketplace. *Banque russo-chinoise* escaped, however, too rapidly from French influence in so far as its German and Russian managers seemed to favour only the Russian interests and did not promote any French bank business with the Chinese State.

Indeed, that latter called on the British and German banks in 1905 when it sought to subscribe the last portion of the indemnity it had to pay to the Powers who intervened during the Boxers war, and this choice aroused strong discontent by the French authorities. *Banque russo-chinoise* ended up competing with *Banque de l'Indochine* in Southern China and opened a branch in

Hong Kong in 1904. This managerial dissent and resultant weakening of the ability of Russian interests to exert strong pressure on China after the military defeat of Russia by Japan in 1905 precluded *Banque russo-chinoise* from playing apart in the great French financial initiative in China. Moreover, when *Banque russo-chinoise* was merged with the Russian *Banque du Nord* into *Banque russo-asiatique*[19] in 1910 and thus rejoined the sphere of influence of French banks (mainly *Société générale*), its successor devoted itself mainly to its Russian and Manchurian business and, in spite of the desires of its managers in China, did not represent any significant strength southwards.

This evolution emphasized the mission of *Banque de l'Indochine*, which outlined a double strategy of reinforcement of its commercial implantation in the south of China and of a breakthrough in the centre and in the north: it thus opened branches in Wuhan and Guangzhou in 1902, in Tianjin on 18 February 1907 and in Beijing in April 1907, just after a change to its statutes in order to adapt them to the practices on the Chinese marketplaces and after an increase of its capital.

Success rapidly crowned this program as these branches, equipped with the comprador system used as an intermediary with the Chinese community, gathered a broad clientele of local traders and bankers for short-term advances in commodities (opium [thanks to the two victorious wars of the first half of the nineteenth century],[20] raw cotton, raw silk, tea), industrial products (cotton and silk fabric) and, depending on location, gold and silver, which explained their profitability. *Banque de l'Indochine*, however, limited its operations to short-term loans, to currency exchange operations and to its participation in issuing securities subscribed abroad, as it refused to let itself become engaged in the construction of a branch network in the Chinese provinces and in the direct financing of local business, then considered as causes of excessively high risks and immobilizations, although the granting of credits to trade houses and even to local bankers implies indeed the indirect financing of indigenous merchants.

Chinese activities provided *Banque de l'Indochine* with 27 per cent of its total operations in 1905 and with 33 per cent[21] in 1910, owing to its advances to local customers; to firms coming from Europe, like the *Compagnie française de tramways & d'éclairage électrique de Shanghai*, companies for public works or building houses, or Franco-Belgian *Crédit foncier d'Extrême-Orient*, owing to the transfers of public money between Indochina and metropolitan France and owing to currency exchange operations); to the trading of remittances and bills, particularly on Shanghai, a place that had become "the heart of the circuits of the *Banque de l'Indochine*, the centre of its network."[22] Beyond that was the clientele of European firms that it had constituted, owing to the 1900 reform of its statutes which allowed it to engage in loans lacking the usual collaterals and credentials, resulting in an outstanding capacity for risk assessment of credit operations with Asian bankers and large merchants.

By their knowledge of the Chinese affairs and their know-how in the exchange techniques that allow them to transfer rapidly the millions subscribed by the French savings or the redemptions of the Chinese government, the agents of *Banque de l'Indochine* brought an organisation and a range of abilities that were necessary to the success of large affairs. We may affirm that never before has "the French Bank" deserved its nickname overseas,[23]

assuming what Michel Bruguière called "flag imperialism", even if from time to time an actual community between French and Belgian (*Banque d'outre-mer, Banque sino-belge,* linked to *Société générale de Belgique*) businessmen[24] was maintained for some of the Chinese financial and railway business.

Notes

1 Pierre Singaravelou, *Tianjin Cosmopolis. Une autre histoire de la mondialisation*, Paris, Seuil, "L'Univers historique", 2017.

2 See Albert Feuerwerker, *The Foreign Establishment in China in the Early Twentieth Century*, Ann Arbor, Center for Chinese Studies, University of Michigan, 1976.

3 Historical Archives, *Crédit agricole,* fund *Banque de l'Indochine,* Wuhan 439AH182 Boîte BVE1047, *rapport-bilan semestriel*, 1st semester 1924, 25 July 1924.

4 Louis Gueneau, *Lyon et le commerce de la soie*, Lyon, L. Bascou, 1932. John Laffey, "Les racines de l'impérialisme français en Extrême-Orient. À propos des thèses de J.-F. Cady", *Revue d'histoire moderne & contemporaine*, April–June 1969. John F. Cady, *The Roots of French Imperialism in Eastern Asia*, Ithaca (New York), Cornell University Press for American Historical Association, 1954. John Laffey, *French Imperialism and the Lyon Mission to China*, Cornell University, 1966. Claude Fivel-Démorel, "The Hong Kong & Shanghai bank in Lyon, 1881–1954. Busy, but too discreet", in Frank King (ed.), *Eastern Banking*, London, Athlone, 1983, pp. 467–516. Henri Brenier, *La mission lyonnaise d'exploration commerciale en Chine, 1895–1897*, Lyon, Alexandre Rey, 1898.

5 Michel Bruguière, "Le chemin de fer du Yunnan. Paul Doumer et la politique d'intervention française en Chine (1889–1902)", first published in 1963 in the *Revue d'histoire diplomatique* and republished in Michel Bruguière, *Pour une renaissance de l'histoire financière, XVIIIe–XXe siècles*, Paris, Comité pour l'histoire économique et financière de la France, 1992, p. 84.

6 Evan Watts Edwards, "British policy in China, 1913–1914: Rivalry with France in the Yangtze valley", *Journal of Oriental Studies*, 1977, n°40, pp. 20–36. E.W. Edwards, "The origins of British financial cooperation with France in China, 1903–1906", *English Historical Review*, April 1971, n°86, pp. 285–317.

7 Hubert Bonin, *Suez. Du canal à la finance (1857–1987)*, Paris, Économica, 1987.

8 Nicole Tixier, "La Chine dans la stratégie impériale: le rôle du Quai d'Orsay et de ses agents", in Hubert Bonin, Catherine Hodeir & Jean-François Klein (eds.), *L'esprit économique impérial (1830–1970). Groupes de pression & réseaux du patronat colonial en France & dans l'empire*, Paris, Publications de la SFHOM, 2008, pp. 65–84.

9 See Jürgen Osterhammel, "British business in China, 1860s–1950s", in Richard Davenport-Hines & Geoffrey Jones (eds.), *British Business in Asia Since 1860*, Cambridge, Cambridge University Press, 1989, pp. 189–227. Robert Bickers, *Britain in China: Community, Culture and Colonialism, 1900–1949*, Manchester & New York, Manchester University Press, 1999.

10 Frank King, *The History of the Hong Kong and Shanghai Banking Corporation. Volume 1: The Hong Kong Bank in Late Imperial China, 1864–1902: On an Even Kneel*, Cambridge, Cambridge University Press, 1987. Geoffrey Jones, *British Multinational Banking, 1830–1990*, Oxford, Clarendon Press, 1993.

11 Kanji Ishii, "Japanese foreign trade and the Yokohama Specie bank, 1880–1913", in Olive Checkland, Shizuya Nishimura & Norio Tamaki (eds.), *Pacific Banking, 1859–1959: East Meets West*, London, Macmillan; New York, St. Martin's Press, 1994, pp. 1–23.

12 Hubert Bonin, "Le Comptoir national d'escompte de Paris, une banque impériale (1848–1940)", *Revue française d'histoire d'outre-mer*, 1991, tome 78, n°293, pp. 477–497.

13 Marc Meuleau, *Des pionniers en Extrême-Orient. Histoire de la Banque de l'Indochine (1875–1975)*, Paris, Fayard, 1990. Let us specify that, without this very book, this text would have considerably suffered from a lack of materials, which explains our gratefulness to Marc Meuleau. Yasuo Gonjo, *The History of the Banque de l'Indochine (1875–1939): French Imperialism in the Far East*, Tokyo University Press, 1985, thesis in Japanese, translated into French and published in 1993 by Comité pour l'histoire économique et financière de la France, Paris.

14 Marc Meuleau, *op. cit.*, p. 145.

15 Hubert Bonin, "The French banks in the Pacific area (1860–1945)", in Olive Checkland, Shizuya Nishimura & Norio Tamaki (eds.), *Pacific Banking (1859–1959): East Meets West*, London, Macmillan; New York, St. Martin's Press, 1994, pp. 61–74.

16 See Frank King, "Extra-regional banks and investment in China", in Rondo Cameron & Valeri Bovykin (eds.), *International Banking, 1870–1914*, Oxford, Oxford University Press, 1991.

17 Jean Bouvier, René Girault & Jacques Thobie, *L'impérialisme à la française, 1914–1940*, Paris, La Découverte, 1986. Jacques Thobie, *La France impériale, 1880–1914*, Paris, Mégrelis, 1982.

18 Rosemary Quested, *The Russo-Chinese Bank*, Birmingham, Slavonic Monographs, n°2, 1977.

19 See Hubert Bonin, *La Société générale en Russie (Histoire des activités financières et bancaires de la Société générale en Russie dans les années 1880–1917)*, Paris, La collection historique de la Société générale, 1994, 2005.

20 Julia Lovell, *La Guerre de l'opium, 1839–1842*, Paris, Buchet Chastel, 2017.

21 See Marc Meuleau, *op. cit.*, p. 238.

22 Marc Meuleau, *op. cit.*

23 *Ibidem.*

24 Ginette Kurgan-Van Hentenryk, "Un aspect de l'exportation des capitaux en Chine: les entreprises franco-belges, 1896–1914", in Maurice Lévy-Leboyer (ed.), *La position internationale de la France, Aspects économiques et financiers, xixe–xxe siècles*, Paris, Éditions de l'École des hautes études en sciences sociales, 1977. Robert Lee, *France and the Exploitation of China, 1885–1901*, Hong Kong & London, Oxford University Press, 1989.

Part II

Years of expansion in French concessions (1900s–1920s)

2 French business and banking in Guangzhou port-city (1900s–1920s)

From an offshoot to embeddedness

Apart from its colonial territories in Indochina and, to a lesser extent, in India, France was a bit of a laggard in Asia as compared to the British commercial hegemony and the Dutch and German strongholds. French banks and trading houses could not think of challenging the domination of British companies and their capital of influence throughout China,[1] all the more because French companies were far less active in Hong Kong[2] and China than their British competitors. Classical and "natural" commercial flows balanced the purchase of staples (silk, tea, etc.) with the delivery of high-end goods (beverages, high-end *articles de Paris*, etc.).

But when the "scramble for China" gained momentum in the 1870s–1890s, with the initial settlements paving the way to a deeper presence there and with perspectives of foreign direct investment and project financing growing in step with Chinese programs of investment into infrastructure and French businesses entering into "pre-globalised" strategies, the French government began having concerns regarding the gap between French ambitions and the weakness of the "toolbox" available to French traders and exporters in the Far East.

As elsewhere, in a bid to counterbalance the strong presence of British trading houses *hongs*) and banks (Hong Kong & Shanghai Bank–HSBC, Standard Chartered), a "triptych: bank, industry, diplomacy"[3] was set up to mobilise the whole range of influence[4] in order to bolster French deployment in the area. For a while, Germany followed the same path (with *Deutsch-Asiatische Bank*, linked with *Deutsche Bank*),[5] as did Belgium (*Banque sino-belge* in 1902, then in 1913 *Banque belge pour l'étranger*, an affiliate of *Société générale de Belgique*, which gave birth in 1934 to *Banque belge pour l'étranger* [*Extrême-Orient*]).[6]

In 1895, the French government required its banking representative in Asia, *Banque de l'Indochine*, to expand from its base in Indochina and to cover the whole Chinese mainland. It was an area where *Comptoir national d'escompte de Paris*–CNEP had established only a few tentative branches as part of its traditional strategy of accompanying French exporters from the Mediterranean area to the territories joined by shipping lines crossing the Suez Canal[7] (like French *Messageries maritimes*). It must be noted that, for decades, French banks had been represented in China by a single bank acting as their ambassador (at first, by CNEP and then *Banque de l'Indochine*) because, very aware of the comparative edge of British banks and especially of HSBC, they wanted to avoid competition among themselves—up to the 1960s–1990s. At the same time, it is true that the Franco-Russian Russo-Chinese Bank, then the Russo-Asiatic Bank, also favoured French interests, but it was mainly in the north-east of China. Therefore, the renewal of the concession agreement between the government and *Banque de l'Indochine* for the issue of money and central banking in Indochina was linked with an obligation for the latter to open branches in the main commercial cities of the Far East, starting with China.[8] No doubt, the first priority was given to wholesale trade flows along the Yang Ze Kiang (from Shanghai[9] up to Wuhan);[10] the second, to the penetration into mainland China via the railway line linking French Tonkin to south-western China; and the third, to the establishment of bridgeheads in the Hong Kong hub.

1. The issue of a breakthrough into the Guandgong cluster

But *Banque de l'Indochine* had also to accompany French traders and exporters who were exploring second-tier marketplaces such as Tianjin in the north-east and Guangzhou in the south-west. Our long-term purpose is to reconstitute the strategy, skills, performance and competitiveness of French banks and businesses in the key Chinese port-cities. We shall investigate the mission entrusted to French bankers there. Did they help French trading networks within South-East Asia in their clearing activities? Were they involved in financing trade in southern China? Did they take part in the life of the regional banking market? Fortunately, we had access to the correspondence between the Guangzhou branch of *Banque de l'Indochine* and its Paris headquarters,[11] which helped us develop the pioneering analysis of Marc Meuleau's history of *Banque de l'Indochine*.[12]

Along such strategic lines, this chapter will first determine how a French bank gained a toehold in Guangzhou; it will then specify the part played by the *Banque de l'Indochine*'s Guangzhou branch in French commerce in southern China, scrutinise the networks woven by the branch all over south-western China, dwell on its connections with Hong Kong's local banking market and, last, reconstitute the growth and evolution of the branch in the midst of short-term economic trends and the political and military environment.

This survey will follow the path of business history as applied to banking history in order to study the evolution of the branch's portfolio of strategic activities and skills and its performance. The successive stages of growth and of diversification follow the evolution of this French bank's "curve of experience" in Asia and, in this case study, in Guangzhou. *Banque de l'Indochine* succeeded in making its portfolio of expertise and skills grow in new areas, either of business or of geography, from Indochina and Paris to bridgeheads all over China— not to speak of "spillover" activities and competences. Its frail breakthrough in Guangzhou against HSBC and the whole British banking and business community had to be transformed into an actual stronghold by seizing growth opportunities along with what business strategists call "SWOT" (strengths, weaknesses, opportunities, and threats).

Using its *Strengths* (built in imperial France, then in a few business market-places in China and in the Far East); becoming aware of its *Weaknesses* vis-à-vis its competitors and the Chinese business world, either on the mainland or through its diaspora connections; looking for *Opportunities* to overcome the *Threats* posed by the competition, mainly in the form of HSBC, Chartered, and a few other path-breakers who tried to transform Chinese markets into bonanzas. Shanghai provided bankers with key leverage for penetrating the mainland Chinese market, in particular through the Yangze River, while Hong Kong constituted a platform for doing business across South-East Asia and a hub for regional business in southern China, thus opening gates for the French banks. The less influential Guangzhou branches of *Banque de l'Indochine* and French trading houses were to conquer market shares all along the Pearl Rivers, deep into the area linking Guangzhou to the western border and moreover at Guangzhou itself, of course.

Actually, the bank was a latecomer. The French consulate had opened its doors[13] in 1861, the city had been open to commerce since 1844 (Whampoa treaty) and 1858–1860 (Tianjin treaty and Beijing convention), and France had been granted access to the Guangdong, Kwansi and Hainan provinces as early as April 1898. But we presume that these trading houses needed time to penetrate the area, that they preferred using Hong Kong as a leverage in south-east China, and that the harbour at Guangzhou was itself far less equipped than its big neighbour, which also explains the small size of the foreign community there (only a few hundred in the 1910s). Such an offensive along the Pearl Rivers couldn't but somehow reverse the path of history: half a century earlier, the Opium Wars had led to the destruction of the Guangzhou area called the "Guangzhou Thirteen Hongs", where foreign merchant houses, French ones among them, had established factories (in French: *factoreries* or *comptoirs*) from 1757 till 1842.[14]

The *Banque de l'Indochine*'s role can therefore be taken as a relevant case study for a French-style port-city—how did a French business community take root and commit itself to the harbour life there?—, and we shall insist on the opportunities of credit, foreign exchange and trade banking which paved the way to the extension of the activities of the bankers on the involved marketplaces. As soon as it, belatedly, took shape at the turn of the 1890s (when its allotment was finally completed among property investors), the Guangzhou concession and business facilities involving French banks and trading houses turned into what François Gipouloux called the "Asian Mediterranean"[15]: the emergence of Guangzhou as a key target for supplementing Hong Kong as a commercial lever in south China.

2. The Guangzhou bridgehead (1902–1918): from a function of support to a community of business

On 7 February 1902, *Banque de l'Indochine* opened a branch in Shameen (Shamian) island[16] where both the UK and France had concessions, along the Sha-Ky canal, a derivation of the Guangzhou River. The manager[17] arrived from Hong

Kong on 31 December, and its first function was to act as an offshoot of the Hong Kong branch. But gradually it asserted itself and grew steadily as a diversified branch, penetrating into local business with the help of a working capital of $1,439,527 provided by the *Banque de l'Indochine*'s Saigon and Hong Kong branches. As usual, it could rely on its own comprador, Leong Dinh Thang (till August 1920) to set up connections within the Chinese community.[18] A dual strategy was defined: to act as a lever to French houses and to become a stakeholder in the banking market. This was in keeping with both an international mindset and a domestic profile, as the development of the "modern" port-city was sustained either by foreign companies or by the growing Chinese "bourgeois" who had commenced to build the basis of capitalism there.[19]

A. The emergence of a Guangdong cluster

Bankers could seize on the opportunities offered by the emergence of the Guangdong cluster or territorial system of exchanges from the 1880s to the 1890s.[20] The overall opening of the West River to foreign trade in 1897 and then that of several doors through treaty ports[21] favoured the trend. Some kind of a unified system of customs (Chinese Imperial Maritime Customs [CIMC],[22] fixed in Guangzhou in 1858) between the mainland and Kowloon (with a CIMC unit in 1887) eased the move for ships bearing foreign pavilions—and also for Chinese vessels hiding behind such pavilions, as a little "hybrid water frontier."[23] Many Chinese merchants also established offices in Hong Kong and managed both pavilions on the West River.[24] Connections with the hinterland were intensified from Guangzhou upwards through the various branches of the so-called West River (south branch and north branch) and their affluents (Liu River, Kwei River), thanks to junks, steam launches, often tugging junks, and several foreign-owned steamers, despite the brakes sometimes put on navigability by climate effects. This explains why a dozen river ports joined the Guangzhou cluster in the 1880s–1900s, up to the frontier regions of Guangxi: Kongmoon/Jiangmen, Samshui/Sanshui, Lungchow (a treaty port in 1899), Kiungshow, Nanning (far westwards, a treaty port in 1899).

A treaty port since 1897, Wuchow/Wuzhu, "the depot for the Guangxi province" and sometimes for some Yunnan cities, was thus "placed at the point where the West River leaves Guangxi to enter Guangdong and join the sea 200 miles from the East."[25] Despite its lower level of development in comparison with the upstream areas along the Yang Ze, Guangxi (and Guilin, its capital) supplied commodities to the West River cluster (silk, sugar, matting, etc.), which broadened the range, reaching Guangzhou (rice, etc.).

The maritime-oriented trade of the West River helped Guangzhou reach a robust commercial and banking position in close connection with Hong Kong, as it remained "the most important trans-shipment port in South China because it was regarded as a foreign port under the Maritime Customs system in China."[26] In the meantime, the downstream ports on the delta itself (Swatow, Kiungchow, Pakhoi) kept up the momentum, even if their growth became lower, for instance that of Pakhoi, all the more because of the railway joining Guangzhou and Kowloon.

Sure British merchants (with three-quarters of the exchanges in 1899, far ahead of the United States) predominated in Wuchow, but all in all the Guangzhou port-city in general and thus banking and *Banque de l'Indochine* could not but take profits from such trade. And only three ships with a French pavilion (*Charles Hardouin, Paul Beau, Robert Lebaudy*) crossed the West River for the sake of *Messageries cantonnaises*, and they were even ceded to the Guangzhou Navigation Company, a Chinese one, in 1913.

B. A leveraging force at the service of the silk trade

Against such a background, this section will tackle a key issue involving French interests much intimately. One must first keep in mind that, at the turn of the century, France and especially the Lyon region was still leading the global silk industry in spite of the fact that Switzerland, Italy and the United States had been putting up some stiff competition since the 1870s. Apart from Lebanon and Japan, China had become a key supplier of raw silk, mainly because it was cheaper and because French silk production had been badly hit by disease. French trading houses had settled in Guangzhou because the port was the outlet for silk producers from several districts such as Nanhai, Zhongshan, Shunde, Xinhui and via merchants from the hinterland. Together, they tackled a huge amount of silk trade, with the total amount being estimated at 25 million francs in 1905. A chain of transfers was reinforced, from the producers of mulberry leaves, breeders of silk worms, Chinese merchants and lenders to French merchants and bankers.

Trade companies from the Lyon marketplace were establishing themselves more and more in Hong Kong and Guanghzou, which became their gateway to the silk cluster in the Guangdong.[27] Two leaders, R. Chauvin and E. Pasquet, competed mainly with the British Jardine Matheson and the German Arnhold Karberg—the latter having been founded in Guangzhou as early as 1866 by German Jakob Arnhold and Danish Peter Karberg. Warehouses ("go-downs") lodged silk, either by merchant intermediaries or at the *Banque de l'Indochine*'s own go-down, well separated from other goods for fear of infection. The bank offered a classical range of credit and first loans pledged by silk balls or cloth piled in the go-downs.

Banque de l'Indochine used an inspector to check the quality of the silk (along "denier") and to determine its value:"Almost all our loans on goods are pledged by silk balls or cloth.They bear a temporary maturation under six months (two to three months generally) and cannot be termed as fixed assets.[28] The bank financed traders to help them purchase silk from Chinese spinning mills.[29] The trading houses welcomed the introduction of such a local branch, which saved them from having to use Hong Kong brokers (with 1/8 percent commission) and banks, as well as sending a constant stream of telegrams, which led to significant cost cuttings. By the summer of 1905, the bank already had an amount of around $1.3–1.4 million. This enticed HSBC to imitate its competitor and set up its own branch in Guangzhou in August 1908.

The exporters draw at four months/vD/P and sell their paper, either to the *International Bank Corp.*, or through Hong Kong brokers, at the usual rate of 1/8%. These sales are made *forward* with delivery in three months and are invariably settled in Hong Kong. In practice, the delivery is almost always made within four weeks at the most and on the other side, the drawees pay (under TB discount) in the course of the month following the arrival of the merchandise. We can thus count, on the average, a month for the delivery, a month in transit and a month of usance. Henceforth, we will synchronize our purchases with sales in Hong Kong delivery three months. Such looped operations will represent for us, for the moment, an investment of 4 to 5% per year on the average. For the present, we will limit ourselves to using the funds that we will not be able to use as local advance which, for this term, amount to two to three hundred thousand dollars. That will suffice to get in touch with European houses in Guangzhou—the French silk houses on their own account for some 25 million francs in FOREX per year.[30]

The new branch was inserted into the chain of trade and credit linking Guangzhou to Europe: transportation; inventories in Marseille, then Lyon; pending sales to French merchants and (weaving) industrialists, which fuelled the remittance of bills of exchange, with the risk on credit (documentary credits) and the risk on foreign exchange (FOREX), for which it was granted autonomy from the Hong Kong branch in April 1910. Part of the exports could also reach other European outlets. Along all these chains of credit, *Banque de l'Indochine* faced competition from HSBC, even in Lyon, where the latter had opened a special branch.[31] It relied on the *Banque de l'Indochine*'s Paris head-quarters or its London branch to support its connections. It also took help from its correspondents in Lyon, especially local banks dedicated to the community of silk merchants (*Veuve Guérin & Fils* family bank)[32] or branches of Parisian institutions such as CNEP, *Société générale* and *Crédit lyonnais*. Banks there received the remitted documents, followed the course of sales, picked up the repayments or repaid the *Banque de l'Indochine* by themselves thanks to their own credits to importers. They transferred the amounts to the *Banque de l'Indochine* in Paris which, in turn, cleared the accounts of its Guangzhou branch in its books.

Business grew slowly: for the first two years (1904–1905), the silk crops were low. But the branch broadened its customership among French trading houses (*Générale des soies*, Gerin & Drevard, *Meurer frères*) despite some short-lived competition from a small but aggressive French bank, *Banque industrielle de Chine* (till its collapse in 1923) and from the German firm of Arnhold Karberg.

It extended its knowledge of the silk business community (from villages and little towns to Guangzhou) and succeeded in coping with the risks. Lastly, it extended its sway by learning how to finance silk exports to the United States, which added new types of risk (finding correspondents in New York, multiplying FOREX risks, etc.). It had to bear the competition of silk brokers of Hong Kong, who tried to short-circuit Guangzhou merchants, especially as the bulk liners charged for Europe-bound silk in Hong Kong itself.

When World War I broke out, French houses made the most of the embargo placed on German trade. *Banque de l'Indochine* profited too[33] and came in touch with the big house of Boyer Mazet & Co. It even convinced the important British house of Reiss & Co. to become a customer (1915). After a few months, clever German firms engineered a transfer of assets and activities to their British sister companies, either directly (Arnhold) or via "neutral" façades. The Swiss Baumann was substituted by Carlowitz, who was himself replaced in Shanghai by his associate, the British Charles Rayner, while the American Alfred Richter replaced Reuter Brockelmann. Thus, *Banque de l'Indochine* granted loans to Rayner against bills on Harth & Co. in Paris.[34] But finally the UK authorities put a stop to trading with such straw companies from January–August 1915. Several debts were suspended in a moratorium in 1916 because of the status of German remittance bills on London and Hamburg owned by the bank: *Meurer Frères* on London and Hamburg, Arnhold Karberg on London. Even during World War I, the branch resisted the uncertainty and maintained its part in the financing of silk trade.

The *Banque de l'Indochine*'s branch thus accomplished the mission entrusted to it: French trading houses and the Lyon market could now avail themselves of an efficient platform to get information, connections, credit, FOREX, international clearing and cash transfers. No doubt they could have found similar facilities elsewhere, in Hong Kong and from British banks, but the fighting spirit and the growing skills of the *Banque de l'Indochine*'s branch undoubtedly eased their *modus operandi* in the region and contributed to the French competitive edge. This led to a partial transfer of activity from Hong Kong to Guangzhou, reinforcing the rise of the latter as a key silk port-city.

C. Financing general activities

The development of the branch's portfolio of skills in that field paved the way for a spillover into other activities. The narrow function which presided over its creation was widened, and *Banque de l'Indochine* became involved in financing general trading. This is also explained by the opportunities arising from the transformation of Guangzhou from a little port-city into a trading hub. The port was expanded, its dockyards refurbished and a railway link established (Guangzhou-Wuhan; work began in 1908; Guangzhou-Hong Kong/Kowloon, operational in 1911; with 45 km in the British colony and 136 km in China, a short stretch joined it to the Tai Sha Tao station of the Guangzhou-Wuhan). Meanwhile, coastal tramping[35] with junks and steamboats went on increasing all along the Pearl Rivers and eastwards up to Hong Kong, with the plying of seaborne trade and the collecting and deporting of goods all along the local tramping routes— whereas, upstream, Guangzhou, as a redistribution centre for imported foodstuff and sundries, intensified its hinterland connections by river or overland.

These multiple ways of transportation opened doors for Guangzhou to intensify its role as a commercial platform, more and more targeted towards satisfying the demand from the hinterland, its medium-sized cities, its middle-class strata and its local authorities. At the same time, the traditional waterway trade was still going strong, with even a French liner plying between Hong Kong and Guangzhou, and later between Wu Chow and Guangzhou—thanks to a subsidy granted by the Indochina General Government to the company which, after two successive failures by its predecessors towards the end of the first decade of the century, reached some stability (under the name *Messageries cantonnaises*)[36] and became a client of the *Banque de l'Indochine*'s branch.

The branch financed loans pledged against various goods (rice, mats, cotton cloth, pistachios, bean oil, sundries, etc.) and welcomed more and more promissory notes with collaterals and advances on securities. A local community of customership was built, under the guidance of the comprador, among the small and medium-sized merchants and bankers. The loan portfolio of Chinese clients reached £1,406,500 in July 1913, of which 706,500 were simply advances against signatures.[37] "Our Chinese clients are on the whole well-established merchants (embroiderers, goldsmiths, silver craftsmen, china manufacturers; silk, tea, rice and coal merchants; pawnshop, steamboat and hotel owners)."[38] The branch even participated in a loan for the Guangdong government in 1911 (HSBC, *Deutsch Asiatische Bank*, *Banque de l'Indochine*) when it was faced with dire budgetary difficulties. It was repaid in November 1913 ($305,000 for *Banque de l'Indochine* itself).

Next, the branch ventured into finance, in 1911, as part of the process of modernising and extending Guangzhou city. It was persuaded to extend four advances totalling $1,510 million (against mortgage guarantee) to a group of Chinese property developers. The company (Guangzhou Land Investment) intended to build new quays, buildings and warehouses along the river as part of a little "Guangzhou *Bund*" project.[39] It proved its commitment to the project of transforming an underclass harbour and petty town into a modern port-city, which could afterwards fuel new business opportunities: "The development is located on the new *Bund*, close to the Kowloon-Guangzhou station."[40] This venture is a clear sign of the confidence in Guangzhou's potential as a commercial and transportation hub, at a second-tier level, behind Hong Kong and Shanghai. The buildings were completed rapidly but did not succeed in getting tenants, and its profitability sank to nil—all the more when the local military troops squatted in the buildings during the civil war and the tensions prevailing in Guangzhou in 1911–1913.

Last but not least, the "Cantonisation" of *Banque de l'Indochine* was complete when it was recognised, in 1914, as a "senior bank" in Guangzhou, allowing it to act as a local bank. Thanks to such a statute, it could take part in the recovery of the salt tax and also in the circulation and clearing of "notes"—even though HSBC kept the leadership—which it collected and stocked in its building for the City's account.

Notes

1 See Jürgen Osterhammel, "Imperialism in transition: British business in China, 1860s–1950s", in Richard Davenport & Geoffrey Jones (eds.), *British Business in Asia Since 1860*, Cambridge, Cambridge University Press, 1989, pp. 189–227.
2 Norman Miners, *Hong Kong Under Imperial Rule, 1912–1941*, Hong Kong, Oxford University Press, 1987. Geoffrey Sayers, *Hong Kong (1862–1919): Years of Discretion*, Hong Kong, Oxford University Press, 1968. Steve Tsang, *A Modern History of Hong Kong*, London, Tauris, 2004.
3 Jacques Thobie, *La France impériale, 1880–1914*, Paris, Megrelis, 1982. Jean Bouvier, René Girault & Jacques Thobie, *L'impérialisme à la française, 1914–1960*, Paris, La Découverte, 1986.
4 Nicole Tixier, "La Chine dans la stratégie impériale: le rôle du Quai d'Orsay et de ses agents", in Hubert Bonin, Catherine Hodeir & Jean-François Klein (eds.), *L'esprit économique impérial (1830–1970). Groupes de pression & réseaux du patronat colonial en France & dans l'empire*, Paris, Publications de la SFHOM, 2008, pp. 65–84.
5 Motoaki Akagawa, "German banks in East Asia: The Deutsche bank (1870–1875) and the Deutsch-Asiatische bank (1889–1913)", *Keio Business Review*, Society of Business and Commerce, Keio University, 2009, volume 45, n°1, pp. 1–20.
6 See René Brion & Jean-Louis Moreau, *La Société générale de Belgique, 1822–1997*, Anvers, Fonds Mercator, 1997. Ginette Kurgan-Van Hentenryk, "Un aspect de l'exportation des capitaux en Chine: les entreprises franco-belges, 1896–1914", in Maurice Lévy-Leboyer (ed.), *La position internationale de la France. Aspects économiques et financiers, xixᵉ–xxᵉ siècles*, Paris, Éditions de l'École des hautes études en sciences sociales, 1977.
7 Hubert Bonin, "Le Comptoir national d'escompte de Paris, une banque impériale (1848–1940)", *Revue française d'histoire d'outre-mer*, 1991, tome 78, n°293, pp. 477–497. Yasuo Gonjo, "The Comptoir d'escompte de Paris in the Far East in the second half of the 19th century", *Kinyu Keizai The Journal of Financial Economics*, April 1979, n°175, pp. 477–497, June 1979, n°176, pp. 97–129 (both articles in Japanese).
8 See Hubert Bonin, "The French banks in the Pacific area (1860–1945)", in Olive Checkland, Shizuya Nishimura & Norio Tamaki (eds.), *Pacific Banking (1859–1959): East Meets West*, London, Macmillan; New York, St. Martin's Press, 1994, pp. 61–74. H. Bonin, "L'activité des banques françaises dans l'Asie du Pacifique des années 1860 aux années 1940", *Revue française d'histoire d'outre-mer*, 1994, volume 81, n°305, pp. 401–425.
9 See Hubert Bonin, "Les banquiers français à Shanghai dans les années 1860–1940", in *Le Paris de l'Orient. Présence française à Shanghai, 1849–1946*, Boulogne & Seine, Albert Kahn Museum, 2002, pp. 113–119. Marie-Claire Bergère, "The geography of finance in a semi-colonial metropolis: The Shanghai Bund (1842–1943)", in Herman Diedricks & David Reeder (eds.), *Cities of Finance*, Amsterdam, Koninklijke Nederlandse Akademie van Wetenschappen, 1996, pp. 303–317.
10 See Ewan Watt Edwards, "British policy in China, 1913–1914: Rivalry with France in the Yangtze Valley", *Journal of Oriental Studies*, 1977, n°40, pp. 20–36.
11 We thank Anne Brunterch, then the head of the Department of Historical Archives of *Crédit agricole SA*, and her team, who opened the large archives of *Banque de l'Indochine* to us.
12 Marc Meuleau, *Des pionniers en Extrême-Orient. La Banque de l'Indochine, 1875–1975*, Paris, Fayard, 1990. To be complemented by Yasuo Gonjo, *Banque coloniale ou banque*

d'affaires? La Banque de l'Indochine sous la IIIe République, Paris, Comité pour l'histoire économique & financière de la France, 1993 (first published in Japanese, Tokyo, University of Tokyo Press, 1985).

13 The Treaty of Whampoa (24 October 1844) opened the ports of Guangzhou, Shanghai, Ningpo, Amoy and Foochow to French merchants and missionaries. France obtained extraterritorial rights allowing it to maintain a separate legal, judicial, police, and tax system in the treaty ports. The Consulate was founded in 1844—thus well ahead of the Tientsin treaty of 1858—but closed in 1847 and opened durably on 18 May 1861 (we thank Nicole Tixier for these details). About French consuls, see Fabrice Jesné, *Les consuls, agents de la présence française dans le monde, XVIIIe-XIXe siècles*, Rennes, Presses universitaires de Rennes, 2017.

14 See the recent museum which opened its doors in 2016 on the very location of these Thirteen Hongs, within the present Guangzhou Cultural Park, now in the Liwan District, and which I visited in November 2018.

15 François Gipouloux, *La Méditerranée asiatique. Villes portuaires et réseaux marchands en Chine, Japon et en Asie du Sud-Est, XVIe–XXIe siècles*, Paris, CNRS Éditions, 2009 (reedited in pocket book, 2017, and also in Chinese in 2018).

16 The plot was purchased for the Catholic Foreign Mission. On one side was the *Bund*, on the other, Central Avenue. The total investment (plot and buildings) reached $38,144. The builing was refurbished in 1925 and extended in 1928.

17 Ardain, replaced in 1906 by G. Poullet-Osier, followed afterwards in 1910 by R.J. Audap, in 1913 by J. Thesmar.

18 Yen-P'ing Hao, *The Comprador in Nineteenth Century China: Bridge Between East and West*, Cambridge, MA, Harvard University Press, 1970.

19 Marie-Claire Bergère, "The Chinese bourgeoisie", in Denis Crispin Twitchett & John King Fairbank (eds.), *The Cambridge History of China, Volume 12, Republican China*, Cambridge, Cambridge University Press, 1983. Marie-Claire Bergère, *L'âge d'or de la bourgeoisie chinoise, 1911–1937*, Paris, Flammarion, 1986. Marie-Claire Bergère, *The Golden Age of the Chinese Bourgeoisie*, Cambridge, Cambridge University Press, 1989. Marie-Claire Bergère, *Capitalismes et capitalistes en Chine, des origines à nos jours*, Paris, Perrin, 2007.

20 Henry Sze Hang Choi, *The Remarkable Hybrid Maritime World of Hong Kong and the West River Region in the Late Qing Period*, Leiden & Boston, Brill, "Brill's Studies in Maritime History", n°3, 2017.

21 Edward Williams, "The open ports of China", *Geographical Review*, 1920, volume 9, n°4, pp. 306–334. Robert Niel, *China's Foreign Places: The Foreign Presence in China in the Treaty Port Era, 1840–1943*, Hong Kong, Hong Kong University Press, 2015.

22 Hans Van de Ven, *Breaking with the Past: The Maritime Customs Service and the Global Origins of Modernity in China*, New York, Columbia University Press, 2014.

23 Henry Sze Hang Choi, *op. cit.*, p. 7.

24 Man-Houng Lin, "Overseas Chinese merchants and multiple nationality: A means for reducing commercial risk (1895–1935)", *Modern Asian Studies*, 2001, volume 35, n°4, pp. 985–1009.

25 Henry Sze Hang Choi, *op. cit.*, p. 59.

26 *Ibidem*, p. 33.

27 Louis Gueneau, *Lyon et le commerce de la soie, op. cit*, 1932. Tse-Sio Tcheng (Zheng Zixiu), *Les relations de Lyon avec Chine*, Paris, L. Rodstein, 1937. Guy Durand, "Le monde des soies: le marché lyonnais des soies asiatiques", *Les Cahiers d'histoire*, 1995, tome 40, n°3–4, special issue *Lyon et l'Extrême-Orient*, pp. 323–335. Lillian M. Li, *China's Silk Trade: Traditional Industry in the Modern World, 1842–1937*, Cambridge, MA, Council on East Asian Studies, Harvard University, "Harvard East Asian Monographs, 97, xv", 1981. Éric Hamaide, *Les relations entre Lyon et la Chine au XIXe siècle. Essai d'histoire commerciale*, PhD thesis, Lyon 2-Lumière University, 1999 [unpublished, digital version http://theses.univ-lyon2.fr/documents/lyon2/1999/hamaide_e#p=0&a=top].

28 The manager of the *Banque de l'Indochine*'s branch to Paris headquarters, 15 August 1913, Historical archives of *Crédit agricole*, fund *Banque de l'Indochine*.
29 Marianne Bastid, "Le développement des filatures de soie modernes dans la province du Guangdong avant 1894", in *Policy and Economy of China: The Late Professor Yuji Muramatsu Commemoration Volume*, 1975, Tokyo, Toyo Keizai Shinposha, pp. 175–178.
30 The manager of the *Banque de l'Indochine*'s branch to Paris headquarters, 22 July 1905, Historical archives of *Crédit agricole*, fund *Banque de l'Indochine*. "When dealing with a local bank, the Guangzhou houses save both on brokerage fees and the cost of telegrams. They also have the advantage of having their foreign exchange without any delay", *ibidem*, 1 August 1905.
31 Claude Fivel-Démorel, "The Hong Kong & Shanghai bank in Lyon, 1881–1954. Busy, but too discreet", in Frank King (ed.), *Eastern Banking*, London, Athlone, 1983, pp. 467–516. Frank King, "The bank's first European 'special agency'", in Frank King (ed.), *The Hong Kong & Shanghai Bank in the Period of Imperialism and War, 1895–1918*, 1989, pp. 135–142.
32 Serge Chassagne, *Veuve Guérin & fils. Banque et soie. Une affaire de famille (Saint-Chamond-Lyon, 1716–1932)*, Lyon, BGA Permezel, 2012.
33 The manager of *Banque de l'Indochine*'s branch to Paris headquarters, 12 November 1914, 5 February 1915, Historical archives of *Crédit agricole*, fund *Banque de l'Indochine*.
34 *Ibidem*, 26 March 1915.
35 See Archibald Blue, "The China coasters", *Journal of the Royal Asiatic Society Hong Kong Branch*, 1967, volume 7, pp. 80–90. Howard Dick & Stephen Ashter Kentwell, *Sold East: Traders, Tramps, and Tugs of Chinese Waters*, Melbourne, Nautical Association of Australia, 1991. Bert Becker, "Coastal shipping in East Asia in the late nineteenth century", *Journal of the Royal Asiatic Society Hong Kong Branch*, 2010, volume 50, pp. 245–302.
36 The manager of *Banque de l'Indochine*'s branch to Paris headquarters, 2 April 1910.
37 "All our borrowers are good for their respective commitments and the loan granted to each is below the credit limit assigned." *Ibidem*, 15 August 1913.
38 *Ibidem*, 19 March 1914.
39 *Ibidem*, 22 September 1911.
40 *Ibidem*, 26 September 1911. The project comprised of a theatre, 55 houses, and a square.

3 Tianjin as a seductive port-city for French business at the start of the twentieth century

Later included within the commercial grip of foreign companies, the port-city of Tianjin, unlike Guangzhou, did not benefit from the proximity of the big hub of Hong Kong and could somehow have suffered from the predominance of Shanghai in central-east China. But it asserted itself as the gate to the Beijing region and took profit from the very natural resources of its own region, along the Hai Ho (now Hei He) River and all along the maritime coast, with enormous production of salt (mainly in the Changlu district), managed by rich merchants who also took up the huge excise tax to be redistributed to the Chinese authorities. Little by little, it became an attractive marketplace, and it could therefore assert its role as a stakeholder in the overall development of commercial networks and activities in north China,[1] all the more that regional industry, with even collieries,[2] craftsmanship, and trade, gathered momentum at the turn of the twentieth century.

1. The institutional background

Tianjin welcomed this *Banque de l'Indochine* branch because it had become a geo-political issue, as the international agreements had attributed a territory to France there.[3] Since the Tianjin treaty of June 1858 (following the second Opium War and signed by France, Great Britain, Russia and the United States) and its signature in 1860 by the imperial state after the agreement concluding the 1859–1860 struggles on the Hai Ho River and then in Beijing between Chinese and Western troops, a French concession had been established in Tianjin in 1860–1862, in parallel with those of the UK and the United States. It had become "an opened city", thus accessible to Western trade houses, and the concession, along the river, had been enlarged in 1895. The "treaty port" and its settlement, granted by the treaties which submitted China to Western Powers, allowed Tianjin to join the group of "city ports" connected to worldwide trade and finance flows.

A. Imperialism versus nationalism (1899–1902)

As Pierre Singaravélou[4] related it, Tianjin suffered some kind of a military and political earthquake in 1899–1900. The huge revolt of the Boxers[5] stirred a nationalist move all over north-eastern China. Whilst the Beijing power itself declared war on the Powers that had imposed the "unequal treaties" in 1860, Boxer troops conquered the Zhili (Hebei) region. They ended by entering the Tianjin city and besieging the foreign concessions. Tianjin epitomized therefore the struggle between imperialism[6] and nationalism and perhaps also between imported modernity and respect for traditional economy and society, all the more because the city had experimented with several paths of modernisation as some kind of a laboratory in the area: telegraph, an arsenal, the Seiyang University from 1895, the Beijing-Tianjin railway since 1898, and so on. The port itself had taken off, with robust revenues from customs taxes. All in all, it could have encapsulated a trend towards the co-production of modernity by Chinese and foreign stakeholders and entrepreneurs, with support from progressive civil servants, and also toward what Niall Ferguson called "anglobalisation"[7] under the British thalassocratic flagship, thanks to interactions and connections between the leading economies represented in the Chinese treaty ports.

One can then well understand the symbolic target of Tianjin, where Boxer troops conquered the Chinese area on 14 July 1900 and besieged the foreign concessions. Foreigners and Christian Chinese were to be eliminated, and concessions suppressed. About 700 foreigners were living there, protected by 2,000 foreign soldiers and 10,000 or 12,000 regular Chinese troops, still hostile to the Boxers. The French concession itself endured a large burning. An internationalised army launched counteroffensives: reoccupying the Dagu fortresses between Beijing and Tianjin, then occupying the Chinese fortress at the heart of Tianjin. An international government administered the city from mid-July 1900 till 15 August 1902, reinstated order, set up police, health and tax administrations, and maintained the security on the river against piracy risks.

But such a victory resulted in the reinforcement of the concessions themselves, along unilateral decisions. Like the British concession, the French one jumped in size (from 28 to 118 hectares) through the annexation of a territory reaching the Haï Kouang Tze canal—and the operation was recognized by China in 1912. The Russian concession was the biggest (327.5 hectares), ahead of the German (150 hectares), the Japanese (131 hectares), the French (118 hectares), the British (103 hectares), and the Belgian concessions (96 hectares). Trade could again commence its long-term growth through the gate to North-Eastern China. From 1901, a commission defined programs to deepen the Hai He River, which was helpful due to the growing size of steamers. And at the heart of the French concession, a metallic bridge was established, built by the French company Fives-Lille (1903) and financed by the provisional government ($200,000).

In fact, the Boxer rebellion helped reinforce the French foothold in Tianjin and provided it greater surface and ability to develop an actual town planning strategy and to foster a process of appropriation of a rationalised territory, which couldn't but profit the overall French community of interests and business.

B. Some later tensions

A key event occurred later on which caused some concerns. In 1916, France seized the "extra-concession", a field bordering the concession which had been disputed for years; it expelled the Chinese police and asserted its authority. A general strike occurred among the Chinese workforce all over the French concession in November 1916. French companies were boycotted, and funds were retired from French bank accounts—until the "victory" of Frenchies.[8] "In Tianjin, a local incident occurred when the Chinese police intervened in the French extra-concession and, probably exploited by German plotting, led to the boycott of French houses and the departure of almost their whole local staff."[9]

C. Local authorities relying on Banque de l'Indochine

A Municipality had been set up to manage French civil residents active there— but there were only about 120 in 1928—and people living and working in the French territory. From 1907, the institution used the *Banque de l'Indochine* branch for its day-to-day needs, drawing overdrafts on its account—even though it was also a customer at HSBC—and it benefited from a four-month 4.5 per cent loan of 100,000 taels in June 1909.

The Municipality also financed French companies contracting with local entities, especially a builder, Brossard Mopin, which got orders from the Municipality or from French institutions for new buildings.[10] A corps of French troops was installed there to watch over the completion of the international agreement following the Boxers revolt—and the *Banque de l'Indochine* branch managed the treasury operations of the French army there.

2. The emergence of the Tianjin port-city and business hub

When the *Banque de l'Indochine* branch was opened, the commercial exchanges through Tianjin had been gaining in substance (see Table 3.1).

Table 3.1 Exchanges through Tianjin as assessed by *Banque de l'Indochine* branch in 1903–1906 (Haikwan taels)

	Import	Export
1903	18,622,406	1,148 246
1904	16,256,651	2,069,362
1905	31,463,208	7,585,982
1906	40,102,558	2,583,800

A. The issue of currencies

One obstacle, the diversity of currencies used in the Chinese area, had to be faced as apriority:

> The bank accounts are held in *hong ping taels* in Tianjin, in *kung fah taels* in Beijing. Despite this difference, in Tianjin, transactions between the two markets are always quoted *hong ping taels* against *hong ping taels*, whereas this currency requires a new conversion in order to be inserted into the accounts in Beijing, which explains boring complexities for accounting entries. Moreover the *hong ping tael* on the two markets have only in common their weight which seems to be of 36,16 grams, but this is 992/1000 in Tianjin whilst it reaches 1000/1000 in the capital.[11]

The *Banque de l'Indochine* branch had to tackle business also in silver Mexican piastres and in *peyi-yang dollars* (delivered in huge quantities by the provincial government).

B. The take-off of the port-city

Obstacles hindered the development of the Tianjin port facilities. Ice during the winter season demanded that the main harbour activities were confined to March through November. The heritage of low marshy and often flooded land had to be overcome, and there were repetitive floodings (in 1917, for example) due to the convergence of half a dozen rivers into the Hai He River.

Anyway, Tianjin asserted itself as "the port of the North", the gateway to Beijing and its area, and as a major transhipment centre for foodstuff, and later on for goods. Historian Gail Hershatter underlined the three main factors explaining the growth of Tianjin: the convenience of transportation, the proximity to the capital, and the location of nearby areas rich in cotton and local products to be exported.

C. Developing banking business in Tianjin

Against such economic, geopolitical and banking surroundings, the Tianjin marketplace appeared within the cross hairs of *Banque de l'Indochine*. But, at first glance, it was then only a little part of the jigsaw puzzle that French bankers were piecing together in China. Its harbour did not match the scope of those at Shanghai and Hong Kong, and the insertion of the Beijing hinterland into the international flows was still far limited in comparison to the Guang Dong and Yang Ze areas. For some years, it was considered a mere experimental tool in complementarity to the Beijing branch, and the Paris headquarters were reluctant to apply a significant working capital to this start-up: its director complained about the scant funding allocated to the branch, which was fixed at £40,000 in 1907 (see Table 3.2).

Table 3.2 Overdraft facilities provided by the Paris head office to the Tianjin branch on 10 October 1907

		Taels
Gold capital	£100,000	635,000
Silver capital	$500,000	360,000
Cash account to be drawn	FRF 1,000,000	250,000
Total		1,245,000
To be deducted as an advance to the Beijing branch		500,000
Actual total for the Tianjin branch		745,000

Tianjin was not perceived as worth too much of an investment because it seem to be a promising market and was subject to stiff competition, with branches opened by the leading British banks HSBC and Chartered and by *Banque russo-chinoise.* This perception was confirmed by reality: at first, the Tianjin branch did not have much business to handle. Initial concerns were also aggravated by the overall economic and financial situation in Asia (and elsewhere in the world) because of a deep slump in 1906–1908, which stopped much transit business.

Treaties paved the way to the inclusion of the Tianjin area in "modern" influence because they signaled the opening of the Beijing region to foreign trade and a revolution in business flows. French interests could not miss such an opportunity; even the "scramble for Tianjin" meant harsh competition among the banks established there. For *Banque de l'Indochine*, a first step was to provide the branch with employees, as a little enclave settled in the immense desert of French influence in this area. The manager (*directeur*)[12] was accompanied by a very few qualified employees (accounting, control, administration) coming from France and thereafter circulating within the Asian network of the bank and by local employees, speaking either French or English, even if accounting skills were often a challenge.

During the first quarter of the twentieth century, flour and cotton mills burgeoned, and Tianjin reached about 6–7 per cent of the whole Chinese cotton spindling capacity, becoming the fourth textile centre after Shanghai (50 per cent), Wuhan and Qindao, all the more because Japanese investments gathered momentum from the turn of the 1930s. Among local merchants and industrialists were the compradors of Western banks (HSBC, Russo-Asiatic Bank) and trade houses (Jardine Matheson, Butterfield, Swire)—as decisive go-betweens and sometimes even investors.[13]

The growth of the population (from 60,000 inhabitants in 1860 to 1.7 million in 1947, from the fifth level among Chinese cities in 1927 to the third in 1935) and the diversification of society and classes opened outlets for Western utilities and equipment or consumer goods. Since the turn of the twentieth century emerged several basic trade flows, mainly cotton yarn, cloth, dyes, sugar, kerosene, opium, and the like—notwithstanding military hardware or gold and jewellery for warlord customers). Then in the interwar period, iron and steel, petroleum, machines and machines parts joined the stream. On their part, raw and semi-processed goods for export progressed: cotton, wool, eggs, and so on. Riverside warehouses flourished, along with the transformation of the former sole bridgehead into a key "port-city", which, in 1937, handled about one-sixth of the level of imports and one-third the level of exports of Shanghai.

D. The issue of the commercial harbour

Little by little, the economic importance of the harbour was reinforced. Tianjin asserted itself as a growing gateway for transit towards north-eastern China, the Beijing area and westward to the Shan-Si region (with a railway from Tai Yuan, Pao Ting and Beijing), thanks to a harbour joining the Hai Ho River, and the Bohai Bay and the Bohai Sea. The Hai Ho River concentrates the Pei Ho and the Tzuya Ho, itself formed by the Ta Ching Ho and the Hou To Ho, thus opening large areas for local commercial river exchanges. The Grand Canal linked the Yang Ze area to Tianjin and was extended by the Ching Chun Ho up to Peitang and to the Chi Yun Ho. The dike of the Canal broke in September 1917, and the whole city was flooded; the French concession laid under water for two weeks.[14]

The Paris protocol in September 1901 had paved the way, for example, for a British and German loan (£1.6 million, or 100 million taels, set up by HSBC and *Deutsch Asiatisch Bank*) in 1908–1911 to build a railway between Tianjin and Fukou, and an entente among French, British and Belgian interests in October 1905 had prepared the concession of the Tianjin–Pou Keou railway.

> Tianjin has for long been only a little port within important business; it had suddenly taken an exceptional importance because the city was used as a supplying basis during the last two wars and because the building of railways has deeply changed the Chinese economic conditions. The new rail lines, to be built, joining Tianjin to Tsinbao [Tsinan or Jinan] and Nankin [Nanjing or Nanking, southwards], will still increase the important of the place, but, balancing these elements of prosperity, have to be taken into account the effects of the four months blockade caused by icing, and would be possible that Chin Wan (or Huan) Tao [now Qinghuangdao], with its harbour opened throughout the year, should surpass the present city, unless we would see emerge two commercial centres as had been the case in France with Le Havre and Rouen, or Saint-Nazaire and Nantes.[15]

This perhaps explains why the French state regained control of its fields located in Chin Wan Tao, which had been leased for a while.

Regional elites extended their scope thanks to key business families (Sun, Zhou, etc.), to salt merchants, a key profession in Zhili, to overall small and middle-sized family companies, and to local bankers (*yinhao* or *qianzhuang*), whilst branches of new modern banks gathered momentum (Daqing Bank,

Imperial Bank of China and Bank of Communications in 1908, Bank of China in 1912).[16] Coastal and interregional trade benefited more and more Chinese merchants, either of native origin or from other regions.[17] An actual constituency thus took shape to which foreign banks could be connected to broaden their activities, and branches in Tianjin became gateways to such prospects.

The overall situation of the port-city evolved positively because Tianjin took profit from the growth of commercial transit in the wake of the foreign investments[18] oriented toward central-northern China, which was less important than Manchuria northward and the Yangze valley southward but maturing significantly.

> Tianjin lived by trade: it was the melting point of five rivers, an important juncture on the Grand Canal, the loading point for sea shipment of goods for north and northwest China, the entry joint for foreign imports and Shanghai goods, and the major northern station of two railroad lines.[19]

Foreign concessions, among them the French, became hives of bustling port activities—about 60,000–70,000 labourers loading or unloading cargo, freight haulers, cart drivers, transport coolies, on the harbour docks or railroad stations and in the warehouses—even though the three largest steamship docks belonged to two British houses, Butterfield & Cooper and Jardine Matheson, and to the Chinese-owned China Merchants Steam Navigation Company.[20]

3. Tianjin as a port-city for the French community of interests

Taking profit from this growth in trade and despite harsh competition, the evolution of the French concession set up a framework for the development of the *Banque de l'Indochine* branch.

A. Taking part in a few basic investments

The commitment of French interests to Tianjin gathered momentum, even from Paris, because there was some geopolitical challenge in their defence and promotion in Tianjin. One example was the fate of *Docks & appontements de Tong Ku*[21] (with its Tong Ku docks and landing quays, competing with the Taku Tug & Lighter Company, originally linked with Russian interests), which was controlled by French entrepreneurs to welcome inland shipping on the Pei Ho and to transport coolies between New Chang and Tong Ku. It had the monopoly on the transport of persons and merchandises between Tianjin and Taku, where big ships stopped. The Taku dock had been the first to set up in north-east China (from 1880/1881) within the coastal defense post established there for the Chinese military naval force, with a naval base earmarked to protect Bohan bay (with the Weihaiwei base and the Liushun port). The Taku dock also began manufacturing ships in 1883 and armaments in 1891 for the

Chinese forces. The daily function of the dock was also to pile up coal for the steamships of the little Chinese Navy.

Docks & appontements de Tong Ku (warehouses and wharfs) got over-indebted and had to be salvaged in 1907 by a syndicated mix of its creditors, among whom was the vice-president, then president of the Municipality of Tianjin, John O'Neill,[22] which provided fresh cash. Further and deeper difficulties led to a liquidation in 1924 and to its succession by a sister company managed by O'Neill and a Chinese team of investors and managers led by Joseph Hsu.[23] The fate of this small company was of importance for French authorities because its quays welcomed the gunboat (*canonnière*) which France maintained there to assert its power on the concession and to support its troops. But it also managed a local fleet of four tugboats and four barges, all under French flag, which practiced tramping downstream and inland shipping, trying thus to bring some French influence to bear.

Another case was the fate of the streetcar and electricity company which had to be modernised. Belgian investors (*Banque d'outremer, Compagnie internationale d'Orient*, Empain) had purchased the company managing the streetcar concession, Electric Lightning & Traction Syndicate, in 1902. Later on, despite discontent among French diplomats and authorities, those Belgian interests were preserved when a new company was set up in 1910 by its managers, which got a 50-year concession of the networks and the plant to be modernised.[24] And it benefited from a permanent line of credit of 100,000 taels at the *Banque de l'Indochine* branch.

B. Religious missions as stakeholders in the local economy

The French community included the Christian missions because French *Missions étrangères* (the international branch of the French Catholic Church) were not active in northern China, leaving room for religious orders (Jesuits, Franciscans, Lazarists). These entities played a key role among the French community of interests,[25] managing somewhat large assets thanks to alms, charities and the revenues of their assets. The *Banque de l'Indochine* branch collected their deposits and even managed their availabilities as a broker: its permanent loan to the new concessionary company for light and tramway in 1910 was thus pledged by the guarantee of the Tianjin Jesuit mission (or *Mission de Sienshien*). Along with *La Procure des Lazaristes*, the other important mission in the city, the Jesuit mission became a minor co-owner (and member of the board) of *Énergie électrique de Tianjin*—the electricity utility (with one-fifth of the equity in 1936).

Conclusion: facing competition successfully

Year after year, the French concession asserted itself as a competing quarter and economic stronghold either against British (or other) interests or beside them. From Victoria Road to *Rue de France*, it became part of the "Wall Street of North China", far from the Shanghai *Bund* but proud of its banking headquarters and trade houses. The newspaper launched in 1902, the *Peking & Tien Tsin Times*, often underlined the high-end activity of the concession, and the *North China Star* evoked in 1920 "Tientsin's Lombard Street."[26]

Notes

1 Linda Grove, "International trade and the creation of domestic marketing networks in North-China, 1860–1930", in Shinya Sugiyama & Linda Grove (eds.), *Commercial Networks in Modern Asia*, Richmond, Surrey, Curzon Press, 2001, pp. 96–115.
2 Ellsworth Carlson, *The Kaiping Mines, 1887–1912*, Cambridge, MA, Harvard East Asian Monographs, 1971. Tim Wright, *Coal Mining in China's Economy and Societies, 1893–1937*, Cambridge, Cambridge University Press, 1984.
3 See Laurent Cesari & Denis Varaschin (eds.), *Les relations franco-chinoises au vingtième siècle et leurs antécédents*, Arras, Artois Presses Université, 2003.
4 Pierre Singaravélou, *Tianjin Cosmopolis. Une autre histoire de la mondialisation*, Paris, Seuil, "L'Univers historique", 2017.
5 Raymond Bourgerie, *La guerre des Boxers (1900–1901): Tseu-Hi évite le pire*, Paris, Économica, "Campagnes & stratégies, n°2", 1998. Lanxin Xiang, *The Origins of the Boxer War: A Multinational Study*, London, Routledge, 2002. Robert Bickers, "1899–1900. Révolte et guerre des Boxeurs", in Pierre Singaravélou & Sylvain Venayre (eds.), *Histoire du monde au xixe siècle*, Paris, Fayard, pp. 373–376.
6 See Robert Bickers, *The Scramble for China: Foreign Devils in the Qing Empire, 1832–1914*, London, Allen Lane, 2011. Lanxin Xiang, *The Origins of the Boxers War: A Multinational Study*, London, Routledge, 2003.
7 Pierre Grosser & Niall Ferguson, "L'empire à la mode Ferguson", *L'Économie politique*, 2004, volume 4, n°24, pp. 106–112.
8 Correspondence between the Tianjin branch and the Paris headquarters of *Banque de l'Indochine* (BIC), 8 and 24 November 1916. *Banque de l'Indochine* yearly report for 1916, Archives of *Crédit agricole, Banque de l'Indochine* fund. We thank their (past) boss Roger Nougaret (and his assistant Annie Deu-Fillon) to have eased our access to such records.
9 Correspondence between the director of the Tianjin branch and the Paris headquarters of *Banque de l'Indochine*, archives DSE 12/1, Historical archives of *Crédit agricole, Banque de l'Indochine* fund.
10 BIC Correspondence, 13 September 1921.
11 *Ibidem*, 30 July 1907.
12 Desvaux, then André Pernotte in 1911, Thesmar, Audap for the interim in 1917, A. Lecot in 1920, L. Chevretton, Joseph Demay in October 1924, etc.
13 Gail Hershatter, *The Workers of Tianjin, 1900–1949*, Stanford, Stanford University Press, 1986, pp. 33–34.
14 BIC Correspondence, 21 and 28 September 1917.
15 *Ibidem*, 25 October 1906. About the economic development of this period, see Marianne Bastid, Marie-Claude Bergère & Jean Chesneaux, *La Chine. 2. De la guerre franco-chinoise à la fondation du Parti communiste chinois, 1885–1921*, Paris, Hatier, 1972.
16 Brett Sheehan, "Urban identity and urban networks in cosmopolitan cities: Banks and bankers in Tianjin, 1900–1937", in Joseph Esherik (ed.), *Remaking the Chinese City: Modernity and National Identity, 1900–1950*, Honolulu, University of Hawai'i Press, 2000, pp. 47–64.
17 See Brett Sheehan, *Trust in Troubled Times: Money, Banks and State–Society Relations in Republican Tianjin*, Cambridge, MA, Cambridge University Press, 2003.
18 Hou Chi-Ming, *Foreign Investment and Economic Development in China*, Cambridge, MA, Cambridge University Press, 1965. See Sherman Cochran, *Encountering Chinese Networks: Western, Japanese and Chinese Corporations in China, 1880–1937*, Berkeley, University of California Press, 2000.

19 Gail Hershatter, *op. cit.*, p. 15.
20 *Ibidem*, p. 118.
21 Now Tanggu.
22 *Banque de l'Indochine* correspondence, 30 October 1907, 7 November 1907.
23 *Ibidem*, 11 March, 27 October 1924.
24 *Ibidem*, 21 April 1910.
25 See Corinne de Ménonville, *Les aventuriers de Dieu et de la République. Missionnaires et consuls en Chine (1844–1937)*, Paris, Les Indes savantes, 2007.
26 *North China Star*, 12 August 1920, p. 13 (Nantes archives of the French Tientsin consulate, 9C1).

4 Tianjin as a leverage to internationalised markets and to Chinese connections

Beyond its regional roots and its function as a gate to inner north-eastern China, the Tianjin marketplace grew in size as it became a lever to gain access to neighbouring internationalised markets, which reinforced *Banque de l'Indochine* as a gatekeeper to some areas, at the service of French business abroad. In parallel, it asserted its proto-globalised scope through several services which joined the portfolio of skills of *Banque de l'Indochine*. In the meanwhile, the French banking offshoot convinced local Chinese businessmen of its quality, reliability, and capability to mobilise its talents not just in favour of foreigners

1. *Banque de l'Indochine* confronted with nationalist eruption and political conflicts (1911–1913)

A first apex of the development of the *Banque de l'Indochine* branch was reached at the start of winter in January 1911, when the capital used climbed to FRF 9 million. But its liquidity was somehow preserved because it could recover 1.5 million of short-term (about four-month) negotiable paper and even 2.5 million on 7 January (or £100,000), complemented by 2.4 million in bills of exchange, which reduced the overdraft on the Paris head office to 1.9 million against an authorisation for 4 million. The branch fostered growth and profit through such purchases of commercial paper.

The key obstacle to reach full success in fact came from political events. First riots broke out in December 1910, when "constitutionalist" students and merchants—among whom even the president of the chamber of commerce, Wang, one of the salt merchants who rapidly afterwards collapsed—demonstrated against the vice-king of Zhili to demand constitutional reform.[1] This paved the way to permanent troubles in the city—like all over China in the 1906–1911 period. A year later, Tianjin was stricken by the general crisis of confidence which halted business: despite political rest there, banks suffered from withdrawals of deposits from customers and even the state.[2]

Species predominated because everyone feared political troubles; the circulation of Mexican piastres and silver metal disappeared. Chinese banks suspended their activities, and a few of them collapsed (Yi Yuan Heng and Yi Ching Heng). All in all, the risks borne by the *Banque de l'Indochine* branch for Chinese merchants and bankers then reached 600,000 taels—among that amount, 40,000 solely for Yu Fong (the customs bank). Commercial exchanges were paralysed, and credit was halted at the end of 1911—even though Tianjin and the Zhili remained faithful to the central Beijing government. The *Banque de l'Indochine* branch tightened its operations in order to recover its loans.

All of a sudden, luckily, military events proved somewhat profitable: it seems that German-friendly interests (the industrialist Skoda Pilsen and the trade house Arnhold-Karberg) issued a £300,000 loan in London to provide money to the Beijing state and Yuan Chi Kai for armaments, against orders.[3] The cash flowed from Europe to China, and then part of it was distributed on the Tianjin marketplace through the *Banque de l'Indochine* branch, and part of it to the state through Commercial Guarantee Bank of China. Anyway, the currency was used as a pledge for an issue of bills, which provided fresh air to the treasuries of Chinese trade and banking houses, then to those of the branches of European banks. But appeasement was short-lived because a revolt, looting and fires shook Tianjin in the beginning of April 1912: warehouses and shops were destroyed, snuffing out the guarantee of bankers' loans. The *Banque de l'Indochine* branch had to face 205,000 taels of thawed commercial credits.[4]

Happily, a rebirth of business took place because the cash provided to the Chinese government in Beijing by the Reorganisation Loan helped it to reimburse numerous debts in the second half of 1913: trust and business regained momentum, even if the *Banque de l'Indochine* branch remained cautious about credits.[5] But the lenient management of the branch in the first half-year of its existence led to the pile-up of bad credits which the bank had to negotiate for about a decade tore cover, pending the sale of goods inventories and mortgaged plots of land.

2. The growing importance of business with foreign houses

Due to the limits of its French customership, the challenge for *Banque de l'Indochine* was to gain access to core businesses among the foreign houses that were pioneering for winning market shares in the area adjoining Beijing and Tianjin, despite the harsh competition from British and American banks—and also of German interests until World War I.

A. The prosperity of FOREX

The portfolio of skills of the *Banque de l'Indochine* branch was enriched rapidly because it wielded far greater autonomy than its colleagues in fixing the values of its exchange operations; it was not a mere relay of the Shanghai head offices and conversely also traded the FOREX operations of the Beijing branch. Its director could therefore develop by himself exchange business and assumed large risks, for instance in June–July 1908 (see Table 4.1).

Table 4.1 FOREX position of the *Banque de l'Indochine* branch in 1908 (FRF)[6]

20 June 1908	274,000
23 June	650,000
2 July	642,000
11 July	1,128,000

But the scale of the Tianjin FOREX remained modest in comparison with Shanghai's:

> There is in China only one market, Shanghai. Tianjin is an important place where are treated numerous exchanged affairs, but it is not the key FOREX market: our place in this respect is only the shadow of Shanghai. Through the quick transmission of rates, we perceive thus here various trends without understanding their motives, because rumours circulate more slowly and we cannot control them. We are therefore submitted brutally to the reactions on the Shanghai market, and the result of such an ignorance of their causes is that, all of a sudden, the market gets paralysed: nobody operates, everybody keeps waiting … And when the exchanges regain momentum, all the banks operate in the same direction and counterparts are lacking.[7]

B. Financing trading houses

In parallel with the development of FOREX, another step was to create a corpus of business because Tianjin had no actual tradition as a foreign banking market, and in such a place *Banque de l'Indochine* had to avoid the syndrome of the "late comer": "Banks concentrate their activities on Shanghai, where the operations of Petchili [the Gulf of Petchili area] and Hubei are usually cleared. Hankeou draws continuously on Shanghai in exchange for its purchase of paper on tea and cereals."[8] The bank got in touch directly with a few traders, for whom it financed bills of exchange. At this time, importers used their own warehouses (go-downs) because the city was not equipped and wares there served as pledges for middle-term loans, which constituted a somewhat heightened degree of risks for bankers. The other side of its activities comprised advances against wares. The branch rapidly reached a positive level of business (see Table 4.2).

Table 4.2 Credits from the *Banque de l'Indochine* branch on 10 October 1907 (taels)

Various advances	1,350,000
Discounted bills	25,000
Bills to be received on short term	30,000
Total	1,405,000

More and more, the *Banque de l'Indochine* branch found customers among the international community attending the Tianjin harbour. Before World War I, the bank had been involved in Manchurian business through the activities of a few wholesale traders who operated there and even in eastern Russia from its Tianjin base in the Russian concession and who spread their activities to Harbin or elsewhere. Both the Batouieff-Zimmerman and Gallusser houses became important clients, but war events or bad management led to their liquidation and losses as soon as 1915, with debts pending for years—Gallusser having brought as guarantees forests and a sawmill which *Banque de l'Indochine* had to sell. Several German-Russian houses had also joined the portfolio of clients for credits in rubles and were also revealed as bad debtors, a situation thatwas aggravated by the depreciation of the ruble. The concept of Tianjin as a door to trading with Manchuria somewhat failed at the *Banque de l'Indochine* branch.

C. Even investment banking?

Some aspects of the commitment to local development among businesses welcoming French interests could even extend to skills in investment banking, but only in limited cases. One can notice, for example, the issuing of a bond for the then large and prosperous Chung Hsing Mines colliery (Yishien, Chantung) (or Chung Hsing Kuang Wu Chu) to finance its purchase of waggons[9] in 1910—even if the management of the firm was German. The next year, the firm issued a loan guaranteed by the Tianjin–Pukow railway; the *Banque de l'Indochine* branch was involved because it took part in a series of credits to the Commercial Guarantee Bank of Chihli (Zhili) (against promissory notes or *billets à ordre*), which itself lent the money to the Mines—and the director of the branch Pernotte had been admitted to the board of the CGBC.[10]

The relationship with the company perdured afterwards, with new packages of promissory notes in 1914–1922 and some advances, reimbursed by bonds issued later on.[11] The *Banque de l'Indochine* branch had thus joined the group godfathering the Mines and brokering their securities among their customers— even if the Mines might have been more dependent on German and Belgian interests than on French ones. But such activities disappeared after World War I when the loan had been repaid (in January 1919), and *Banque de l'Indochine* focused on its commercial banking activities.

3. *Banque de l'Indochine* as a local bank for Chinese in Tianjin

Such analysis leads to an obvious conclusion: the *Banque de l'Indochine* branch could not find enough business among French firms because the part played by France and the number of French companies was small, and it could not compete on a broad scale with Japanese, British or American bankers to finance trans-Pacific exchanges—even in this niche it supported the French house Olivier. Such an intermediary conclusion explains the development of the influence of the *Banque de l'Indochine* branch among Chinese business.

A. **Banque de l'Indochine** *embedded in Tianjin*

The bank had to embed itself in such business communities in order to convince them of the creditworthiness of an institution still unknown in northern China beyond the finance circles of the state in Beijing and to promote the reputation of what was called southward "the French bank". It had to appear as equipped with cash enough to meet their needs for loans in booming periods and as a reliable banker able to assume satisfying terms of credit beyond merely very short-term activities. These were conditions to conquer the embeddedness required to become a key player on a banking market.[12]

> The success of our special business is linked to the attitude which we shall adopt during the negotiations with Chinese merchants; the exchange operations should not be taken into account when the time will come for them to assess the value of our institution, and the authorities will attribute a moral credit to our bank only along with the level of the resources they will find in our house.[13]

Sure, *Banque de l'Indochine* lacked the amount of cash provided to HSBC by its advantage in collecting deposits in the Tianjin marketplace (constituting about four-fifths of the liabilities of the HSBC branch). But it could also draw depositors from the French community (the Municipality, the power company, the Jesuit Mission) and use the "clearing" between banks to get available on call. The basic task was to acquire a basis of local customers, which was the commonplace function of its comprador.[14] A classic approach was to determine how and how much *Banque de l'Indochine* ploughed back money into the indigenous sector of the Tianjin economy, notably by using the networks of its comprador—his art of *"guangxi"*, or art of entertaining connections among business communities—as an intermediary between a foreign bank and the domestic sector, in which were the business of the comprador and his family. But constraints had often to be overcome because risk assessment of local loans ("chop loans" especially) faced difficulties when "ethnicity" habits had to be considered, that is, credit and accounting uses which did not fit European standards.

B. The comprador's business before World War I

Along with a traditional *modus operandi*, the comprador Wei (and his deputy Liu, who had worked with a German bank, then with *Banque russo-chinoise* in Tianjin) was financed by *Banque de l'Indochine* to provide loans to its own network of Chinese merchants and bankers (what were called the *qiang huang* banks)[15] and to manage his own staff of clerks (to cover the banking operations with Chinese clients), boys and "shroffs" to dispatch documents and also to watch over customers' go-downs, where pledged goods were stored. Chinese purchased imported wares against "native orders" which the comprador rediscounted with local Chinese banks. He himself used its treasury to speculate on wares on his own side.

The comprador seems to work well, but Chinese business is far from representing the diversity found in Shanghai: it is impossible there to use money for short-term operations, as is practiced in the South with Chinese bankers. The shorter advances there are on two to three months, and more generally on six months to a year [with interest rates at almost 10 per cent].[16]

The 1910–1911 troubles reveal the involvement of the *Banque de l'Indochine* branch in the financing of salt traders.[17] They had become key customers of both the Tianjin and the Beijing branches, among them Wang, the president of the Tianjin Chinese chamber of commerce and Ho Ping Chan—because the Changlu salt field was among the main producers of salt in China. They were organised in a "Committee of salt traders", who borrowed money against the pledge of the salt tax collection, under the supervision of the salt *tao bai*[18]—and the credit reached a level of 50,000 taels at the end of 1910. The salt business with the comprador had been extended to investments in salt trading, which were led in common by the compradors in Hankeou and Beijing:[19] in January 1911, the importance of this business led to uncertainty because the merchants were on the brink of collapsing.

The debt owned by salt leaseholder merchants (Quang, the chairman of the chamber of commerce, Li, and others) grew in 1907–1910 and indeed became "bad loans" because both Beijing and Tianjin branches took the easy way of granting trust to this layer of customers (and to the comprador as a go-between) in order to gain customership in the area and to assert the brand image of the bank, freshly established there.[20] The Tianjin comprador was unable to repay the bank for its borrowing (50,000 taels just for the month of December 1911). In order to prevent its salt customers and a majority of the small Chinese banks of the area from failing, *Banque de l'Indochine* had to renew its credits: 90,000 taels from its Beijing branch and 189,000 from Tianjin—whilst the Tianjin Russo-Chinese branch bore a loan of 200,000. "All our availabilities are now fixed in loans to Chinese, bankers or salt merchants. Impossible to get any funds on this side. We are even debtors to the banks of the place"[21]—this at a time when all the salt merchants were collapsing because sales of salt apparently declined harshly and the gabelle system was no longer functioning efficiently (see Table 4.3).

Table 4.3 Locking up of funds with the salt gabelle system on 1 April 1911 (taels)

Banque de l'Indochine branch in Tianjin	549,500
Banque de l'Indochine branch in Beijing	1,310,000
Banque de l'Indochine branch in Shanghai	1,100,000
Russo-Asiatic Bank	1600,000
Deutsch Asiatisch Bank	1,000,000
Yokohama Specie Bank	1,000,000
Sino-Belgian Bank	300,000
Chinese banks	3,000,000
Total	9,000,000

The state took drastic measures with the salt merchants: inquiries about their properties to seize them as pledges, imprisonment of about ten reluctant ones, and finally repayment by the state itself of 7 million taels of their debt in August, mainly thanks to a 6 million loan by the Ka Ta Ching Bank in July 1911. Finally *Banque de l'Indochine* came up with 3 million taels for its branches in Beijing and Tianjin, which were the creditors of ten big merchants.[22] This unexpectedly favourable result ended the involvement of the *Banque de l'Indochine* branch in the financing of the salt business; it was then resolved to dedicate its efforts to more day-to-day commercial operations and to avoid incurring large bad debts, thanks to an improved "capital of experience".

4. The results of a steadfast banking strategy in Tianjin in the 1910s

Such a sectorial survey of the business covered by the *Banque de l'Indochine* branch leads to a consideration of a global assessment of the results reached on the Tianjin marketplace beyond the day-to-day management of a branch, was it of any interest to set a French bridgehead there? In fact, one even has to wonder how such a branch could resist the shocks of its political and economic environment. But business in northern China was rich with adventures and at the heart of hot history-in-the-making, and traders, bankers and financiers who succeeded somewhat there had to resist such jolts and become acute intermediaries between military and political clans which tried to control the area. Despite its relatively satisfying management and business, the *Banque de l'Indochine* branch did not become the keystone of the *Banque's* activities in Asia or even in China. Its relative weight against the total returns (frequently at 2 per cent) remained far from those of the Shanghai and the Hong Kong branches, as shown in Table 4.4.

Table 4.4 Returns of the main *Banque de l'Indochine* branches at end of the 1910s (percentage)[23]

	First term 1916	First term 1919	Second term 1919	First term 1920
Indochina and Cambodia	44.6	50.9	47.3	41.6
China	23.6	22.8	17.4	18.5
South China (Guangzhou, Mongtze and Hong Kong)	11	9.2	11.2	5.6
Guangzhou	2.4	2.7	3	−5.8
Mongtze	5.3	5.3	6.2	3.8
Hong Kong	3.3	1.2	2	7.6
Shanghai	7.8	10.5	4.1	11.3
Hankeou	3.9	−2.2	−0.2	0
Tianjin	**1.8**	**5.5**	**1.9**	**2.4**
Beijing	−0.9	−0.2	0.4	−0.8
Singapore	4.7	2.7	16.1	3.6
Paris	14.2	6.2	4.7	4.4

But the strategic purpose defined by the Paris office and the French government was achieved: even in this Tianjin city where business prospects had not been high, the flag of a French bank succeeded in competing with the British ones, and the interests of the French concession had been well served, all the more because the port-city opened its doors more and more internationally as Pierre Singaravélou analysed it.[24]

The branch took root within the Tianjin market: it built the corporate image of the bank there; it carried the French flag to the heart of a French territory supposed to express the dominance of power at the entrance of the empire and provided services to French stakeholders there. It also constituted a base of customers among Chinese interests, especially bankers, salt merchants, trade houses, and even a mining company. It seized a market share of financing export–import trade and foreign exchange. It worked often in closed linkage with the Beijing branch, thus confirming the economic partnership between both markets. Throughout these accomplishments, it asserted its autonomy against the tutelage of the Shanghai branch, which predominated over the other branches in China, except Hong Kong.

Surely bankers served as leverage to foreign (and thus "imperialist") interests' penetration into several layers of Chinese economy,[25] even in the northern areas despite their far less commercial importance than the central and southern areas for foreign companies. And the *Banque de l'Indochine* branch was used by French interests first to penetrate into the area adjoining Tianjin and Beijing, with breakthroughs westwards towards the Shansi or elsewhere, and second to prospect in Manchuria despite the reversal of influence there, from Russian to Chinese and finally to Japanese stakeholding. Such a branch complemented the Shanghai leverage force established by *Banque de l'Indochine* and constituted a bridgehead into north-eastern China, either for business or, almost so much importantly, for getting information about the evolution of balance of powers, of economic trends, of currency moves, and of the orientation of trade exchanges.

Notes

1 *Banque de l'Indochine* correspondence between the Tianjin branch and the Paris Head Office, archives of *Crédit agricole, Banque de l'Indochine* fund, 22 December 1910.
2 *Ibidem*, 7 November 1911.
3 *Ibidem*, 23 February 1912.
4 *Ibidem*, 6 April 1912.
5 *Ibidem*, 12 July 1913.
6 *Ibidem*, 11 July 1907.
7 *Ibidem*, 5 February 1936.
8 *Ibidem*, 21 March 1907.
9 *Ibidem*, 7 April 1910.
10 *Ibidem*, 19 October 1911.
11 *Ibidem*, 17 April 1912.
12 See Mark Granovetter, "Economic action and social structure: The problem of embeddedness", *American Journal of Sociology*, November 1985, volume 91, n°3, pp. 418–510.

Mark Granovetter & Richard Swedberg, *The Sociology of Economic Life*, Boulder, West-view Press, 2001 (2nd edition).

13 *Banque de l'Indochine* correspondence, 7 February 1907.
14 See Yen-p'ing Hao, *The Comprador in Nineteenth Century China: Bridge Between East and West*, Cambridge, MA, Harvard University Press, 1970.
15 See Linsun Cheng, *Banking in Modern China: Entrepreneurs, Professional Managers and the Development of Chinese Banks, 1897–1937*, NewYork, Cambridge University Press, 2003. Brett Sheehan, *Trust in Troubled Times: Money, Banks, and State-Society Relations in Republican Tianjin*, Cambridge, MA, Cambridge University Press, 2003.
16 *Banque de l'Indochine* correspondence, 21 March 1907.
17 See Kwan Man Bun, *The Salt Merchants of Tianjin: State-Making and Society in Late Imperial China*, Honolulu, University of Hawai'i Press, 2001.
18 *Banque de l'Indochine* correspondence, 22 December 1910.
19 *Ibidem*, 13 January 1911.
20 Letter from the French Consul to the head of the *Banque de l'Indochine* branch, 7 April 1911, Nantes Consulate archives, 9C1.
21 *Banque de l'Indochine* correspondence, 9 February 1911.
22 *Ibidem*, 11 May 1911, 17 June, 7 July, 15 July, 23 August 1911.
23 Minutes of the Board of *Banque de l'Indochine*, 25 October 1916, 29 October 1919, 28 April 1920, 24 November 1920.
24 Pierre Singaravélou, *Tianjin Cosmopolis. Une autre histoire de la mondialisation*, Paris, Seuil, "L'Univers historique", 2017.
25 Clarence Davis, "Financing imperialism: British and American bankers as vectors of imperial expansion in China, 1908–1920", *Business History Review*, 1982, volume 56, n°2, pp. 236–264.

5 French trade and banking footholds in Wuhan

Challenging British hegemony up the Yangtze (1903–1914)

In the massive port-cities of Shanghai and Hong Kong,[1] the French business and banking communities were very active, and bridgeheads had been established in Tianjin and in the Guangdong by French businessmen and bankers around the time of World War I. Conversely the river port-city of Wuhan was a remote marketplace in upstream Yangtze/Yangzi Jiang, far from the core interest of French imports, exports and money flows. Though this study presents a challenge, it will serve to complement our survey of the initiatives, successes and limitations of French economic expansion in China in the first half of the twentieth century. It will reveal French entrepreneurs' ability to resist and overcome the competition and to join the group of major stakeholders.

At the same time, we shall also sketch the outlines of the "open economy" which took shape in the more remote regions upstream. But, as elsewhere, here too events conspired to hamper the development of the Wuhan port-city: the revolutionary movement and the subsequent civil war, the tensions created by the division of Republican China and the various social and political crises in Shanghai which hindered trade between Wuhan and its outlets abroad.

The issue revolves around the ability of the French to establish, in the name of economic patriotism, a bridgehead upstream of the Yangtze in the face of the strong British hegemony in trade, transport and banking.[2] In this text we hope to describe the foundations of French trade and banking in Wuhan, the methods followed to garner market share and weave networks of relationships with foreign and local merchants and the role played by compradors and intermediaries in penetrating the Chinese business community. We'll analyze the French bankers' skills portfolio, including the ability to control and avoid risks, the insertion of managers and intermediaries into the Wuhan–Shanghai axis regarding money and commodity operations and their growing FOREX operations.

Finally, we shall also assess the diversification in their clientele in order to determine how these French bankers succeeded in becoming stakeholders in the river port-city's business over and above merely serving the interests of the French business community. To gauge the "transnational" dimension acquired, we shall scrutinise the balance between French, non-French (German, Belgian, etc.) and Chinese business in the growth of French bankers' assets. This will also help profile the "imperial", "global" and "local" banking models. As bank regulations and risk management changed dramatically in 1920, we will focus on only the first 17 years of the *Banque de l'Indochine*'s branch.

1. How important was it to be embedded in Wuhan?

Though there is no doubt that, in this twenty-first century, being active in Wuhan represents a key advantage as the city is rich with more than 9 million inhabitants, supervises a fast-developing region in terms of energy, industry and services (with key French interests like Peugeot-PSA (automobiles), Valeo (car equipment), Alstom (electrotechnics) and Carrefour (retail), business prospects there were rather dim in the first decades of the previous century. The neighbourhood lacked substance, the range of commodities and minerals was limited, and the trade along the Yangtze River was restricted to local exchanges and specialties—a far cry from the scale of the "big" business and trade that had already taken shape downstream around Shanghai. Moreover, the region had just emerged from the Boxers uprising, which had been supported there by the reformist and nationalist viceroy himself, till he set limits to its spread.[3]

2. Wuhan: towards an "open" economy

The core issue laid in the hope that Wuhan[4] could turn into a regional hub with an "open economy", that the Yangtze axis would grow to have adequate substance for exports and imports and, last, that Wuhan could enter the network of Asia's "modern" hubs.[5] Two objectives prevailed: increasing trade between Wuhan and Shanghai on the domestic front and improving foreign trade and transforming the region into a major outlet for exports to Europe, Japan or the United States (like Tianjin), be they of high value (Guangzhou silk) or not. Apart from the port-city itself, trading could be extended into the Hunan province, where opportunities in mining, railways or commodities could be exploited to fend off Russian and German ambitions.

Before World War I, a 500-km railroad connecting Wuhan to Chángshā/ Tchang Cha (capital of Hunan province, with 500,000 inhabitants) already existed. The latter was a hub for collecting commodities and goods bound for the northern river shipping connections, which made Wuhan an important trans-shipment point linking rail to river traffic. A second track was laid in 1903–1905 connecting Wuhan to Beijing with the aid of Belgian (and French) finance, rail equipment and public works—the station in Wuhan, *Han kou da che men*, was designed by a French architect.[6] Subsequently, it was bought over by the state thanks to the Peking–Wuhan Railway Redemption Loan Agreement settled on 8 October 1908. These connections helped open up the area, with immediate effects on the degree of competition, services offered and a reduction in interest rates (from 12 to 10 percent in 1907 according to *Banque de l'Indochine*), which stimulated trade and led to the development of the Wuhan marketplace. Lastly, the building of the section linking Wuhan and Guangzhou commenced just before World War I.

One of the issues faced by bankers and traders was weaning the Wuhan market away from its dependence on Shanghai, its main rival. Traditionally, contracts (exports, boarding, financing) were signed in Shanghai, where the various stakeholders had been active for decades, leaving nothing for the bankers upstream except to be loan recovery managers. Though gradually the diversification of service equipment increased value addition in Wuhan, only some 20 million taels were "engineered" in Wuhan of the total 26 million exported in the first half of 1911 because a quarter of them were processed in Shanghai and transited through Wuhan warehouses and harbour only as trans-shipments.[7]

3. Which local resources to feed exchanges?

Foreign interests were mainly centred around tea, with Russia and Tibet as main clients and France not really involved. Still, the cash generated increased imports and helped French traders find outlets. It was only slowly that a wider range of goods and minerals began to figure in the list.

A. Rural resources

The staples traded epitomize the port-city's rural roots. It had become an outlet for commercial agriculture thanks to enterprising and open-minded peasants and craftsmen. Hides topped the list: cow hides (78,805 piculs[8] in the first half 1906 and 109,856 in the first half of 1907), buffalo hides (22,539 and 18,694) and goat hides (3,024,183 and 2,370,171 units). As Chinese trade intermediaries grew in size and scope, so did the opportunities for bank loans. The goods traded included vegetal and animal tallow (for candles and machinery), wood oil (for the manufacture of linoleum in Germany and United States and of varnish in the United States), pig bristles, sesame seeds (110,000 tons in 1908), gall nuts (to Germany and the United States), musk and jute[9] (see Tables 5.1 and 5.2).

The growing trade increased the need for credit, for both exporters and importers: equipment was imported for modernising villages (motorised winnowers for seeds, hydraulic presses and dryers for hides, steam heaters and

Table 5.1 Exports of rural commodities through Wuhan in the first half of 1911 (million taels)

Total value	26	
Sesame seeds	8	40% towards The Netherlands, 17% to France, 13% to Germany, 11% to Italy
Cowhides	4,5	French firm Olivier, Italian Chinese Export
Wood oil	4,5	Hegemony of US firm Gillespsie
Cotton	2,1	For Japan and other Chinese provinces

Source: Archives of *Banque de l'Indochine*, historical archives of *Crédit agricole*, BE 1047, 439 AH 179, *rapports-bilans semestriels*, 27 July 1911

Table 5.2 The major trading houses in Wuhan for the export of rural
commodities in 1908

Cowhides (piculs)		Sesame seeds (tons)
Carlowitz	45,000	15,000
Melchers	20,000	20,000
Arnhold Karberg	9,000	26,000
Racine Ackermann (French)	3,500	4,000
Olivier (French)		3,000
And also: Schweitzer,		
Furhmeister, Kolkmeijer,		
Evans Pugh, *Societa*		
Coloniale Italiana, Meyer,		
Theodore Rawlins		

Source: Crédit agricole archives, Fund Banque de l'Indochine, lettre, 1908

Table 5.3 The leading commodities exported
from Wuhan in 1915 (piculs)

Sesame seeds	1,770,025
Beans and broad beans	1,407,137
Wood oil	602,128
Cotton	461,112
Vegetal tallow	210,884
Cow hides	227,026
Ramie and jute	203,162
Gall nuts	57,449
Buffalo hides	14,961
Pig bristles	22,801

Source: Fund *Banque de l'Indochine*, historical archives
of *Crédit agricole*, BE 1047, 439 AH 179, *rapports-bilans
semestriels*, second half of 1915

tanks for oils and fatty substances). Because of growing competition and lower
profit margins, the cotton business gave way to the export of beans and horse
beans towards the end of the 1900s. France emerged as a major outlet for a few
commodities like sesame seeds and cowhides (sesame seeds came from Hebei
also), which constituted a peculiar aspect of this stage of the global economy at
the start of the twentieth century (see Table 5.3).

B. Black tea

Wuhan's biggest export was, of course, black tea with 278,426 piculs (556,852
"half-chests" or strong boxes) exported in 1906 and 350,709 piculs (701,418
"half-chests") in 1907. But as Russia was the biggest client of "brick tea"
(till the end of the 1910s), *Banque de l'Indochine* had to scramble to prevent

Table 5.4 Exports of tea from Wuhan in 1908 (lb)

To Nikolaievsk	8,797,700
To Vladivostock	7,430,500
To Odessa	4,423,200
To London	1,489,000
To Ohotsk	850,000
To Saint Petersburg	600,400

Source: Fund *Banque de l'Indochine*, historical archives of *Crédit agricole*, BE 1047, 439 AH 179, *rapports-bilans semestriels*, 1 February 1909

Russo-Chinese Bank[10] from assuming leadership in that field. Being the centre of the Chinese black tea trade, Wuhan attracted Russian tea traders who set up factories in the early 1860s to manufacture "brick tea", made from tea dust. Three of the four brick tea factories in Wuhan were owned by Russian businesses: SW Litvinoff & Co (known locally as Shun Fung), Tokmakoff, Molotkoff & C° (Hsin-Tai) and Molchanoff, Pechanoff & Co (Fu Cheong). Shipments from Wuhan went via steamers directly to Odessa and St Petersburg or were transported overland on the Tea Road via Mongolia and Siberia to Moscow. It finally succeeded in grabbing some market share from the leading bank and in seducing a few tea traders such as Trading C°, Theodor & Rawling and *Popoff Frères* (1915) (see Table 5.4).

4. Little flows of imports

Imports at the start of the century were still stagnant as the smaller Chinese traders were used to dealing directly with their Shanghai suppliers. As elsewhere, cotton cloth and spun cotton was imported for local craftsmen, joined later by velvet cloth. The progress of copper, iron, cement, machinery, oil and railway equipment illustrates the gradual diversification of the industry, the extent of the public works undertaken in the area and the complementarities between Wuhan and Shanghai as the doors to upstream Yangtze. As soon as the "open economy" spread across the countryside and into the merchant cities of Hebei and its neighbouring provinces, imports increased rapidly, transforming Wuhan from a hub for collecting commodities to a dispatching centre for imported goods, equipment and material. Some houses even specialised in this import trade which served as a lever for the issue of commercial paper, managing bills of exchange and remittances to clearing houses in Europe.

5. Competition as elsewhere

But despite their high ambitions, the French had to face the real balance of power. For instance, the French shipping company connecting Hong Kong and Shanghai had to stop its river services upstream in June 1911 and to yield to the

China Navigation Company's hegemony on the Yangtze. British and German houses[11] had long established themselves all along the river and its corresponding relays, the Yellow Sea[12] and the East China Sea. Their concessions in Wuhan were also much better entrenched compared to those of the French, especially as the *"hongs"*[13] exerted great influence from their base in Shanghai: Jardine Matheson and Swire & Butterfield had been very active in Wuhan since before World War I.

The British HSBC and the Russo-French *Banque russo-chinoise* had preceded *Banque de l'Indochine* upstream of the Yangtze: the former as the arm of British interests all across China, and the latter due to the heavy tea purchases by Russian traders in the provinces.

> No doubt that given equal rates, traders prefer certain banks, and for generations the Hong Kong [HSBC] and the *Russo-Chinoise* banks have grabbed the lion's share. But it is also because they too reciprocated in kind, advancing the sums required for purchases. We too can build ourselves a solid clientele. We are the only one, apart from the Hong Kong Bank, to have locally available funds—a big advantage in the eyes of the traders here. We just need to set right the misconception, still widespread, that we only deal with the Chinese, and to convince the Europeans that we would welcome them with the same facilities offered by other banks.[14]

The Japanese business community had established itself with ardour, with a federative trade house, a shipping company and the support of its Yokohama Specie Bank.[15] In 1907, there were around 1,600 Japanese in Wuhan. They were influential at the court of the viceroy of Hubei/Hou Peh and even managed to convince him to commence investing in modern city equipment—a rarity in those days. There were two types of Chinese banks: small and local, on one side, and, on the other side, the larger, medium-sized ones (about 25) mostly from Chansi or one of the nine "mandarin" banks linked to the Administration. Gradually they gained in size and stability, as was proven during a sharp

Table 5.5 Current accounts by banks in Wuhan at the end of June 1907 (thousand taels)

	Cash (deposits)	Loans to Chinese bankers
Yokohama Specie Bank	150	500
Russo-Chinese Bank	80	700
Deutschasiatisch Bank	500	200
Chartered Bank	200	?
HSBC	400	1,200
Banque de l'Indochine	75	1,080
		290 (for the account of the Saigon branch)

Source: Fund *Banque de l'Indochine*, historical archives of *Crédit agricole*, BE 1047, 439 AH 179, *rapports-bilans semestriels*, 9 August 1907

monetary crisis in Wuhan in October 1907: "Thanks to the resources gained over the past two to three years, Wuhan had a large reserve of liquid capital. Chinese houses have made great strides in creditworthiness."[16] This explains why *Banque de l'Indochine* lagged far behind the stakeholders of the Wuhan market in 1907: they had a long way to go! (see Table 5.5).

Notes

1 Hubert Bonin, "French banking in Hong Kong: From the 1860s to the 1950s", in Shizuya Nishimura, Toshio Suzuki & Ranald Michie (eds.), *The Origins of International Banking in Asia: The Nineteenth and Twentieth Centuries*, Oxford, Oxford University Press, 2012, pp. 124–144. Hubert Bonin, "Les banquiers français en Chine (1860–1950): Shanghai et Hong Kong, relais d'un impérialisme bancaire ou plates-formes d'outre-mers multiformes?", in Laurent Cesari & Denis Varaschin (eds.), *Les relations franco-chinoises au vingtième siècle et leurs antécédents*, Arras, Artois Presses Université, 2003, pp. 157–172.

2 Robert Lee, *France and the Exploitation of China, 1885–1901*, Hong Kong & London, Oxford University Press, 1989. Jacques Weber (ed.), *La France en Chine, 1843–1940*, Nantes, Presses académiques de l'Ouest-Ouest Éditions, Nantes University, 1997.

3 John Kelly, *A Forgotten Conference: The Negotiations at Peking, 1900–1901*, Geneva, Droz, "Travaux de droit, d'économie, de sociologie, n°5", 1963.

4 See William Rowe, *Wuhan: Commerce and Society in a Chinese City, 1796–1889*, Stanford, Stanford University Press, 1984.

5 François Gipouloux, *The Asian Mediterranean: Port Cities and Trading Networks in China, Japan, and Southeast Asia, 13th–21st Century*, Cheltenham, Elgar, 2011. François Gipouloux, *Gateways to Globalisation: Asia's International Trading and Finance Centres*, Cheltenham, Elgar, 2011.

6 See Ginette Kurgan-Van Hentenryk, *Léopold II et les groupes financiers belges en Chine*, Brussels, Palais des Académies, 1972. Ginette Kurgan-Van Hentenryk, "Un aspect de l'exportation des capitaux en Chine: les entreprises franco-belges, 1896–1914", in Maurice Lévy-Leboyer (ed.), *La position internationale de la France. Aspects économiques et financiers, XIXe–XXe siècles*, Paris, Éditions de l'École des hautes études en sciences sociales, 1977.

7 Fund *Banque de l'Indochine*, historical archives of Crédit agricole SA, BE 1047, 439 AH 179, *rapports-bilans semestriels*, 27 July 1911 [BIC, then onwards].

8 A *picul* (or *tam*) was a traditional Asian unit of weight, defined as "a shoulder-load", "as much as a man can carry on a shoulder-pole". As for any traditional measurement unit, the exact definition of the picul varied historically and regionally: In imperial China and later, the unit was used for a measure equivalent to 100 catties, or around 60 kg (*Wikipedia*).

9 Fund *Banque de l'Indochine*, historical archives of *Crédit agricole*, BE 1047, 439 AH 179, *rapports-bilans semestriels*, 9 August 1907.

10 See Olga Crisp, "The Russo-Chinese bank: An episode in Franco-Russian relations", *The Slavonic and East European Review*, 1974, volume 52, pp. 197–212. Nobutaka Shinonaga, *La Banque russo-chinoise et les relations franco-russes, 1896–1910*, Tokyo, Daito Bunka University, "The Economics Society", 2012.

11 Britten Dean, *Sino-British Diplomacy in the 1860s: The Establishment of the British Concession at Hankow*, Cambridge, MA, Harvard-Yenching Institute, 1972. Ewan Watt Edwards, "British policy in China, 1913–1914: Rivalry with France in the Yangtze valley", *Journal of Oriental Studies*, 1977, n°40, pp. 20–36.

12 See Torsten Warner, "Der Aufbau der Kolonial Stadt Tsingtau: Landordnung, Stadtplanung und Entwicklung (Building the colonial city of Tsingtao: Land regulation, city planning, and city development)", in Hans-Martin Hinz & Christoph Lind (eds.), *Tsingtau. Ein Kapital deutscher Kolonial Geschichte in China, 1897–1914*, Paderborn, Schöningh, 1985, pp. 188–191 (2nd edition).

13 Maggie Keswick (ed.), *The Thistle and the Jade: A Celebration of 150 Years of Jardine Matheson & Co*, London, Octopus Books, 1982. Robert Blake, *Jardine Matheson: Traders of the Far East*, London, Weidenfeld & Nicholson, 1999. Stephanie Jones, *Two Centuries of Overseas Trading: The Origins and Growth of the Inchcape Group*, London, Macmillan in association with the Business History Unit, University of London, 1986.

14 Fund *Banque de l'Indochine*, historical archives of *Crédit agricole*, BE 1047, 439 AH 179, *rapports-bilans semestriels*, 9 August 1907.

15 Norio Tamaki, "The Yokohama Specie bank: A multinational in the Japanese interests, 1879–1935", in Geoffrey Jones (ed.), *Banking as Multinationals*, London, Routledge, 1990. Kanji Ishii, "Japanese foreign trade and the Yokohama Specie bank, 1880–1913", in Olive Checkland, Shizuya Nishimura & Norio Tamaki (eds.), *Pacific Banking, 1859–1959: East Meets West*, London, Macmillan; New York, St. Martin's Press, 1994, pp. 1–23.

16 *Ibidem*, 15 February 1918.

6 Wuhan banking between economic patriotism and overall business

With Wuhan turning into a "pioneering front" for French businesses, I'll follow the emergence of French pioneers there and see how they built themselves a strongly rooted community in that developing market. The opening of the *Banque de l'Indochine*'s branch in 1902 (made autonomous in January 1904) epitomized the strategy drawn by French experts in Paris. Let us recall that the institution managing the currency and business banking in Indochina was assigned the mission of opening branches there in return for the renewal of its status in the colony. It took up the task in earnest at the turn of the century[1] to help the French compete against British, German, Japanese, Russian and, later, American trading, shipping and banking firms.

1. *Banque de l'Indochine* at the core of French business in Wuhan

The *Banque de l'Indochine* branch—headquartered on Dubail Street,[2] today *Dongting Jie*[3]—acted as the spearhead for an efficient penetration of French interests into Hubei province. Like its counterparts, the French concession[4] (set up in 1896 within the framework of the Treaty Ports)[5] was located within the settlements area in Wuhan long the HanRiver, close to the two other areas of Wuchang (*Outchangou*), on the right side of the Yangtze, and to Hanyang on the other side of the Han River.

A. A new business community

The branch was a cornerstone of the French concession which, in 1910, was headed by a French Consul who looked over 30,000 inhabitants spread over 361,000 square miles. It was relatively isolated, with a letter to Paris taking 21 days through Siberia or 40 days via the Suez Canal. "Imperialism" was very much at stake with the French flag fluttering proudly over the newly built *Hôtel municipal* and visits by warships like the *Dupleix* which came in June 1911 for the inauguration of the building. The manager of the *Banque de l'Indochine* branch, like the consul (for example, Joseph Réau,[6] consul and head of the French Municipality from 1910 to 1916 and Lecomte), entertained lavishly, both formally and informally, in order to consolidate their rooting and to foster solidarity now that a business "bourgeoisie" had taken shape. The *Cercle gaulois* and the Wuhan Club (which managed the race rack) were also social watering holes.

Like in all French concessions, business "bigwigs" (heads of trading and real estate houses) were the main stakeholders of the settlement (Brandt, O'Neil, Lehman, etc.). Though partners in economic patriotism, their continued success depended on their ability to respect basic management rules and good practices. The fragility of some of them, especially in the face of recessions, prevented the concession from attaining some degree of permanent economic stability.

B. Human and financial resources

Thus, the survival of this little French community depended in no small measure on the quality and competence of the *Banque de l'Indochine*'s branch manager. Most had already acquired some experience elsewhere before moving to this job: Trouillet graduated from the Bangkok branch to replace the Wuhan branch's founder, Joseph Pernotte, in 1909. He brought with him Lehman (promoted to deputy-manager in Saigon in August 1912) and Delaunay as deputies. The branch was given a credit line from Paris of 1 million dollars, complemented by advances from the Saigon branch (FRF 100,000 on 30 June 1904) and further contributions from Paris in addition to current profits. In 1908, FRF 1.4 million in capital and 7.8 million in cash advance helped the manager to achieve a breakthrough in the market. Sometimes he was also helped by his counterpart in Shanghai, where the availabilities were often abundant: for example, an amount of 14.6 million taels was lent (at 4 per cent interest) in December 1916.[7]

2. A dynamic strategy: the French offensive in the Wuhan region

The issue was well put by the first branch manager in 1907:

> Are we [not] here to take an increasingly more active part in the business affairs knowing that, despite the present difficulties, they have a brilliant future? I remember how pained I was to see, some years back, how isolated our branch had become from any European business and looking, for all intents and purposes, like an old retiree in the middle of this young and vibrant colony bursting with life and activity.[8]

Pernotte, the branch manager—who would later leave *Banque de l'Indochine* to head the smaller *Banque industrielle de Chine*[9] and stir up what he felt were over-conservative mindsets—spearheaded French entrepreneurship in the Yangtze region.

> Wuhan has entered the industrial stage of its economic development. This will gradually open up major opportunities for European industries for the

supply of all the material required by this growth. There is little doubt that, as elsewhere, here too the French industry will let itself be forgotten, stuck in its ivory tower, while the big English, German and American houses have already begun sowing the country with their agents and agencies. And, seeing the facilities offered by them—which sometimes border on sacrifice (as in the case of Borsig [German] for the pumps of Tan-San-Wan)—one has the distinct impression that they have realized the massive potential of the region and are prepared to fight tooth and nail. Meanwhile, our poor French houses, so timid and mediocre, are incapable of any sustained effort towards an as-yet far-off result.[10]

An offensive strategy was asserted: "We must never hesitate to accept an operation without profit if it could result in luring other advantageous ones."[11]

A. Trade finance and commercial banking

A dual strategy was to be deployed: "To prospect houses demanding credits for their export business at the expense of other banks, and managing bills to be discounted or paid for the account of houses with imports business."[12] Advances on bills amounted to £5.268 million in June 1909 (probably Shanghai pounds).

B. Advances without formal collaterals

The export houses found a rapidly developing market in advances on bills, paid by them to their regional suppliers, pending the loading of these goods on ships. As collateral, the goods kept in warehouses were scrutinised and checked by bankers, either for the usual warrants (registered in the books with documents) or for overdraft facilities or "advances on bills" which were less formalised, as they linked stocked goods and classical overdrafts without formalised pledges: "Loans against bills of exchange. We think that your bigger loans are all well covered by the merchandise specified in your statements and whose existence you have ensured by conducting regular visits and inspections."[13] In 1909, the branch took part in an agreement[14] between banks to tighten the conditions for loans: every check would be guaranteed by a formal "letter of linkage" and, at the end of each month, by a letter of recapitulation of the goods pledged. But competition forced banks to break away from this agreement and dabble in greater risk.

In any case, all this was not possible for tea because it required testing and sampling of the product and some heavy negotiations regarding price. "It goes completely opposite to the other goods such as hides, grains, oils, fats, fibres, etc., that is, all that we classify under the name 'general cargo'. For these articles, everything is done by 'forward' contracts in which the Wuhan trader acts as the link between the entire set of Chinese sellers and their European buyers."[15] Risks increased with price fluctuations because compradors, who maintained

Table 6.1 Amount of overdrafts on unpledged goods from the branch of Wuhan in 1905–1912 (taels)

	Our payments	Clients' repayments
1905	215,617	155,237
1906	859,510	785,062
1907	2,643,836	2,423,638
1908	7,214,616	6,750,797
First semester 1912	1,635,606	821,522

Source: Fund *Banque de l'Indochine*, historical archives of *Crédit agricole* SA, BE 1047, 439 AH 179, *rapports-bilans semestriels, passim*

relations with both European buyers and the local sellers, began speculating. Lastly, there were the risks of quality: "The goods we dispatch end up almost worthless: they lose in weight and quality, the hides have holes, the grains smell rotten, etc."[16] Tense negotiations were undertaken among dispatchers, experts and arbitrators, with major losses at stake.

The advantage of this type of credit was the rapid recovery of the loan—immediately after the trade house had sold and transferred the goods on board. The turnover of the capital involved was supposed to be rapid—except when recessions in Shanghai or tides on the Yangtze blocked exports downstream. "The money invested as advances on bills to be delivered was reimbursed and turned over more than three times in the same semester. The goods involved did not remain, on average, more than a month and a half in the go-downs."[17] Whatever the balance between security and commercial spirit, the take-off of this line of products was rapid from the first years of the branch (see Table 6.1).

Despite recurrent risks, *Banque de l'Indochine* had to admit Wuhan's profitability. It became a key stakeholder of that region, with a wide range of clients (see Table 6.2).

C. FOREX *operations*

Each *Banque de l'Indochine* branch dealt directly with FOREX operations not only because each was (relatively) free to add value to its cash treasury but also because each had to anticipate the fluctuations of the half dozen currencies used and in the prices of gold and silver for its coverage operations. The branch manager sent orders by telegraph to his partners in Shanghai, Hong Kong, Paris and London. Bills of exchange to be discounted and mainly remitted (in Europe or Asia) opened doors to clearing flows also involving FOREX operations. The branch had to get rid of its currencies as soon as their amounts commenced, posing some risk. Thus, in order to remain competitive, *Banque de l'Indochine* began to routinely buy and sell them on the Wuhan market.

Table 6.2 Major customers of the *Banque de l'Indochine* branch in Wuhan for advances on bills to be delivered in 1912 (taels)

German houses	
Schwarz Gaumer	151,314
Arnhold Karberg	88,768
Carlowitz	73,972
Melchers	3,881
French houses	
Miffret	17,466
E. Bouchard	8,186
Olivier	5,023
From various countries	
Mitsui Bussan Kaisha	59,498
New Chinese Antimony	17,556
Louis Göring	4,251 +
	192,760
J.K. Panoff	192,760
Alff	7,815
Total	664,437

Source: Fund *Banque de l'Indochine*, historical archives of *Crédit agricole*, BE 1047, 439 AH 179, *rapports-bilans semestriels*, July 1912

This trading of bills of exchange became a leading activity of the *Banque de l'Indochine* branch. For example, in the second semester of 1907, it bought bills for FRF 11.116 million (compared to only 1.802 million in the second semester of 1906) and sold bills for 5.176 million (0.303 in 1906). It included the support of FRF 10 million on paper for direct exports—for trade between Wuhan and other markets—supplemented by 2 million negotiated with the houses using Shanghai for managing their exports.[18] "This paper had been supplied to us mainly by the principal houses of Wuhan, whose patronage was eagerly sought after by all the major banks such as Arnhold Karberg, Carlowitz, Jardine Matheson, The Trading Company, etc."[19]

Losses and disappointing results alternated with massive profits. The manager struggled to balance the currencies against the risks. For example, in 1909, contracts to sell pounds in Shanghai and Tonkin were concluded in the Shanghai currency, with uncertainties on the value. In 1910, the temptation to jump on opportunities was fortunately curbed as the speculative positions could have threatened the branch:

It was due to this that we allowed our competitors to grab Carlowitz's FOREX contracts. As this house only dealt with big parcels, the fear of a lack of funds made us lose this business which, through interest on loans against bills to be delivered and FOREX profits, though small, was always profitable.[20]

Still, the branch's capital of expertise continued to increase, and the little boom preceding World War I was marked by sound FOREX operations on bills of trade, with an amount of FRF 12.1 million in the first semester of 1914 (compared to 8.4 million and 11.112 million in the first and second semesters of 1913, respectively). The branch acquired export paper, consisting of bills to be drawn on European banks as representative of the exporting trade houses, and the profits from these FOREX operations amounted to 28,974 taels in the first semester of 1914.

FOREX operations depended on loans against bills of exchange as it was only by negotiating its bills with a bank that it could expect to get overdraft facilities from it. This was perhaps the only type of loan that existed between banks and European traders. It was a result of the work conditions imposed by the region's circumstances. The largest export market of Western and Central China was Ha. All goods shipped over the Yangtze and its tributaries ended up here, as did the products from Honan after the opening of the railway line. Prior to their arrival here, the goods were handled the absolute minimum required for this short trip and it was at Ha, before being dispatched towards foreign ports, that they underwent the final preparations required by European markets. The time taken for this preparation varied by product. For example, the drying of hides sometimes required weeks, especially during the rainy season, while the cleaning of sesame seeds, which took place indoors, took little time. Chinese sellers received 80% of the amount from their European customers at the time of delivery.

It is for this that the latter needs to approach a bank, promising to pay back from his proceeds from the same merchandise which he already supposes [is] sold in Europe. Thus, the duration of this loan is theoretically the time taken between the reception of the goods from the Chinese and its dispatch either directly or via Shanghai. If one has the misfortune of dealing with an unscrupulous trader, the risks can be big as there are many ways of cheating: loans from several banks against the same merchandise, bigger loans than the real value either in quantity or quality, loans against merchandise he does not actually own, etc. This type of credit is thus much more of a personal loan than a real loan. Everything depends on the client's honesty, something which the English have well expressed by their term for these transactions—"in trust". It is a question of faith in the individual. Thus, it is imperative for the manager to know personally the people he deals with and to not miss any opportunity that could shed light on their sense of business ethics.[21]

3. Widening the customer base

Step by step, the small team (three Frenchmen, a comprador and their employees) succeeded in luring customers and established the institution in Wuhan's market. As a sign of its competitiveness, *Banque de l'Indochine* succeeded in drawing a part of the bills discounted between Wuhan and Shanghai for cotton exports:

> Our purchases of discounted bills on Shanghai have more or less doubled following the establishment of Spunt & Rosenfeld in Wuhan. It buys cotton and dispatches it to its Shanghai headquarters, replacing the Japanese houses which, till recently, had dominated these 15-day loan operations, the time to do the packaging, then replaced by term discounts of ten days on Shanghai.[22]

A. Belgian customers

Belgian companies, pioneers in the region, were the logical first target: getting them would quickly build *Banque de l'Indochine*'s reputation and help its entry into the local network. Railways had been useful tools for prospecting fresh markets: French interests were involved in railway projects in the wake of Belgian initiatives.[23] In the 1910s, French and Belgian interests had jointly managed the Lung–Tsing–U-Hai railway track, with bonds issued and capital raised in Belgium and France, and Seynot, a Frenchman, as chief engineer. *Banque de l'Indochine* conducted business with Belgian Trading, a trading house hungry for credit on bills (for the export of hides).[24]

It provided major loans to J.K. Panoff, a Belgian firm from Brussels, which exported minerals (antimony) for its own plant or for importers in Anvers. From 1915 it also processed a part in the Seven Mile Creek foundry in the Russian concession.[25] *Banque de l'Indochine*'s total risks with the group attained 734,394 taels in 1914 (mainly advances on bills to be delivered, on goods, bills), almost 1 million in 1915 and 921,000 in 1918 (FRF 5.5 million).[26] It also accounted for 70 per cent of the loans to Chinese Antimony in 1910. Via the intermediation of the Paris merchant bank *MM. De Neuflize*, Panoff also found an outlet in France:

> Major contracts with Stibium, *Usines de Brioude, Compagnie La Lucette*, Cookson, etc. which had been won through the intermediation of *MM. De Neuflize* were interrupted by the War. Large quantities of minerals have been detained in the ports of Lisbon and Alexandria. A part of it goes to De Neuflize and some other houses for which the operations had been conducted. Another part belongs to Panoff himself. His Belgian partner has asked his agent to pursue the restitution of this merchandise, on which there is considerable value-addition.[27]

L. van der Stagen came through during World War I as Belgian Trading Cy's representative in Wuhan and used the *Banque de l'Indochine* for imports.

B. Native prospects

In 1889, Zhang Zhidong/Chang Chi Tung was transferred as Viceroy of Liang-guang (Guangdong and Guangxi provinces) to Viceroy of Huguang (Hunan and Hubei provinces). He governed the province for the next 18 years (till 1907) and called for big plants to open up the path to modernity. While he ended his tenure on a more conservative note, his successor, Tchao Tse Chouan, rekindled the reformist spirit. Despite the cash flow crisis lived through by the State cotton mills, it paved the way for *Banque de l'Indochine* to join the informal consortium of bankers providing them loans.

That was the case for a cigarette plant (MAT), the Hanyan Plants (steel manufacturing, with 6,000 employees—from 1909 for *Banque de l'Indochine*, with collaterals on property documents), the Hupeh Cement Works (from 1912) and (in the French settlement) the Ching Long Flour Mill (from 1908/1914) set up by a group of Chinese investors managed by the French A. Brandt house—and the same for the Wuhan Waterworks, a Chinese company (Sun). In 1910, Hanyang Steel benefited from advances on rails to be delivered to the Tianjin–Pukow railway, repaid through remittances on London. Despite the offer for sale of the Ching Long Flour Mill in 1914, their production went on without any crisis with their banker,[28] which was not the case of Hupeh Cement, which was forced to close down in 1914 because of its Japanese creditors—but *Banque de l'Indochine* got back its advance (16,800 taels) thanks to a pledge on a cement stock.

Moreover, as it was practiced in other places, *Banque de l'Indochine* began offering advances in piasters to native bankers, with a risk on exchange (from 1907). It used its own go-down in the building of its branch to store the goods pledged against these advances but also rented other go-downs (*Pao-Tong* go-downs, since 1905). Prior to World War I, it relied on a comprador, Liu Sing Seng. Trustworthy connections were extremely important as Wuhan had only just begun to introduce modern accounting practices and transparency and local capitalism still lacked the scale. The "absence of strong indigenous houses presenting solid guarantees for credit and able to serve as intermediaries between the European trader and the Chinese retailer."[29] "The resumption of these operations since last September has been of considerable benefit for us. Moreover, we have transferred the short-term loans, whose flexibility is valuable for our cash balance, from Shanghai to Wuhan."[30]

Like its fellow banks, *Banque de l'Indochine* widened its trade network by dispatching imported goods all across the province and its neighbourhood: discounting paper spread deep into the countryside. Though profit per operation was meagre, the aim was to accumulate these quick returns to amortise the resources (deposits, advances from Paris) mobilised in such businesses:

> Our branch itself absorbed some six million taels on average every year which, along with millions more brought by the other banks, disappeared in the Chinese hinterland or returned in part to settle import accounts. In

any case, they came back to us in the form of francs credited to us in Paris only six to eight months later. This unavoidable cycle is the result of the unique conditions of this place (large number of imports) which requires a constant supply of funds to function.[31]

4. Credit to import/export houses

The French bank did not hesitate to pick up business and credit opportunities among the challengers of French companies, mainly German and British competitors.

A. German trading houses

German customers made a beeline to the *Banque de l'Indochine*'s branch, happy to extend their credit line for their overall trade. Their needs were high as they accounted for 30 per cent of the overall Wuhan trade in 1910. The branch was patronized by both modestly sized companies (Schnabel-Gaumer, Lautenbach, S. Wurch, Kolmeyer & Rockstroh, etc.) and large ones (Melchers & C° since 1912). Moreover, Carlowitz and Arnhold Karberg (set up as early as 1866 in Shanghai), both present in several port-cities, frequented the branch with success before World War I, getting credit to finance their imports in Europe, China and Wuhan. They were very active in imports, purchasing cotton cloth in Manchester and selling them in Shanghai and Wuhan. "It was to avoid the big risks run by the German houses when they extended to the Chinese very long credit lines that the importers of Manchester preferred going through the Germans as intermediaries."[32]

As in other provinces, they gave the British a run for their money, and the *Banque de l'Indochine* had to be involved unless it wanted to miss the boat. In 1915, a *Banque de l'Indochine* report related *ex post* the extent of the German competitive spirit:

> We have given our complete support to the French houses here. And after the disappearance of the Germans, all of them have made big profits. The commissions, which earlier had been below the improbable, have returned to normalcy. It was because the Germans had worked not so much to make money as to monopolize the market and destroy the competition at all costs.[33]

B. British trading houses

The 1910s were marked by the arrival of British customers like Harvey & C°, which used the *Banque de l'Indochine* as their sole banker to finance their imports from Liverpool to upstream Yangtze:

> This house only does imports. All of its credit lines opened in Europe pass through our hands. This type of business is not an immobilisation, but a

continuous rolling to which we have set an upper limit. Every check is, so to say, a new business as it guarantees us new merchandise, and every payment becomes a part or full repayment of an earlier loan. This rolling also brings us FOREX business and presently, we have £17,000 in sales contracts.[34]

Spunt & Rosenfeld, a house based in Shanghai, established itself in Wuhan during World War I. In May 1916, *Banque de l'Indochine* bought large quantities of bills to be remitted on Shanghai. In the first semester of 1916, the firm accounted for a fourth of all cotton exports to Japan, financed through *Banque de l'Indochine* (1.4 million taels).

J. Spunt is a big house specialized in the cotton trade. It works for the Shanghai house and settles our accounts from its discounts on Shanghai: 444,000 taels as loans against remittances in Shanghai at the time of the cotton harvest in September 1916.[35]

The powerful English house of Dodwell, which managed the tea business of the *Anglo-Asiatic* trading house in Wuhan and which had the opportunity of granting overdraft facilities for the transfer of bills to Europe through the *Banque de l'Indochine*'s services, also joined the fray during World War I.[36] After 1915, Burtenshaw,[37] taking advantage of the German withdrawal, forged ahead, relying completely on the *Banque de l'Indochine*'s branch: he was the main importer of Belgian plate glass, and his boss was an important investor too, in *Pharmacie centrale*, Central Stores, *Patell Frères*, and a plant for carbonated water.[38] The firm amassed 421,000 taels[39] at the start of 1918, favouring advances on goods by *Banque de l'Indochine* for an amount of 47,000 taels (2,000 crates of window glass, lighting equipment and electrical appliances).[40] A few houses complemented this core set of clients. In 1914, the Swiss Louis Göring and his mining company (Göring-Laidrich/Wan Chen Chu) were treated as big clients for their tin export business. The China-Java Export Company was also accompanied in its development.

Notes

1   Yasuo Gonjo, *The History of Banque de l'Indochine (1875–1939): French Imperialism in the Far East*, Tokyo, Tokyo University Press, 1985, thesis in Japanese, translated into French and published in 1993 by the *Comité pour l'histoire économique & financière de la France*, Paris. Marc Meuleau, *Des pionniers en Extrême-Orient. Histoire de la Banque de l'Indochine (1875–1975)*, Paris, Fayard, 1990. Hubert Bonin, "The French banks in the Pacific area (1860–1945)", in Olive Checkland, Shizuya Nishimura & Norio Tamaki (eds.), *Pacific Banking (1859–1959): East Meets West*, London, Macmillan; New York, St. Martin's Press, 1994, pp. 61–74. Hubert Bonin, "L'activité des banques françaises dans l'Asie du Pacifique des années 1860 aux années 1940", *Revue française d'histoire d'outre-mer*, 1994, volume 81, n°305, pp. 401–425.

2   The building itself is today the *Victori & Café*.

3 From the name of a battle in 1854 where Chinese troops won over foreign ones during the Taipin war, as if anti-imperialism had to be proclaimed against a past when the Powers had predominated.

4 Dorothée Rihal, *La concession française de Hankou (1896–1943): de la condamnation à l'appropriation d'un héritage*, PhD thesis, directed by Nora Wang, 2007.

5 Rhoads Murphey, *The Treaty Ports and China's Modernization: What Went Wrong?*, Ann Arbor, University of Michigan, Center for Chinese Studies, 1970. John King Fairbank "The creation of the treaty system", in Denis Twitchett & John King Fairbank (eds.), *The Cambridge History of China*, volume 10, part I, Cambridge, Cambridge University Press, 1970, pp. 213–263.

6 "Last evening, I dined at the *Banque* [*de l'Indochine*], with the O'Neil, the Brandt and Bondeuf. This evening I will dine with the Brandt and tomorrow with the Hervy", 10 June 1912, in Philippe Marchat, *Raphaël Réau, consul à Hankéou pendant la Révolution chinoise et la Grande Guerre, 1910–1916*, Paris, L'Harmattan, "Mémoires asiatiques", 2013, p. 112. On 12 June, Réau had dinner with the Brandt, the O'Neil and Lehman [the deputy-head of the *Banque de l'Indochine* branch]. "Lehman invited me to the bank along with the O'Neil, very nice", *ibidem*, 15 June 2012. Réau was promoted to Hong Kong.

7 Fund *Banque de l'Indochine*, historical archives of *Crédit agricole*, correspondence and statistics from the branch to the headquarters, 439AH535, 30 December 1916.

8 Archives of *Banque de l'Indochine*, historical archives of *Crédit agricole*, BE 1047, 439 AH 179, *rapports-bilans semestriels*, 9 August 1907.

9 Frank King, "Sino-French *Banque industrielle de Chine* between 1900–1922", in Peter Hertner (ed.), *Finance and Modernization: A Transnational & Transcontinental Perspective for the Nineteenth and Twentieth Centuries*, Farnham, Ashgate, 2008. André Joseph Pernotte, *Pourquoi et comment fut fondée la Banque industrielle de Chine, ses difficultés, ses ennemis, politique et finance*, Paris, Jouve, 1922.

10 Fund *Banque de l'Indochine*, historical archives of *Crédit agricole*, BE 1047, 439 AH 179, *rapports-bilans semestriels*, 15 February 1908.

11 Fund *Banque de l'Indochine*, historical archives of *Crédit agricole*, correspondence and statistics, 439AH535, 5 April 1907.

12 *Ibidem*, 4 April 1903.

13 Fund *Banque de l'Indochine*, historical archives of *Crédit agricole*, correspondence and statistics from the branch to the headquarters, 439AH535, 24 March 1914, 11 March 1911.

14 *Ibidem*, 2 April 1909.

15 *Ibidem*, 11 March 1911, 24 March 1914.

16 Fund *Banque de l'Indochine*, historical archives of *Crédit agricole*, BE 1047, 439 AH 179, *rapports-bilans semestriels*, 15 February 1908.

17 *Ibidem*, January 1916.

18 *Ibidem*.

19 *Ibidem*.

20 *Ibidem*, January 1911.

21 *Ibidem*, 15 February 1908.

22 *Ibidem*, January 1916.

23 See Ginette Kurgan-Van Hentenryk, "Un aspect de l'exportation des capitaux en Chine: les entreprises franco-belges, 1896–1914", in Maurice Lévy-Leboyer (ed.), *La position internationale de la France, Aspects économiques et financiers, XIXᵉ–XXᵉ siècles*, Paris, Éditions de l'École des hautes études en sciences sociales, 1977.

24 Fund *Banque de l'Indochine*, historical archives of *Crédit agricole*, correspondence and statistics, 439AH535, 5 April 1908.

25 *Ibidem*, 18 March 1914, 31 March 1915.

26 *Ibidem*, 7 April 1918.

27 Fund *Banque de l'Indochine*, historical archives of *Crédit agricole*, BE 1047, 439 AH 179, *rapports-bilans semestriels*, July 1915.

28 Fund *Banque de l'Indochine*, historical archives of *Crédit agricole*, correspondence and statistics from the branch to the headquarters, 439AH535, 24 March 1914.
29 Fund *Banque de l'Indochine*, historical archives of *Crédit agricole*, BE 1047, 439 AH 179, *rapports-bilans semestriels*, 9 August 1907.
30 *Ibidem*, 20 July 1909.
31 Fund *Banque de l'Indochine*, historical archives of *Crédit agricole*, BE 1047, 439 AH 179, *rapports-bilans semestriels*, 1 July 1916.
32 *Ibidem*, January 1916.
33 *Ibidem*, July 1915.
34 Fund *Banque de l'Indochine*, historical archives of *Crédit agricole*, *Lettres-bilans*, from the headquarters to the branch, 439AH535, 19 April 1913.
35 Fund *Banque de l'Indochine*, historical archives of *Crédit agricole*, BE 1047, 439 AH 179, *rapports-bilans semestriels*, January 1917.
36 Fund *Banque de l'Indochine*, historical archives of *Crédit agricole*, correspondence and statistics from the branch to the headquarters, 439AH535, 2 April 1909, 13 March 1916, 12 September 1916.
37 *Ibidem*, 7 September 1917.
38 Fund *Banque de l'Indochine*, historical archives of *Crédit agricole*, correspondence and statistics from the branch to the headquarters, 439AH536, 20 January 1918.
39 At this time, the tael was valued at seven francs.
40 Fund *Banque de l'Indochine*, historical archives of *Crédit agricole*, correspondence and statistics from the branch to the headquarters, 439AH536, 20 January 1918.

7   *Banque de l'Indochine*'s breakthrough in Wuhan (in the 1900s–1910s)

Against such a promising background, *Banque de l'Indochine* scrambled to seize part of the business opportunities on the Wuhan banking marketplace. Its very success crowned the strategy defined by the French State and by *Banque de l'Indochine*'s Board to accompany French business on key Chinese port-cities, this one upstream on the Yangze.

1. Privileged French customers

A thorough analysis of the *Banque de l'Indochine*'s contribution to French interests is not possible, but there is no question that the French business community was a priority target. All six Catholic missions active in the area were clients (for their deposits of 37,253 taels in 1911) as was the concession's Municipality as regards its cash flow and some borrowings after 1911 (with a debt of 85,106 taels in June 1918). *Crédit foncier d'Extrême-Orient*, a Franco–Belgian financial institution linked with real estate investors in French concessions, borrowed in Wuhan (60,000 taels in June 1918). Though *Banque de l'Indochine* had no monopoly and French firms were often also clients of HSBC, for instance, several houses approached it regularly, happy to use its connections to the main Chinese port-cities and Europe.

Banque de l'Indochine also dealt with several local companies like Monbaron (1909), Adolphe Grosjean & Cie, Cossantelis Brothers (a Greek house from Marseille, active in Calcutta and Wuhan) and A. Miffret—which financed its entire export of hides through *Banque de l'Indochine* in 1912: "This house made great progress by dealing with Europe and America in its speciality of leather and hides using open and documentary letters of credit. It uses the services of the International Banking Corporation for its business in the United States."[1]

Wuhan also hosted the offshoots of bigger companies that were active in several port-cities such as Racine-Ackermann: "This house is extremely methodical and prudent and has done very well over the past few years. Its balance with us this semester attained 260,000 taels. It has since remitted 130,000 from HSBC and 130,000 in Europe."[2] The branch also worked with Olivier, the largest French trading house in China and its maritime neighbourhood: "This house too has done very well over the past few years. Originally established in the English concession, it has migrated to the free lands of Tachimen [Tai Chi Man], where the hide business is not forbidden, and has built there a first class establishment."[3]

On a smaller scale, the branch also serviced retailers like the chemist Picca, the clockmaker *Dubois* and the Italian foodstore Cozzi (till 1916, when the Italian Chinese Import & Export bought it), expressing the intimacy between the bank and daily life in the settlement. Established in Wuhan, *Société franco-chinoise de distillerie*—set up in 1909 by Yao Foo Chen—became a permanent client, with advances on securities (1911) and overdrafts. For a while, the branch was in touch with Bouchard, the manager of a colliery. In Wuhan as in other provinces, a few French entrepreneurs and investors tried (and often succeeded) in exploiting local mineral resources, even on a small scale.[4]

All things considered, *Banque de l'Indochine* satisfied the demands for a banking form of economic patriotism by actively supporting its French customers in the Wuhan riverport-city. World War I was a first apex for this development, thanks to the temporary elimination of German competitors: "The French houses—notably Grosjean, Racine-Ackermann and Miffret—are presently passing through a period of unmatched prosperity. A string of businesses that have resulted in profits they could never have known without the disappearance of the German houses from European markets."[5] Meanwhile, *Banque de l'Indochine* kept its feet firmly on the ground, financing other foreign houses active on the Yangtze to an equal amount—if we focus on the special "credit product" available at the port, that is, advances in blank, pending the issuing of formal bills (see Table 7.1).

The *Banque de l'Indochine*'s Shanghai branch was a permanent commercial partner too. Both branches acted with a large degree of autonomy (except for a very few years). The Wuhan branch used its cash treasury to purchase bills to be

Table 7.1 Breakdown of credit amounts of advances on bills to be delivered at the *Banque de l'Indochine*'s Wuhan branch in May 1916 (taels)

French houses	
Racine Ackermann	2,045,226
Grosjean	556,141
Miffret	446,817
Olivier	304,047
Subtotal	3,352,231
Foreign houses	
Italian Chinese Import & Export	1,317,428
Spunt & Rosenfeld	1,067,931
Mitsui Bussan Kaisha	98,931
Panoff	627,212
Subtotal	3,111,502

Source: Fund *Banque de l'Indochine*, historical archives of *Crédit agricole*, correspondence and statistics from the branch to the headquarters, 439AH536, 13 May 1916

drawn on Shanghai through the Shanghai branch. The latter mobilised its own cash as deposits by its sister branch, which managed some means of payment on a daily basis and, more importantly, by organising the transfer of the amount of the salt tax collected in Hebei and its neighbourhood.

2. Hurdles on the path of expansion

Several barriers had to be overcome in the course of a successful implementation of a developmental business strategy in Wuhan.

A. The effects of the general crisis of 1907

Within a few years of its establishment, the *Banque de l'Indochine* branch had to face the turmoil caused by the severe recession that struck the United States, then Europe, and last Shanghai and a few port-cities. Exports fell in 1908, and the collapse of several firms in Wuhan affected many banks, notably the branch of the Russo-Chinese Bank which was badly hit by the fall of its comprador—though the other banks were all repaid in that last case, except HSBC. *Banque de l'Indochine* had to curtail its advances, even though it could not give up on its weakened customers in the midst of the crisis. FOREX operations turned uncertain, with the bank and its clients having to bet on a revival in valuations which made the "situation difficult for our branch. On one hand, we cannot refuse FOREX to our clients who are themselves straining to guard themselves against the expected hike, and on the other, it is almost impossible for us to cover ourselves."[6]

B. Local worries in the first semester of 1910

Apart from the world's economic conditions, China was confronted with its own "regional" disturbances. In the first semester of 1910, several houses collapsed in Shanghai and, by domino effect, in Wuhan. The rapid expansion after the 1907–1908 crisis led to over-deleveraged operations among Chinese traders, who had benefited from too many loans by mainly German houses and bankers. A few compradors, unable to recover their assets, fled (at China & Java Export). German houses had failed to implement the rules of loan balancing and the monitoring required on the quality and quantity of stocked goods. Some of them ended up with bad debts, which affected their bankers. *Banque de l'Indochine* itself declared immobilised loans to Fuhrmeister (13,000 taels) and to Kolkmeijer & Rockstroh (76,000 taels, among them some 20,000 for the export of wood oil to the United States). Fortunately, the branch manager had refused to extend FOREX credits to German clients.[7] But these claims were to load its accounts for a while.

C. The effects of the Wuchang Uprising (1911)

A ferocious mini-civil war broke out in the area in 1911: the so-called Double Ten insurrection (or Wuchang Uprising)[8] was launched by local revolutionary groups on 10 November against the Qing imperial regime—as in Guangzhou, it was nationalism against imperialism. Heavy fighting between the official army and the insurgents followed the flight of the Viceroy Rui Cheng: from 17 October to 1st December, the revolutionary army and local volunteers defended the city in the Battle of Yangxia against the better armed and more numerous Qing forces commanded by Yuan Shi Kai. The latter seized Wuhan (except the concessions) and Hanyan, but not Wuchang, as by then the revolt had spread all across central China to Nanking (30 November), and negotiations led to an agreement which would eventually bring about the Republic (ushered in on 19 December after the Regent was deposed). All in all, it was one month of hard infighting in the port-city, two and a half months of local war followed by a huge fire in November and the destruction of more than a third of the town. Even after that, anarchy prevailed as the Republicans could not maintain order, and regional trade came to a grinding halt.

Delegates of foreign settlements—including French consul Raphaël Réau[9]—succeeded in convincing the belligerents not to bomb them and to provide better healthcare to injured soldiers. Meanwhile, precautions were also taken in the form of French military ships with troops steaming up the Yangtze (the *Décidée*, then the *D'Aberville*). Troubles resurfaced when the Yan Shi Kai regime parted ways with their former revolutionary partners. Once again, purges and revolts rendered the trade roads insecure. *Banque de l'Indochine*'s major clients were badly affected: public works came to a halt affecting the tin mines of Louis Göring and the Hupeh Cement Works.[10]

A mass of unpledged advances were suddenly frozen, leading the *Banque de l'Indochine*'s Paris headquarters to place its branch under the direct supervision of the Shanghai manager (1912 to 1st July 1913). Numerous Chinese clients failed to repay their debt, and the guarantee shouldered by the comprador had to be committed. But he himself was short of funds, and his own debt amounted to 1,312,000 taels in 1916 along with the irrecoverable claims on his Chinese connections. But all things considered, the effect on the *Banque de l'Indochine* branch was not severe, and business regained momentum in 1913–1914.

3. Was it worth investing in the Wuhan market?

It is always difficult to understand the strategic and financial mindset which leads companies to form developmental strategies, either in skill portfolios or in new regions. Grazing for bits of business in far off regions might seem a shallow business model. The history of companies, the core of business history, is rife with questions like: was it worth committing so many human and financial resources to such petty commitments?

A. Banque de l'Indochine *stirring fresh competition*

Banque de l'Indochine fought to gain access to French and foreign companies active in these fields, and its progress was rapid: in fact, the opening of the branch filled a void, and the Wuhan trading community felt happy to have a new supplier of credit. In *Banque de l'Indochine*'s own words: "These figures represent about one sixth of the overall exports, which is an encouraging result if we take into account the considerable part of HSBC."[11] The branch experienced several years of rapid growth, with 15 per cent in 1908–1909 (after a recession) and a doubling of exports of hides in 1910. For goat hides only, the *Banque de l'Indochine*'s branch accounted for 47 per cent of all loans in 1912, thanks to its client *China Java Export* (with German interests) (see Table 7.2).

B. A sustainable offshoot

The rapid upward move of the *Banque de l'Indochine* branch was crowned with success—or so it seemed. Its new head in 1908–1909, Trouillet, swore[12] that he had improved risk control, as in the case of Arnhold Karberg: he personally checked the elasticity of the account and followed the balance on a daily basis. "We are following our client's daily movements with the utmost attention and thus have a clear idea of their business activities."[13] Go-downs (warehouses) were visited either by the boss (for example, to Racine-Ackermann, Schwarz-Gaumer, and Miffret in April 1909) or by his deputy Delaunay. Liquidity was the chief concern: "Our old advances against goods are a continuously rolling

Table 7.2 Part of *Banque de l'Indochine* in the financing of exports from Wuhan in 1909–1915

	During the first semester 1909 (piculs)			In the second semester 1909	In 1915
	Banque de l'Indochine	Total bank financing	Per cent	Per cent	Per cent
Goat hides	330,000	2,138,000	15.43		
Sesame seeds	372,000	1,386,000	26.84	25	8
Beans	45,000	525 000	8.57	17	
Wood oil	18,600	269,000	6.91		0.5
Cow hides	17,600	132,000	13.33	14	14
Vegetal tallow	38,000	125,000	30.40	25	14
Ramie (China grass, also called "Chinese plant" or "white ramie") (for fabric manufacturing)	7,000	66,000	10.61		
Gall nuts	2,400	21,000	11.43		3 or 4
Buffalo hides	2,900	20,000	14.50		2
Pig bristles	1,380	6,281	21.97	36	18
Cotton					8.5
Ramie and jute					2

Source: Fund *Banque de l'Indochine*, historical archives of *Crédit agricole*, BE 1047, 439 AH 179, *rapports-bilans semestriels*, 1909, 1910, 1915

business where the pledged merchandise is constantly changing. Import stocks are renewed as soon as they are depleted."[14] Concern for liquidity, struggle against the risk of asymmetry of information and commonplace attention given to collaterals and to the risk of reputation among customers belonged to the classical toolbox of the bankers.

Such a capital of experience and skills exerted beneficial effects on the curve of profitability of the *Banque de l'Indochine* branch. Despite inevitable ups and downs, it proved to be somewhat of a financial success (see Table 7.3).

But this *Banque de l'Indochine* branch was not a cornerstone in the life of the overall bank as its return did not even attain 5 per cent of the total returns of the *Banque de l'Indochine*'s branches in 1916. In 1907, the capital (FRF 1,393,531) and the overdraft drawn on Paris (FRF 7,826,531), totalling FRF 9,220,062, generated returns of FRF 285,843 over the two semesters of 1917; that is an ROCE (return on capital employed) of 3.1 per cent, which is low considering the risks undertaken and the distance between the branch and banking hubs in China (Shanghai, Hong Kong), London and Paris (see Table 7.4).

4. A piece within a large jigsaw puzzle

Still, business and banking histories have to take a much wider view in order to arrive at a more balanced assessment. First, let us remind ourselves that

Table 7.3 Profits and losses of the *Banque de l'Indochine*'s Wuhan branch in 1904–1914

| | FRF | |
	Profits	Taels
1904 First semester	125,881	40,541
1904 Second semester	128,789	
1905 I	?	
1905 II	?	
1906 I	146,370	
1906 II	396,000	
1907 I	146,130	
1907 II	139,713	
1908 I	424,189	
1908 II	236,914	111,352
1909 I	83,198	27,733
1909 II	139,107	
1910 I	?	
1910 II	109,943	
1911 I	161,135	50,804
1911 II	Around 205,000	68,339
1912 I	268,573	77,847
1912 II	111,497	
1913 I	77,167	
1913 II	154,173	

Table 7.4 Returns of the major *Banque de l'Indochine* branches
in the first semester 1916 (percentage)

Indochina and Cambodia	44.6
Singapore	4.7
Paris	14.2
Total of China	23.6
South China (Guangzhou, Mongtze, and Hong Kong)	11
Guangzhou	2.4
Mongtze	5.3
Hong Kong	3.3
Shanghai	7.8
Wuhan	**3.9**
Tien Tsin	1.8
Beijing	−0.9

Minutes of the Board of *Banque de l'Indochine*, 25 October 1916

economic patriotism was at stake, which meant that *Banque de l'Indochine* had to open and manage branches in every port-city and provide for French trading, shipping and insurance companies. In that regard, the implantation in Wuhan was a success, with about a dozen French houses relying on the branch, its three French-speaking bankers, its warehouses and services.

Second, the complementarity between *Banque de l'Indochine* branches profited from the development of the Wuhan branch. The Saigon branch invested cash while the Shanghai branch worked closely with its sister upstream for trade finance and FOREX operations and the management of payment and remittances. For the "house of *Banque de l'Indochine*", it was an opportunity for mutualising the management of its twin offshoots.

Third, on the scale of the entire firm, any multinational company could find complementary services in that branch in favour of their multiple bases in Chinese port-cities: think of German, French or British firms active in the Yangtze valley and elsewhere (Olivier, etc.). Offering a banking presence across so many markets added to the French bank's reputation and cemented its international position and brand image. In the eyes of its customers, *Banque de l'Indochine* was almost equivalent to a "*Banque de Chine*".

Fourth, the amortisation of the entire banking firm, on a global scale, was favoured by the development of the Wuhan branch. Specialised departments, business units in market banking, FOREX, trade finance, documentary credit, management of means of payment and money flows and so on could incorporate the small flows engineered in Wuhan and the regions upstream of the Yangtze into the "big machine" of their "organisation of firm" at the scale of *Banque de l'Indochine*. The little bits of business brought by the Wuhan branch contributed to reducing the overall cost of exploitation of the banking firm as a whole, be it in Shanghai, London or Paris. Here, there were no "noble" products like the silk tackled by the Guangzhu branch, no sheer amounts like those of Indochinese rice managed by the Hong Kong branch. As in Tianjin, low-key products were the norm, but each one, like pig bristles or hides, fuelled business and contributed in its small way to the building of *Banque de l'Indochine* in Asia and European.

Fifth, as the Wuhan branch gathered momentum, its managers and employees formed part of the managerial team, which reinforced the portfolio of skills and the capital of competence of the *Banque de l'Indochine* as a firm. Generally speaking, at the scale of this modest competitor to HSBC, it enhanced the over-all Asian corporate culture of the institution, as has been studied by Frank King regarding HSBC.[15] Details such as the joining of a senior employee at Wuhan as deputy manager at the Saigon branch exemplify the spillover of "good prac-tices" in risk management and of the portfolio of skills throughout the *Banque de l'Indochine*'s network of branches in China.

Competition was fierce, especially from HSBC.[16] After a promising start, the Wuhan branch endured great difficulties in the second half of the 1910s. But all in all, it succeeded in gaining ground against the banking bigwigs. In fact, it survived both its rivals: first Russo-Chinese Bank and then (from 1910), Russo-Asiatic Bank. The latter was weakened by bad business in Wuhan and by the Russian revolution, and the second, *Banque industrielle de Chine*, collapsed in 1923 (though succeeded by *Banque franco-chinoise*, it was later amalgamated into *Banque de l'Indochine*). The "Darwinian syndrome", so effective in business history, did not apply to *Banque de l'Indochine* or its branch.

Notes

1 Fund *Banque de l'Indochine*, historical archives of *Crédit agricole*, BE 1047, 439 AH 179, *rapports-bilans semestriels*, January 1917.
2 *Ibidem.*
3 *Ibidem.*
4 Fund *Banque de l'Indochine*, historical archives of *Crédit agricole*, *Lettres-bilans*, from the headquarters to the branch, 439AH535, 11 April 1914.
5 Fund *Banque de l'Indochine*, historical archives of *Crédit agricole*, BE 1047, 439 AH 179, *rapports-bilans semestriels*, January 1916.
6 *Ibidem,* "Year 1908", 1 February 1909.
7 *Ibidem,* 27 July 1910.
8 Wuhan was known as the birthplace of the *Xinhai Revolution*, named after the Xinhai year on the Chinese calendar. There are several museums and memorials to the revolu-tion and the thousands of martyrs who died defending the revolution.
9 Nicole Bensacq-Tixier (ed.), "Réau Raphaël", in *Dictionnaire du corps diplomatique et con-sulaire français en Chine, 1540–1911*, Paris, Les Indes savantes, 2003, pp. 469–471. Philippe Marchat, *Raphaël Réau, consul à Hankéou pendant la Révolution chinoise et la Grande Guerre, 1910–1916*, Paris, L'Harmattan, "Mémoires asiatiques", 2013. Dorothée Rihal, "Raphaël Réau: un consul français au cœur de la révolution de 1911", *Matériaux pour l'histoire de notre temps*, n° 109–110, "Le premier moment révolutionnaire: Chine, 1911–1913", 1st semester 2013, pp. 10–18.
10 Fund *Banque de l'Indochine*, historical archives of *Crédit agricole*, correspondence and sta-tistics from the branch to the headquarters, 439AH535, 13 November 1911.
11 *Ibidem,* 1909.
12 Fund *Banque de l'Indochine*, historical archives of *Crédit agricole*, correspondence and sta-tistics from the branch to the headquarters, 439AH535, 2 April 1909.

13 *Ibidem*.
14 *Ibidem*, 18 November 1913.
15 Frank King, "Does the corporation's history matter? Hongkong bank/HSBC holdings: A case", in Andrew Godley & Oliver Westall (eds.), *Business History and Business Culture*, Manchester, Manchester University Press, 1996, pp. 116–137. Frank King, "The transmission of corporate cultures: International officers in the HSBC group", in Anthony John Heaton Latham & Heita Kawakatsu (eds.), *Asia Pacific Dynamism, 1550–2000*, London & New York, Routledge, 2000, pp. 245–264.
16 See Frank King, *The History of the Hong Kong & Shanghai Banking Corporation. Volume 2: The Hongkong Bank in the Period of Imperialism and War, 1895–1918:Wayfoong, the Focus on Wealth*, Cambridge, Cambridge University Press, 1988.

Part III

The rebirth of business in the French concessions in the 1920s

8 A community of business interests resisting civil war in Guangzhou

Slowly but steadily, the *Banque de l'Indochine*'s branch asserted itself at the vanguard of French business in south-west China: "Our bank, the oldest in Shameen, occupies a pre-eminent position there because of the importance of its activities."[1] Far from the "imperialist" type of penetration conceived of by French interests in the Yunnan from the Tonkin stronghold and along the railway,[2] the breakthrough realized in Guangdong respected the rules of open competition between banks and trading houses from several countries. Whereas it remained a lesser duplicate of the international markets of Hong Kong and Shanghai, Guangzhou port-city grew as a beacon for an "open-door" policy in the area.

Its role was broadened when the port became more and more closely connected with the hinterland, adding railroads to the existing rivers and roads. In contrast to Tianjin, it lacked the proximity of a large city like Beijing and had to respect the economic and financial predominance of Hong Kong, often acting as a relay for many operations involving Guangzhou business. In any case, though lagging far behind its Hong Kong counterpart, the Guangzhou business community grew steadily, with French representatives becoming more and more consistent.

1. *Banque de l'Indochine* as a gate to the Guangzhou marketplace

Several merchants and the *Banque de l'Indochine*'s manager spun informal connections around the French consul in their day-to-day relationships. Mutual trust predominated, either locally or through the correspondence networks joining Guangzhou to Paris, Lyon and London. Because everyone had to rely on compradors and Chinese merchants or clients, some sharing of information was necessary—for instance about the quality of silk products, the price lists, the actual costs to Chinese suppliers and intermediaries and the like. Several forms of economic intelligence were thus at stake, which naturally characterized business life in such a port-city, where so many types of Chinese merchants (languages, rural communities, family networks, etc.) were committed as stakeholders in the emergence of Guangzhou as an autonomous rival to Hong Kong.

The French community, for instance, received news on projects regarding the laying of railway lines in south-west China, linking Kwansi and Guangdong, which were being studied[3] in 1904–1905, and followed the prospects of the Guangzhou-Hankeou line, in 1905–1906, when foreign (American) interests considered being involved before it was re-attributed to a Chinese concern, and orders for rails passed to American, Japanese and Chinese firms while loco-motives and waggons came from the United States. All through 1910, French merchants struggled to create and support a "French line" between Guangzhou and Hong Kong, despite financial tensions, with three steamboats (*Charles Har-duin, Paul Beau, Robert Lebaudy*). It was not to enhance a "French pavilion flag" but to have some reliability in the face of the erratic local shipping practices, not to speak of coastal piracy. In April 1910, in addition to the FRF 226,000 subsidy granted by the Indochinese government, *Banque de l'Indochine* led a FRF 220,000 loan to the *Messageries cantonnaises* (a shipping company) in order to prove its commitment; after all, the greater the traffic, the greater the extent of its activities.

Apart from its French commercial customers, *Banque de l'Indochine* became the banker to the entire French community. It managed the funds for French schools (*École Pichon, École de médecine franco-chinoise*), the Catholic Church and the missionaries (very active there as in the other concessions), the Doumer hospital, the French Post, several doctors, the Doumer Hotel, French army and navy officers and the *Cercle des marins français*. And, of course, it managed the accounts of the French authorities and of the consul himself. This explains why, when a French Chamber of commerce was set up in Guangzhou in 1915–1916, with representatives from the silk merchant houses of Gérin-Drevard, Boyer-Mazet, *Meurer frères*, Albert & Wullschleger and Th. Varenne, and when all the French Chambers of commerce merged with the Chamber of Shanghai in 1919, the Guangzhou committee preserved the autonomy of the local community. As a mark of his influence, the *Banque de l'Indochine*'s manager, Gaudiot, was elected chairman[4] in 1916, a post he retained till his departure for France in January 1919. He was succeeded by Eymar, the head of Boyer-Mazet.

This emerging solidarity was necessary for a number of reasons: first, to tighten the links between French businessmen in a port-city still lacking power and stature; second, to resist the belligerent German and British practices; and last, to provide some common reinsurance in the face of growing tensions in the city and the province. French businesses shared information during the social unrest of 1906, when "guilds" became more and more influential and demonstrated for wage increases, challenging the authority of the viceroy in Guangdong. It was the same when, in 1910, financial difficulties in the province caused panic, with doubts cast even on government notes. When the empire collapsed in 1912, a power vacuum threatened local peace because Yuan Shi

Kai's authority was contested by the local warlord Chan Kwing Ming. Dem–onstrators and autonomous armed bands protested the Shameen concessions. British troops were sent in, and fights broke out here and there in the province, hampering trade and credit lines, fuelling distrust and instigating the transfer of the Chinese capital to Hong Kong.

> From the economic point of view, it is certain that the present revolution will further compromise the already strained local business. But provided events don't turn completely tragic and the city of Guangzhou is not put to the sword like Wuhan in 1891, it is very likely that the Europeans will not suffer too much. The major business here is the export of silk and, in its raw form as delivered by the mills, it has no value in the hands of looters who much prefer attacking rice and liquor stores. It is well-known fact that in this pirate-infested region, silk, which is the main product, has always been respected.

"The main thing is that the government must have sufficient authority to maintain order in the Province so that the local trade, disturbed for so long, can gradually return to normalcy."[5] In August 1913, an offensive against the warlord led to four days of internecine fighting, before a motley group of forces ransacked the city for about five weeks—but happily, the concessions, well pro-tected, were preserved.

> On 27 July, the central government asked the Tutuhs of the three Provinces of Yunan, Koetcheou and Kwansi to send troops to Guangdong and quell the revolt. Meanwhile, Chan Kwing Ling had not remained inactive: he had gathered 30 to 40,000 troops at Guangzhou, and had expedited some of them to Sanshui, an important strategic point at the confluence of the Western and Northern Rivers in order to block General Ling, commander-in-chief of the Kwangsi army. Stationed at Wuchow, this army could sail down the river in three or four days and threaten Guangzhou at any moment. At the same time, understanding that the public opinion, which had been against him from the beginning, was turning hostile, Chan Kwing Ling unleashed a veritable reign of terror in Guangzhou, which spread panic through the population. The inhabitants fled in mass, business came to a complete halt and everyone was busy only in hiding away his assets ... It was exactly at this critical juncture that an unexpected incident changed the whole situ-ation. On the morning of 4th August, Chan Kwing Ling had an artillery colonel shot because he doubted the officer's loyalty. The General's entire division mutinied in protest and the majority of the army joined them. In the ensuing battle that broke out between the mutineers and those who still

remained loyal to the Tutuh, the latter were defeated. The victors marched on Yamen, which they had already bombarded and Chan Kwing Ling knew that all was lost. He fled to the Catholic Mission (*Missions étrangères de Paris*) where the fathers gave him refuge till nightfall. Then, they disguised him and led him through the Chinese town and into the French section. The French Consul, who was naturally extremely annoyed by the embarrassing situation he found himself in, had no other option but to bundle Chan Kwing Ling onto one of our gunboats (*La Vigilante*) as a political refugee and have him taken to Hong Kong. But as the British government had shut its colony's doors to all rebels, the fugitive could not disembark and had to directly board a German mail-boat bound for Singapore. Thus, in a flash, the leader of the Guangdong revolution was gone ... The town plunged into anarchy. For the next several days Guangzhou lay helpless as the leaderless soldiers ran a mock.[6]

Still, commerce remained paralysed for several months, and law and order in the countryside and, more importantly, along the waterways and the coastline—because of piracy—took a long time to be re-established.

The Cantonese authorities will now direct their efforts against the pirates of the delta. The repeated recruiting and disbanding of troops over the past two years, the disturbances in rural services, the misery and ruins accumulated in certain regions have led to fresh outbreaks of brigandage almost all over. In Guangdong and Kwangsi especially, piracy has attained unbelievable proportions. At one point, looters even attacked the very suburbs of Guangzhou.[7]

A few guerrilla skirmishes went on for many months. Such events, followed by World War I, put the brakes on business and banking, though some "business as usual" gained momentum somewhat. Human and business solidarity prevailed on Shameen island which, being insulated from the countryside, has both a disadvantage (losing business connections) and an advantage (being able to be evacuated by the British fleet if necessary).

In contrast to Hong Kong, Guangzhou port-city like some "Far West" trading post. The Guangzhou branch of *Banque de l'Indochine* had not become a powerful leverage force within the banking firm, as its returns accounted for only about 3 per cent of overall revenues. Still, it had proven itself to be a viable and active bridgehead in south-west China, in keeping with the expectations of the French authorities and the bank's headquarters since its opening in 1902 (see Table 8.1).

Table 8.1 Returns of the *Banque de l'Indochine*'s main branches at the turn of the 1920s (percentage)[8]

	First term 1916	First term 1919	Second term 1919	First term 1920
Indochina and Cambodia	44.6	50.9	47.3	41.6
China	23.6	22.8	17.4	18.5
South China (Guangzhou, Mongtze and Hong Kong)	11	9.2	11.2	5.6
Guangzhou	2.4	2.7	3	-5.8
Mongtze	5.3	5.3	6.2	3.8
Hong Kong	3.3	1.2	2	7.6
Shanghai	7.8	10.5	4.1	11.3
Hankeou	3.9	-2.2	-0.2	0
Tianjin	1.8	5.5	1.9	2.4
Beijing	-0.9	-0.2	0.4	-0.8
Singapore	4.7	2.7	16.1	3.6
Paris	14.2	6.2	4.7	4.4

2. Crisis looming over the port-city at the beginning of the 1920s

Just after World War I, competition increased because HSBC lowered its rates, *Banque industrielle de Chine* (which opened a branch in Guangzhou in September 1919) intensified its drive for risky, low-cost loans, and Bank of Taiwan, the International Banking Corporation (ICB, a US bank)[9] and Yokohama Specie Bank[10] floated shares. In a nutshell, profit margins were generally very low:

The profit margins remain rather limited due to the competition brought by the other banks, especially the Yokohama Specie Bank. And unless one wanted to be constantly speculating, it was difficult to get anything more than 0.5 per cent from any normal operation. The margin was then further diminished by our debit balances and interest on our capital account.[11]

Naturally, it was our branch that was the most affected by the competition regarding the franc and I found myself in a most delicate situation. First, some of our clients, such as the *Compagnie générale d'Extrême-Orient, Générale des soies*, Boyer Mazet, Meurer brothers did not want, in principle, to go to the *Banque industrielle de Chine*. As its rates were known by all, to quote anything different would have meant penalizing them for their loyalty, which would have been disastrous. On the other hand, it was important to keep in close touch with the market at such an active time and to monitor our competitor's actions. I was thus constrained to conduct deals at similar rates to his. My purchases of the first fifteen amounted to, in these conditions, to around seven million francs. I estimate that *Banque industrielle de Chine* did double of this figure. As for what concerns us, the cover was inevitably expensive. The assistance from the Saigon subsidiary was very limited, and I had to sell Sterling in Hong Kong and Shanghai. The condition of my funds and the fear of a rise in the Paris-London rates forced me to operate ready for September. I will get back to the consequent losses when our monthly statement is made. I am convinced that nowhere else will they find any significant compensation. Perhaps by giving my competitor the impression that I was following him closely and that my quotes were not far from his, I flatter myself to think that I caused him to quickly exhaust the resources we had set up for him at favourable rates and thus to have helped in getting back to normalcy. Since then, our competitors' policy has remained the same concerning the Sterling paper. For Francs, they first limited themselves to follow the increase of [telegraphic transfers] TT on London. But, since a few days, though the hike in the cross rate seems to have been annulled for the moment at least, I have the impression that they are coming close to parity and I can do business as close to normal, but without profit. Henceforth, we are faced by new litigations, and the struggle for foreign exchange transactions is becoming more difficult than ever in our market. But I have the firm hope that, thanks to the faith that people have in our establishment, in the facilities that we provide, especially regarding loans, our clientele will mostly remain loyal to us and that we should be able to maintain, along with our rank on the stock market, our normal turnover and profits.[12]

A. The dire post-war recession

The biggest impact was caused by the post-war recession which, like elsewhere in the world, halted Guangzhou business for several terms.[13] The overall economic situation weighed on the port-city. Orders from Europe fell as companies struggled. They had to depreciate their inventories (in Asia, on the way to Europe, or in European ports) and incurred bad loans and losses, and some of them collapsed. The result was a drastic reduction in the trade managed by the Guangzhou platform: "Silk exports have almost completely stopped, the dispatches delayed, and we ask ourselves what rates will we get for the goods in transit or in stock which have been bought here at the highest rates."[14]

Several big merchant houses went through trying times, with their branches having to bear thick layers of pending bills of exchange (Gérin Drevard: $50,000; General Silk Importing Inc., with a mortgage on a Shameen building against a

$45,000 loan, etc.). Hogg Karanja finally collapsed in 1921, each of their own-
ers owing *Banque de l'Indochine* large amounts ($88,000 for Hogg).[15] Albert &
Wullschleger was liquidated in 1924. The pending debit accounts reached the
equivalent of FRF 44 million in mid-1920, before dwindling to 20 million in
the fall of that year. Throughout 1920–1921, the motto was "cut risk"—pick
up immobilised credit, scrutinise clients' business and inventories, look for more
pledges and collaterals, and so on.

B. The effects of civil war and disorder

Local problems continued with sporadic internecine fighting as every warlord's
authority was endlessly contested: rebels came from Yunnan[16] and in 1920 dis-
mantled the legal powers before fleeing to Hong Kong. Various troops marched
into and out of the city in 1920–1922 under the leadership of Cheng Kio Ming/
Jiongming, even though Sun Yat Sen was in the city as Chinese president
(without territory) in April 1921. After some authority was re-established in
1921–1922, rampant piracy struck the coasts and even the railway to Kowloon.
Revolutionary demonstrations and workers' strikes added a "leftist" touch to the
uncertainty—with Sun Yat Sen coming back for a while in January 1923, toppling Cheng Kio Ming and, along with his son Sun Fo as mayor, trying to restore
order, under a "red power" unifying Guo Ming Dang and communist forces.

But his forces (recruited in Yuannan and Kwangsi) were resisted by those of
Cheng Kio Ming/Jiongming in the countryside.

> The situation of the town and the Province remains precarious. Pirate
> bands—former soldiers—stalk the countryside. The Hong Kong–
> Guangzhou railway line is not safe. There are frequent strikes. The workers
> have come together in syndicates which depend on a municipal association
> which is itself attached to a veritable Chinese CGT [a French leftist trade
> union: *Compagnie générale du travail*] … There is fear that Sun Yat Sen will
> return and that, with brief periods of relative calm, the town will be in a
> constant state of revolution.[17]

Soldiers ransacked the city once again. Armed gangs stalked the countryside,
terrorizing merchants and transporters, who had also to help finance Sun's mer-
cenaries. Armed French and British ships had to rush in December 1923 to prevent Sun from seizing the Guangzhou Customs headquarters and its revenues
which had been earmarked since the 1900 treaty to the concessions. Tensions
came to a head on 19 June 1924 when a bomb (by an Annamite conspirator
Pham Hong Thai) struck the reception building where the French Governor
of Indochina, Martial Merlin (in transit between Japan, China and Indochina),
was welcoming his guests at the Victoria Hotel.

The French community lost five of its representatives, including the sub-
accountant of *Banque de l'Indochine* (Rougeau) and other leading business

personalities (H.G. Gérin, of Gérin Drevard; André Demaretz, from General Silk Importing Company).[18] A near civil war resumed in the fall of 1924 between Sun's troops and militia armed by the merchant guilds and the Labour Party. There was much looting and killing. A flood of refugees descended on Shameen before Sun's clan won and he restored some order till his death in March 1925. Then anarchy prevailed, the city was torn by civil war, the concessions were besieged from June to October 1925 and the Nationalists in Hong Kong imposed a general boycott of "imperialist" business for 16 months.

C. Disappointment about Chinese business

Banque de l'Indochine's embeddedness in the port-city's domestic business met with major disappointments. First, the real estate assets in the Chinese Land Investment lay frozen due to the occupation by unofficial troops which prevented the assets from being used commercially, especially as the development of the harbour facilities were not oriented towards that area. The bad debt still clung to its $560,000 in principal (and the $296,000 in interest). Even though the troops evacuated the area in July 1920 (but came back in August with lots of prostitutes!), the property had lost value severely. Negotiations with the governor underwent ups and downs and became somewhat gridlocked. Some buildings were sold to Chinese investors, but the bank had to keep 22 houses, which were rented.

Second, the comprador Leong Din Shan, who had accompanied the branch's growth from the beginning, turned up to be a rogue intermediary.[19] He fled Guangzhou in 1920, leaving behind some deficit, around $650,000 in promissory notes which were declared as losses, and bad credits on inventories as the quality silks in the go-down had been replaced by cheaper products (amounting to a loss of $215,000). The ex-comprador's guarantors assumed their collateral ($60,000), and part of the loans by Chinese businessmen was repaid. This led to new rules requiring frequent checking of the goods in stock and the books themselves.

The new comprador, Wai Tsuk Ling,[20] pledged to respect drastic standards of credit, especially for the advances on goods (cloth, mainly). Wai had been a shipping clerk to a Chinese company (Joo Tek Seng) in Hong Kong for ten years, then the comprador of *Deutsche Asiatische Bank* in Guangzhou in 1912–1917, before occupying jobs at two merchant houses. His first guarantor was Lee Hy San, who won the tender for the leasehold on opium trade in Macao. His second was Fong Chung Tong, one of the richest silk merchants in Guangzhou, and altogether the comprador of the French firm Ch. Poisat & C°. He remained the guarantor of the next *Banque de l'Indochine* comprador, Mak Fook Cho. His Chinese corner could rely on a dozen employees in 1922, promising to broaden its domestic basis. The recession worsened the situation because the value of goods was often cut harshly.

Notes

1 The manager of the *Banque de l'Indochine*'s branch to Paris headquarters, Historical archives of *Crédit agricole*, fund *Banque de l'Indochine*, 28 January 1920.

2 Michel Bruguière, "Le chemin de fer du Yunnan. Paul Doumer et la politique d'intervention française en Chine (1889–1900)", published in 1963, *Revue d'histoire diplomatique*; re-edited in Michel Bruguière, *Pour une renaissance de l'histoire financière, xvIIIᵉ–xxᵉ siècles*, Paris, Comité pour l'histoire économique & financière de la France, 1992.

3 The manager of the *Banque de l'Indochine*'s branch to Paris headquarters, 8 April 1904, Historical archives of *Crédit agricole*, fund *Banque de l'Indochine*.

4 *Ibidem*, 29 October 1910.

5 *Ibidem*, 28 July 1913, then 15 August 1913.

6 *Ibidem*, 20 August 1913. Ling Chai-Kwong entered Guangzhou and was promoted by Yuan governor of Kwantung.

7 *Ibidem*, 7 November 1913.

8 Minutes of the Board of *Banque de l'Indochine*, 25 October 1916, 29 October 1919, 28 April 1920, 24 November 1920.

9 Ayumu Sugawara, "American international banking in China before World War II: Beijing, Tianjin and Guangdong branches of international banking corporation", *Tōhoku Management & Accounting Research Group*, 2007, n° 78, pp. 1–19. Citicorp, *Citicorp in China: A Colorful, Very Personal History Since 1902*, New York, Citicorp, Citibank, 1989. Peter Starr, *Citibank: A Century in Asia*, Singapore, Didier Millet & Citicorp, 2002. ICB was set up in 1902 and opened its Guangzhou branch in 1904, second after Shanghai.

10 See Kanji Ishii, "Japanese foreign trade and the Yokohama Specie bank, 1880–1913", in Olive Checkland, Shizuya Nishimura & Norio Tamaki (eds.), *Pacific Banking, 1859–1959: East Meets West*, London, Macmillan; New York, St. Martin's Press, 1994, pp. 1–23. Norio Tamaki, "The Yokohama Specie bank: A multinational in the Japanese interests, 1879–1935", in Geoffrey Jones (ed.), *Banking as Multinationals*, London, Routledge, 1990.

11 Report on the first term of 1928 by the general manager of the *Banque de l'Indochine* branch.

12 *Ibidem*, 29 September 1919.

13 See Marie-Claire Bergère, "The consequences of post-First World War depression for the China treaty-port economy, 1921–1923", in Ian Brown (ed.), *The Economics of Africa and Asia in the Inter-War Depression*, London, Routledge, 1989, pp. 221–252.

14 The manager of the *Banque de l'Indochine*'s branch to Paris headquarters, 30 July 1920, Historical archives of *Banque de l'Indochine*. "There are no orders which have come to Guangzhou, neither from Lyon or America", *Ibidem*, 18 November 1920.

15 *Ibidem*, 30 July 1920, 26 September 1922.

16 "Nothing remains of the South Chinese government and the tuchuns are the uncontested masters of our provinces", *Ibidem*, 31 March 1920.

17 *Ibidem*, 9 October 1922.

18 "Assassination at Guangzhou: Dastardly outrage at the Victoria hotel", *The Hong Kong Daily Press*, June 1924.

19 The manager of the *Banque de l'Indochine*'s branch to Paris headquarters, 18 June 1920.

20 *Ibidem*, 15 November 1926.

9 The rebirth of the Guangzhou port cluster

Its fragile equilibrium between external and internal forces and the crisis that shattered Chinese political and commercial areas had led the Guangdong economy through hard times and the crumbling of opportunities for trade, profit and banking. But the 1920s benefited from a kind of rebirth, with effects on the turnover and the returns of the *Banque de l'Indochine* branch in Guangzhou.

1. The return of prosperity: a first apex of Guangzhou port–city

As soon as the recession was over (with silk exports gaining 23 per cent between 1922 and 1923) and despite some uncertainties about the political and military stability around the Guangzhou area, the port–city resumed its commercial growth. It also benefited from a program of investment into roads, streetcars, running water and sewage systems as the local authorities intended to imitate the "process to modernity" of neighbouring Hong Kong and to take part in the "New China" spirit, intent on modernisation and taking on the Japanese challenge. Two loans, of £2 million each, were concluded in 1922 with the Anglo-French China Corporation, a "syndicate" of bankers and financiers (HSBC, Bank of Liverpool & Martins, Yokohama Specie Bank, International Banking Corporation, Asia Banking Corporation, Chinese Bank for Industry & Communications— but without *Banque de l'Indochine*), for the city's investments.[1]

No doubt, the political and social troubles of 1925–1927, which were part of the general unrest in China, undermined confidence and business. Harsh anti-European mindsets sparked a general strike in Hong Kong and Guangzhou in June 1925–October 1926. A boycott choked both harbours, compelling merchant houses to transport silk to Shanghai to be exported. The housing development owned by *Banque de l'Indochine* was occupied by strikers and even set on fire. Internecine challenges for power led to the toppling of the warlord and his successor in 1927:

> Our region was quite disturbed for a while after the conflicts between the rival generals who, having agreed to share power in the beginning, now wanted to have it all, especially the direct profits. When General Li Chai

Shum who, with the support of the Ironsides, had governed Guangzhou rather wisely for a year, had gone for a conference to Shanghai, he found himself deposed by his former collaborator, Wong Ki Cheung, General of the ironsides.[2]

Leftist militia occupied the city in December 1927. The number of casualties was estimated at a few thousand by the *Banque de l'Indochine*'s manager:

> After Wong Ki Cheung, General of the Ironsides, had ill-advisedly sent the majority of his troops out of Guangzhou in order to quell the pirates, he himself had to hurriedly quit the city at the end of December when, overnight, it fell into the hands of communists led by Russians. Though these communists were there only for a short time, within three days they had looted enormous sums, massacred 3,000 people and burnt 3,000 houses. On the third day, the Ironsides, with the help of General Li Fook Lam's (governor of the island of Honam) troops, retook the city and restored order …. The Ironsides and Li Fook Lam completed the work begun by the communists by looting another three million dollars before leaving. The government notes, issued by the Central Bank of China, which, just three months back were trouncing the divisionary currency, were now worth barely 50 per cent of their face value. That is why traders now prefer to wait rather than be paid in a currency which was depreciating day by day.[3]

Many spinning mills were forced to close down, either permanently or temporarily (a total of 170 were active at beginning of 1928). Happily, order was restored in the first quarter of 1928:

> Calm and tranquillity returned to Guangdong. The governor of the province, Marshal Li Chai Sum, who had returned to Guangzhou at the beginning of January, managed to impose order and stamp out piracy from the neighbourhood of Biass Bay as well as from the interior. He also made commendable efforts to reorganise the economy …. The provincial government, with its back to the wall, imposed all sorts of taxes on imported goods, which have had or will have serious repercussions on imports.[4]

"Business as usual" resumed for a few years:

> Meanwhile, the silk trade continues in a more or less normal fashion with Europe and America making some offers. The stock of spun silk as of 31 December [1927] stands at 7 to 8,000 balls and the cocoons still to be spun will make another 7,000 balls, which gives a total of 15,000 balls, enough to last till the new season which begins towards the end of April.[5]

Such an environment required from the branch manager and his small team (four till 1925, then three expatriates only: a cashier, a controller, a head of accounting, with local employees, of course) some balance of temper and a relevant command of risks.[6]

2. The *Banque de l'Indochine* branch's triumph in silk trade banking

Taking full advantage of the rebirth of commerce and its portfolio of skills and connections, the *Banque de l'Indochine*'s branch proved itself a major player in the port-city's silk trade. Over the first quarter of 1923, it financed three-quarters of all silk balls sent to Lyon (6,000 of a total of 7,550/8,000).[7] In France, since the mid-1920s, artificial silk (rayon) began replacing natural silk for commonplace cloth, which forced merchant houses to redefine their business model. They had to demand higher-quality raw silks to be delivered to high-class weavers and luxury houses in Lyon. The Guangdong constituency of traditional spinning mills had to redeploy themselves to take into account such moves, thus causing a few troubles: Chinese bankers became wary of their credits to such customers and sifted them attentively.[8]

Another point was the *Banque de l'Indochine*'s focus on French houses because, during the 1921–1924 crisis, British houses (Jardine, Griffith, Arnhold, Reuss, etc.) had depended heavily on advances from British banks, which afterwards demanded that they remain loyal to their traditional banks and not go to the competing French bank.[9] The *Banque de l'Indochine*'s key advantage lay in its permanent funds (allocated by its mother company) which allowed it to grant increasing amounts of loans on silk balls, which in turn allowed its merchant clients to repay their suppliers without long deadlines (see Table 9.1).

The clientele was a classical one and also offered a renewed profile, as a few houses fell back or even disappeared (Leynaud, Arnhold & C°). Ahead of a bunch of little and medium-sized merchants, the leaders provided banks with

Table 9.1 Advances on silk balls by the *Banque de l'Indochine*'s Guangzhou branch in 1926–1930 ($)

	Amount		Number of pledged balls	
	Through the comprador	Indirect	Through the comprador	Indirect
June–October 1926	Boycott and general strike			
October–December 1926	1,665,750	225,000	2,535	385
1927	1,624,400	778,000	2,795	1,284
1928	1,356,200	1,345,580	2,158	1,794
1929	1,909,250	1,827,568	3,034	2,776
1930	626,000	162,500	1,525	305

Source: Special report-letter from the Guangzhou *Banque de l'Indochine* branch, 3 September 1935

large amounts of business: Guangzhou Silk & C°, South China Trading C°, Madier-Ribet (with FRF 2.3 million in credit in July 1931, for exports to Japan and Lyon), *Comptoir franco-chinois* (Servanin, an ancient manager of Madier-Ribet), Central Produce & C°, Hogg & C°, J. Cassa, Gérin-Drevard, Boyer-Mazet (whose building was adjacent to that of *Banque de l'Indochine*).[10]

Madier-Ribet (with its managers Henry Madier, Joseph Madier and Adolphe Ribet) was the leading French silk trade house at that times, with branches in Guangzhou, Yokohama and Shanghai and its headquarters in Lyon. Its Asian headquarters was in Shanghai, where it led the raw silk business, ahead of Jardine Matheson and Mitsui Bussan in the 1920s. But it ranked also first in Guangzhou, ahead of Paskille and Griffith, and thus covered the whole chain of silk trade, till Lyon, where the families were also influential (at the *Chambre syndicale des acheteurs de soie*, for instance, chaired at a time by a Madier).[11]

The *Banque de l'Indochine* branch's advances (see Table 9.2) on raw or spun silk climbed to HK$1,748,600 on 15 December 1926—before falling to 575,750 on 15 December 1927 (because of the political situation and the caution of Chinese bankers). Loans to silk traders were estimated at FRF 2,205,000 on January 1930. At the height of the boom, Gérin-Drevard (an association between Michel Drevard and Guillaume Gérin) was granted HK$275,000 for its local silk trade (against 325,000 as pledges), which allowed the firm to pay its Chinese suppliers, pending shipping its staples abroad. Some of these houses practiced general trading on sundries and, apart from silk, also purchased local goods from Chinese partners (hides, hen feathers, etc.) for a few overseas outlets.

Because of its contacts with French merchants or thanks to the comprador, the *Banque de l'Indochine*'s branch was revealed as a "domestic" bank because it had a large constituency among Chinese merchants. The 1920s marked a strong

Table 9.2 Status of advances on goods by the *Banque de l'Indochine* branch in Guangzhou on 30 May 1923

	Amount of the advance ($)	Number of pledged balls of silk	Value of the pledge ($)
French merchants			
Gérin Drevard	174,000	365	209,160
Hogg & C°	20,125	30	20,835
Comptoir franco-chinois	27,000	40	23,640
Chinese merchants			
Hing Cheong Wo	260,500	500	293,280
Wing Wo	135,000	270	152,230
Tin Po Lun	22,500	45	25,380
Hip Hing Loong	19,000	40	22,560
Yue Hing Cheong	15,500	50	28,520
Wo Shing Hing	11,500	25	14,100
Wong Man Sang	7,000	15	8,460
Wing Tai Loong (17 July 1923)	40,000	100	52,000

Source: Special report-letter from the *Banque de l'Indochine*'s Guangzhou branch, 14 January 1924

renewal of the insertion of the Chinese community as stakeholders in the port-city's commercial life, and a few local merchants reached a creditworthiness which allowed them to be granted big credits (see Table 9.3), even though the level of guarantee required was higher than that for French houses.

A fact to be reported is the competition that the Chinese houses are beginning to give to the European establishments. Presently there exist five in Guangzhou: Wong Man Sang, Guangzhou Silk Trading Co., Guangzhou Silk Exporting Co., Central Produce Co. and Wing Tai Loong, whose turnover has been impressive ... . Among these heterogeneous houses, three stand out: Wong Man Sang, Guangzhou Silk Trading Co. and Wing Tai Loong. Because of their honesty, their fair prices and punctual deliveries, they have earned themselves an excellent reputation in Lyon and New York and have achieved a massive turnover. It goes without saying that this competition is not going down well with the European houses who have been forced to reduce their profit margins and agent commissions. Still, it is unlikely that they succeed in eliminating them or even cutting them to size as these Chinese firms are presently treated by European banks with the same high regard as towards any of their other precious clients.[12]

Table 9.3 Amount of silk commercial paper purchased by the *Banque de l'Indochine*'s Guangzhou branch to each merchant house connected to the Lyon market in 1928–1929 (thousands FRF)

	During the first term of 1928	*During the second term of 1929*
Total	49,920	37,138
Madier-Ribet	14,250	8,712
Comptoir franco-chinois	6,440	234
T.E. Griffith	6,433	2,139
P. Leynaud	5,912	—
Boyer-Mazet	4,027	1,181
Jardine-Matheson	3,841	684
Wong Man Sang	2,830	4,821
J. Cassa	2,200	/
Gérin-Drevard	1,939	3,179
Reiss-Massey	958	4,489
Hogg	111	4,210
Wing Tai Loong	/	3,001
Guangzhou Silk Trading C°	/	1,277
Guangzhou Mercantile C°	/	1,013
Central Produce C°	/	716
Guangzhou Raw Silk C°	/	564
Mitsui Bussan Kaisha	/	372
Etc.		

Source: Report for the first term of 1928 by the manager of the Guangzhou *Banque de l'Indochine* branch

The connections between Guangzhou and Lyon regained momentum,[13] and *Banque de l'Indochine* resumed the use of its French counterparts there (*Société générale, Crédit lyonnais,* CNEP) as bearers of the pending documentary credits till the sale of imported goods:

> The credit establishments at Lyon are very well organized and provide document-holders with all facilities for the financing of their maturities till the moment of actual delivery of the merchandise. As such, these establishments can easily monitor traders' commitments, the growth of their business and consequently, are fully informed regarding their situation and that of the market.[14]

In the first quarter of 1928, the branch's operations attained around FRF 50 million (stabilised 1928 gold francs) (see Table 9.4). The amount jumped to 102 million during the first quarter of 1929, one apex of the boom cycle (see Figure 9.1).

This boom explains why some of them overstretched their positions as they used leverage on credit to bolster their market share at the expense of their financial stability, thus causing either icing of debts (stirring concerns at *Banque*

Table 9.4 Guangzhou exports of raw silk balls in 1926–1929 (May–April)

1926–1927 season	66,679
1927–1928 season	54,848
1928–1929 season	58,163

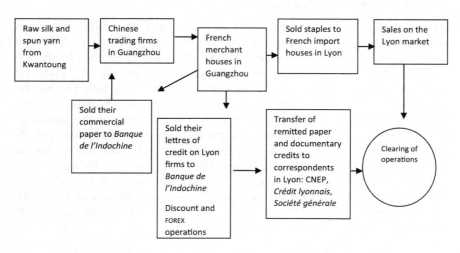

Figure 9.1 The circuit of commercial paper flows from China to Europe

de l'Indochine) or losses on the values of inventories and cargoes in Europe. On April 1929, the *Banque de l'Indochine*'s branch carried $286,000 "in trust blank advances"—with goods piled up in the merchants' warehouses instead of at the bank's—which was considered a growing risk at the height of the boom cycle. *Compagnie générale française pour le commerce & l'industrie*, for instance, was granted $120,000 as advance in 1922 for its business between Guangzhou, Shanghai and Europe. It acted as a trader at its own risk, a silk merchant on behalf of Lyon houses, and a consignee for various goods. Such general trading took off massively after the recession and was a hallmark of the port-city's renewed prosperity and scope, even if it required larger allocations of financial resources (see Table 9.4).

But *Compagnie générale française pour le commerce & l'industrie* had to cede its mortgaged building to *Banque de l'Indochine* in November 1923 as part payment of its debt ($121,000), whereas the *Marthoud frères*, also active in Shanghai and Guangzhou, closed its doors in October 1923 (leaving a $25,000 in debt to the *Banque de l'Indochine*). Another merchant house, *Veuve Brun Pons*, was also strained in 1923 because of lengthy bills of exchange lines with two French houses (J. Sauvayre and P. Servanin), with belated payments.[15] Albert & Wullschleger was rubbed out in 1924. Hogg Karanja, which had collapsed in 1921, was replaced by Karanja, but the new company, active with US and Lyon importers, remained overcharged by debts towards HSBC ($524,000) and *Banque de l'Indochine* ($155,000, pledged against $235,000 in goods till *Banque de l'Indochine* discovered that the stock had been sold to reduce the HSBC debt), which ended restructuring the credits to $537,000 over seven years, with a $533,000 mortgage on the client's buildings.[16] The wellknown and ancient house of *Charles Meurer* went bankrupt in 1927.

3. New scope for silk trading: a port-city on two international legs

The renewal of silk trading was based on new connections. While European outlets maintained their momentum, the US market opened up a whole new dimension for Chinese exports, in the wake of the stature attained by the US economy from the start of the twentieth century, the growth of a high-end consuming bourgeoisie and the luxury industry around New York. During the 1923 season, silk exports from Guangzhou to the United States attained 47,342 units against 18,298 to Europe and Lyon.[17] A good client of the *Banque de l'Indochine* branch, the General Silk Importing C°, shared its silk exports equally between Lyon and New York in 1928. An approximate balance was reached in 1926 and 1928 when 23,239 and 18,005 balls, respectively, left Guangzhou for the United States and 20,316 and 17,625 for Europe. Between May 1926 and December 1927, Gérin-Drevard, the biggest French firm there, sold 3,096 balls to Lyon and 5,895 to the United States, Arnhold respectively 909 and 4,320, and the whole business, 45,634 and 55,792.

All in all, the French bank had to evolve in parallel: as an offshoot of French interests along the Pearl Rivers, it couldn't but join the growing China–US connections, where the port-city was strongly involved, thus changing its scope from Asia–Europe habits to Asia–US business. But such developments required its insertion into a new "financial system", with FOREX operations no longer linked to the French franc and the British pound (through the Hong Kong dollar or the Chinese-Mexican silver dollar) but rather to the US dollar. Far from the stature of Shanghai and Hong Kong, Guangzhou had to diversify its banking *modus operandi* (see Table 9.5).

Massive FOREX contracts had to be set up with maturities up to one year or more. Beyond volumes and maturities was determining:

> *Compagnie des soies de Guangzhou 1920–21*, which has already been engaged by America, will probably give rise, from the coming month, to major FOREX contracts. The major part will be in pounds or in Guangzhou dollars and will mature towards the end of the current year, if not in 1921. Such long-term settlement dates represent for us, from solely the cross rate point of view, a major gamble. It is not possible for us to sell sterling at such deliveries, as much because of the limitation of our funds as for the rarity of the very long-term transactions on the Hong Kong and Shanghai markets.[18]

But the *Banque de l'Indochine*'s branch could not act on its own because of its lack of correspondents in New York—and it faced harsh competition from National City Bank, which even managed to lure French houses (bigwig Madier-Ribet) with its better bank interest conditions:

> The National City Bank of New York, probably going bearish, picked up the major portion of the American transactions by constantly offering extraordinary rates. We know by experience how vain it is to want to keep an exchange clientele. We also let it be, voluntarily relinquishing many USD

Table 9.5 Guangzhou from a mere China–Europe port-city to a trans-Pacific one in 1928–1929

	Towards Lyon		Towards the United States		Towards Italy
	May 1928–April 1929	May–December 1929	May 1928–April 1929	May–December 1929	May 1928–April 1929
Export of raw silk balls	21,773	15,079	26,972	34,061	
Silk waste products	21,084		21,825		6,817

Source: Report from the *Banque de l'Indochine*'s Guangzhou manager for the first and second terms of 1929

deals. Through its comprador, it advanced four or five million dollars on silk balls at the rate of 7 percent per annum. At the moment, it has begun to occupy a dominating position on the market.[19]

By chance, French transatlantic interests moved decidedly forward in the immediate post-war period and led, in 1919, to the foundation of the French American Banking Corporation, which federated initiatives by a bank which was then the most involved in non-European international operations, *Comptoir national d'escompte de Paris*. This affiliate became thus the correspondent of the *Banque de l'Indochine*'s Guangzhou branch in 1920—owing to a security deposit of $500,000 by *Banque de l'Indochine* Paris in the name of its Guangzhou offshoot. Now the trade houses exporting to the United States could onward-transfer their letters of credit and trading documents (for documentary credit) and rely on that platform to clear the banking operations[20] with their US counterparts (Serrell Brothers, etc.).

> Since the major growth in silk paper negotiations in the United States, our account with our New York correspondent generally showed a very high debit balance: on average, since the beginning of this year, one million in gold dollars. It is not possible for us to meet in a proportionately large measure the delivery of our TT sales with our credit discounts. Not only do we have to wait four months for the maturity of our bills, but as a large part of our remittances are non-instalment or discountable as soon as they arrive in New York, we still have there a difference in delivery (purchases and sales) which is difficult to account for exactly. Our purchase contracts are almost always deliverable in two or three months. Our sales contracts are mostly on one month delivery. The limited Hong Kong and Guangzhou markets only allow us to do our counterparties by close delivery.[21]

The bills ("silk paper") arrived in New York and were paid for in cash or, pending their repayment, were rediscounted locally for a few months (three to four), and acceptance operations complemented the process[22] with about a final 0.5 per cent profit margin.

> The discount rate in the United States and the interest rate on our debit balance that is being charged by the French American Banking Corporation (presently 5.5 percent), makes these operations very difficult. Nevertheless, given that the paper drawn on the United States is exclusively on letters of credit and thus gives us a high level of security in our transactions, it would be a mistake to withdraw from this domain of our local business, and my intention is to continue these purchases to the extent that they leave me with a normal margin.[23]

During the first term of 1928, the branch purchased commercial paper on the United States for $2,063 million, for French (Madier-Ribet, Gérin-Drevard, etc.), British (Arnhold, T.E. Griffith, Mac Neary, etc.) and Japanese (Mitsui Bussan Kaisha) houses. All in all, the operations completed in US dollars by the branch rose significantly from the first (4,538 million) and second (5,874 million) terms of 1928 to the first term of 1929 (8,529 million): it "walked on two legs"—Lyon and New York. A precise breakdown of the silk credit activities of the branch for the first term of 1925 shows the *Banque de l'Indochine's* involvement on both international markets, with about a fifth (18.4 per cent) of the total financing of Guangzhou's silk exports (see Table 9.6).

The evolution of the branch thus epitomized the port-city's three-fold dimension, with operations with France, London and New York and the whole range of FOREX and clearing markets in their wake, all the more when the branch commenced purchasing credit papers on London and New York issued in Guangzhou by trading houses, whether or not they were its customers: it wagered on pure FOREX operations without any direct link to the operations of its own clients. But competition was harsh: one example was the commitment of National City Bank to finance the French firm Gérin-Drevard, which was revealed as National's main creditor when it collapsed in August 1931.

Table 9.6 The *Banque de l'Indochine's* participation in the financing of Guangzhou silk exports in 1925 (US dollars)

Trading firms involved	Towards France	Towards the United States	Total (including other countries)	Credit negotiated by the Banque de l'Indochine branch
Arnhold	208	389	597	50
Boyer-Mazet	752	—	752	437
Clerici Bedoni	309	15	324	237
Comptoir d'achat de soies & Varenne Proton	941	277	1,345	905
General Silk Imports	—	790	790	436
Gérin-Drevard	278	915	1,193	45
T.E. Griffith	957	1,926	2,883	180
Holyoak Massey	380	1,061	1,489	—
Jardine Matheson	385	125	510	—
Karanjia	100	2,305	2,405	645
Madiet frères & Madiet Ribet	1,857	4,286	6,148	547
Mitsui Bussan	508	1,889	2,397	—
Nippon Ki Ito	152	355	507	—
J. Pasquier	1,024	415	1,439	170
Ch. Poisat	639	—	639	317
P. Servanin	375	20	395	195
U. Spalinger	50	/	170	33
Total (with other small houses)	9,348	15,571	25,361	4,667

Source: General report of the *Banque de l'Indochine* branch in Guangzhou, for the first term of 1925

Customers were not so faithful, despite economic patriotism, or they wished to share their credits among several banks and to put them into competition for interest rates and fees.

4. Guangzhou as a regional platform

In parallel, the Guangzhou area intensified its domestic activities along the rivers upstream[24] (Xi Jiang, Xun Jiang, Pei Kiang) to Wou Tcheou/Wu Chow, Fu/Wuzhou, LiouTcheou/Liuzhu, Chao Chow Fu or Nanning, with fuelled credit, remittances, management of means of payments, all in all ending partly in the office of banks and *Banque de l'Indochine*. This eased somewhat the comprador's job (Mak Fook Cho since 1926). By adding to the connections between foreign and Chinese merchant houses, he made up for his predecessor and reinserted the branch into the domestic market, fuelled by local activities and by the flows linking the port-city to the hinterland, either by waterway or roads. With a dozen employees in 1930 and a joint building, he could find fresh opportunities of credit and check clearing, bolstering the revenues in interests and commissions and, more importantly, contributing to the creditworthiness of *Banque de l'Indochine* in the Guangzhou marketplace. The total amount of the advances guaranteed by the comprador reached $448,500 (against 507,600 as goods pledged by the clients and 56,000 by the comprador himself).

"The silk trading chain", comprised of those Chinese merchants working with the French houses, also benefited from the *Banque de l'Indochine* credits; for example, in 1930, Cheong Ke or Wong Man Sang reflected the structuring of a local Chinese capitalism that reached a relevant size and creditworthiness, and were more and more partners of international connections around each port-city.[25] In 1929, the branch informed Paris that it had been developing business with Chinese houses which "had been recently set up" and which were "improving their involvement in the exports business to Europe", which required the manager to make a drastic selection among his clients based on the FOREX risk, but he underlined the high quality of a group of customers, Wing Tai Loong, Wong Man Sang, and Wo Hing Silk Trading. "We are working mainly with the first one, who is very serious and sends silks only to the US against letters of credit; he has been our bestseller of USD over the last term."[26]

They were also in touch with their French counterparts for import operations, partly from Japan and mainly from Europe, regarding consumer goods (cognac, etc.), and they acted as wholesale intermediaries before redistribution in the hinterland. But German houses (Reuter Brockelmann, Carlowitz) had come back in the 1920s and seized key roles in the import trade. British and German agents tackled the market for armaments, prospering from the endless internecine fighting and the "investments" made by the warlords in modern equipment (in Guangzhou and Guangdong, in neighbouring Kwansi, both clans struggling one against the other in 1928–1929 when the former, rallying the Guo Min Tang Nanking government, trounced the latter).

5. Guangzhou and Hong Kong: sister port–cities

As our study dedicated to Hong Kong published in another book[27] has already indicated, the business activities at Guangzhou were quite independent of and complementary to the Hong Kong market.[28] Its harbour depended on the 160–200 British steamers calling at Guangzhou every month from Hong Kong, as the hub of international transportation remained located in the British colony. Cheap but extensive transportation connections joined both harbours with two-way trade depending on availability and price lists. This explains the cooperation between both of the *Banque de l'Indochine*'s branches in Guangzhou and Hong Kong—all the more because the latter was involved in financing the import trade of Indochinese rice which was subsequently redistributed to the whole of south-east China and the Guangzhou area, which also received big cargoes of flour from the colony. The former frequently purchased commercial bills and documentary credits paid there by French merchants (for their collection in the area for exports) to be remitted to Hong Kong, depending on clearing needs. "On several occasions, we have had the opportunity of buying francs for the Hong Kong account on conditions that this agency would not have found elsewhere: purchase of documentary paper of four years, ceded to the agency, without it having to incur any risks."[29]

The connection between the two cities also favoured currency trading, acting both in parallel or sometimes through clearing between themselves, with each branch taking profit from the spread on currency exchanges between the two places (Mexican dollars, Hong Kong dollars, US dollars, pounds, etc., and silver/gold). The Guangzhou branch developed active trading activities alongside the small differences between the various dollars circulating in the area and, moreover, succeeded in relevant (low-key, anyway) speculations on arbitrages against gold and silver[30] in 1927–1929—even if it endured a big loss once in May 1929, when it bet bullishly on the tael currency whereas HBSC helped push the Hong Kong dollar upward.[31]

6. Assessing the niche strategy of *Banque de l'Indochine*

If we use our SWOT analysis to gauge the performance and competitiveness of the *Banque de l'Indochine*'s branch in the Guangzhou port-city, we can say that the belated initiative to open an offshoot there was full of promise.

Threats were to be found in the under-equipped and old-fashioned city and harbour (before intensive investments were made to modernise them), the intense competition from British banks (HSBC and Chartered) and more and more from Yokohama Specie Bank and City Bank, the hegemony of the Hong Kong international commerce and banking centre and, last, the successive military and political civil wars which hindered confidence, transportation and security.

Opportunities were to be seized in the growing production of silk in southwest China, the emergence of Chinese intermediaries oriented towards their hinterland and, for a few, committed to developing international connections.

Far from keeping its "local" dimension, Guangzhou asserted itself as a proto-global port-city, practicing business with Europe (Lyon, London), Japan (Yokohama) and, increasingly, New York. No doubt that a large number of small steamers and junks had to fuel the Honk Kong harbour where the main transoceanic shipping liners handled trans-shipment. But Guangzhou was involved directly in international trade, FOREX, and banking connections.

The *Banque de l'Indochine's* **weaknesses** lay, first, in the difficulty to tackle the risks posed by the comprador—which explains the losses in the post-war years. It also lacked expatriates (four, then three), and its managers did not stay for more than a few years, and all of them were not brilliant. The branch lacked permanent funds to follow the growth of business in the 1910s and then in the second half of the 1920s, which meant costly re-funding by its Hong Kong, Saigon and Paris sister concerns. Last, Guangzhou was not the bank's priority in Asia and remained as a second-tier type of outlet as compared to Shanghai and even Tianjin.

Still, little by little, the *Banque de l'Indochine's* **strengths** became leverage forces which drew a large clientele and captured some solid market share. Its embeddedness in Guangzhou's foreign business community and the commitment of its successive managers paved the way to a deep and long-lasting cooperation with the French merchant houses active in the region (mainly in silk trade), although these firms were not averse to benefitting from offers made by other banks. *Banque de l'Indochine* was sufficiently equipped on an international level to compete with HSBC, Chartered and IBC-City Bank in the domains of FOREX, remittance of exchange bills, documentary credit, clearing transfers, among other areas, thanks to its bases in Paris and London.

The creation of FABC (French American Banking Corporation, set up by *Comptoir national d'escompte de Paris* in 1919) in New York helped enhance this competitiveness when the American market became a key outlet for silk merchants, including the French. Both networks (Paris/Lyon and London on one side, to New York on the other) were forms of proto-globalisation inserting the port-city of Guangzhou in a worldwide trading system, though, of course, far behind Hong Kong and Shanghai in size. The Guangzhou branch's refinancing capacity was often consolidated by fresh contributions from its parent house in Paris or from its big branches in Saigon and Hong Kong, which were always rich with ready funds (see Table 9.8).

Admittedly, the development of Shameen island, its port and concessions in the first quarter of the twentieth century will not foster broad considerations about the history of globalisation. But several dozen European merchants and bankers showed a fighting spirit and the entrepreneurship to seize the opportunities offered by the diversification of the worldwide silk production system. Guangzhou became their bridgehead in south-west China. We could claim that such an open-minded offensive revealed itself far more promising and profitable than the long-dreamed Franco-French penetration of western China along the Mekong or the French railway!

The "official" or "institutionalised" north–south axis, so highly touted by the French Indochina authorities (Governor Paul Doumer, in the first decade of

Table 9.7 Position of the Banque de l'Indochine's main Chinese branches in the first term of 1930

	Net profit	Profit on interests and commissions	Profit on FOREX trading	Returns on interest	Interest charged on advances	Returns on commissions and interest	Commissions and interest paid by the branch	Revenue from the rediscounting of bills of exchange
Tianjin	216	31	241	76	538	2,608	439	4
Hong Kong	645	51	681	100	647	6,146	426	0
Guangdong	**37**	**21**	**65**	**48**	**347**	**642**	**223**	**0**
Shanghai	788	412	511	625	1310	11,681	2,441	1
Beijing	35	18	91	26	115	699	55	0
Hankeou	39	4	70	11	104	703	72	0
Mongze and Yunnanfu	605	33	882	396	253	769	52	
Total for Banque de l'Indochinecompany	30,315				29,535	78,168	22,788	5,978
Total of raw profits at Banque de l'Indochine	107,705							

Source: Fund Banque de l'Indochine, Archives of Crédit agricole, 339AH53 profits and losses on first term of 1930

Table 9.8 Growth of the *Banque de l'Indochine*'s Guangzhou branch in 1926–1929

	First half 1926	Second half 1926	First half 1927	Second half 1927	First half 1928	Second half 1928	First half 1929
Completed operations (million HK$)	3,067	3,890	3,559	3,543	16,261	21,029	30,222
Net profit (thousands $)	19,930		35,177	18,133	12,551	−9,879	−36,167 (big loss on a bad currency exchange operation)
Total amount of local operations (million HK$)	1,085	1,450	1,919	1,463	1,335	2,308	2,977
Advances on goods (thousands $)	39	568	634	235	237	743	816
Overdrafts (thousands $)	561	580	592	681	694	708	723

Source: Data mined in the term reports of the Guangzhou branch, but with errors and discontinuity

the century, for instance), which went from Hanoi to Mongtsé/Mengze and Yunnan-Sen (along the railway or via the Mekong or the Red River/Song Koi), never really took off. It was little by little challenged by the east–west axis which took shape from Guangzhou. Instead of relying on protectionist "*chasses gardées*" or state protectorates, the framework of the greenfield offensive in Guangdong/Kwangsu was designed along open competition among trading and banking houses. This little "scramble for China" benefited from almost no protective help—beyond the mere spot of the concessions on the small Shameen island. This axis grew informally by merchant connections, on waterways (You-Kiang River upstream to Nanning and Po-Se; Si-Kiang River) or on roads from Guangzhou (and Fo-Chan) to Ou-Tcheou, then to Nanning westwards—but independently from the French settlement in Kwang-Cho-Wan/Kouang-Tcheou on the southern coast of the Tonkin gulf.[32]

The setting up of a subsidiary at Fort Bayard was discussed in 1923:

The traffic between our port and that of Kwang Tcheou Wan was never of any great importance. Sea-going junks had sufficed all these past years till the fear of pirates forced us to abandon that route. Even otherwise, the route had never been developed to any great extent because the entrance to the port of Kwang Tcheou Wan was hindered by a solid sandbar which made it dangerous for large junks or even barges. Today, the trade between Guangzhou and the Territory takes place exclusively via Hong Kong by the means of small coastal steamers which ply between Fort Bayard, Hong Kong and Macau. Our province exports to Fort Bayard products manufactured here and of daily Chinese consumption, jams, cotton fabrics, silk, incense sticks, or imported products: sugar, flour, oil. Guangzhou especially imports packing mats or bags, poultry, pigs, sheep. There are steamboat services which go up Guangzhou's West River to Wuchow, a major Chinese town which itself is linked by steamboats to Lun Cho and Nanning, that is to say, the receiving and distributing centres directly to the north of the Lui Chow peninsula, which depend economically on Kwong Tcheou Wan. Opium is Kwong Tcheou Wan's only major business.[33]

The destiny of the Guangzhou port-city relied therefore on its very insertion in this proto-globalised network of connections. Japanese and American firms joined French and British competitors there, and the German ones, sidelined for a while due to World War I and its aftermath, came back in the 1920s as importers of European goods. The ultimate high-watermark of the "global" span attained by the port-city was the fact that a dozen Chinese merchants themselves turned into "big players" on the international silk market. Shameen/Guangzhou was thus not only an island of "imperialist" settlements; it became a kind of informal school for a proto-globalised "business model", connecting the bank's portfolios and trading skills—despite the string of obstacles posed by civil wars, revolutionary/anti-imperialist demonstrations and strikes and piracy.

7. Guangzhou harbour and banking into "proto-globalisation"

The development of Guangzhou as a port-city[34] can therefore be gauged through the growth of its banking business itself: the more credit, FOREX and cash transfers gathered momentum, the more the river and maritime exchanges of the harbour were extended. From a mere relay between the countryside and the British Hong Kong big offshoot, Guangzhou emerged slowly but steadily as a regional hub by itself. Sure, the main commercial flows toward Europe or the United States were to transit through Hong Kong facilities, and a majority of the maritime connections of Guangzhou actedas "feeders" to the international lines reaching Hong Kong.

But we can pretend that the first third of the twentieth century transformed radically the function of the seaport: it acquired more and more independence, and its Chinese bourgeoisie broadened its basis, scattering its links deeply into the Pearl Rivers and its affluent, alongside the commercial roads penetrating the countryside. Because of this move towards some kind of a "first globalisation", this commercial penetration stimulated the production of commodities for exports, mainly silk, some little mining ores and a few other agricultural products. As Lyon (in France) and the United States became intimate customers of the area, the port-city changed its stature and jumped into a worldwide dimension.

This led to the building of a new commercial city centre, equipped with far more warehouses, belonging to Chinese intermediaries or, sometimes, as for *Banque de l'Indochine*, to banks or their compradors. What is amazing is that, throughout the political and military events striking at the heart of the city, every municipal body and power struggled to pursue the extension of the construction of a modern commercial port and port-city, far beyond the sole European concessions in Shameen island, even if the latter was also included within this breakthrough of business modernity (with regional headquarters of banks, trading houses, insurance companies, or other organizations).

Thanks to the impulse of European and American capitalism, "East met West" in Guangzhou too, through a visible and regular process which imposed its rhythm on the local society, despite the arguments about Chinese nationalism and model versus the import of the Western model. Certainly the investments into a modern city favoured grafts and thus the financing of the political and military cliques which succeeded one another at the head of the region. But, all in all, Guangzhou came out of these decades as a competitive port-city, far behind the starring Hong Kong and Shanghai business and financial centres, but at the level of Tianjin or Wuhan, for example, justifying that *Banque de l'Indochine* and its competitors clung to their strategy of establishing a small but robust banking centre there—even if refinancing by Hong Kong supplemented the capabilities of these branches.

A major proof of such commitment and success was supplied by the development of a local bourgeoisie, either in the countryside (silk merchants, general trading houses) or in the city itself. Even a few houses commenced to assert themselves in the 1920s as international players, as stakeholders to the exports of silk, mainly oriented towards the United States. Such a proto-globalised trans-Pacific connection eventually led to the building of "modern" layers of business society, in Guangzhou and its surroundings, somewhat independent from the military cliques managing customs revenues or racketeering the trade houses. Such a social revolution fuelled the extension of banking customers and therefore that of *Banque de l'Indochine*, which included them in its "niche strategy", either directly or, more generally, through the intermediary of its comprador.

Far from passively accompanying the building of a "modern" economy and society and remaining mere companions to foreign companies, several dozens of "modern" Chinese houses also joined the in the effort and contributed to the embeddedness of "capitalism" in the port-city and in the upstream areas. And this gave the European banks strong clients, able to broaden the limit of the "niche" as they inserted it more and more into the proto-globalised transoceanic exchanges and FOREX. This ended naturally in the transformation of the Guangzhou harbour from an export tool to a point of import leverage for foreign goods, thus explaining the parallel growth of European importing houses (among them several French ones, supported by *Banque del' Indochine*) and of Chinese houses, thanks to a process of diversification of Chinese involvement in the opening of the Guangzhou port-city.

Notes

1 The manager of the *Banque de l'Indochine*'s branch to Paris headquarters, 20 October 1922, Historical archives of *Crédit agricole*, fund *Banque de l'Indochine*.
2 Report on the second term of 1927 by the manager of *Banque de l'Indochine* branch.
3 *Ibidem*.
4 Report on the first term of 1928 by the manager of the *Banque de l'Indochine*'s branch.
5 Report on the second term of 1927 by the manager of the *Banque de l'Indochine*'s branch, pp. 24–25.
6 The managers of the *Banque de l'Indochine* branch were successively J. Thesmar, Grenard, Émile Le Carduner (1920), Barrau (1930).
7 The manager of the *Banque de l'Indochine*'s branch to Paris headquarters, 3 December 1923.
8 *Ibidem*, 22 December 1927.
9 Report on the second term of 1927 by the manager of *Banque de l'Indochine* branch.
10 The manager of the *Banque de l'Indochine*'s branch to Paris headquarters, 6 April 1929.
11 See *La soierie de Lyon*, February 1933, 16th year, n°2. Allister Macmillan, *Seaports of the Far East: Historical and Descriptive, Commercial and Industrial, Facts, Figures, & Resources*, London, W.H. & L. Collingridge, 1907 (1st edition), 1926 (2nd edition) (608 pp).
12 Report by the manager of the *Banque de l'Indochine*'s branch to Paris headquarters for the first term of 1929.
13 See Tse-Sio Tcheng (Zheng Zixiu), *Les relations de Lyon avec Chine*, Paris, L. Rodstein, 1937. Lillian M. Li, *China's Silk Trade: Traditional Industry in the Modern World, 1842–1937*, Cambridge, MA, Council on East Asian Studies, Harvard University, series "Harvard East Asian Monographs, 97, xv", 1981.
14 Letter from the *Banque de l'Indochine*'s Paris headquarters to the manager of the *Banque de l'Indochine*'s Guangzhou branch, 24 September 1930.
15 The manager of the *Banque de l'Indochine*'s branch to Paris headquarters, 17 March 1923.
16 *Ibidem*, 9 May 1925, 19 August 1925.
17 *Ibidem*, 3 December 1923.
18 *Ibidem*, 18 March 1920.
19 Report from the *Banque de l'Indochine*'s Guangzhou manager on the second term of 1929.
20 *Ibidem*, 15 August 1923.
21 The manager of the *Banque de l'Indochine* branch to Paris headquarters, 23 April 1920. "We thus hope to take a significant part of the deferred letters of credit in £ and $ which will be placed on our market for the *campagne des soies 1920–21*."
22 "Acceptance by an American company of remittances on irrevocable confirmed credit drawn by Gérin Drevard on a few banks of the New York clearing houses", *Ibidem*, 26 January 1931.
23 Report of the manager of the *Banque de l'Indochine*'s branch for the first term of 1928.

24 See Ho Pui-Yin, "Les marchands du delta de la rivière des Perles et de Chaozhou au Guangdu", in Yves Chevrier, Alain Roux & Xiahong Xiao-Planes (eds.), *Citadins et citoyens dans la Chine du xxᵉ siècle (Essais d'histoire sociale)*, En Hommage à Marie-Claire Bergère, Paris, Éditions de la Maison des sciences de l'homme, pp. 207–226.

25 See Sherman Cochran, *Encountering Chinese Networks: Western, Japanese and Chinese Corporations in China, 1880–1937*, Berkeley, University of California Press, 2000.

26 Letter from the manager of the *Banque de l'Indochine*'s Guangzhou branch, report on the first term 1929.

27 Hubert Bonin, *French Banking and Entrepreneurialism in China and Hong Kong, from the 1850s to 1980s*, Abingdon, Routledge, "Banking, Money & International Finance", 2019.

28 See Ming Chang, "Historical dimensions of the Hong Kong-Guangdong financial and monetary links: Three cases in politico-economic interactive dynamics, 1912–1935", paper for the HKMRJ banking and monetary history conference, April 2007.

29 The manager of the *Banque de l'Indochine*'s branch to Paris headquarters, 22 October 1924.

30 Report on the second term of 1928 by the *Banque de l'Indochine*'s branch manager.

31 The manager of the *Banque de l'Indochine*'s branch to Paris headquarters, 5 July 1929.

32 Antoine Vannière, *Kouang Tchéou-Wan, colonie clandestine. Un territoire à bail français en Chine du Sud, 1898–1946*, Paris, Les Indes savantes, 2020..

33 *Ibidem*, 23 January 1923.

34 See Robert Lee, "The socio-economic and demographic characteristics of port cities: A typology for comparative analysis?" *Urban History*, 1998, volume xxv, n°2, pp. 147–172. Frank Broeze, "Port cities: The search for an identity", *Journal of Urban History*, 1985, volume xi, n°2, pp. 209–225.

10 *Banque de l'Indochine* in the Tianjin marketplace in the 1920s

Though with less fame than Shanghai or Guangzhou, the Tianjin French concession commenced emerging as a key platform to penetrate into the communities of business in north-eastern China in order to extend the connections with the Beijing big city, a centre of power and a large consuming area. French bankers and businessmen therefore invested much energy to include the port-city in their strategy of promoting economic patriotism in Asia. French houses coalesced in any case to challenge their foreign competitors; relying on banking support, they had set up a somewhat strong business community of interests, often linked to Christian and military institutions. And they even set up a French fair in 1923 to promote French production, the *Foire française d'échantillons de Tientsin*.[1] The fair was held 13–31 October 1923, and a well illustrated booklet was even printed. But despite these resilient efforts and the continuity of this core customership, the *Banque de l'Indochine* branch could not counter-play the weight of figures: the French contribution to the life of the Tianjin harbour and trade was insignificant and occupied only "niches", and it was not the hub of the marketplace.

An important event occurred in Tianjin in January 1919: the defeat of Germany led to the sequestration of German assets in the French concession but also to the Germany's loss of its concession, which eased the penetration of foreign real estate investors in the area which Chinese authorities managed by themselves henceforth—and they also recovered the management of the Russian concession in June 1920. The immediate after-war period fuelled regained momentum for local, foreign and French business and banking in the city-port. It was the end station for the railway Tianjin–Pukow, itself linked by ferry to the Shanghai–Nankin, and it was joined by the Pei-Ning Railway (Beijing–Liaoning), itself joining in Mukden the Manchurian railways and finally the *Trans-Siberian* at Manchuli.

1. Competition as a background

In any case, *Banque de l'Indochine* had to face more intense competition, even if the branch of Russo-Asiatic Bank closed down because of its Bolshevisation in Russia.[2] First, in 1920–1922, *Banque industrielle de Chine* rushed to surpass *Banque de l'Indochine* on several opportunities. Then from 1923, the successor of *Banque industrielle de Chine*, *Banque franco-chinoise*, opened its doors in Paris on October 1922 and in China on February 1923, with branches in Beijing, Shanghai, Tianjin and Hong Kong. It disposed of a brand new building at the corner of *Rue de France* and *Rue Saint-Louis*, which was inaugurated[3] on 2 June 1928. The Belgian *Banque sino-belge*[4] and the Italian and Chinese Bank also settled there. Such intense competition raised discontent with *Banque de l'Indochine*, along with complaining by the authorities about its legitimacy as "the French bank" there.

In 1923, the following banks were thus active in Tianjin: *Banque de l'Indochine, Banque sino-française*; HSBC, Chartered; Japan: Yokohama Specie Bank, Bank of Chosen, Exchange Bank of China, Bank of Tien Tsin; United States: International Banking Corporation, Asia Banking Corporation, Chinese American Bank of Commerce, American Oriental Banking Corporation; *Banque belge pour l'étranger* (opened on 13 September 1912); Sino-Italian Bank; *Deutsch Asiatisch Bank*; the Russo-Asiatic Bank (till 1926). These foreign banks were supplemented by a dozen Chinese banks.

2. Catholic missions reinforcing the French basis

The leader of the Jesuit mission, the Reverend Jacquart (in 1921–1929), then Reverend René Charvet, was part of influential circles in the city, and the manager of the bank treated regularly with him because he had become more and more some kind of an institutional investor and even a financial "godfather" of the French community of business interests.[5] The Mission invested funds in several companies of Tianjin: Tianjin Realty; *Société foncière franco-chinoise de Tianjin*[6] (intimately linked with a driving leverage force on the property market in China [Shanghai] and Hong Kong); *Crédit foncier d'Extrême-Orient*, a Belgian financial holding; *Société française de librairie & d'édition* (a publisher); Tianjin Trust; General Dairy & Farm; Chihli Press; *Huileries de Tianjin*; and a few trading houses (Arnoult [chaired by the Reverend himself], J. Gully or Battegay, etc.).[7] Moreover, the Mission served as an endorser bringing its guarantee of several advances by *Banque de l'Indochine* to local companies, for instance *Union immobilière de Tianjin*, a real estate investor[8] created in 1925.

The Mission took part in several projects in real estate on the one hand for its offices (*École des hautes études industrielles et commerciales*,[9] *Musée du Hoang Ho-Pai Ho*, laboratories, chapel, offices) and on another hand because it invested as a property owner in several concessions or ex-concessions. They owned properties and fields in the ex-German concession and in the French concession, adjacent to the British one—the revenues from their properties in the French concession even reaching $52,000 later on in 1935. These assets provided it with important revenues from renting, and their head was some kind of a financial assets manager too, with a thick portfolio of securities, for example American ones, thus fostering deposits and loans to companies. But its management was not crowned with success, and several companies which it supported crumbled in the 1920s. Reverend Jacquart had been pushing too much, too speculative and too close to businessmen (Jean O'Neill in particular). A drastic reshuffling of the strategy was imposed in the 1930s to alleviate bad investments and to recover more revenues from the portfolio, in fact favouring real estate activities.

3. Promoting a portfolio of banking skills

The *Banque de l'Indochine* branch picked up within its portfolio of skills to promote its brand image in the Tianjin marketplace.

A. Entertaining the foreign exchange specialty

The need for currency in cash was felt several times because the Tianjin marketplace was so sensitive to commercial and monetary events in Shanghai and Hong Kong. An intense FOREX crisis thus occurred in 1927, during the upsurge in Shanghai: the dollar fell, nobody purchased taels, everyone rushed after silver. "The main factor which replaced the levels on almost normal rates was the certitude that British war ships would leave Shanghai to Tianjin to bring golden dollars for British and Japanese banks."[10] At the same time, the *Banque de l'Indochine* branch had to sell with losses in order to face a run on its deposits because the French cruiser *Jules Michelet* failed to transport cash from Shanghai for *Banque de l'Indochine* and British banks refused to refinance it or to help it change its silver *sycées* (or taels) into silver or golden dollars.

B. Commercial banking enhanced

Banque de l'Indochine had to resort to a more lenient policy of credit, although the ground for business depended on relatively middle-sized and fragile companies, managed by people who were more "adventurers" than long-term developers and who were prompt in seizing opportunities to reach agreements without pondering their disadvantages. That was the case for the public works company Brossard & Mopin, which got orders from French authorities and created two plants (ship engines in Tianjin and a small shipyard in Takou-Sin Ho in 1918, with 3,000 employees) without great success but consuming a few advances in the process.[11]

The branch had also to support the trade houses Galussère in 1920–1921 in order to get a share of its credits against *Banque industrielle de Chine* and, throughout the 1920s, a few other French houses (Arnoult, Colinet, Racine), which constituted a very limited basis for a prosperous and durable activity of advances on goods against promissory notes. They had set a little community of business at the very centre of the city (see Table 10.1).

C. Olivier as a close client of Banque de l'Indochine

The main target anyway was trade houses, but the French presence in Tianjin was scarce, all the more because of the might of foreign competitors, from

Table 10.1 A few important French trade houses in Tianjin at the end of the 1920s

	Location in the French concession (depending on two different sources)		
	In 1926	*In 1929*	*In 1932*
Olivier	Rue de Takou	35 rue de Verdun	
G. Colinet	58 rue de l'Amirauté	23 rue de l'Amirauté	6 rue Henry Bourgeois
J. Battegay	26 rue de l'Amirauté		
Racine	137 quai de France	18 quai de France	
J. Ulman			99 rue de France
La Mutuelle (J.-P. Ferrer)			
J. Gully			54 rue Henry Bourgeois
J. Lafitte		rue de l'Amirauté	
Compagnie générale d'Extrême-Orient	?	Rue Dillon	
Moyroux			41 rue de France
E. Médard	?	?	
Arnoult	?	?	
Galussère	?	?	
Vernaudon	?	?	

the UK (Jardine Matheson, Perrin Cooper, William Forbes,[12] etc.), from the Danish (and partly German) Arnhold, or from the United States (Andersen Meyer, etc.):[13] there were about 34 French trade houses against a total of 625 in the mid-1920s. The sole important company active there was the international wholesale commission trader Olivier, very active in Asia from its bases in Paris, London and Milan, which opened offices and warehouses (go-downs) in Tianjin (financed by *Crédit foncier d'Extrême-Orient*). E. Charlot from the Olivier house, was, for example, the chairman of the Tianjin section of the French Chamber of Commerce in 1922. The branch financed its Tianjin activities[14] from the 1920s, even if Olivier faced a permanent treasury crisis; it had to require guarantees on inventories piled in a special go-down dedicated to goods serving as pledges for its "packing credits" (then $125,000),[15] that is, advances on merchandises transiting through the warehouses.

Despite a temporary failure of Olivier in March 1922, it restarted its operations and remained a faithful customer of *Banque de l'Indochine* in Tianjin. It exported through Tianjin basic goods (wools, walnuts) but also high-valued "exotic" goods: goat beards, horsetails, bristles (pork hair), animal casings, stumps (drawings on special paper), carpets, furs, straw braids, egg albumine, among others, often sold in New York. For example, the company Standard Casing manufactured hog and sheep casings in its factory in Tianjin (on the territory of the Russian concession) and used Olivier to export them to the United States.[16] Despite the constant support from *Banque de l'Indochine* in Paris—as its house banker—and in Tianjin, the bank complained that Olivier also used other banks to finance its exports; for example, the current overdraft advances were shared, with 43 per cent for *Banque de l'Indochine*, against 42 per cent for HSBC and 12 per cent for *Banque industrielle de Chine*.[17] But it favoured in fact a sound division of risks, and *Banque de l'Indochine* remained the key banker with two-thirds of the 1.5 million taels borrowed by Olivier through packing credits in 1924–1925.

D. An internationalised marketplace

After World War I, everyone took profit from the unfolding of German interests— even if some of them rebounded under other names and Danish flags, notably to import chemicals—which had been so important before the war. It played, for example, some part in the business of American firms, always desiring to broaden their credit basis; it began by financing China American Trading (878,000 taels in 1917), a large import house (cars, tires, carpets, office equipment, machines, coats, etc.), which in 1921 was the largest overdraft of the branch and kept its rank durably. Its debt amounted to 1,480,000 taels in 1918, 446,000 in October 1922 and 606,000 on 10 February 1923, and 358,000 on 6 January 1925.

But it was revealed as a bad affair because its repayments took years through monthly instalments, even if the firm went on trading. The bank had to use the mortgaged offices and warehouses of China American Trading to be paid for part of its debt. In any case, the *Banque de l'Indochine* branch could join the pack of bankers supporting the exports from Tianjin to the United States, with large amounts of bills drawn on American banks, even if the Paris office, from the start of the 1930s, established drastic lists of the New York bankers considered solid enough, which reduced the flexibility of the branch and *in fine* its customership.

E. The comprador business after World War I

A new comprador had to be recruited in June 1915 when the first one died; Tzu Chih Fu, himself the son of the comprador of a German house, Tzu Hsen Tang, was recommended by the *Banque de l'Indochine* comprador in Shanghai, Nicolas Tsou, and pledged by the comprador of the trade house Liddel Brothers.[18] But these guarantees appeared as nil when his son lost on his side about $60,000, and he had to resign as soon as May 1920. He was replaced by Ling Chi Hsiang, first an executive at the Chinese bank Ye Yung Cieng, then the treasurer of the army of Li Hung Chang and finally the comprador of a French insurance company in Tianjin, *La Mutuelle*. In fact, he developed rapidly his own business under the cover of *Banque de l'Indochine*, and the branch had to handle large amounts of "native orders" for his own clients.

But his operations brought cash through broad deposits either from the comprador himself or from his customers, thus providing a collection of more than 200,000 or 300,000 taels because such amounts have to be repaid during a little run in July 1927, and his operations were concluded in success and profitability, as it appeared at his death in 1933.

The background of the French concession was broadened by the emergence of local industrialists, entrepreneurial companies evolving from small-scale production to factory systems, even if they remained fragile due to a lack of a "structured" form of capitalism,[19] "a weak, transient capitalist class",[20] burdens resulting from bad finance (the cotton merchants "defaulted"[21] in Tianjin in 1923), dependence on warlords' connections and finance,[22] and a weakened condition from the civil war in the 1920s, with its heavy exactions levied by competing warlords' governments to authorise and protect the flows of goods[23] till the unification in 1928 by the Guo Min Dang.[24]

4. Big business for French industrialists?

In the mid-1920s, *Banque de l'Indochine* became a partner of a group intending to conquer public orders for telecommunication equipment, *Société française des téléphones interurbains* (SFTI). SFTI had installed the networks in Tianjin, Harbin and Mukden (in Manchuria), and it transferred its headquarters from Harbin to Tianjin in 1925 because, from an Anglo-Russian company, it had become a French one in September 1924 even if it had kept links with the British Far Eastern company, a supplier to the Chinese Eastern Railway. Its purposes were to redeploy its activities from Manchuria to the broader north-eastern areas of China. It won the contract for the telephone and wireless link between Tianjin and Shanghai for the Tianjin–Pukow railway (Chinese Eastern Railway).

If it had issued a loan to finance this investment, it needed bank credits to finance its purchases in Europe and the United States (copper, equipment) and in Manchuria (wood poles) and to its day-to-day operations in China as a representative of French telecommunication firms, with advances[25] of G$ 148,000, £11,000 and 10,000 taels in 1926. Such an opportunity seemed relevant to *Banque de l'Indochine*.[26] In the summer of 1926, it was modestly involved in a large agreement between European and Chinese banks and SFTI to provide big advance pledges of seven years of revenues from the network to be set up, but *Banque de l'Indochine* provided it with advances (69,000 taels) pending the first instalment of credit—with the pledged equipment in a warehouse.

Part of the equipment was ordered in France from *Câbles de Lyon* (today Nexans), part in the UK to Siemens UK.[27] Another contract took place in October 1927: the Far Eastern Bank (through a G$175,000 documentary credit and a global G$400,000 advance) financed the telephone equipment of Mukden (the exchange centre and 3,000 automatic units).[28] The group led by Pavlovski enlarged its scope, and its subsidiary *Le Matériel technique* could propose anything to customers: eleven *Potez 25* with Lorraine engines were even sold to the Szechuen government in 1932, transported by boat to Haiphong and assembled there, but military troubles suspended the completion of the operation, co-financed by *Banque de l'Indochine* through confirmed credits.

Such business ought to have changed the scale of *Banque de l'Indochine* in Tianjin, but it had to consider the slowness of the process for such operations and moreover the fragmentation of Chinese power and influence networks, which led to huge amount of graft: the telephone contract consumed G$237,000 against a total amount of G$859,000:

> No state operation could be concluded in China without considerable 'squeezes' to deliver, as soon as the signature of the contracts, to those who negotiate them. This explains why big German firms (Siemens or Carlovitz, and Danish-German Arnhold Karberg) had won before the war the monopole of large industrial firms in the country. Far from having changed, the method has been excessively amplified because of the colossal appetite of present politicians who are the first interested by the conclusion of such operations. Large orders of planes, trucks, railway equipment, etc. are reached along with such way. We have to accept such constraints and close our eyes if we wish to work in this country.[29]

In the interwar period, even if it lost the contract for the Japanese concession in 1928, *Énergie électrique de Tianjin* prospered under the management of Clément Bourgery, its co-owner and manager; its net assets of $2,347,000 were the basis of large profits (£12,500 in 1924–1925) and dividends, part of them being used to invest in French Indochina. Such a business was reinforced because the firm sold its electricity to the big *Compagnie des tramways & d'éclairage de Tianjin*, which distributed it in the Belgian concession and in the Lao Si Kai territory (*de facto* included in the French territory) but also supplied the whole Chinese city.

Less pacific trade was also developed, when armaments were involved, owing to the fragmentation of military and political power at the turn of the 1930s. The French firm Hotchkiss received an order from the Hei Lung Kiang government for a hundred machine guns,[30] and *Banque de l'Indochine* brought its local guarantee ($80,000) while the Paris office opened a confirmed credit (USD 78,000). But the development of such business was obviously hindered by the military and political evolution of China and moreover by a disturbing position of the French state, which refused to bring a public guarantee from credit insurance for the suppliers, because it required that the Chinese 1902 loan be repaid in golden francs and not in current francs, which paralysed export prospects.

5. The Manchurian French dream from the Tianjin city-port

From the 1920s, some French business circles dreamed of getting a share of the growing Manchurian economy, in line with the interests they had developed there before World War I through *Banque russo-chinoise*, then *Banque russo-asiatique*. The Sovietisation of the Russian zone of influence did not disturb them, and as early as 1924—after France had recognised USSR—they tried to establish a relationship with Russian state institutions, the Far Eastern Bank and its sister in Harbin on the Chinese side, *Banque d'Extrême-Orient* (or Dalbank).[31] Some years later, *Banque de l'Indochine* studied a project of opening a branch in Manchuria because there the French banking influence had dwindled since the liquidation of *Banque russo-asiatique* by its French shareholders: two missions were achieved in the country by the director of the Tianjin *Banque de l'Indochine* branch,[32] in March 1928 and in March 1933.

This latter emerged thus as a lever to prospect the whole north-eastern area, as an information collector for the sake of the French business community, far beyond its initial function to finance day-to-day local exports. But Manchurian business was far riskier: some trade houses failed there (Silverberg in 1929, with *Banque de l'Indochine* losing 11,000 taels on a total of 127,000),[33] and competition was intense, even from French bankers because the *Banque russo-asiatique* assets there had been purchased by their managers and transformed into *Banque franco-asiatique* in Harbin and Mukden.[34]

Some French businessmen rushed to Manchuria and set up *Union commerciale & industrielle pour la Mandchourie* in 1928 to prospect among local authorities for railway orders or other opportunities. But American industrialists and bankers won some contracts in 1930, all the more because the French state refused to bring its guarantee against political and military risks to such business. This offensive was halted by the Japanese invasion of Manchuria in 1931. A second offensive took shape when French firms tried to convince Japanese authorities to consider orders. Tensions between China and Japan and the refusal by France to recognize Manchukuo did not hinder the *Banque de l'Indochine* branch in becoming involved in such canvassing in the wake of French industrialists, and it joined a group which competed with another one to induce Nippon potentates (general Koiso Kuniaki, for example, in 1933) in ordering railway equipment to modernise the lines linking Manchuria to northern China or public works schemes.

Such a division, the frailty of financial arrangements and the will of Japan to favour its own exports limited success. SFTI won a contract for tramway cars for the Streetcar Company of Harbin, and *Banque de l'Indochine* financed the operation (USD 36,000).[35] It was set up at the very branch of Tianjin because of the SFTI office there, then developed on a worldwide scale: the Harbin company paid its debt to Bank of China in Harbin, which remitted it to the Harbin account of National City Bank, then to City Bank New York, then to French American Banking Corporation (a joint venture between two French banks, among them *Banque de l'Indochine*) in New York, then to France (*Ateliers de constructions électriques de Jeumont*).

6. Business despite uncertainties in the 1920s

The *Banque de l'Indochine* branch lost its director, André Pernotte, who had been judged as pushing too hard and as lacking in "risk-aversion", but such a move helped it to succeed in resisting reckless risk taking. Either because of instructions from the Paris headquarters or because of lucid management, it avoided the fate of the branch of *Banque industrielle de Chine*. This harsh competitor of *Banque de l'Indochine* in China and particularly in north-eastern China had been led by Pernotte himself [36] after its departure from *Banque de l'Indochine* and had rapidly broadened its operations to numerous French, non-French and even Chinese business, without apparently respecting sane rules of risk assessment—because it often linked financial prospects and large overdrafts to its future clients for investment banking projects.

The collapse of *Banque industrielle de Chine* troubled the *Banque de l'Indochine* branch[37] because it stirred a crisis of trust and a run on deposits from Chinese customers who confused *Banque industrielle de Chine* and *Banque de l'Indochine*, all the more because a few Chinese trading houses working with *Banque industrielle de Chine* failed and because French authorities demanded *Banque de l'Indochine* to take part in a rescue refinancing of its rival. But rapidly *Banque de l'Indochine* emerged safe and even drew depositors fleeing *Banque industrielle de Chine* or its successor (which opened its Tianjin branch in February 1923).

Globally, the banking business profited from the relative growth of Chinese economy[38] and from the development of the Beijing area (because of the modern urbanisation process) and of the Tianjin hinterland (Shansi, etc.), thanks to the railway networks and even somewhat to Manchurian orders. The *Banque de l'Indochine* branch could thus finance more Chinese business, beyond the scope of the French concession and its close neighbours. For a while, the military struggles took place far southwards, and the Tianjin area benefited from the relatively stable government of a few warlords balancing their power with that of the central government. In any case, the civil war imposed its dire effects on the *Banque de l'Indochine* branch, which suffered from uncertainty and bad debts over Chinese houses: "All the trading houses of our place are struggling against important troubles."[39] And Kuominchun troops occupied Tianjin for a while in 1925.

But the concession itself ended welcoming thousands of rich people fleeing the civil war because Chinese families wished to escape despoliation from warlords,[40] and trading with the hinterland was resumed nevertheless—despite the exchange crisis in Shanghai in 1927: "Tianjin, like the other northern ports, benefited from a relative tranquillity. The volume of transactions was thus growing despite the halt on transit of goods from Mongolia which use now the Eastern railways and the Dairen and even Vladivostock ports"[41] (see Table 10.2).

Signs of deflation prevailed anyway because of the climate of risk, and the Paris office required the repatriation of cash assets between November 1925 and September 1926 (to Shanghai), then again in January 1927 in January 1929 (to London, about £85,000, then 600,000 taels) in order to preserve the assets from geopolitical threats, which was well anticipated:

This [1928] year, Tianjin has directly suffered from the regaining of hostilities, and the Chinese city has been particularly hit by massacres and destructions. To the horrors of civil war was added starvation, and misery is high among a population charged with taxes. The lack of transport means, which hinders the circulation of goods, and robbery have impeded the imports from the hinterland and, except a few articles, the majority of export products were shortened a lot.[42]

Table 10.2 Situation of the *Banque de l'Indochine* branch of Tianjin on 31 December 1928

Resources	
Deposits	1,703
Capital account	1,238
Various creditor accounts	702
Clearing creditor accounts by other banks	127
Money coming to the branch from internal resources of *Banque de l'Indochine*:	
Deposit from Paris (£ account)	795
Deposit from the Beijing branch	54
Deposit from the Shanghai branch	423
Total of resources from *Banque de l'Indochine*	1,386
Total liabilities	3,831
Assets	
Advances on exterior business	2,427
Advances on bills of exchange	183
Local business	2,791
Among which advances pending:	
Advances on promissory notes in taels and dollars, among which:	774
Crédit foncier d'Extrême-Orient	157
Catholic Mission	37
Chinese clients through the comprador	385
Advances on goods	384
Advances to Olivier house in China	12
Among which advances to Chinese houses through the comprador	130
	100
	26
Advances on securities	274
Advances on current accounts	230
Among which *Énergie électrique de Tianjin*	139
Among which advances to the Mission of Tianjin and its *Union immobilière de Tianjin*	50
Among which advance to trading house Arnoult	81

The flight of dictator Chan So Ling spurred a cash crisis on the Tianjin place in January 1929 because its clan drew huge amounts from its banking accounts in Chinese banks, themselves threatening their deposits in European banks. *Banque de l'Indochine* had to be cautious and could not thus take profit from a strong and stable growth, but its accounts were preserved sane.

Banque de l'Indochine faced huge handicaps due to the competitive edge of British banks, the frail influence of French business in north-eastern China in comparison with southern China) and the meagre number of French trade houses involved there. The branch was devoted to supplying financial means to the French concession indeed. But business history shows that even companies hindered by harsh handicaps did succeed in encroaching on market shares: return-led managers looked out for business opportunities, curtailed niches

Table 10.3 Position of the main Chinese branches of *Banque de l'Indochine* during the first term of 1930

	Net profit	Profits on interests and commissions	Profits on FOREX trading	Returns on interests	Interests charged on advances	Returns on commissions and interests	Commissions and interests paid by the branch	Revenues from the rediscounting of bills of exchange
Tianjin	216	31	241	76	538	2,608	439	4
Hong Kong	645	51	681	100	647	6,146	426	0
Guangdong	37	21	65	48	347	642	223	0
Shanghai	788	412	511	625	1310	11,681	2,441	1
Beijing	35	18	91	26	115	699	55	0
Hankeou	39	4	70	11	104	703	72	0
Mongze and Yunnanfu	605	33	882	396	253	769	52	
Total for *Banque de l'Indochine* company	30,315				29,535	78,168	22,788	5,978
Total of raw profits at *Banque de l'Indochine*	107,705							

Sources: Fund *Banque de l'Indochine*, Historical archives of *Crédit agricole*, 339AH53, profits and losses on first term of 1930

and, because of their adaptability and flexibility, explored new territories of business and followed such a path in Tianjin, which transformed the *Banque de l'Indochine* branch into an active and profitable hub of banking business despite high risks, bad debts and dire military events—even if its part in the life of the bank did not reach a key position, as it provided only 0.71 per cent of its profits on the first term of 1930, for example (see Table 10.3).

Notes

1 (Nantes French Consulate archives, TT47). "French Minister opens *Foire fran-çaise d'échantillons de Tientsin* in presence of hundred visitors", *North China Star*, 14 October 1923.
2 Russo-Asiatic Bank was liquidated in Paris on 1 October 1926 and in China on 17 October 1926. The Tianjin branch closed its doors on 27 September 1926 (*North China Star*, 27 September 1926), and its premises were sold to Bank of Communications in December 1928 (see *Peking & Tientsin Times*, 16 October 1929).
3 "Inauguration du nouvel immeuble de la Banque franco-chinoise à Tien Tsin", *Le Tient-sinois*, 8 August 1928, Nantes French Consulate archives, 619C.
4 Fund *Banque de l'Indochine*, Archives of *Crédit agricole, Banque de l'Indochine* correspond-ence, 6 January 1933.
5 See Corinne Dehoux-Dutilleux, *Les Hautes Études industrielles et commerciales de Tianjin (Tianjin Gongshang xueyuan* 天津工工商学院)*, 1923–1951: un exemple de l'action éduca-tive des Jésuites en Chine*, thesis presented on 15 June 2018 at the Bordeaux Montaigne University, in Bordeaux-Pessac.
6 *Société foncière franco-chinoise de Tianjin* had been created in 1919 and was owned by O'Neill, but *Mission de Hsien Hsin, Mission catholique de Tientsin* and *Mission des Lazaristes* had bought stakes, along with Chinese investors (Nantes French Consulate archives, 212, 3 July 1926). And Father F. Desrumeaux, the *Procureur des Lazaristes*, succeeded to O'Neill as the chairman (*ibidem*, 27 March 1930); two other priests were then direc-tors, R.P. Charvet, *Procureur de laMission de Hsien Hsin*, and R.P. J. Molinari., *Société foncière franco-chinoise de Tianjin*, and owned warehouses, residence houses and apartment buildings.
7 *Banque de l'Indochine* correspondence, 17 December 1928.
8 *Ibidem*, 24 November 1930.
9 Louis Samarcq was the manager of *Société foncière franco-chinoise de Tianjin* but also the *fondé de pouvoirs* of *Crédit foncier d'Extrême-Orient*, located on 45 *rue de France*.
10 Fund *Banque de l'Indochine*, Archives of *Crédit agricole, Banque de l'Indochine* correspond-ence, 26 July 1927.
11 *Ibidem*, 5 April 1918.
12 William Forbes also represented the French line *Messageries maritimes*.
13 The French Consul identified 625 non-Chinese trading houses in Tianjin in the mid-1920s (Nantes French Consulate archives, TT46): 372 Japanese ones, 85 British, 40 Ger-man, 37 American, 28 Russian, 16 Belgian, 11 Italian, 5 Dutch, and 34 French ones.
14 With a global advance of 127,000 taels, 28 April 1921.
15 Fund *Banque de l'Indochine*, Archives of *Crédit agricole, Banque de l'Indochine* correspond-ence, 1 October 1921.
16 Nantes French consulate archives, 9B2, 1928.
17 Fund *Banque de l'Indochine*, Archives of *Crédit agricole, Banque de l'Indochine* correspond-ence, 26 May 1925.
18 *Ibidem*, 16 June 1915.
19 Gail Hershatter, *op. cit.*
20 *Ibidem*, p. 140.

21 Nantes French consulate archives, 9B3.
22 Gail Hershatter, *op. cit.*, pp. 31–32.
23 *Ibidem*, p. 32. From 1916 to 1928, several warlords succeeded one another (Wu Peifu, Zhang Zuolin, Li Jinglin, Feng Yuxing), before the Shanxi warlord Yan Xishan acquired control of Tianjin.
24 But then the French Consul (Nantes archives, 9B2) underlined the tax extortion by the Zhili provincial administration at the end of the 1920s and the start of the 1930s or the new "consolidated taxes" on cotton yarn, cement, matches, etc.
25 Fund *Banque de l'Indochine*, Archives of *Crédit agricole, Banque de l'Indochine* correspondence, June 1926.
26 *Ibidem*, 15 July 1926.
27 *Ibidem*, 26 August 1926.
28 *Ibidem*, 27 October 1927. But *Banque de l'Indochine* was not directly involved.
29 Fund *Banque de l'Indochine*, Archives of *Crédit agricole, Banque de l'Indochine* correspondence, 9 February 1927.
30 *Ibidem*, 23 July 1930.
31 *Ibidem*, 16 May 1924.
32 *Ibidem*, 29 February 1928.
33 Fund *Banque de l'Indochine*, Archives of *Crédit agricole, Banque de l'Indochine* correspondence, 25 February 1929.
34 *Ibidem*, 16 July 1929.
35 *Ibidem*, 4 and 26 April 1932.
36 See André J. Pernotte, *Pourquoi et comment fut fondée la Banque industrielle de Chine, ses difficultés, ses ennemis, politique et finance*, Paris, Jouve, 1922. Nobutaka Shinonaga, *La formation de la Banque industrielle de Chine et son écroulement, un défi des frères Berthelot*, Paris, 1988. Le Duc Léouzon, *Le procès de la Banque industrielle de Chine. Plaidoirie de M. Léouzon Le Duc*, Paris, 1926. Jean-Noël Jeanneney, "La Banque industrielle de Chine et la chute des frères Berthelot, 1921–1923", in Jean-Noël Jeanneney, *L'argent caché*, Paris, Seuil, 1984, pp. 128–168.
37 Fund *Banque de l'Indochine*, Archives of *Crédit agricole, Banque de l'Indochine* correspondence, 9 July 1921.
38 See Thomas Rawski, *Economic Growth in Prewar China*, Berkeley, University of California Press, 1989.
39 Fund *Banque de l'Indochine*, Archives of *Crédit agricole, Banque de l'Indochine* correspondence, 6 January 1925.
40 *Ibidem*, 1 May 1925.
41 *Banque industrielle de Chine* annual report for the 1927 year.
42 Fund *Banque de l'Indochine*, Archives of *Crédit agricole, Banque de l'Indochine* correspondence, 1928.

11 The effects of World War I on the Wuhan branch

Even if World War I did not involve Asia for a few terms, it exerted indirect effects on the overall business. It therefore affected the Wuhan trade despite the fact that China entered the war against Germany only in 1918. For instance, the submarine war hampered free navigation, and some liners and cargo ships such as the *Ville de La Ciotat*, of the *Messageries maritimes* line, were sunk in the Mediterranean before or after crossing the Suez Canal in December 1915. The Suez transit was suffering somewhat from military and naval events.[1] And the outlets throughout Europe had to be reconsidered because of the division of the continent and of the militarisation of the economy itself, escaping to market rules.

1. The issue of German business

Of great importance was the suspension of payment by German houses active in China because they were considered as "enemy" by the Allied powers managing foreign concessions. Their assets were sequestered in warehouses, hampering export. Because these houses had halted their relations with China, their European headquarters and their local delegates reneged on their pledges.

> The present situation is no less delicate, with the hostilities complicating it further. Being in a neutral country, it is difficult to say what should our goal be. The recently enacted laws tell us to abstain from all business with houses belonging to an enemy nation. You thus cannot continue to work with the numerous German houses that formed part of your clientele. On the other hand, the recovery of pledges covering your overdrafts would be possible, we believe, in only very few cases because it is probable that they were retained in trust by your borrowers. Make the most of any opportunities that come your way. At the same time, do not forget that certain German houses claim a neutral nationality under the pretext that their founder or a partner belonged to that country, for example, Arnhold Karberg & C°— the Bank of England has told us that it is actually a German house. Make it a rule of attributing every house the nationality that it was registered under before the start of hostilities ... The present situation will make it very difficult for us to realise the remittances drawn on France or England

by German houses here as we will need to establish for each of them that it is money owed to us and not a case of cashing their credit.[2]

This was the case of Arnhold Karberg, a big house active in all the open port-cities (with 101,000 taels still pending in April 1920), Lohmann (from Bremen, FRF 57,000 pending in June 1919), Carlowitz, Max Mittag and the more modestly sized Schnabel Gaumer, Lautenbach, S. Wurch (with a total debt of 57,741 taels in 1916) and Siemssen, Diederichsen, China Java Export, Talge & Schröter, and Garrels Börner. Conversely, German authorities impounded a large consignment of antimony sent to Antwerp by Panoff, which reduced the value of the pledge against the loan granted by *Banque de l'Indochine* for this operation.[3] Overall, German customers turned into pools of immobilised, even bad assets.

> Business with German houses has declined. With respect to shipments of cargo to cover our debit balances, the customs trouble us at every step due to the name of the dispatchers and often the goods are sequestered. You cannot consider our bills of lading as a clearance of accounts.[4]

Twelve German houses were involved in June 1912 for a total of 640,563 taels of unpledged advances and 280,554 marks on bills of exchange (FRF 2.867 million). In China, *Banque de l'Indochine* had to wait until the end of neutrality to start legal action.

> Outstanding loans to German companies: the settlement of some German loans could not be pursued till 1917 due to the neutrality assumed by China. Now that the situation has changed in this regard, we need to look into the measures to be taken for liquidating our commitments to enemy houses.[5]

Lawyers in Paris (and London) were mobilised to assert its rights over European assets in several ports and banks. It took several years, till 1918/20, to get back a few thousand taels (for instance, from Arnhold Bros, the official British successor of Arnhold Karberg) or to amortise losses with the pending debts.

2. The issue of cash

Because of the lack of liquidity caused by the economic war in Europe, the *Banque de l'Indochine*'s Paris headquarters slashed internal refinancing, and Shanghai had to follow suit. This resulted, from 1916, into a cash crunch in Wuhan, which was forced to reduce the amount of discounts. "Due to the complete stoppage of cash supply from our Shanghai branch, we have had to do the same to our export clients and our purchase of paper on Europe."[6] Resources fell from FRF 3,974,366 in the second half of 1915 to 2,628,488 in the first half of 1916 (−33 per cent). Despite a rebound in the second half of 1915, business fell dramatically between 1914 and 1917 (−75 per cent) (see Table 11.1).

Table 11.1 Total operations by the *Banque de l'Indochine* Wuhan branch in 1914–1917

	FRF	Taels
1st semester 1914	12,031,099	
2nd semester 1914	5,401,619	
1st semester 1915	6,371,579	
2nd semester 1915	11,287,420	
1st semester 1916	6,582,640	11,953,874 or 10,784,464
2nd semester 1916	3,172,000	7,163 758
1st semester 1917	Around 3 million	7,110 088

Consequently, several clients went over to rival banks for their discount and remittance business with Europe. Between the second half of 1915 to the second half of 1916, Grosjean went from FRF 2,315,000 to zero, Racine-Ackermann from 2,334,000 to 47,000, and Italian Chinese from 3,668,000 to 196,000.[7] "It became impossible for us to adequately supply Spunt which, previously, dealt only with us and which today conducted most of its business with the *Banque russe (Russo-Asiatique)*."[8] "Our single biggest seller was Miffret, with 1.484m in paper drawn almost entirely on documentary letters of credit issued by banks in London and New York."[9]

3. The issue of European war

Business dwindled further as the war was prolonged: "Lacking resources, our Export account is almost stopped" (January 1918), with meagre FOREX operations and the barriers imposed by the Allies to exports from west Europe (not to speak of German trade, which was completely blocked).

> The first half of 1918 was, for us, a repetition of the conditions that had prevailed over the preceding years. The problems and difficulties faced by businesses only increased month after month as the Allies kept adding newer measures and restrictions and to siphon all resources into the war. Being farthest from Europe and supplying only a small part of essential commodities, the Chinese market was completely neglected as regards freight and saw British tonnage being reduced to a trickle.[10]

Customer debt accounts fell from 1.316 million in the second half of 1916 to 0.875 million taels in the first half of 1917.

4. Risks due to regional civil wars

Moreover local military events aggravated the situation: regional civil wars broke out when local troops, taking advantage of the mobilisation of the Powers in Europe, began controlling a few territories and set off the process of

Table 11.2 Dwindling operations at the *Banque de l'Indochine* Wuhan branch in 1916–1919 (million FRF)

	Liabilities	Resources
1st semester 1916	3,794	4,144
2nd semester 1916	/	/
1st semester 1917	1,666/3,904	2,285/2,818
2nd semester 1917	1,284	1,550
1st semester 1918	3,158	2,004
2nd semester 1918	1,024	1,120
1st semester 1919	0,618	0,756

fragmentation of the Chinese Republic that went on till the second half of the 1920s. Warlords (*dojun*) set up feudal systems which were nothing more than modern trade rackets.

> Business communication has been difficult because of the civil war between the Northerners and Southerners. This civil war is nothing more than a war of pillaging and robbing caused by the incapacity, intrigues and petty jealousy between the leaders of the fighting troops. The rich lands which regularly supplied Wuhan with their products have fallen prey to banditry and anarchy. Sichuan and Hunan are no more in contact with our port because of the bands which pillage the junks and convoys, paralysing all traffic to the Upper Yangtze.[11]

Railroad tracks like the Wuhan–Beijing and the Wuhan–Guangzhou lines (under construction) fell under the control of these cliques.

> At the Beijing-Wuhan line, the number of Europeans employed by this railway company declined every year. The management, which will soon be composed entirely of Chinese, is showing itself to be more and more incompetent and disorganized. [But] the volume and value of the goods transported is increasing by the year. The equipment and the tracks are in a pitiable state. The Northern troops hold on to this railroad track like some conquered property, which only adds to the confusion .... Canton–Wuhan railroad, Hupeh–Hunan section: no progress was made on this section in 1918. No delivery was made. On the contrary, the hostilities caused much damage. The rolling equipment was requisitioned by the belligerents who use it without the least care or concern. It will take many months to restore it. Without these hostilities, the line between Wuhan and Changsha could be used without needing to change trains.

5. Hardships for the Wuhan branch

The *Banque de l'Indochine* branch could no longer cross such dire hardships without a thorough reassessment of its accounts and of its management.

A. The quasi-paralysis of the Wuhan branch (1917–1920)

Bad debts piled up with too many immobilisations. Moreover, interest on the latter had to be put in a "pending loans account". Amortisations became a necessity in every semester between 1916 and 1918. The first accounting loss was declared in the first semester of 1917, another one in the second semester, with successive deficits all through 1920 (see Table 11.3), which had to be borne by the Paris headquarters. The upshot of this analysis was the first thorough screening of the assets in 1918: loans were amortised for FRF 1.1 million; the claim over the failed *Panoff* firm ended by the accounting amortisation of FRF 3.5 million,[12] and its bad debts stayed at 795,000 taels in December 1919.

An accurate assessment of the actual balance sheet of the branch was difficult in 1918–1919 because of fluctuations in prices, shipping freight and commercial orders, which led to a re-evaluation of the real value of goods and pledged securities and a subsequent delay in repayments. "The year [1919] began with a slowing down of business in Wuhan. Prices in Europe and America were too erratic and the problem was compounded by the slowness of telegraphic communication: it took at least three weeks for an answer to an offer made in China. Restrictions were lifted gradually and freight and insurance rates decreased."[13]

> Business with France was greatly reduced except for a few large deals regarding sesame seeds with Marseille, almost entirely handled by foreign houses. Our French clients had to bear with unfavourable conditions regarding business with France. Due to the lack of money, foreign banks reserved their loans almost exclusively for firms from their country, something that we could not do ourselves.[14]

FOREX rates climbed all through 1919. Chinese traders stocked silver because of concerns regarding currencies. There was no credit to be had in Wuhan (or Shanghai) and imports were stagnating, which confirmed the hesitation among native and foreign trading houses. French houses could not get the required shipping for Europe and China: resolving bad debts had become impossible in the short term.

This explains the gloomy situation of the *Banque de l'Indochine* branch at the turn of 1920: the immobilised assets had reached 3.553 million taels against a total asset value of 4.339! Bad debts of 2.940 million needed to be liquidated, and claims against German houses stood at 96,000 taels. Conversely, "good" assets were only of 49,000 taels for advances on goods, 61,000 tales for

Table 11.3 Amortisation of bad debts by the *Banque de l'Indochine* branch in Wuhan in 1918 (FRF)

February 1918	1,091,133	711,532 for Panoff, Schnabel-Gaumer, S. Wurch, Lautenbach
19 December 1918	2,500,00	Panoff

overdrafts and 480,000 taels through remittances operations with the Paris (and London) headquarters. Business was in the doldrums.

The branch had to repay Shanghai its advance (850,000 taels as of July 1918) and transfer its losses to the Paris headquarters, which cleared them against the current capital affected to the branch, thus reducing the amount of that capital: "Our capital and the Wuhan branch's various resources are immobilized and practically unproductive regarding interest. Our branch can no longer function, but will have to liquidate. Under these conditions, our figures will continue to fall."[15]

B. The branch manager challenged

In fact, the manager admitted falling prey to the "infantile disease" of over-growth with the resulting overleveraged balance sheet and immobilised loans. Risk taking had been foolhardy. A few unsound customers had subverted the monitoring of warehouses and had extracted bigger loans compared to the value and quality of the collateral.

> We have seen at Tianjin just how dangerous these types of overdrafts [advances against bills] can be. You are no better placed at Wuhan than at the port of Pei-Ho to oversee and monitor our pledges; you do not have enough people and, most importantly, they do not have the required technical knowledge to evaluate the merchandise. Your clients' honesty is your only safeguard. The losses due to Fafa, Kolkmeyer & Rockstroh are there to remind you that you are no better placed than anyone else regarding such mishaps.[16]

Managers in Paris came to an obvious conclusion:

> We readily grant that, due to your efforts, your branch has seen a significant increase in its turnover over the past few years. We hope now that your finances have improved, you will be stricter regarding your choice of operations. In the past, apart from the overdrafts to Chinese banks, you have often credit lines to clients who did not deserve them. Our situation in the recent past has allowed us to liquidate a part of our German clients' arrears but, as regards the other assets, we are, as you yourself admit, stuck for the long term.[17]

An exhaustive assessment of the branch's assets took place in 1917–1918: because of the difficulties caused by World War I in Europe (and Russia, an important outlet for Hebei province) and by the recession in Hong Kong and other port-cities, the balance sheet was jeopardized. A few clients were also passing through hard times, either because of the death of the boss (Göring, *Distillerie franco-chinoise*) or an associate (Kolkmeyer & Rockstroh; the death in 1911 caused a debt of 103,115 taels to be frozen). Though losses on FOREX arbitrages mounted in the second half of 1916 (22,324 taels), there were profits on gold and silver arbitrage in the first half of 1919.

Even several "normal" clients caused disappointment and immobilisations, like Adolphe Grosjean, which had to be liquidated in December 1918 and purchased by *Société maritime & coloniale du Pacifique*. Burtenshaw (with numerous goods in stock) was hurt by the death of its boss Burtenshaw himself in 1919, which left the firm with a debt (as overdrafts) of 49,283 taels, covered by guarantees of 40,579 taels (on electrical equipment for 47,000 taels and on securities for 7,840 taels). Losses mounted after the second half of 1917. Trouillet, head of the branch for a decade, painted a sombre picture and was dismissed in the summer of 1918 (see Table 11.4).

The year 1918 was earmarked for the liquidation of bad claims left by manager Trouillet: "We cannot earn anymore, only liquidate."[18] Overextended loans were subject to constraints, like the advances to Burtenshaw, whose figure fell from 85,000 taels in December 1917 to 44,000 in December 1918 (repayment of 2,000 taels per month). Such a hard stance might seem to go against commercial ambitions as it cuts deep into the "flesh" of the branch. What would have been the result of a more open, a more accommodating policy? The perennial issue of strict discipline and lucidity in risk management versus commercial progress with over-flexibility (in French: *laxisme*) remains dramatically unresolved when we consider the fate of *Banque industrielle de Chine*, a *Banque de l'Indochine* competitor headed by ex-*Banque de l'Indochine*

Table 11.4 Profits and losses of the *Banque de l'Indochine*'s Wuhan branch in 1904–1920

FRF			Taels
	Profits	*Deficits*	
1914 I	Around 140,000		46,521
1914 II	16,674		5,930
1915 I	121,754		41,173
1915 II	432,739		127,276
1915	Around 506,000		168,548
1916 I	287,505		127,276
1916 II	438,146		−97,366
1916		Around −38,000	−12,805
1917 I	84,560		32,814
1917 II		−623,186	−103,864
1917			−71,050
1918 I		−383,897	−60,036
1918 II		−413,517 FRF	−41,357
			Or:−58,242
1919 I		−349,898	−42,932
1919 II			−3,359
1920 I			−57,031
1920 II			−26,979

manager Pernotte: after rapid gains over its rivals, it collapsed in 1923 because of the Chinese economic crisis of 1921–1923. What could be seen as pusillanimity and shortcoming might end as being seen as foresight and wisdom.

6. Misfits and disappointment (1916–1920)

The *Banque de l'Indochine* branch's return to Wuhan had dwindled and did not even attain 5 per cent of the total returns of the overall branches in 1916. In 1907, the capital (FRF 1,393,531) and the overdraft drawn on Paris (FRF 7,826,531), totalling FRF 9,220,062, generated returns of 285,843 FRF over the two semesters of 1917, that is, a ROCE (return on capital employed) of 3.1 per cent, which is low considering the risks undertaken and the distance between the branch and banking hubs in China (Shanghai, Hong Kong), London and Paris.

Losses at the turn of the 1920s negated the revenues. The capital allotted to the branch was almost swallowed by the losses that piled up in 1916–1920. Many bad debts had to be amortised and claims immobilised over several semesters. The manager was dismissed, and operations were paralysed for four–five years. The customer base shrank because many of them found elsewhere what *Banque de l'Indochine* could not provide. Disappointment prevailed (see Table 11.5).

Tensions were also fired by a fierce post-war competition, especially from HSBC.[20] After a promising start, the Wuhan branch had thus endured great

Table 11.5 Returns of the branch of Wuhan in comparison with the major *Banque de l'Indochine* branches at the turn of the 1920s (percentages)[19]

	First semester 1916	First semester 1919	Second semester 1919	First semester 1920
Indochina and Cambodia	44.6	50.9	47.3	41.6
Singapore	4.7	2.7	16.1	3.6
Paris	14.2	6.2	4.7	4.4
Total of China	23.6	22.8	17.4	18.5
South China (Guangzhou, Mongtze and Hong Kong)	11	9.2	11.2	5.6
Guangzhou	2.4	2.7	3	−5.8
Mongtze	5.3	5.3	6.2	3.8
Hong Kong	3.3	1.2	2	7.6
Shanghai	7.8	10.5	4.1	11.3
Wuhan	**3.9**	**−2.2**	**−0.2**	**0**
Tianjin	1.8	5.5	1.9	2.4
Beijing	−0.9	−0.2	0.4	−0.8

Source: Minutes of the Board of *Banque de l'Indochine*, 25 October 1916, 29 October 1919, 28 April 1920, 24 November 1920

difficulties in the second half of the 1910s. But all in all, it succeeded in regaining ground against the banking bigwigs. First, it survived both its rivals: first the Russo-Asiatic Bank, which was weakened by bad business in Wuhan and by the Russian revolution. Second, *Banque industrielle de Chine*, which had led the contestability move against *Banque de l'Indochine*, collapsed in 1923 (though it succeeded the *Banque franco-chinoise* for a few years). The "Darwinian syndrome", so effective in business history, did not apply to the Wuhan branch of *Banque de l'Indochine*, even in such terrible circumstances.

Notes

1 "Le canal et la Compagnie de Suez face aux défis géopolitiques, maritimes et économiques de la Première Guerre mondiale" (chapter XX), in Hubert Bonin, *La France en guerre économique en 1914–1919*, Geneva, Droz, 2018, pp. 463–476.
2 Fund *Banque de l'Indochine*, historical archives of *Crédit agricole*, BE 1047, 439 AH 179, 29 October 1914.
3 *Ibidem*, 31 March 1915.
4 *Ibidem*.
5 *Ibidem*, 18 March 1919.
6 Fund *Banque de l'Indochine*, historical archives of *Crédit agricole*, BE 1047, 439 AH 179, *rapports-bilans semestriels*, 1 July 1916.
7 *Ibidem*, January 1917.
8 *Ibidem*.
9 *Ibidem*.
10 *Ibidem*, 31 July 1918.
11 *Ibidem*.
12 *Ibidem*, 7 February 1918, 4 April 1918, 25 October 1918.
13 Fund *Banque de l'Indochine*, historical archives of *Crédit agricole*, BE 1047, 439 AH 179, *rapports-bilans semestriels*, 12 August 1919.
14 *Ibidem*.
15 *Ibidem*, 31 July 1918.
16 *Ibidem*, 31 March 1915.
17 *Ibidem*.
18 *Ibidem*, 31 January 1919.
19 Minutes of the Board of the *Banque de l'Indochine*, 25 October 1916, 29 October 1919, 28 April 1920, 24 November 1920.
20 See Frank King, *The History of the Hong Kong and Shanghai Banking Corporation. Volume 2: The Hongkong Bank in the Period of Imperialism and War, 1895–1918: Wayfoong, the Focus on Wealth*, Cambridge, Cambridge University Press, 1988.

12 A turbulent environment for the Wuhan marketplace in the 1920s

Once the tensions of the war in Europe and at sea had subsided and shipping activity had been fully resumed in the Mediterranean and the Suez Canal, banks and businesses revived their geo-economic ambitions. The Shanghai market once again became a key target, and consequently the Yangtze valley again became part of the strategy of "economic patriotism" that encouraged these players to get involved in commercial and banking activity in central China.

1. The Wuhan marketplace: appeal versus tensions

From that point on, the Wuhan marketplace became a target for the ambitions of players keen to expand into the remote Far East, including, in particular, *Banque de l'Indochine* and the specialist trading firms, notably Olivier. It made a highly attractive hub for export flows towards these regions of the Upper Yangtze. But the fact that it was increasingly proving to be a rich source of products useful to the European and North American economies also swayed French trading firms in its favour.

A. Wuhan, a highly attractive marketplace

The resumption of normal maritime relations after the end of the war, the rapid growth in demand in the countries of Europe and North America, and the relative prosperity of companies with a focus on the colonial empires and Asia were among the factors driving growth but also competition in the foreign concessions in Wuhan. French trading firms and banks therefore battled to regain their pre-war positions and fend off their competitors. The fact is that in 1924, the Wuhan urban area had 1.646 million inhabitants, ahead of Shanghai (1.5 million), Canton (0.9 million) and Tianjin (0.8 million). The city capitalised on its interregional connections, the busy city port of Shanghai at the mouth of the Yangtze Kiang and even its links with Beijing.

As a railway hub it was hard-hit by the deterioration of the Beijing–Wuhan railway line, which had reportedly suffered from a lack of maintenance funding since being taken back by the Chinese in 1908: the purchase (for 12 million Belgian francs) in 1924 of 40 new carriages supplied by Belgium more or less revived it. The other major line, the Canton–Wuhan railway, remained in "a deplorable state", which kept traffic to a low level, and the stretch between Hangchow and Yangchow was not completed. Other lines offered opportunities for commercial activity: the Longhai crossed the Jinghan at Chengchow/Zhengzhou; the Shanchow–Chengshow link extended 261 km out to the west; the Shanchow–Soochow line stretched out 342 km to the east, and all the way to Unjo (71 km further). Thanks to these networks, the city was able to capture some of the traffic from the provinces of Henan, Shaanxi, Gansu and the south of Shanxi. Cotton, peanuts and hides were increasingly transported by rail.

However, the development of this denser rail network drew in competitors from outside the Wuhan communities: "Traders and bankers from Canton, Shanghai and Shantung are arriving in the Zhengzhou region and gradually taking the place of agents from Hupei. The Wuhan market has only kept the far south of Honan, plus the southern part of Shensi and of Kansu, in the Han basin."[1] But it maintained close links with Changsha, the capital of Hunan, in the south-west on the Xiang River, and it remained a transit centre for Dongting, in the hills to the west.

Nevertheless, the river port continued to see high levels of activity since the transportation of goods and commodities by boat proved good value for money. The shipping companies operated the *Si Kiang* on the Yangtze, while the *Fook Lai*, under the command of the Chiris colonial posts in May 1924, flew the French flag rather than the Chinese (China Merchants China Company, etc.). Wuhan remained well positioned in the port rankings based on customs receipts and traffic levels (see Tables 12.1 and 12.2).

Table 12.1 Port rankings by maritime customs receipts in 1923–1925 (million taels)

	1923	*1924*	*1925 (two different sources)*	
Shanghai	23,904,400	27,547,700	27,548,000	26,023,700
Tientsin and Chwangtao	7,263,400	7,414,700	7,414,000	8,950,700
Wuhan/Wuhan	4,285,400	5,595,700	5,596,000	5,393,000
Dairen			5,412,000	
Canton			3,471,000	
Kiapchow			3,211,000	

Source: *Rapport-bilan*, 2nd half 1924, 18 February 1925; *Rapport-bilan*, 2nd half 1925, 8 February 1926

Table 12.2 Maritime customs receipts in some ports in 1923–1925 (taels)

	1923	*1924*	*1925*
Shanghai	23,904,400	27,547,700	26,023,700
Tianjin and Ching Wang Tao	7,263,400	7,414,700	8,950,700
Wuhan	4,285,400	5,595,700	5,393,000

B. A fragile environment

The early 1920s saw a drop in export business in the market. In the first half of 1920, high exchange rates and delays in the transmission of telegrams to and from Europe made businesses cautious. Moreover, the region itself was facing difficult circumstances:

> There are a few paper purchases now starting to happen, but the worry is that the troubled political situation in which China finds itself will make it almost impossible to make purchases inland since our region is falling victim to soldiers and brigands who are holding the locals to ransom and imposing huge fines on merchants.[2]

In the second half of 1920, business with inland China was reported to have ceased altogether due to the political troubles:

> Communications have been severed for nearly a month (June-July) between the North and the Yangtze Valley, preventing any transactions. Just when the situation was showing signs of improving, the effects of the economic crisis currently buffeting Europe and the entire world made themselves felt here, and put a stop to all export business.[3]

This sparked a major commercial crisis and speculation on a rise in silver while gold was losing value at a rapid rate, leading to losses among the Chinese in this market:

> These traders are refusing to honour their commitments and are thereby putting foreign trading firms and banks in a very serious position. The troubled situation in Szechuan, one of the main importing provinces, has prevented it from continuing its purchases for the time being, so vast stock-piles of goods remain in Shanghai, depreciating daily. The liquidation of these stocks will inevitably entail heavy losses for the European firms.[4]

Moreover, "the famine raging in Chi Li, Hunan and Chensi has caused a sharp rise in cereal prices, and the situation in these three provinces is appalling". Business came to a halt "in November and December [1921], when the presence of Wu Peifu's army in Wuchang and on the Yangtze prevented goods from arriving in Wuhan on a regular basis."[5] Calm was gradually restored in 1922, and business and exports picked up, but reports continued of disorder in Szechuan, Honan and Hunan.

C. Business hampered by internal tensions in China (until 1925)

The Wuhan region, too, was faced with a civil war in which truces alternated with periods of fighting. "The political situation is exceptionally bad", the branch manager declared in July 1920. During an encounter between two enemy leaders "a few days ago on the Kin-Han line near the city, numerous shots were fired, and stray bullets landed on the concessions, one of which embedded itself in the staircase used by our branch management."[6] In the first half of 1923, a "slump in business" was noted, caused by the following: "As far as Hupei is concerned, this province is constantly being preyed on by small gangs roaming the area, who often come within a few dozen kilometres of Wuhan, from where they engage in banditry and take foreigners hostage for ransom."[7] Communication routes were often blocked as well:

> The three main routes are in the hands of the *tuchuns*[warlords]. Two of them, the railway lines from Wuhan to Beijing and from Wuhan to Guang-zhou, are blocked by Wu Peifu's soldiers who are wholly in control, stopping trains at will, never paying for the goods they need transported, and even collecting the receipts for their own profit. At present, the Yangtze is almost blocked on the frontier between Szechuan and Hupei by the troops of Wu and his adversary Liu Tcheng Chuen, *tuchun* of Szechuan. On several occasions, troops fighting in this region have seized Chinese vessels for their own transport, and are threatening to commandeer foreign steamers, which have to be constantly protected by foreign gunboats."[8]

In fact, the China Navigation Company (Butterfield & Swire) and Indo-China Steamship Navigation (Jardine Matheson) declared heavy losses in 1922.

In the second half of 1923, "the general situation has worsened further in Hupei and Honan; there has been no reduction in banditry. In Hunan, civil war has erupted between the *tuchun* Chao Geng Ti, a partisan of Wu Peifu, and General Tan Yen Kai, supported by Sun Yat Sen", leading to looting. "In Szechuan, the war has continued between General Yang Sen, a partisan of Wu Peifu, and General Yung Kou Wu; Yang Sen has succeeded in recapturing Chungking",[9] resulting in a contraction in business and lending and a rise in interest rates, as well as adding to traders' hesitancy, which was only aggravated by a monetary crisis in Shanghai, causing large fluctuations in the port-city's tael. Shanghai itself was encircled by a civil war from September 1924, and the "gradual breakdown of central government"[10] was noted, before the emergence of the "threat of the establishment of Wu Peifu from his operations centre in Wuchang [a district of Wuhan] in November–December", which fortunately was averted by his death at the beginning of 1925.

Paradoxically, though, business carried on in Wuhan, "which leads us once again to note that China is the only country where general business prosperity is not dependent on the political situation."[11] But bankers had to be vigilant, as the head of the *Banque de l'Indochine* branch commented: "As the situation in China has deteriorated, I have sought to gather in our funds, as a precautionary measure",[12] resulting in a stock of liquid funds at all the banks, a plethora of money and a general stagnation in banking business itself in the second half of 1924. Nevertheless, prudence was required: in the first half of 1925, an order came from Paris suspending advances to foreign banks in that market, given that there was no let-up in the crisis in the Shanghai and Szechuan regions, with civil war reignited by the return of Wu Peifu in October 1925. Although "the organised boycott of British and Japanese boats and products along the entire river is having little effect in Wuhan",[13] trade did suffer as a result of the almost complete halt in traffic on the Kin-Han railway, which Wu Pei had seized control of: "For a year, there has no longer been a single, direct railway line, but a series of sections run for personal profit by the military or by the gang leaders whose territories they pass through",[14] prompting an increase in river traffic in 1925.

> This half-year [January–June 1926] has been marked by an almost complete halt in traffic on the Wuhan to Peking railway line. On the rare occasions when non-military train services have been partly resumed, this has had virtually no effect because of the excessive taxes levied by the military for the hire of railway trucks. It is hard for products from Honan to get through to here [Wuhan], particularly hides and eggs, which cannot survive a long journey by trucks often overheated by the sun and regularly left standing in sidings for long periods at a time. The civil war, which seems to have become the normal state of affairs in China, has not ceased and Wuhan, whether it finds itself within the theatre of operations or on the outside, is inevitably suffering as a result of this constant anarchy.[15]

D. Wuhan at the heart of political struggles in 1926

The civil war intensified in 1926, and Wuhan found itself occupied by Cantonese troops from August/September and under the authority of the government of the Republican left. "General Tang Shen She, with the backing of Wang Sing Huei, persuaded the Nanjing government to put him in control of these two provinces [Hupei and Hunan]. As soon as he achieved what he was after, he ... declared himself independent. This new rift prompted the government in Nanjing to send an expedition against Wuhan."[16]

That led to the creation of workers' unions within companies and to unrest in factories from September 1926, which more or less paralysed business. In 1927, banks were hit by a workers' strike, as the unions, including the bankers' union, stepped up their demands. This strike forced the closure of the *Banque de l'Indochine* branch from 19 or 21 March to 1st May 1927. It then remained closed because of the embargo declared on silver bullion on 20 April and the obligatory exchange rate on banknotes from the Central Bank, the Bank of China and the Bank of Communications. Unrest multiplied, bringing business to "an almost complete standstill", with a drop in half-year profits to 7,268 taels from 38,129 taels in the second half of 1926, followed by the "transfer to Shanghai of all liquid assets on account of the unrest".

Action had to be taken to protect the concessions, so French warships moored nearby. "It would not surprise us if, before long, the French concession, through which armed Chinese troops now march freely with bands playing and flags flying, is no longer a place of refuge for foreigners living there, and we find ourselves in a dangerous situation. Apart from the arrival of a few Annamite police officers, the concession has seen no increase in the means of defence at its disposal. We still have only two small French warships moored nearby, one aviso and one gunboat from the Upper River—no more than we had before the situation degenerated." [17]

Everything changed in the first half of 1927. The British concession was invaded by the Chinese population in January, leading to the Chen–O'Malley Agreement for the definitive return of the concession to China. The city suffered "appalling mis-management by the new municipality". The police force was in a state of collapse: "The soldiers do what they like". All ships were requisitioned by different factions, and the staff of several foreign firms had to be evacuated. Some 150,000 coolies were reportedly out of work in Hunan, and there was a "general lack of confidence in the Southern government", [18] as the power relations between the military factions (including that of Marshal Feng Yu Siang) became strained.

E. Testing times in Wuhan with the war of the factions (1927–1929)

The crisis was resolved with the expulsion of the communist faction (led by the Russian Mikhaïl Borodine) in July 1927, the end to union activity and a rapprochement between the Nanjing and Hunan governments. [19] Betrayed by most of his lieutenants, Tang Shen She, who moreover was extremely unpopular here due to his communist tendencies and financial demands, soon gave in and had to flee the country on a Japanese ship. [20] It took a long time for the situation to settle down:

> No sooner was the new Wuhan government in place in our port than it had to quash numerous plots hatched by Russian and Chinese communists aiming to establish a Soviet regime in this region. The Chinese authorities in Nanjing, seeing where events were heading following the coup in Canton, decided to take action against the "red" element with mass arrests and executions .... On 16 December, there was a raid on the Russian consulate and on the main sources of Soviet propaganda. Several hundred communists were arrested and numerous executions followed. The Russian Bolshevik element was expelled from our port. [21] In Changhsa, the situation has improved in the wake of the massacre of the student working-class element by General Hokien's troops. Business is picking up and foreign [traders and manufacturers] are returning. [22]

It would be many more months before the situation would ease sufficiently for business to return to normal. After the abuses committed by the communists, the anti-Northern campaign has plunged transport connections, both the rail routes and the Yangtze river routes, into chaos. The occupation by troops from the main centres, along with ever higher taxes, levied at will, based on

needs at the time, have prevented growth in commercial activities in this port or even a normal continuation of activity [with banditry and piracy still rife].[23]
In the second half of 1928:

> the resumption of hostilities between General Yang Sen (Wu Peifu's deputy chief) has led to the almost complete interruption of traffic on the Upper Yangtze. The river has been mined on the Chungking side by General Liu Hsiang's troops, who are occupying the town. Ongoing piracy and gun battles are preventing vessels flying foreign flags from venturing into the upper reaches of the river unless accompanied by gunboats [while Japanese vessels were boycotted] ... Goods shipped by river can no longer be transported by junks because of piracy and, most recently, privateering by small boats. Things do not bode well for the future, and this port [of Wuhan], which is so well served, has been suffering for two years as a result of a crisis from which it will not easily recover, despite its privileged situation.[24]

It was not until the year 1929 that central order was restored in Wuhan. "The uprising by the main Guangxi clique in Wuhan" was followed by the "victory of the nationalist armies who have taken Wuhan" in April. However, the head of the *Banque de l'Indochine* branch[25] noted at the time that the "highly anti-communist" administration that had been driven from power seemed to have been more warmly disposed towards foreign business communities than his successor, who wished to put an end to extraterritoriality—in place till 1st January 1930. Anyway, economic activity regained momentum once order was finally restored, although fighting continued against rebel armies in several neighbouring territories in December 1929.

2. Fierce inter-banking competition

The branch referred to "overly strong competition"[26] from the two British banks and the American International Banking Corporation, while the office of the Sino-Italian Bank closed in 1923. HSBC opened its new head office in Wuhan in 1921, followed by *Banque belge pour l'étranger* in 1924, also in the British concession. In addition, as of the second half of 1921, "German institutions have reappeared in the market and are highly active". Schnabel Gaumer, which had paid off its debt of 49,694 taels and put plots of land up for sale in Shanghai, reappeared on the scene: "This firm has started operating in China again, initially under the guise of O. Klein, which has just taken the name of Kai Lee Gung Tse, a new German company operating in Shanghai and Wuhan. The former directors of Schnabel Gaumer are authorised agents of the new company."[27] In 1927–1928, the company had at its disposal a foundry in Changsha, as well as utensil, furniture and machinery plants in the Tachimen district, with engineers brought over from Germany; it was a client of *Banque de l'Indochine*.
It is true that the Germans had lost their own concession in 1918, like the Russians, who returned their concession to China on 1st July 1924. In 1924,

though, they took back possession of the buildings they had owned there. *Banque industrielle de Chine*, meanwhile, kept up French competition. Although it did collapse in Paris in 1923, it rose again from the ashes (with the support of the investment bank Paribas), and an office of the *Banque industrielle de Chine* management company opened in Wuhan in January 1924. Chinese competitors also stoked competition by opening branches in Wuhan, so that by December 1923 there were 16, including Bank of Canton (set up in Hong Kong in 1912), Continental Bank (in Tianjin in 1918) and Kuo Ming Bank (in Hong Kong in 1920). In July 1924, there were 11 foreign banks and 13 Chinese banks operating in the market. It is interesting to note the fragility of the majority of the local institutions: of the 170 banks (native banks) active in Hunan in the winter of 1927, only 60 were still in existence in July 1927.

All the same, the *Banque de l'Indochine* branch had to fight hard to remain competitive:

> There are no clients here who demonstrate loyalty to banks or even recognition for services rendered. For an added 1/16%, even on G$, trading firms have no scruples in abandoning the banks that have helped them on numerous occasions, and switching to competitors. During periods when business is stagnating, like the one we are currently experiencing [at the beginning of 1924], business is so difficult and earnings from it are so low that the banks are forced to make big concessions to trading firms to encourage them to give them their paper.[28]

HSBC and Chartered benefited from competitive advantages: "Your situation as an independent branch will never be enough to counterbalance the advantages that your British rivals gain from their issuance in China and their low-price deposits both in Shanghai and Hong Kong", which forced the bank to set itself apart by "focusing on the quality of the paper, be it bankers' acceptances or commercial paper, on London and New York",[29] with better profit margins. Strategic optimism was maintained:

> We believe that, while still continuing the policy of prudence which has been justified hitherto and cannot yet be abandoned, it is possible, with reduced risks, to attract a large proportion of the [commercial] paper in our market. By reduced risks we mean risks reduced to the discount on the paper, without assignment of fixed-limit packing credits. Our privileged situation as an independent branch with an adequate intelligence network should enable us to operate wisely in the market as the best buyer without needing to agree packing credits to acquire the paper of major foreign firms, as our rates alone should attract them. At most we might need to allow two- or three-day shipping credits, each applying to specified shipments. This policy was launched in the second part of this half-year [1929] with the negotiation, without packing credit, of paper from Arnhold and from Mitsui Bussan Kaisha.[30]

At any rate, every company and every bank took care to spread its risks: "Our regular clients Racine, *Olivier-Chine* and Vanderstegen kept up their usual reduced activity, sharing their paper between *Banque belge pour l'étranger*, Hong Kong Bank, Chartered Bank and us, based on the best rates."[31] Even flows destined for France could be handled by a non-French bank: "Theodor & Rawlings, a large tea [exporting] company, is financed almost exclusively by Chartered, which negotiates all its paper drawn on the Marseille firm (documentary paper)."[32] In 1928, its good client Olivier definitely held a substantial volume, namely SH$110,000, in advances on bills to be delivered, with foreign exchange contracts in the same amount in pounds, but "it is working with National City Bank for the same amount."[33]

Each firm shared its business among various bankers, like Vanderstegen & Crooks, which "did not take much advantage of the unsecured packing credits we granted it, and is seemingly dependent, instead, on two British banks."[34] And all traders naturally sought to negotiate an increase in their credit lines by asking several banks: when times were tight, *Banque de l'Indochine* "refuses to increase the volume of advances on packing credits granted to our current clients and to make advances available to new firms wanting us to grant them funds in addition to those already placed at their disposal by our competitors."[35] Customer loyalty, though tricky to secure, was maintained, as in the case of Olivier, and Schnabel & Gaumer: "This firm, despite many approaches by our competitors, has remained loyal to us and is handing us a large share of its business, [hence the] negotiation of its drawings 60 days after sight D/P [documents against payment] on America, on confirmed credit lines."[36]

Notes

1   *Rapport-bilan* from the Banque de l'Indochine branch, first half of 1924, 25th July 1924, *Banque de l'Indochine* fund, archives of *Crédit agricole*.
2   *Rapport-bilan*, first half of 1920, 20 July 1920.
3   *Rapport-bilan*, second half of 1920, 15 January 1921.
4   *Ibidem*.
5   *Rapport-bilan*, second half of 1921, 26 January 1922.
6   *Rapport-bilan*, first half of 1920, 20 July 1920.
7   *Rapport-bilan*, first half of 1923, 15 August 1923.
8   *Ibidem*.
9   *Rapport-bilan*, second half of 1921, 30 January 1924.
10   *Rapport-bilan*, second half of 1924, 18 February 1925.
11   *Ibidem*.
12   *Ibidem*.
13   *Rapport-bilan*, first half of 1925, 15 August 1925.
14   *Ibidem*.
15   *Rapport-bilan*, first half of 1926, July 1926.
16   *Rapport-bilan*, second half of 1927, 30 January 1928.
17   *Rapport-bilan*, second half of 1926, January 1927.
18   *Rapport-bilan*, first half of 1927, July 1927.
19   *Rapport-bilan*, second half of 1927, 30 January 1928.
20   *Ibidem*.

21 *Ibidem.*
22 *Ibidem.*
23 *Rapport-bilan,* first half of 1928, July 1928.
24 *Rapport-bilan,* second half of 1928, 15 February 1929.
25 *Rapport-bilan,* first half of 1929, July 1929.
26 *Rapport-bilan,* second half of 1923, 30 January 1924.
27 *Rapport-bilan,* first half of 1922, 24 July 1922.
28 *Rapport-bilan,* first half of 1924, 25 July 1924.
29 *Rapport-bilan,* first half of 1929, 7 August 1929.
30 *Ibidem.*
31 *Rapport-bilan,* first half of 1929, 7 August 1929.
32 *Rapport-bilan,* first half of 1924, 25 July 1924.
33 *Rapport-bilan,* first half of 1928, July 1928.
34 *Rapport-bilan,* second half of 1928, 15 February 1929.
35 *Ibidem.*
36 *Ibidem.*

13 The Wuhan branch serving French and foreign companies

Despite the political, military and monetary uncertainties, and faced with intense competition, the *Banque de l'Indochine* branch in Wuhan capitalised on the bank's expertise, its relations with the Shanghai branch and its own skills legacy. It offered a complete range of corporate banking services. Its aim was to promote French interests in the name of economic patriotism as the same time as developing its own business, which would require it to approach all potential clients in the area.

1. The difficult job of rebuilding commercial banking (1920–1922)

However, *Banque de l'Indochine*'s business versatility was restricted by the legacy of 1914–1918: it had too many creditors with frozen debts, which dented the resources the bank had at its disposal to fund its commercial banking activities.

A. A tough period dealing with the legacy of the war years

At the beginning of the 1920s, the branch's priority was to manage the portfolio of debts at risk due to the poor situation of the debtors—in other words, collect the balance of the "advances still outstanding". The first issue was the skills of the comprador himself, as he proved to be a weak link. He emerged from the war years virtually insolvent, which hampered the revival of relations with the Chinese market: "Meanwhile, we are not able to engage in Chinese business since we have as comprador a man who owes us more than \$3 million and, moreover, is not active in the market at all."[1] Indeed, he had granted sizeable advances to bankers in Wuhan, on behalf of *Banque de l'Indochine*, using funds provided by the Wuhan and Shanghai branches. The debts were estimated at 1,454,000 taels for the former and 470,000 for the latter.[2] Therefore the first job was to recover the interest due from the official comprador, Liu Sin Seng, on liabilities estimated at 3.073 million in December 1920 (for example, 137,088 taels for 1919, 90,488 for 1920, 48,515 in the first half of 1922).

Importantly, the plots of land owned by Liu, which served as collateral, gained in value in 1921 because they were located in the former German concession, whose return to China opened up opportunities for property development. Liu sold some of these, enabling him to settle part of his debt (HK$ 170,000 in the first half of 1922), which still stood at 3,016,258 taels in December 1921. With that said, as late as 1924, the branch complained that it could not rely on a "real comprador because the official comprador, Liu, is mainly occupied with his own business and hardly ever turns up, resulting in a loss of revenues since other banks (*Banque belge pour l'étranger*, *Banque industrielle de Chine*) do a lot of business with Chinese bankers."[3]

At the same time, several trading firms remained cash-strapped, with debit balances on advances on bills for forward delivery. Fortunately their situation did improve, as in the case of Grosjean:

> We have removed from our books our exposures with the firm Grosjean, consisting of an advance of 16,349 taels, which had been non-performing since August 1919, and three foreign exchange contracts amounting to 920,000 francs, also outstanding—Grosjean having been bought by *Société maritime & commerciale du Pacifique* (connected with Gallusser) in 1919. The firm Vanderstegen, which was no longer doing business with us, has also repaid the bulk of its overdraft (9,515 taels).[4]

Arnhold Bros, the former German firm directly active in China, paid 39,885 taels in settlement of its three frozen advances. So the sum of outstanding debts to be recovered plummeted from 53,869.30 in June 1919 to 819 in June 1920: Grosjean went from 21,781 to zero, Petersen from 624 to zero. When repayments of the Panoff debt were completed in December 1920, the bank was pleased to have avoided a heavy loss.

The branch had to take firm action to get its traditional business—advances on goods—back on track.[5] It managed to reduce its unrecovered debts from 556,838 taels on 1st January 1919 to 385,090 on 30 June 1919, to 402,775 on 1st January 1920 and then to 394,428 on 30 June 1920. However, the advances on goods account remained burdened by the debts of two clients who alone accounted for the bulk of the outstanding sum of 394,428 on 30 June 1920: the Franco-Chinese Distillery, located in Chiao Kow (345,000 taels, rising to 377,000 in December 1920, with a further 71,404 added by December 1925), and Burtenshaw (49,000), two effectively dormant accounts.

The French distillery company's attempt to get back on its feet was hampered by problems in selling alcohol due to the civil war, but production resumed in the first half of 1921, and a loan was guaranteed by the *Distilleries de l'Indochine*. The Burtenshaw debt, meanwhile, was absorbed into general bank debt, with no priority given to recovering the goods in stock that served as collateral: the company's bankruptcy led to an irrecoverable sum of 35,797 taels in June 1921, when only 12,398 taels were recovered.

The branch's balance sheet situation remained fragile. The branch essentially lacked current resources since its liquidity had been tied up in debts that were, if not irrecoverable, then at least frozen. Many Chinese clients froze their repayments in 1920–1921, as local business was hit by a crisis. The distillery company was carrying a huge volume of debt. Therefore cash contributions were requested from the Saigon branch (864,000 taels outstanding in December 1921), the Beijing branch (200,000 taels) and the Shanghai branch (558,358 taels). But then it had to pay the interest, which ate into its final profits, and attempt to repay these funds. It managed to pay the Shanghai branch 157,395 taels in July 1920 and 250,000 taels in the second half of 1920.

The balance sheet had to be stabilised and any now irrecoverable receivables removed from it, resulting, for example, in 531,569 taels in write-offs in the first half of 1921 for account auditing purposes.[6] In the first half of 1922, 394,682 taels were written off on the distillery's account, 24,654 on Olivier's, and 22,822 on Burtenshaw's, making a total of 453,157 taels, the aim being a "massive stabilisation of the accounts".

In the early 1920s, the branch had little room for manœuvre, which put a damper on its expansion: "Since our financial situation did not permit us to grant attractive overdrafts to the export houses operating in the market, these firms turned instead to banks that were able to finance them."[7] "For a time, to maintain competition with *Banque industrielle de Chine*, we accepted deposits at 6 percent. It was awkward that we seemed to be profiting from the disappearance of this establishment when we lowered our interest rate to 4.5 percent; this resulted in some discontent among our clientele."[8] These efforts were worthwhile since the total debit balances on advances on bills for forward delivery amounted to 355,099 taels in December 1922 versus 102,789 in 1921. A policy that was both combative and prudent was called for to get through these difficult periods without risking the branch's position in the Tianjin market. The widespread recession had in any case reduced clients' needs:

> As far as your branch is concerned, the tie-up of your old capital and the fact it is impossible for us to provide you with new capital at present, either in gold or silver, is necessarily limiting business. Given the crisis affecting your market, this state of affairs is not so much of an issue at present.[9]

B. Uncertain profitability (1920–1922)

The combination of a fragile balance sheet, interest charges payable to branches that had advanced money, a business recession and political uncertainties resulted in patchy profitability. The years 1920 and 1921 saw accounting losses, followed by a sudden surge in 1922, as the situation gradually resolved itself. The manager was thus heartened by the "good business" conducted in the second half.

It would take several six-month periods for the branch's situation to stabilise: "In 1921–1922 your predecessor was able to restore the branch's position in the market and forge firm relationships with export houses, which was not easy after such a long absence—and finally draw a line under the era of losses."[10] In the end, those testing times were endured with perseverance and resilience, until the situation finally returned to normal at the end of 1922: "Commerce in your market now seems to be on a healthier footing and seems to be gradually returning to normal."[11] In the second half of 1923, the branch even managed to complete the repayment of the cash advances provided by its sister branches.

An accounts summary covering the three years shows the branch operating at a loss, with overly risky gold arbitrage business, inadequate current business and, in particular, excessive write-offs of frozen or irrecoverable receivables, highlighting the need to overhaul a balance sheet that had come under severe strain at the end of the 1910s (see Table 13.1).

2. The power of foreign exchange business

Foreign exchange business had traditionally been part of the lifeblood of the *Banque de l'Indochine* branch, which sometimes worked with the foreign exchange firm Pearce & Garriock, "the brokers with the largest clientele in Wuhan" (in 1925). In the early 1920s, this business took advantage of fluctuations in the price of sterling. But a competitor arrived on the scene, in the form of *Banque industrielle de Chine*, which, "having recently established itself in our market, is offering very attractive rates to win over all clients dealing in francs."[12] In the second half of 1920, priority was given to "gold and silver arbitrage, the only areas that generate decent profits", and again in the second half of 1921 (with gains of 40,106 taels). The overdraft granted by the Shanghai branch was kept at 250,000 taels and helped fund the foreign exchange operations. In order to expand gold business, an arbitrage account was opened in 1921 with *Banque de l'Indochine*'s American co-subsidiary, French American Banking Corporation (FABC), to negotiate bills in New York.

In 1922 the branch conducted "speculative foreign exchange transactions with Théodore Sopher & Co, large sesame seed transactions involving the purchase and sale of pounds sterling. The Sophers are Shanghai Jews, related to the Sassoons and the Ezras, who are rich."[13] It was thanks to *Banque de l'Indochine*'s know-how and connections that "almost the entirety of our profits comes from our foreign exchange operations" in the first half of 1924—112,713 francs compared with 46,115 the previous half-year—taking advantage of fluctuations in the exchange rate of the British pound in association with its correspondent bank, National Provincial Bank, in London, "by speculating on a rebound in the franc on the basis of telegrams from Paris",[14] by means of a large number of contango transactions in pounds (ready purchases and forward sales) in London or with French American Banking Corporation.

There were also regular transactions involving gold (with French American Banking Corporation and in the London City) and silver (in conjunction with the Shanghai branch). As a full-scale military crisis gripped the region, *Banque de l'Indochine* managed to take advantage of the improvement in its liquidity to bolster its market share: "Our branch, which was one of the few banks with liquid funds available at the time, was able to profit from this rise in the interest rate by entering into contango transactions at exceptionally lucrative rates."[15]

Table 13.1 Situation of the Wuhan branch of *Banque de l'Indochine* in the early 1920s (taels)

	First half of 1919	Second half of 1919	First half of 1920	Second half of 1920	First half of 1921	Second half of 1921	First half of 1922	Second half of 1922
Final result	−42,932	−3,359	−57,031	−26,979	−46,505	−9,840	40,041	50,813
Profit from gold arbitrage			Losses 818	9,704		40,106	63,126	68,400
Outstanding debit balances for advances on bills for forward delivery	53,869					102,789		355,099
Outstanding advances on goods	385,090	402,775	394,428		405,973 (of which 330,000 was frozen)			404,143
Outstanding discounts on commercial paper			53,986					
Write-offs effected during the half-year					531,569		453,157	
Productive business			223,090	251,900				27,784,774
Total assets				3,288,000		7,003,000 (of which 2,626,000 was frozen)		6,885,460
Interest and commission						−26,106	13,627	8821
General expenses						23,839		

Source: Half-yearly *rapports-bilans*

In the first half of 1925, profits on arbitrage amounted to 46,147 taels (£22,488, $11,280, FRF 7,584). Currency arbitrage business often accounted for a substantial share of the branch's profits: 48,795 taels in 1924, which constituted the bulk of the final profit, which was just 40,437 taels after expenses and losses. These activities were marked by highs and lows: volume reductions in silver were unavoidable in the first half of 1925 because "the market is very nervous" due to the tensions in the Shanghai area. But business quickly picked up again in 1926: "Overall, concluded foreign exchange transactions (gold) of 4,088,325 for $227,970 made us a profit of $12,570, giving a percentage of 5.513%."[16]

3. *Banque de l'Indochine* promoting French interests in Wuhan

Although the economic and banking climate was rather subdued, especially given the tensions caused by the military and political battles in the region, the *Banque de l'Indochine* branch saw its business pick up at a rapid rate. In addition to the foreign exchange and discount business, part of the traditional repertoire of any bank concerned about its liquidity and adept at "transactional banking", it expanded its commercial banking business, with added risk, to encompass more "relational banking" elements, broadly based on relationships of trust with clients seeking support in the form of overdrafts, advances on goods and the like. Above all, the branch was able to act to further French interests in the name of economic patriotism, far from Parisian home soil, in the heart of the regions of the middle Yangtze.

A. Banque de l'Indochine *within the French community*

Getting business up and running again in 1920–1923 may have been difficult, but fortunately the *Banque de l'Indochine* branch still had a solid base it could rely on: the French business community in Wuhan. The offshoot, which had several managers in succession (Ruyters, A. Brugh, De Broc, Branotel) underwent a major renovation in 1927–1929, turned it into an imposing building on the corner of *Quai de France*, the Wuhan *Bund*, and *Rue de Hanoi* (today Cheshan Lu Street), close to *Rue Dubail* (Dongting), home to the consulate (in a building still standing today, constructed in 1892, at number 81, Dongting Street) and the head office of the Racine trading house (another building still standing).

Unfortunately, the Wuhan concession did not enjoy the same vitality as others. Military and political crises took their toll on commercial and river business in the early 1920s, resulting in something of a decline: the "departure of several members of the French colony, which is diminishing each year"[17] was noted. There were only 87 French nationals living in Wuhan in June 1924. The city was home, at the time, to thirteen French houses and eight "protected" foreign houses. The consular catchment area, which covered four regions, served 219 French nationals and 88 "protected" persons.[18]

The branch manager remained on close terms with other key figures in the concession. Thus the French consul, Georges Lecomte, was granted a small advance in 1921, as was his deputy, G. Eynard, and G. Goubault, consul in Foochow/Fuzhou. Loans were also extended to the Municipality (to buy land in 1924, etc.), to the Apostolic vicariate of central Chihli, and to the Catholic Missions in Hunan and eastern Hupeh. The branch also provided finance to the French army by funding its gunboat supplies and furnishing its currency requirements. It also supplied the advance needed for the construction of a barracks for the Annamite infantrymen in 1929. Meanwhile, on 7 October 1920, *Crédit foncier d'Extrême-Orient* received a loan of 45,000 taels from three French banks (*Banque de l'Indochine, Banque industrielle de Chine, Banque russo-asiatique*) earmarked for the reconstruction of the *Cercle gaulois* building—the French expatriates' club—by the property developer.

Advances were granted to Racine in December 1923 totalling 95,897 taels to finance the construction of buildings on *Rue Dubail*, "currently under development, with plans for the lease of apartments and shops", next door to the *Banque de l'Indochine* branch office. The branch also financed building by *Crédit foncier d'Extrême-Orient* in the French concession to the tune of 100,000 taels, as well as buildings in the Chinese part of the city.

B. A larger French clientele

Amid the difficult circumstances prevailing in the early part of the 1920s, the branch had to balance business sense with prudence: "I endeavoured to bring clients back to us by always offering more attractive rates than the other banks, while at the same time being particular about the quality of the paper I was negotiating."[19] Hence, in the first half of 1921, it bought £250,000 of paper on London and New York, which was successful but not very profitable. The re-establishment of a sterling account led to transactions worth £376,128 (or 2,164 taels).

Fortunately, *Banque de l'Indochine* was able to take advantage of its legacy from the first two decades of the century, when it had some good French clients. The top client in the upper Yangtze region seems to have been Olivier, whose Wuhan branch employed six European agents,[20] headed by A. Maillard and then, in 1928, by Lordereau, an ex-agent of Chiris trade house in Chungking. Business had seen a "marked increase"[21] between 1914 and 1925. This justified the resumption of advances on goods, in particular for the import of cloth (twills) and scrap iron, as well as *Michelin* tyres through the *Banque de l'Indochine's* Shanghai branch, which was *Michelin's* consignee, a representative of the big tyres firm of Clermont-Ferrand in central France (Auvergne).[22] "The considerable quantity of remittances negotiated through us by Olivier testifies to the regularity of their shipping activity."[23] In December 1920, outstanding advances on bills for forward delivery amounted to 33,145 taels. Even so, the branch placed great importance on clarity and prudence, especially when the security for the advances appeared risky (like eggs) or when the state of the economy called for a healthy diversification of risk: "We do not wish to have any capital locked up in this company, and we consider that the advances on goods that we are granting it under existing credit lines amount to be sufficient help in the current circumstances."[24]

The branch kept up business with its good clients from past years: "Our cash balance stands at almost 160,000 taels, part of which we can make available to the French houses Olivier and Racine, for the purpose of export-related foreign exchange business."[25] "Our liquidity has improved quite markedly; we have made an effort to resume business with the trading houses that have not worked with our branch for several years. We have thereby managed to renew our business relationships with the French firms Olivier and Racine, which we have granted advances amounting to 50,000 and 40,000 respectively",[26] with 37,797 taels and 4,895 taels respectively outstanding in June 1921, "secured by goods to be shipped shortly".

In 1921, Olivier was granted an advance of 23,985 taels for the export of "preserved whole eggs;" advances on bills amounted to 43,450 taels in July 1922. Business between China and the United States was handled directly from France, by Olivier's Paris office: its shipments to the United States were worth 734,000 taels versus 290,000 for sales in Europe.[27] It was able to call on the Chungking and Chang branches for help and had an agreement with French line *Messageries maritimes* to set up a company to handle its river transport. In 1928 it was principally exporting pig bristles, cowhides, goat hides, dried egg whites and egg yolks, and tripe, but no wood oil, beans, antimony, cotton or sesame seeds. As "French trade dwindled further and further [in 1928], Olivier was the only firm engaging in business in connection with its Wuhan interests. One of its representatives recently admitted to us that its Tachimen establishments were all that was keeping it active on the Yangtze."[28]

Sometimes risks weighed on this relationship, as in the second half of 1926: at Olivier, "business has been much reduced as a result of the troubles which have stopped or delayed the arrival of goods. Its campaign had barely got going in December before it came to an end in April; it was during these six months that it registered the bulk of its exports, involving goat hides."[29] In the first half of 1928, the branch received authorisation "to grant Olivier, in addition to its overdraft of SH$110,000 relating to the loan of ten million francs, packing credits for its transactions on America, covered by bank loans, [which] will enable you to substantially expand your business in G$ [gold-dollars]."[30] In 1928, "we are maintaining close relations with this firm and closely following business entered into with it". Its debit balance reached 135,000 taels in December 1928, following "advances granted on presentation of letters of credit concerning negotiated remittances denominated in USD."[31]

However, it had to remain clear-headed; even a firm so heavily involved in representing French interests in China did not see itself as a defender of all-out economic patriotism; it promoted its own budgetary interests and sought optimum efficiency by means of level-headed competitive tendering. The *Banque de l'Indochine* branch admitted this itself in 1927: "The firm Olivier, which National City bank is granting a large overdraft, prefers to use that institution for its transactions in G$ [gold dollars]. It uses us for its purchases of paper in pounds on francs, for which the American bank cannot offer at attractive rates. Nevertheless, we urged the head of the Olivier China branch to let us handle at least part of its business in G$."[32]

In December 1922, "credit lines provided for the account of Messieurs. Racine & C°" were the reason why total discount effects amounted to 627,135 taels (including 102,360 for collection). "All our goods are imported on contracts, in other words sold in advance. We are well placed for window glass and iron, imported mainly from Belgium."[33] The firm had go-downs near the river and furthermore is the agent for *Messageries maritimes* in Wuhan. In the first half of 1923, the branch bought 1.5 million taels' worth of bills from Racine: "We are pleased to note the increase in your export turnover with these good clients."[34]

But Racine appeared to falter in the mid-1920s: "Be it USD or francs, Racine is no longer in the market and it is true to say that, for the last six months, business has been practically at a standstill."[35] "The decline of this firm over the last six months [1925] has only got worse. We have bought all the export paper it had to sell. It is continuing to slowly liquidate its stock of window glass, imported in early 1925."[36]

The client portfolio was gradually expanding: Antoine Chiris, based at his Chungking branch, became a regular client again (with 33,547 taels outstanding in advances on bills in June 1921, 30,187 in December 1921, and 98,819 in July 1922), with "shipments of goat hide from Shanghai that are already sold in Europe and for which foreign exchange contracts have been entered into with us."[37] A. Gaussin & C° owed 6,844 in December 1921, secured by a fleet of imported cars. Along with *Pharmacie générale* (J. Mesny, a drugstore) (3,544 taels in June 1922), the firm Ch. Monbaron, situated on Chinese territory next door to Olivier in Tachimen, joined the ranks of the branch's clients in 1922 (13,622 in advances on bills in July 1922), as it needed to bolster its resources, hitherto funded by HSBC and Chartered.

Then Monbaron withdrew at the end of 1925, handing over its business to Vanderstegen, a Belgian firm which, until then, had been Dodswell & Crooks's representative in Wuhan but was also a former authorised agent of Monbaron. It was a "serious firm, managed by one man who is both the proprietor and the manager",[38] specialising in exports of pork intestines and bristles to the United States, with an eggwhite factory leased from the Chiris colonial trading post. *Banque de l'Indochine* granted it a mortgage loan of 56,000 taels in 1925 to renovate its facilities. But as early as 1926 it proved to be "an unfortunate deal", resulting in "the closure of lines" and a "loss to be reduced to 30,000 taels by the realisation of goods pledged to the banks and currently being sold", while its owner, F. Stucki, was shown to be insolvent.[39]

4. Discount business thriving

Still another traditional area of business was the purchase of commercial bills exchanged between China and other continents. London remained the main hub of this business. But *Banque de l'Indochine* had to carry these bills for several months, which constituted an accounting risk, even though it had to pay the sum in question without delay because the transactions were handled by telegraph:

> Our paper purchases only procure us funds in London five or six months after the signing of the foreign exchange contract, which makes it difficult for us to hedge them at such far-off dates. Especially as now the Shanghai banks have substantial gold and silver reserves and are showing a general preference for purchases of telegraph transfers on London with immediate delivery.[40]

Therefore the branch had to pay cash to one of the parties and wait several months for the other to reimburse it. So it asked the head office for advances and paid it debit interest, which dented its own balance sheet:

> The profits on arbitrage are often, in some cases at least, more apparent than real because debit interest is not sufficiently taken into account, especially on sterling accounts. To get an accurate picture of arbitrage results, it is important to bear in mind the interest on accounts involving advances on bills for forward delivery that are linked to foreign exchange transactions and settle the sterling debit interest in the local currency. Advances on bills for forward delivery entail a lot of risks. However, they, and foreign exchange transactions, remain our main source of earnings. Indeed we cannot restrict ourselves to mortgage investments or current account advances without relinquishing our role as banker in the form considered the norm in the Far East.[41]

But it complained that interest is low on this arbitrage, especially since "we can only obtain paper if our rate is at least 1/16 below the rates of the rival banks, namely HSBC, Chartered and *Banque belge pour l'étranger.*"[42]

At any rate, discount business advanced substantially. "Remittances of commercial paper on one to four months' sight" totalled 1,760,088 in francs, 316,327 in pounds and 1,379,504 in gold dollars (G$) in June 1923. But an impediment to traditional discount flows emerged: the franc was expected to fall against the pound, and the branch noted a:

> decline in the French franc account. Our commercial paper purchases only amount to 782,175 francs. This is because importers in France are increasingly asking their sellers in the Far East to draw on them in sterling. Moreover there are few transactions with France. I think nearly all the commercial paper in francs on France is negotiated by us. *Banque industrielle de Chine* is not involved in the market, *Banque belge pour l'étranger* and HSBC are not generally good buyers of francs.[43]

Overall, the franc was "used very little in transactions in our market."[44] The firms Vanderstegen & Crooks (1.246 million taels), Arnhold (163,076), Olivier (50,887) and Racine (63,475) constituted the quartet of clients for the branch's purchases of remittances in francs in 1925.

The rising fortunes of the *Banque de l'Indochine* branch allowed it to raise its ceiling for discount transactions, leading, for example, to "the purchase from Mitsui, Arnold and Liu Brothers of 600,000 taels of Shanghai remittances on either ten days' or thirty days' sight, relating principally to cotton shipments."[45] The branch intensified its partnership with FABC. In 1924, transactions entered into with it (purchases of remittances on the United States, settlements) totalled 2,930,945 in US dollars and 3,823,152 in taels—giving a profit of 15,790 taels, equivalent to an estimated annual return of 0.826 per cent (see Table 13.2).

In 1925, a brisk short-term market fuelled "fierce competition from banks wishing to use, at any price, the abundant funds at their disposal",[46] resulting in a fall in interest rates.

> Between June and December [1925], commercial paper has become increasingly rare due to the troubled situation we have experienced, and the banks' determined rivalry for this business has narrowed the safety margin between the possible purchase price and sale price in Shanghai to the very minimum. Nevertheless, we have been determined to stay in the market and although our paper purchases are lower overall than in the previous half-year, there is no doubt that the bank's proportional share of total transactions in our market is larger than it was in the first half [1925].[47]

Banque de l'Indochine did hold its own, though, versus its rivals:

> We—that is the Hong Kong branch and our branch—are still the two banks whose rates shape the market. Chartered does not always follow our lead and, for USD especially, has often been 1/8 to 1/4 above our rates. It is these three banks that are competing for purchases of commercial paper. *Banque belge pour l'étranger*, which is very energetic and well informed, is sometimes hampered in its transactions by a lack of adequate funds, and confines itself to the purchase of TTs in return for transactions concluded direct from

Table 13.2 Purchases of commercial paper on one to four months' sight by the Wuhan branch of *Banque de l'Indochine* in 1921–1922

	Second half of 1921	*First half of 1922*
Francs on France	135,000	214,500
Pounds on London	407,000	256,000
US dollars on New York	529,449	1,900,000

Source: Half-yearly *rapports-bilans*

Table 13.3 Transactions involving remittances of commercial paper ("gold" applications) at the Wuhan branch of *Banque de l'Indochine* in 1924–1925

	Francs	£	USD
Second half of 1924	456,895	202,349	576,174
First half of 1925	413,784	293,731	1,206,906
Second half of 1925	1,168,497	231,627	834,403
Transactions involving purchases of commercial paper ("gold" applications)			
Second half of 1924	425,417	236,123	779,756
First half of 1925	486,009	321,275	1,265,825
Second half of 1925	1,175,041	228,707	823,662

Source: *Rapport-bilan* for the second half of 1925, 8 February 1926

Table 13.4 Transactions involving remittances of commercial paper by the Wuhan branch of *Banque de l'Indochine* in the mid-1920s

	Francs	£	$
First half of 1925	413,784	293,731	1,206,906
Second half of 1925	1,168,497	231,627	834,403
First half of 1926	1,512,931	269,733	594,603
Second half of 1926	1,860,470	202,415	586,227
First half of 1927	195,578	103,043	363,464
Second half of 1927	/	49,123	31,918
First half of 1928	/	103,902	/
Second half of 1928	/	98,441	70,558

Source: Half-yearly *rapports-bilans*

Table 13.5 Transactions involving purchases of commercial paper at the Wuhan branch of *Banque de l'Indochine* in 1926–1928

	Francs	£	USD
First half of 1926	1,568,392	263,423	590,634
Second half of 1926	1,688,000	201,027	711,239
First half of 1927	5,125	64,806	97,144
Second half of 1927	/	66,282	3,801
First half of 1928	/	102,356	/
Second half of 1928	/	101,582	129,464

Source: *Banque de l'Indochine* fund, *Crédit agricole* archives, BE1037 439AH195: *rapports-bilans*

London, Paris, New York and San Francisco. The Japanese banks serve a particular clientele, and they are content with that. And International Banking Co. has been just as inactive as last year. *Deutsch-Asiatische Bank* [from the *Deutsche Bank* group] is focused on its national [German] clientele, whose business has slowed considerably given the economic stagnation

Table 13.6 Commercial transactions of the Wuhan branch of *Banque de l'Indochine*: Negotiated "gold" remittances in 1923–1925

	Remittances in £					Remittances in USD					Remittances in FRF				
	1923	1st half 1924	2nd half of 1924	1st half 1925	2nd half of 1925	1923	1st half 1924	2nd half of 1924	1st half 1925	2nd half of 1925	1923	1st half 1924	2nd half of 1924	1st half 1925	2nd half of 1925
Olivier	143,022	29,690	25,133	15,634	34,509	86,407	45,235	77,955	158,063	40,451	224,750	114,000	75,300	50,887	59,295
Racine	9,969	7,850	10,364	11,879	1,578	292,525	150,003	132,030	0		1,751,802	564,967		63,475	
Monbaron	13,227	7,217	11,176	5,334	2,658	43,013	9,225	4,483	39,688	51,565	954,098	250,369	460,010	136,342	59,295
Van der Stegen	7,920	1476	3,771	0	2,879	34,360	45,310	20,267	46,383						
Mitsui Bussan	23,922	14,773	3,475	10,145		240,015	57,742	5,723	90,922	100,344					
Mitsubishi Shoji	7,471	0	13,393	1,360	565	162,851	0	243,846	131,206	50,000		0			
Harrisons King & Irwin			22,309	2,103	26,864	0									
Theodor Rawlins			5,869	0		0									
Kai Lee Gung Tse			33,437	90,678	65,538			32,140	232,693	216,720					
SIM			9,581	63,422	60,630										
Arnhold			11,900	55,953	14,997				122,994	100,068			34,727	163,078	
International Export															
Asiatic Trading			5,717	11,280											
Chungkin Export			1,659	11,113	7,354										
Central China Export									100,345	55,108					
Pacific Orient (Edlin)									91,897	70,605					
Jardine Matheson									79,292	21,123					
David Sassoon			16,000		8,000										

Source: *Rapport-bilan*, first half of 1924, 25 July 1924

and scarcity of capital in Germany. *Banque russo-asiatique* is vegetating and is not expected to cover its general costs; it is still regarded with mistrust.[48]

The latter closed its doors in 1926, and its building was taken over by the Central Bank, the Cantonese government bank, which controlled the region for several months.

In the first half of 1926, Olivier was the branch's best client in terms of remittances of commercial paper in dollars (with $153,021), ahead of Vanderstegen, Arnhold, Jardine Matheson, and Pacific Orient. "We do not have any competitors for the purchase of French commercial paper"[49] from Vanderstegen & Crooks, Arnhold, Olivier, and Racine. *Banque de l'Indochine* was fortunate enough to be able to mobilise the whole of its network in order to ensure effective compensation capable of containing the risks and the costs: "We are tending to sell ready francs, while our purchases tend to be paper at usance with fairly long delivery dates. We are hedging our French sales *in situ* with sales of £ at three months conducted via *Banque de l'Indochine* Paris, to take advantage of the high contango rates in Paris."[50] The Wuhan branch could also call on the assistance of its sister branch in Shanghai: "Our account in Shanghai serves above all to facilitate our gold transactions. We use the funds we obtain here for hedging purposes or for contango investments."[51] Hence *Banque de l'Indochine*'s discount banking activities in the Wuhan market prospered in the second half of the 1920s, with some remittances in francs and many in pounds and dollars (see Tables 13.3–13.5).

Discount business and bill remittance business fluctuated a great deal depending on the needs of each client and the macroeconomic factors affecting a particular export market or collection market and a particular output. The statistics do not display any growth logic because what mattered was the ability to bounce back after setbacks, the capability to get these bills into circulation thanks to the clients' good reputations. About twenty such clients formed the basis of the branch's ongoing commercial business in 1923–1925. It stabilised the operating basis of a branch working at the very farthest reaches of France's banking and capitalist influence, in the upper Yangtze region, where it hoisted high the flag of French economic patriotism (see Table 13.6).

Notes

1 Summary letters sent by head office, *Crédit agricole* archives, *Banque de l'Indochine* fund, 439AH 535, 28 February 1925.
2 *Ibidem*, 1 June 1921.
3 *Rapport-bilan*, first half of 1924. 25 July 1924.
4 *Rapport-bilan*, first half of 1920, 20 July 1920.
5 *Ibidem*.
6 *Rapport-bilan*, first half of 1921, 27 July 1921.
7 *Rapport-bilan*, first half of 1920, 20 July 1920.
8 *Rapport-bilan*, first half of 1922, 24 July 1922.
9 Letter from head office to the branch, 13 June 1919.

10 Letter from the Paris head office to the branch manager, 15 July 1924.
11 Letter from the branch manager, 30 April 1923.
12 *Rapport-bilan*, first half of 1920, 20 July 1920.
13 *Rapport-bilan*, first half of 1922, 24 July 1922.
14 *Rapport-bilan*, first half of 1924, 25 July 1924.
15 *Rapport-bilan*, second half of 1923, 30 January 1924.
16 *Rapport-bilan*, second half of 1926, January 1927.
17 *Rapport-bilan*, second half of 1923, 30 January 1924.
18 Economic report on Hupeh by *Banque de l'Indochine*, July 1924.
19 *Rapport-bilan*, first half of 1921, 27 July 1921.
20 Summary letters sent by head office, *Crédit agricole* archives, *Banque de l'Indochine* fund, 439AH 535, 28 February 1925.
21 *Ibidem*, 11 June 1925.
22 *Ibidem*, 8 March 1926.
23 *Ibidem*.
24 Letter from the branch manager, 13 October 1921.
25 *Rapport-bilan*, first half of 1920, 20 July 1920.
26 *Rapport-bilan*, second half of 1920, 15 January 1921.
27 *Rapport-bilan*, second half of 1925, 8 February 1926.
28 *Rapport-bilan*, second half of 1928, 15 February 1929.
29 *Rapport-bilan*, second half of 1926, January 1927.
30 *Rapport-bilan*, first half of 1928, July 1928.
31 *Rapport-bilan*, second half of 1928, 15 February 1929.
32 *Rapport-bilan*, second half of 1927, January 1928.
33 Letter from Racine to *Banque de l'Indochine*, 28 January 1925.
34 Letter from head office to the branch, 20 November 1923.
35 *Rapport-bilan*, second half of 1925, 8 February 1926.
36 *Ibidem*.
37 *Rapport-bilan*, second half of 1921, 26 January 1922.
38 *Rapport-bilan*, first half of 1925, 15 August 1925.
39 *Rapport-bilan*, second half of 1926, January 1927.
40 Summary letters sent by head office, *Crédit agricole* archives, *Banque de l'Indochine* fund, 439AH 535, 1 June 1921.
41 *Ibidem*, 28 February 1925.
42 *Ibidem*.
43 *Rapport-bilan*, second half of 1923, 30 January 1924.
44 *Rapport-bilan*, second half of 1925, January 1926.
45 *Rapport-bilan*, first half of 1924, 25 July 1924.
46 Letter from head office to the branch, 22 December 1925.
47 *Rapport-bilan*, second half of 1925, 8 February 1926.
48 *Ibidem*.
49 *Rapport-bilan*, first half of 1926, July 1926.
50 *Rapport-bilan*, second half of 1926, January 1927.
51 *Ibidem*.

14 Corporate banking flourishes in Wuhan in the 1920s

Besides its traditional activities, namely foreign exchange, discount and short-term banking, *Banque de l'Indochine* deployed its full array of corporate banking services to enable it to play an active part in business in the Wuhan region and become even more involved in international trade: the story of its connections is both a geopolitical one, on account of the French concession, and a geo-economic one.

1. Active support for international trade

Despite the at times uncertain environment, the branch did a good job of re-establishing its position in the market. In the first half of 1922, "we continued to purchase as much commercial paper as possible." But competition was intense: "The numerous banks operating here are engaged in fierce local competition. If we happen to quote 1/8 of a penny lower than HSBC, there is always a competitor ready to offer the same price as us or even lower."[1] "I endeavoured to bring clients back to us by always offering more attractive rates than the other banks, while at the same time being particular about the quality of the [commercial] paper I was negotiating."[2]

A. The key role of advances on bills

The market for advances on bills was a decisive one in terms of banks' positions locally. Therefore the *Banque de l'Indochine* branch had to strike a balance between taking risks to stay competitive and employing prudence, particularly in relation to advances on bills for forward delivery:

> It is clear that excessively large facilities granted by some banks to their export clients are having an appalling effect. On the other hand we cannot show ourselves to be too inflexible otherwise we may forfeit some foreign deals. We say "some", because there are a few exporters who will negotiate paper with you without taking advances for it, like Jardine Matheson and Arnhold Bros; others like Mitsui normally only ask for a moderate sum. For the others, your policy must be to facilitate your exposures and

monitor their situation closely. To this end, stay in contact with your colleagues in Shanghai and Tianjin and see to it that the three offices periodi-
cally inform each other of their respective exposures with clients working
in these three localities and pass on any information they can glean about
the business performance of the firms in question.[3]

Every banker basically had to cope with one-sided information and make
use of his networks to collect data on the risks associated with each client in the
different markets of northern and central China. The Paris head office regarded
the system of advances on bills with suspicion, but it was such an established
practice locally that not participating in this market would amount to a crip-
pling handicap. In fact the *Banque de l'Indochine* branch noted this in 1927 when
it obeyed the head office and cut back strongly on its advances on bills:

> Apart from the company *Olivier-Chine*, whose packing credit of around
> 10,000 to 12,000 taels we have continued, all our accounts relating to
> advances on undisputed bills for forward delivery have been repaid to us
> in full in the course of this [first] half of 1927. We will not conceal from
> you the fact that this request for repayment, though presented in the most
> conciliatory terms possible, was greeted with annoyance by most of our
> clients, who interpreted it above all as indicating a lack of trust in their
> firm's standing. One of our clients, Pacific Orient, a respectable firm enjoy-
> ing a good reputation locally, saw our action as a distinct mark of mistrust
> towards it, and it is already clear that it will no longer be using our bank for
> its future business dealings.[4]

So the Paris head office was forced to make concessions as a matter of
urgency:

> Your telegram of 7 June authorised us to resume advances on bills for
> forward delivery on a limited basis, but only with firms with unquestion-
> able credit standing, in other words which will honour all their commit-
> ments, whatever happens. It is impossible, in practical terms, to know for
> sure whether, at the present time, such and such firm in our market can
> be considered able to meet all its commitments, whatever happens. We do
> not have all the information we need for this. The few highly creditwor-
> thy firms, like Asiatic Petroleum C°, Standard Oil and so on are British or
> American. These firms tend to work only with British banks or National
> City Bank, and there is no way for us to win lucrative business from them.
> Therefore we are obliged to stick to the other trading houses, particularly
> the German houses, whose credit standing is very hard for us to gauge.[5]

Risk-taking depended on constantly upgrading the pool of client data, but there
was a lack of transparency, particularly with regard to flows in these regions,
where corporate accounting and good balance sheet practices were not to be

relied on. Moreover commercial banking business formed a single whole: all activities were interconnected: the short-term activities that were profitable and not too risky and the medium-term ones that came with higher risk. Dispensing with the latter would cause the bank to lose the former:

> Most of these firms work with foreign banks operating locally which are not afraid to grant them large overdrafts and accept the associated risks. If we, for our part, do not seek to attract them by offering them funding, these firms will have no reason to speak to us about the discounting of their commercial paper, since they will find facilities with all the other banks operating here. Consequently our foreign exchange business will shrink to nothing, or almost nothing, and this branch's profits will vanish altogether.[6]

The firms targeted were Vanderstegen, *Olivier-Chine*, Vanderstegen & Crooks, Schnabel Gaumer, Mitsu Bishi Shoki Kaisha, Stiff, and Jess, as their cumulative debit volumes fell from 317,829 taels in December 1926 to 70,135 in December 1927. So "Pacific Orient C° [of San Francisco] is operating using packing credits only. Given the problem we had with this firm when we requested repayment of its advance on bills for forward delivery, it is doubtful whether it will resume business with our branch. We will try, nonetheless, to bring this about, as this well-managed company is regarded locally as being of good credit standing."[7] Therefore, in the second half of 1927, some easing of ceilings was consented to with respect to "houses of excellent credit standing" that were "very solid", even if they worked principally with their main bank, be it British (including HSBC) or American. The *Banque de l'Indochine* branch basically kept business rolling only by capturing a minor share of its clients' business, resulting in a fall in volumes and especially in profits.

B. A branch with an international outlook

It is worth pointing out that, in Wuhan as elsewhere, France's overall position in international trade remained modest (see Table 14.1). Therefore, in the same way as prior to 1914–1918, the *Banque de l'Indochine* branch succeeded in stabilising its business volumes not only by providing for the needs of the French players in the concession but also by developing a

Table 14.1 Overseas exports of some regional products from Wuhan in 1928

	France	United Kingdom	Japan	United States	Germany	Italy
Cowhides (piculs)	7,051	4,941	1,659	9,092	23,861	30,946
Buffalo hides (piculs)	866	1,078	101	1,155	5,407	0
Goat hides (items)	2,780	362	0	7,381	0	172
Pork bristles (piculs)	1,425	1,174	1,077	1,840	475	50

portfolio of clients from all over the Wuhan marketplace. It made approaches to foreign trading houses. In 1924, it added the British company, International Export Company, to its client base, offering it overdrafts in the form of credit lines (packing credits), as well as Edlin, among others. It remained on close terms with the American company Gillespie and the Chinese Liu Brothers. Mitsubishi, of Japan, became a major client, with 1.911 million taels outstanding, reduced to 176 in December 1924 following some repayments. One of its main clients was still Central China Export (run by Henkel), which exported goat hides, among other things, to the United States: its outstanding debt stood at 25,826 taels[8] in 1926. In 1924, "in less than two months, confirmed credits of USD 100,000 were taken out with us by Heidelbach Ickelheimer & C°, of New York."[9]

Sesame, beans, wood oil (for varnishes), tea, pork bristles (88,000 tonnes exported in the first half of 1920), egg products—often destined for the United States—leathers and hides (for Japan), and the like were sources of credits. This business involving advances on goods (advances on bills for forward delivery or packing credits) called for ongoing vigilance because these were "very risky transactions due to the impossibility of monitoring the quality and value of the goods."[10] The manager went so far as to assert that "this kind of business should be avoided altogether."[11]

> It consists of advances on existing goods, stored in our name or left 'in trust' with the exporter, the shipment of which in the relatively near future has resulted in a foreign exchange contract with your branch, rather than advances, following the signing of a foreign exchange contract, for the purpose of purchasing goods inland.[12]

The year 1922 saw a marked improvement in exports, especially to the United States, the main buyer of products passing through Wuhan, with sales of pork bristles, egg yolks, egg whites, and wood oil. In 1924, *Banque de l'Indochine* got involved in the sesame market: "We bought 71,493 taels' worth of remittances from Kai and Olivier out of a total output value of 1,750,000."[13] "We negotiated 63,200 taels on broad beans and other beans from Mitsubishi (out of a total of 1,672,596 exported)". "The main exporter of leathers and hides, Central China Export, which was set up recently, seems to be keen to give us the majority of its business."[14] The branch was also involved in the trade in egg yolks, handling 15,800 of the total of 1,197,130 taels, and in pork bristles, with 210,360 taels out of a total of 1,840,040, destined for the United States.[15]

The Wuhan market and consequently *Banque de l'Indochine*'s business were highly internationalised:

> In analyses of exports by country, France has always only had a minor role. However, a slight increase can be seen in most products compared to 1925: buffalo hides, vegetable tallow, gallnuts, pork bristles, sesame seeds, beans, wood oil, egg white, tea and, above all, antimony. For the latter, about

40 percent of the unrefined exports and 9 percent of the babbitt being shipped overseas are destined for France.[16]

In 1929, *Banque de l'Indochine* provided finance to Schnabel Gaumer in connection with a large sale of broad beans to *Grandes Minoteries d'Alfortville*, on the outskirts of Paris.

The bank was well established in these markets, as it indicated in 1925: "We—that is HSBC and us—are still the two banks whose rates shape the market. Chartered does not always follow our lead and, for USD especially, has often been 1/8 to 1/4 above our rates. It is these three banks that are competing for purchases of commercial paper, while Japanese banks serve a particular clientele."[17] *Banque belge pour l'étranger* was short of funds, and International Banking Corporation [from US Citibank] was to some extent stagnating. *Banque de l'Indochine* worked with Kai Lee Gung, whose headquarters was in Wuhan: "Thanks to the impetus it has had from its managing director, O. Klein, this company remains one of Wuhan's top export houses and enjoys excellent credit standing due to its punctuality in meeting its commitments."[18] It exported ores and metals acquired by its branch in Changsha, along with a variety of other products: egg white, pork bristles, wood oil, vegetable tallow, ramie and pork intestines.

It "remains one of Wuhan's top export houses and enjoys excellent credit standing due to its punctuality in meeting its commitments". In the niche market for remittances of commercial paper, "Kai Lee Gung Tse remains our main client with more than £77,000 of paper delivered"[19] in 1926, while "Pacific Orient is becoming our biggest client in USD",[20] for example for imports of crockery. In 1917, this company had taken over Cowen, Heineberg & Co. (established in 1902 and based in San Francisco), with branches in Wuhan, Tianjin, Harbin and Kobe, while its boss in Asia, Jacob Heineberg, was a shareholder and board member of Pacific National Bank.

2. Financing flows of Chinese mining products

The Yangtze was being used more and more for transporting ores downstream from the regions. "Exports of antimony have recommenced, and the Changsha mines are being worked again."[21] Hunan benefited a great deal from the trade in ore from Changsha, with zinc making its way from there to Hamburg and Antwerp. "Zinc from Hunan is bought from the Chinese mines and exported principally by two companies, one French one, *Société hounanaise de traitement de minerais*, and one German one, Kai Lee Gung Tse, set up by the Hamburg firm Schnabel Gaumer."[22]

Banque de l'Indochine was pleased at the appointment of a French agent in October 1923, Gestreaux, to represent *Société d'importation de minerais* (Company for the Import of Minerals, with headquarters in Levallois-Perret, near Paris, and in China, in Canton, and later in Changsha and Wuhan). He was succeeded, on his death in 1925, by Colonel Peirlot, who relocated the operational headquarters from Wuhan to Changsha, the centre of the antimony market. The head office authorised the branch to work with *Société d'importation de minerais* in April 1925.

Société d'importation de minerais bought wolfram produced in southern Kiangsi which, however, was then exported via Kiukiang (18 km from Hong Kong), so in 1924 it turned its attention to purchases of babbitt (from refined antimony), unrefined metal, wolfram (260 tonnes in March–June 1924) and zinc, sold in advance to *L'Asturienne des mines*.[23] "We are its only bankers in Wuhan."[24] *Société d'importation de minerais* sold this wolfram to *Comptoir français de ferro-tungstène*. In 1924 it started purchasing zinc ore. *Société d'importation de minerais* made its mark in the region, becoming the local representative of the French metallurgical trade, which was lacking in non-ferrous metals. This explains the increase in capital to 1 million francs (with contributions from its owners, Lemoine, Biès & Harang of Paris).[25]

Its rapid growth meant prudence was called for: "However much we want to help a French business whose representative in China is a perfectly honourable and conscientious man, in these circumstances we felt obliged to demonstrate a measure of reserve in our commitments."[26] However, *Société d'importation de minerais* "continues to sell us all its paper",[27] that is, commercial remittances. Suddenly, in the second half of 1929, the company was liquidated, but its debts had a guarantor (Lemoine, Biès & Harang). Its debit balance with the branch came to 6,844 taels and $26,530.[28] In addition, a French agent, Bouvet, set up in business in Changsha in 1922, buying babbitt and linen "notably for the account of Olivier, Vanderstegen, J. & M., and Monbaron", resulting in a number of loans. But the major buyer, the German firm Schnabel, used the services of *Banque belge pour l'étranger*.

3. *Banque de l'Indochine* supporting import flows

The Wuhan market was "connected" by the very fact that so many firms imported goods and equipment intended for industrial purposes, for the

Table 14.2 Imports into Wuhan in 1926–1928

		1925	1926	1928
Cotton fabric	Items	1,741,621	1,570,958	128,869
Cotton yarn	Piculs	233,441	229,788	142,418
Velvet	Yards	103,020	157,271	10,638
Woollen material	Yards	192,820	144,128	142,664
Various metals	Piculs	385,242	840,738	374,574
Machine parts	Value in taels	626,302	1,014,147	233,499
Oil	Gallons	21,996,424	29,296,315	15,756,392
Sacks	Items	1,569,510	1,462,123	738,119
Sugar	Piculs	2,228,364	1,527,768	1,033,731

Source: Half-yearly *rapports-bilans*

running of cars and machinery, but also for current consumption, as in case of cotton fabric. From as early as 1920, the import business started to get going again,[29] with several years of "growth into an open economy", although it nowhere near matched the major Japanese and European producer regions.

In the first half of 1923, the market suffered a drop in imports of cotton fabric because outlets were contracting due to the "political disarray that reigns throughout China and in particular in Szechuan and Honan."[30] Other contributing factors were the collapse of Reiss & Co., which had been operating in China for over a century and had a large turnover, and a crisis at the Shanghai mills. In the end, part of the market was captured by the Wuchang mills, which were experiencing a period of growth thanks to the equipment they had recently received from Europe and the United States. The Wuhan region became a centre for the modern textile industry: 1923 marked the arrival of the equipment for the Wuchang mills (machinery and electrical equipment), and in the meantime a new power station was being constructed in Changsha (with equipment imported by Jardine Matheson).

One piece of good news was the establishment of the Japan Cotton Trading mill downstream on the Han. It acquired equipment from France from *Société alsacienne de constructions mécaniques* [in Alsace] for making cotton fabric, as well as velvet spindles: "This equipment was paid for at the point of shipping in France, and did not entail any foreign exchange transaction in our market."[31] It was installed at the turn of 1924. The bad news was that *Banque de l'Indochine* did not participate in the financing:

> The funds sent to the Lyon agent of Japan Cotton Trading came from Japan. The company paid *Société alsacienne de constructions mécaniques* 50 percent of the order value at the time the order was placed, and 50 percent on delivery (understood to mean presentation of the shipping documents, once the equipment was on the train in Belfort) and *Société alsacienne de constructions mécaniques*'s representative in Wuhan was accredited with *Banque industrielle de Chine* [due to links with Paribas in France].[32]

So cotton was imported in 1924 with the support of Japanese banks (Yokohama Specie Bank, Sumitomo and Bank of Taiwan).

The *Banque de l'Indochine* branch played a part in the financing of oil imports linked particularly to the boom in car sales: "Again, even more so than in the last quarter, we have been selling TTs [telegraphic transfers] on Shanghai to the import houses Standard Oil and especially Asiatic Petroleum C° (amounting to nearly 1.5 million SH-taels) to repatriate our liquid assets"[33] to the lower Yangtze.

4. The pace of growth of the *Banque de l'Indochine* branch

After the crisis surrounding the adjustment and recovery of frozen receivables in 1919–1922/1923, business at the *Banque de l'Indochine* branch went through various phases.

A. Strengthening and diversification of the client base (1922–1925)

It was in 1922 that the branch began to diversify its client base again, having restored itself to its pre-war position (see Tables 14.3 and 14.4).

Table 14.3 Current loans outstanding by *Banque de l'Indochine* in Wuhan in 1922–1923 (taels)

	December 1922	June 1923	December 1923
Current account advances on bills for forward delivery			
Total	355,009	288,772	89,262
French companies			
Olivier	118,501	97,717	58,664
A. Chiris	96,758	20,395	
Racine	33,341	12,996	
Ch. Monbaron	14,554	44,163	
Crédit foncier d'Extrême-Orient		24,289	
Pharmacie centrale		13,063	
A. Picca		6,573	
Gaussin			7,473
Foreign companies			
China Java Export	40,553		27,671
Gillespsie	25,427	59,731	
Fearon Daniel	7,859		
Mitsui Bussan Kaisah	18,105		
Current account advances			
Olivier		26,971	
A. Chiris			
Racine			
Ch. Monbaron			
Crédit foncier d'Extrême-Orient		24,289	
Pharmacie centrale		13,063	
A. Picca		6,573	
E. Roumagoux		4,089	
Advances on goods			
Total	404,143		
Olivier	24,654 on dried egg yolks		
Gaussin	7,897		
Distillerie	388,000		

Source: Half-yearly *Rapport-bilan*, 2nd half 1922, 27 January 1923; 1st half 1923, 15 August 1923

Table 14.4 Debit accounts of the *Banque de l'Indochine* branch in Wuhan in 1925–1926

	31 December 1925	31 December 1926
Vanderstegen	16,545	35,967
Olivier	124,953	95,090
Ch. Monbaron	29,560	
Kai Lee Gung Tse	9,185	
Central China Export Cy	25,826	
SIM	39,938	
Pacific Orient	11,186	49,258
International Export	419	
Melchers China Corporation	26	
Vanderstegen & Crooke		23,739
Schnabel Gaumer		19,882
Mitsui Bishi Shoji Kaisha		62,025
Alff		10,383
Jess		21,485
	257,637	317,829 wuhan dollars

B. Enduring a slowdown (1926–1928)

Owing to political and military tensions, business proceeded at a more uncertain pace for some sectors in 1926–1927. Flows of goods for export now merely passed through Wuhan from upstream without being handled by local traders, leading to a decline in earnings from credit business. Given the lack of takers for loans, banks' liquid assets were underutilised, as the traders were handling a lower volume of business and could fund themselves from their own resources.

> At the end of the half-year, the slowdown in export business came as a big change for us from the attractive situation that went before. Our buyers, encumbered with unproductive liquid assets, started terminating their contracts, putting us significantly in debit in London and New York, and are abnormally augmenting our cash resources. At the beginning of the half-year, our buyers of £ and USD (principally the Bank of Taiwan) did not take delivery of their contracts as soon as the timings specified in the contracts extending over several months allowed them [resulting in a large cash balance at the branch caused by this decline in productive advances]. The abundance of capital caused by a marked slowdown in business translated into an increase in our unproductive liquid assets locally and a decrease in assets of 600,000 taels relative to the second half of 1925 and of 270,000 relative to the first half of 1926.[34]"

Secondly, political and military events brought business activity to a standstill locally and in the neighbouring regions, especially where advances on goods were concerned. The report lamented the:

> considerable decline in business transactions in our market. The difficulty of transporting goods on the Yangtze and its tributaries, the almost complete halt in train traffic on the Kinhan and Houkouang lines, the continual

tax hikes both on entry to our port and on exit, the demands of the worker element [the trade unions], the imposed exchange rate [of the tael], the embargo on silver and the instability of the political situation in the Yangtze valley have been the main causes of the noticeable slowdown then almost complete halt in business in this port.[35]

Some business was maintained, including tea destined for Russia and cotton. But "these products are for the most part shipped directly to Shanghai, as the Chinese merchants currently prefer to sell them there. Also, that port is now the only place where foreign exchange rates on these deals are static, and this business is completely passing us by."[36]

Given military, political, social and monetary events, the year 1927 proved unconducive to business growth.[37] Foreign transactions slumped in the first half, before virtually ceasing in the second. Advances on goods (packing credits) disappeared, local lending was minimal, and the bulk of the *Banque de l'Indochine* branch's liquid assets was used for book carry-forwards, with low margins of 1/16. There was still the odd business opportunity, in the form of foreign exchange transactions and some bill collections (Optorg on its representative in Hunan).

Gloom prevailed in the first half of 1928: although the branch conducted some arbitrage transactions with Shanghai and some contango operations, there was little in the way of local investments and advances on bills. The branch no longer engaged in purchases of paper on the United States or import bills in francs and recorded only "meagre remittances by the consulate or the navy for the purchase of coal and food supplies or purchases of remittances in pounds on Shanghai. In addition, "for several years now, the branch has not been allowed to engage in Chinese business."[38] As it no longer had a real comprador (due to the bankruptcy of Liu Sing Seng), it did not have access to sufficient intelligence on the Chinese communities in that marketplace and lacked embedded connections. But there were still a few opportunities of business: *Compagnie du Kin-Han* had 60,000 sleepers delivered for the overhaul of its railway lines with the aid of an advance from *Banque de l'Indochine*.

All in all, prudence was called for:

> We approve of the reserve you have demonstrated with respect to exporters in your market. Given the political and economic situation in which central China finds itself, they are bound to be faced with considerable risks, and the financing of their business, particularly in the usual form of packing credits, would cause your branch more troubles than benefits.[39] Undoubtedly it would have been easy for us to use more capital locally by increasing the volume of advances on packing credits granted to our current clients and agreeing to make advances available to new firms wanting us to grant them funds in addition to those already placed at their disposal by our competitors. We judged it imprudent, in these troubled times, to increase our risks in Wuhan and we are afraid that the series of events that is still ongoing will force our branch to continue with our present policy for some time to come.[40]

C. A lacklustre year for French banking in Wuhan in 1929

Throughout 1929, the watchword was prudence due to the tensions persisting in the region, uncertainty about the global trade climate, marked by a fall in commodity prices, and also the first signs of the crisis in the United States in October. Business was maintained over the summer, "in July to September, during which the nationalist government seemed to have control of the Yangtze valley and the surrounding area, at least as far as our city, during which the overseas markets situation seemed more or less normal in terms of their potential purchases in China".

There was a breakdown in "October to December, during which the nationalist government stopped enforcing its laws even around the capital, fighting over our territory continued without interruption, cutting all our port's communications with the producer countries, and the New York stock market crash and its repercussions in Europe upset external economic conditions."[41] Yet "October to December are normally the months of hard, income-generating work here, during which the market for export products coming down from the neighbouring provinces is established. Consequently the internal and external crisis raging at that time created a particularly serious situation locally."[42]

This prevailing gloom was the reason for the slump in the banking market, narrow margins and excessive competition. The report laments:

> The steady fall in the price of silver from 24 deniers on 30 June to 21–25/26 deniers on 31 January, which harmed our business rather than helping it, as buyers reduced their offer prices in the hope that sellers, profiting from the decline in the currency, would succeed in meeting their needs. So, apart from the odd exception, the buyers' top prices were 1 to 2 per cent below the prices that could be obtained from Chinese owners of goods, and many export houses operated without earning anything other than freight commission in order to bridge the gap between supply and demand and keep their staff busy.[43]

> Exporters' client bases are very much reduced. There are just six British firms, two American, two Belgian, four Japanese, seven German, two French, one Italian and two Russian firms involved in exports in gold currencies, served by two British banks, one American, one Belgian, three Japanese, one German, and one French bank. Several major Chinese firms operated with the aid of American credits.[44]

The market was essentially divided into two groupings: the first consisted of the banks "that operate (HSBC, National City Bank) in the same way as the chetties [Chinese banks]: the amount of interest collected and the increase in profits from foreign exchange make it possible to accept as normal a percentage loss on arranged overdrafts, a method facilitated by the issue of bills, which procures them usable capital cheaply". The second group consisted of "those that operate prudently (Chartered Bank, *Deutsche Bank, Banque belge pour l'étranger* and ourselves) by only authorising small overdrafts and reducing their income in order to safeguard it."[45]

The manager of the *Banque de l'Indochine* branch harboured traditional doubts over the viability of an active overdraft banking policy and especially over its profitability in the medium term. But HSBC seemed to him to be acting as a lever of economic patriotism: "In our market, even during troubled periods, it accumulates foreign and Chinese exposures, thereby attracting numerous clients and, at its own risk, extensively sustaining declining British trade."[46] But we know that the Paris head office of *Banque de l'Indochine* demanded sound management, which ruled out any conduct that would mark it as an "easy bank", as it was termed in France at the time to qualify a bank as easy to open its credit books to customers.

Therefore every banker had to fight hard to win any slice, however small, of a now lacklustre market:

> The banks have battled each other for the small amount of paper on offer locally; so, throughout the second part of the half-year, we often preferred to withdraw from the market rather than operate at a loss if [credit] lines had to be immediate, or to stick to speculating when, despite the inevitability of the fall in the price of silver, a fall led by Shanghai, local political events served to delay this price slide for a long time. More than once during the half-year, with the aim of securing turnover, banks in our market quoted prices which, on a sight basis, were significantly lower than the hedging rate in Shanghai. We did not follow suit by adopting this policy, and waited before taking on business until, due to various factors, we were able to compete with them while at the same time earning a profit. This policy has proved sound in terms of generating a return.[47]

Business was slow across the board, including in the leather and hide export business, due to a delay in the collection campaign. This gloomy climate had a rapid impact on the *Banque de l'Indochine* branch: "For the last three months, our branch has been operating at a reduced pace owing both to the halt in business as a result of the disastrous domestic political situation and the economic crisis in the buyer countries, and to the trouble I had in reducing our risks to a minimum by the start of 1930, when things were looking ominous for foreigners in China."[48] The manager reduced overheads and weighed up loan applications. Once again, he fell back on longstanding clients. But "*Olivier-Chine* did not use much of its packing credit facility (20,000 taels)".

"Racine, meanwhile, is in need of new blood. Managed in a way that can no longer be called prudent, but risk-averse, it no longer counts in our market where the local managers are lacking in stature and experience". Anyway Borioni & Cie saw business expand. "As with the other firms operating locally, we only grant them advances on bills for forward delivery in the case of specific deals with specialised accounts, with repayments monitored on a deal-by-deal basis. This method means balances are not left to stagnate, something that can often lead to surprises later on"[49] (see Table 14.5).

Table 14.5 Core operations of the Wuhan branch of *Banque de l'Indochine* in 1924–1929 (taels)

	Second term 1924	First term 1925	Second term 1925	First term 1926	Second term 1926	First term 1927	Second term 1927	First term 1928	Second term 1928	First term 1929	Second term 1929
Currency transactions											
Gold arbitrage	46,322	41,352	46,322	35,559	44,666	33,857	18,249	23,034	23,118	26,761	45,681
Of which:											
FRF accounts	10,605	7,854	6,075	6,585	12,570		1,150	2,626	1,724	3,523	3,962
£ accounts	19,926	22,488	24,959	21,145	27,518		13,903	19,768	19,136	21,102	28,956
$ accounts	15,790	11,280	15,266	7,829	4,578		3,196	640	2,238	2,136	12,763
Silver arbitrage	2,475	4,795	4,016	2,234	1,629	2,717	1,297	1,748	2,659	1,054	888
Trade operations											
Interest and commission	19,095	18,885	18,846	29,486	21,701	1,042	5,493	6,116	7,144	4,595	3,934

Table 14.6 Accounts of the *Banque de l'Indochine* branch in 1924–1929 (taels)

	First term 1923	Second term 1924	First term 1925	Second term 1925	First term 1926	Second term 1926	First term 1927	Second term 1927	First term 1928	Second term 1928	First term 1929	Second term 1929	First term 1929	Second term 1929
Total income				67,890		69,162	67,279	67,996	37,616	25,039	30,900	32,921	32,410	50,503
Write-offs					8,000		7,847	8,999	7,268		5,493	6,116	7,144	4,595
Net profit	21,479	53,313	53,314	40,437	40,332	36,182	30,890 Or: 32,242	38,129		−4,778	1,257	752	3,018	23,747
Funds used		5,306,000		5,972,550	5,834,648	5,239,006	4,805,648	4,659,392	3,779,988	3,686,589	3,730,203	3,583,526	3,224,293	3,435,810

Source: Half-yearly *rapports-bilans*, *Crédit agricole* archives, *Banque de l'Indochine* fund, 439AM204

In the mid-1920s, the balance sheet of the *Banque de l'Indochine* branch was healthy again, stable and even profitable. Hence the branch was able to record a gross return on gold-currency assets of 4.5414 per cent per annum for the second half of 1925. The uncertainty faced in the second half of the 1920s resulted in fresh write-offs of irrecoverable debts, but the amounts remained modest after the woes of the very early 1920s: 8,999 taels in the second half of 1925, 7,847 in the second half of 1926 (see Table 14.6).

The situation improved substantially from the 1923 balance sheet onwards: that year, the gross operating profit amounted to 84,452 taels on official capital of 1.6 million taels, supplemented by advances from sister branches and the head office; the gross operating return came out at 17.9132 per cent, and the net return on actual capital employed (942,896 taels) at 6.0918 per cent. In July 1924, spirits were high because the branch's profit for the first half of 1924 (53,314 taels, or 693,077 francs) was its best since the first half of 1916! In the second half of 1925 and the two halves of 1926, the net return stood at 3.259 per cent, 1.711 per cent and 5.513 per cent, respectively: despite the sudden economic changes, the branch remained profitable.

Profits were recorded almost every half-year. The level of write-offs of frozen credits remained under control. This was good news for the branches, which had previously had to supply their sister branch with liquidity, especially the for head office. From then on, it could feel worthwhile making the effort to support a branch operating in a market in a far-flung corner of the geo-economic map drawn by the business community in the name of French economic patriotism.

Conclusion

This outpost of the capitalist struggle became part of the "economic war machine" of French bankers, merchants and manufacturers. Of course, Olivier could have survived without engaging in exports from Wuhan to the United States, French industry without the ores from *Société industrielle de minerais*, the *Banque de l'Indochine* without the revenues from its branch on the upper Yangtze. But the business going on in Wuhan and the surrounding regions formed a point of connection between the business operations of the companies involved; it complemented them and counted as useful rather than necessary.

The extra costs generated by it were roughly offset by the marginal income it provided for the activities of the sales and banking branches in Shanghai, for which Wuhan was more or less a bridgehead, or more generally for the commercial and banking system of the firms forming a link between the Asian markets and New York, San Francisco, Paris, London or Hamburg. This business generated only marginal costs, so it ultimately proved profitable. It also illustrated the gambles taken by French capitalism as regards the potential for development of these regions of central China. Had they not been thwarted by the events of the 1930s and 1940s, these initiatives would have confirmed the spirit of enterprise fostered at the time by the demands of economic patriotism, a spirit that effectively manifested itself in the way the *Banque de l'Indochine* branch integrated itself and took root in the Wuhan marketplace.

Notes

1 *Rapport-bilan*, first half of 1922, 24 July 1922, *Banque de l'Indochine* fund, archives of *Crédit agricole*.
2 *Rapport-bilan*, first half of 1922, 24 July 1922.
3 Letter from head office to the branch, 2 May 1924.
4 *Rapport-bilan*, first half of 1927, July 1928.
5 *Ibidem*.
6 *Ibidem*.
7 *Ibidem*.
8 Summary letters, 8 March 1926.
9 *Rapport-bilan*, second half of 1924, 18 February 1925.
10 *Ibidem*.
11 Letter from the branch manager, 13 October 1921.
12 *Ibidem*.
13 *Rapport-bilan*, second half of 1924, 18 February 1925.
14 *Ibidem*.
15 *Ibidem*.
16 *Rapport-bilan*, second half of 1926, January 1927.
17 *Rapport-bilan*, first half of 1925, 15 August 1925.
18 *Rapport-bilan*, second half of 1925, 8 February 1926.
19 *Rapport-bilan*, first half of 1926, July 1926.
20 *Rapport-bilan*, second half of 1926, January 1927.
21 *Ibidem*.
22 *Rapport-bilan*, second half of 1922, 27 January 1923.
23 *Rapport-bilan*, second half of 1924, 18 February 1925.
24 *Rapport-bilan*, first half of 1924, 25 July 1924.
25 Letter from Gestreaux, managing director of *Société d'importation de minerais*, to the manager of *Banque de l'Indochine* in Wuhan, 25 January 1925.
26 *Rapport-bilan*, second half of 1925, 8 February 1926.
27 *Rapport-bilan*, first half of 1926, July 1926.
28 *Rapport-bilan*, second half of 1929, 10 February 1930.
29 *Rapport-bilan*, first half of 1920, 20 July 1920.
30 *Rapport-bilan*, first half of 1923, 15 August 1923.
31 *Rapport-bilan*, second half of 1923, 30 January 1924.
32 *Rapport-bilan*, first half of 1924, 25 July 1924.
33 *Ibidem*.
34 *Rapport-bilan* for the first half of 1926, July 1926.
35 *Rapport-bilan* for the first half of 1927, July 1927.
36 *Ibidem*.
37 *Rapport-bilan* for the second half of 1927, 30 January 1928.
38 *Rapport-bilan*, first half of 1928, July 1928.
39 Letter from head office to the branch, 23 May 1929.
40 *Rapport-bilan*, second half of 1928, 15 February 1929.
41 *Rapport-bilan*, second half of 1929, 10 February 1930.
42 *Ibidem*.
43 *Ibidem*.
44 *Ibidem*.
45 *Ibidem*.
46 *Ibidem*.
47 *Ibidem*.
48 *Ibidem*.
49 *Ibidem*.

Part IV

Facing crisis and wars in the 1930s

15 French business and banking in the port-city of Guangzhou in the 1930s

Banque de l'Indochine was entrusted with the mission of assisting the development of French business with the aid of its Chinese branches[1]—a mission which its Guangzhou branch fulfilled amply. In the years 1910–1920, it accompanied French silk traders who used Guangzhou as their supply base to get raw silk, spun silk and silk waste for export to Lyon and subsequently to the United States, which turned out to be the main market for such high-value goods. It also wove close ties with Chinese merchants in the silk sector as well as in general trading, thereby turning itself into a "local" bank.

Four chapters will look at the intimate connections between business history and banking history, at the evolution of the portfolio of strategic activities of this branch, its portfolio of skills and its performance. Till the events of the 1930s, it benefited from *Banque de l'Indochine*'s "curve of experience" in China and in Guangzhou: its portfolio of expertise and skills was faced by the harsh tensions prevailing then—military, political and economic—because of the overall crisis. The progress achieved since 1902 and the position attained after the growth surge in the 1920s have been investigated. Why and how did *Banque de l'Indochine* and the entire French business community maintain their presence and activities in a city shaken by wave upon wave of crises and tensions?

I'll investigate the strategy and tactics used to face the dire times, the skills used in the management of risk and the penetration into the Chinese community, the intensity of the business community in mixing banking and trading in Guangzhou and its surroundings. I'll determine how the "port-city" succeeded in preserving its commercial position, its international business connections, its basic vocation as a "driving" force collecting local staples (and ores) for non-Asian ("imperialist") interests, its function as a bridgehead for non-Asian exports of consumer or equipment goods in south-west China. Lastly, I'll study its role as a platform favouring the "spillover" of non-Chinese entrepreneurship, business reliability and creditworthiness (against "rogue" practices) within the emerging Chinese capitalism during the interwar period (the existence of 19 Chinese banks in Guangzhou in 1936 epitomized this breakthrough).

1. French businessmen and bankers caught in a worrying environment

After three decades of a steady, if chaotic growth of modern capitalism in the port-city, the 1930s presented a more worrisome backdrop. As in many marketplaces all over China, Guangzhou businessmen and bankers had to jump from the little golden age of trade in the second half of the 1920s to the dire 1930s, when so many hurdles were placed in the path of free business. The fate of Guangzhou as a "proto-globalised" port-city was therefore at stake. Since the turn of the century, it had gained a position as a key export centre of raw silk, spun silk and silk waste, either towards Europe (Lyon, Italy) or towards the United States and New York. This dual trade and banking architecture, built and oriented towards Europe and North America, was challenged by a variety of small and large crises.

A. Guangzhou gathering momentum as a modernised city

No doubt, the Pearl Rivers, the Si-Kiang (to Wuchow Fu, Nanning or Liou/ Tcheou) and the Pei-Kiang (to Chao Chow Fu), remained the main access route for drawing local produce from the countryside upstream to the port-city. The port-city itself remained a regional hub and depended mostly on Hong Kong for its open sea trade, but its traffic soon gained substance, for instance with Shanghai, Formosa and even Tianjin (see Table 15.1).

Table 15.1 Vessels having entered and cleared at the Guangzhou port in 1933–1934

	1933		1934	
	Number	Tonnage (thousand tons)	Number	Tonnage (thousand tons)
Open sea steamers	1,813	2,624	2,067	3,040
River steamers	4,201	4,356	4,015	4,350
Small boats	522	97	679	119
Distribution of flags and tonnage of vessels entered and cleared at Guangzhou				
Total	7,288	7,102	10,041	7,578
British	4,893	5,367	5,458	5,857
Chinese	1,313	783	3,526	897
Portuguese	349	160	376	167
Norwegian	261	441	182	339
Japanese	120	166	130	176
Dutch	66	70	43	51
French	38	49	25	32

Source: Archives of *Crédit agricole, Banque de l'Indochine* fund, 323 DES 36/2, Letters and reports, second half of 1934

In the meantime however, the economic environment for business changed as several tools became available. First, a telephone line was set up between Guangzhou and Hong Kong in 1931, allowing for better trading operations:

> Thanks to the telephonic link with Hong Kong, we have been able to demonstrate to our European and Chinese clients that it was in their interests to place firm orders valid for one or two hours. That has allowed us to negotiate a large portion of the remittances drawn following credit from good American houses at better rates than those of our competitors.[2]

Second, the opening of the (681-mile) railway line joining Guangzhou to Wuhan in July 1936 cut the journey time down to forty hours and extended the port-city's scope northwards. Third, a new line was opened on September 1937 at Chuchow station linking Nanchang (Kwangsi) to Pingshiang (Hunan) and extending the already active route between Pingshiang and Chuchow, which indirectly enhanced Guangzhou's reach as a regional hub. Fourth, the first air link between Guangzhou and Hanoi was set up by *Air France* on 14 February 1936: every Friday, business exchanges between the concession and the colony could be done via airmail.

B. Power struggles in Guangdong

Unfortunately, several hurdles and pitfalls got in the way and stalled the business momentum. Guangzhou was engulfed in military and political turmoil. First, relations between the Guangdong authorities and the central Nanking power became uncertain, as it had in the mid-twenties. Local chieftains were given some form of autonomy to keep order in the region, but that soon led to local rearmament and rekindled the phenomenon of warlordism. They were also constrained to finance part of the national war through transfers of cash to the Guomingdang armies. Both facts led to higher taxes being levied on business, often arbitrarily.

The prospects of Guangzhouese business, which had arrived at some sort of peaceful balance by the end of the twenties, were once again mired in gloom. Uncertainty intensified in April 1931 when a change in the Guangdong government (with warlord Chen Ji Tang/Chen Chai Tong) declared war on Nanking and took a hard stance against the Japanese, denouncing the agreement arrived at by Chiang Kai Shek with them regarding Manchukuo and the contracts he had negotiated to preserve his influence on Guangdong. This imposed a policy of extreme rigor on bankers: "A policy of extreme prudence is still required."[3]

These troubles sometimes even affected the safety of the journey between Guangzhou and Hong Kong, requiring strong precautions, for instance the protection of the small warship *Argus*, based in the South China Sea: "Transporting funds to Hong Kong is too risky without the protection of the warship *Argus*, which has not been seen in Shameen for the past several months."[4] A few years later, the Guangdong clique was toppled by an internecine coup (August 1936):

Marshall Chan Chai Tong, who favoured more autonomy from the Nanking state, had to flee, and Guangdong came under the central power—while in Kwangsi, Li Chung Jen,[5] an ally of Chan, stayed at the helm: "The only result of the revolution of July 1936 fomented by the two *Kwangs* against the central authority was to allow Nanking to have complete power over Guangdong after the hurried departure of Marshall Chan Chai Tong and his clique."[6]

The main result of this was the spreading of the central currency, the national Chinese dollar, into Guangdong between August 1936 and February 1937. This meant that three currencies were now used in the port-city: the dollar of the Kwangsi-Guangdong, the Hong Kong dollar (for notes), and the national dollar, which was rejected by the users of the other two. Still, the national dollar grew in popularity due to the inflow of refugees from the northern regions, the Shanghai and Nanking areas and the firms fleeing from the occupied zones. "Internal exchange" operations grew, but the *Banque de l'Indochine*'s branch did not get much involved due to its weak resources in national dollars,[7] even though the head of Postal & Savings Bank (De Sercey), being French, chose to open a deposit account with *Banque de l'Indochine*. However, it had to take into account all these moves because the State imposed a control on FOREX in Guangzhou in August 1938.

C. The effects of the Sino-Japanese war

The deepening rift between the Japanese and Chinese powers greatly hampered business. After the invasion of Manchuria, the Chinese set up a boycott of Japanese goods, which put a halt to several trades between Guangzhou and the rest of Asia. Then the military penetration or offensive into the Republic of China greatly disturbed Guangzhouese business connections, as the maritime lines and tranquillity were often disrupted, and insecurity gripped the daily life of the harbour. No sooner was order re-established that military events ("the North war") struck the port-city in the summer 1937: the outbreak of the war with Japan forced Japanese houses, banks (Yokohama Specie Bank, Bank of Taiwan) and people to leave Guangzhou post-haste and trade with Japan disappeared. Such events weighed on the day-to-day fate of merchants and bankers (and the population) just as air raids started targeting the harbour, with the first occurring on 18 August 1937.

War finally came to Guangdong when three warships entered the Pearl Rivers on 6 September 1937.[8] The Japanese fleet tried to blockade the maritime route between Guangzhou and Hong Kong and all traffic on the Pearl Rivers, mainly to stop the import of armaments. Aerial bombings increased, targeting the railways, the industrial and harbour areas (for instance on 21–23 September).[9] The Kukong port (150 km north of Guangzhou) was destroyed in October. A major target was the Guangzhou–Kowloon railway line, but the bombings failed, whilst the Guangzhou–Wuhan was struck a few times.[10] Anyway, the offensive lacked efficiency: the river, maritime and railway connections survived.[11] On 30 September, Chinese troops themselves blocked the rivers to protect the harbour against any Japanese offensive, thus hindering foreign ships from getting to Hong Kong till 30 November 1937.

Meanwhile, Chinese nationalism turned actively against foreign "imperialism" when anti-Japanese reactions were somehow extended to the whole foreign presence. At the beginning of September 1937, Chinese demonstrators invaded the concessions on the mainland, but the British and French area on Shameen was saved when a military force was mobilised and the gunship *Argus* was stationed within firing range—though the wives of the two French managers of the branch were transported to safer Hong Kong. The branches of Yokohama Specie Bank and Bank of Taiwan had to close, and their staff and business were transferred to Hong Kong.

Business uncertainties prevailed, capital fled the area and a moratorium had to be imposed by the authorities. Happily, *Banque de l'Indochine* bore no risks on Japanese and Chinese banks at that time, which appeased the concerns of its Paris headquarters: "Our branch has no risk with Chinese or Japanese banks, whether it be FOREX contracts, deposits, clearing or settling discounts."[12] But "business as usual" could not continue because of the panic caused by the bombings and naval offensives. Three-quarters to four-fifths of the population of the port-city fled, with only about 300,000 remaining behind. Even though foreigners noticed the Chinese "determination" to resist the Japanese, the normal circuits of production and commerce were disturbed in the last four months of 1937 in the whole of South China. The *Banque de l'Indochine*'s branch comprador could no longer siphon business towards the branch: "Four-fifths of the population have fled the city and only the poor are left behind. Business has therefore almost completely dried up. Where there is nothing, the comprador can obviously do nothing."[13]

Then history caught up with Guangzhou when the Japanese army seized the city on 20 October 1938. Normal trade towards Hong Kong and Indochina was practically snuffed out. Chinese Nationalists held the centre of the Kowloon–Guangzhou railway line, while the Japanese controlled both ends.[14] The river was blockaded, and communication halted with Macau and Hong Kong, whilst the telegraph lines fell under Japanese control. Moreover, the final battles had destroyed part of the harbour and the warehouses, causing major losses to merchant houses. The *Banque de l'Indochine*'s bigger clients could no longer continue doing business: "Since the fall of Guangzhou, the *Société commerciale asiatique*'s Shameen branch is no longer working as it is no longer possible to dispatch anything from Guangzhou. But the SCA has kept its Hong Kong bureau active."[15]

The bank decided to stop loans on silk bales so long as the war lasted[16], thereby cutting deeply into its appetite for risk. Instructions were sent to convert the assets of the branch into US dollars bought in Hong Kong and transferred there on creditor accounts, at the *Banque de l'Indochine*'s branch or by other banks[17]—in order to anticipate the depreciation of the Nanking dollar (NK$). Between 27 October and 16 November 1939, the assets in Nanking dollars were reduced from 1,300,373 to 634,000. When all-out full war broke out,

Hong Kong served as a shelter for Chinese savings at the expense of Guang-zhou: "Hong Kong has now become a haven for refugee capital as a result of the war. Chinese funds are seeking safety there and vast sums are being invested in real estate business and industry."[18] In 1938–1939, the *Banque de l'Indochine*'s branch relied on the French consul (Philippe Simon) to keep its telegraphic connection and its postal envoys (through the diplomatic bag) and to ease cash transfers of Hong Kong dollars (HK$) and national dollars to Hong Kong.[19]

2. New business opportunities

Despite the gloom, a few opportunities were offered to businessmen and bank-ers which allowed them to fill the hole.

A. Financing the armaments trade

In 1929, the *Banque de l'Indochine*'s branch became involved in the sale of armaments by French (and Belgian) companies: as the orders from the Guangdong authorities grew in size, so did FOREX activities and cash transfers (repayment in Europe of the receipts paid by Chinese clients), offering good returns through commissions. In 1929–1930, order in Guangdong was not yet fully re-established because General Chan Fat Kwei, a warlord of Kwangsi, wanted to return as head of the Guangzhou government. He was finally defeated, and the local State came to an agreement with the Nanking State to act as its delegate in the region: "The agreement between the nationalist government and our own seems to be perfect, with ours enjoying an almost total autonomy."[20]

In any case, the fights, the repression of the bandits who had proliferated during the local wars and several rearmament programs provided major busi-ness opportunities for French business: "It is probable that in three years, the Kwang Tung and its satellites, the neighbouring provinces, will make up a sig-nificant force, equipped and armed with the best of modern weapons. It is the French and Czechoslovak factories which would have supplied the major part of this material."[21] A cause was that "the major part of the resources is spent on the military and on the buying of arms and ammunition."[22] What favoured Guangdong's finances was the fee imposed on the opium trade which used Guangzhou as its export harbour for goods coming from the provinces of Yun-nan, Kweichau and Sechuen, through the Kwangsi, towards Swatow, Amoy and Shanghai.[23]

On one side, *Banque de l'Indochine* practiced normal banking: The import of airplane engines for the Guangdong air force in 1930 resulted in a fat bill of exchange (FRF 833,000) to be discounted. Similarly, when the house of *Pinguet* acted as an intermediary to sell armaments to the warlord, another bill of exchange (£16,000) drawn on the Reuter-Brockmann house was discounted by the bank, with a collateral in cash for 75 per cent.[24] Another service com-prised of FOREX facilities, as was the case in 1931 for an order of armaments, emerged thanks to the *Banque de l'Indochine*'s art of FOREX: "Sale of dollars to the Guangzhouese Military Headquarters for the purchase of arms (USD 519,000). We have been able to give our clients exceptional rates which have allowed them to close deals which they would not have managed with the usual rates."[25] "The import of arms has continued to be productive and has procured very interesting [FOREX] hedging."[26] The total amount[27] overseen by *Banque de l'Indochine* during the first half of 1932 reached USD 760,000.

For the major orders, *Banque de l'Indochine* assumed no risk at all, except the "risk of execution": "The preceding contracts involved no risk for the *Banque de l'Indochine*, which acted only as a cashier and as an agent for the transfer of the funds due to the French seller."[28] For example, in 1932, the two brokers tackling these armament deliveries, Ott and Krebs, had to fuel cash on a current account in Europe beforehand as an actual guarantee.[29] *Banque de l'Indochine* partnered larger operations in 1932: sale of armaments by the French firms Schneider and Hotchkiss (and also consultancy to the Belgian Herstal). E. Ott, a Swiss heading the Industrial Export C°, acted as an intermediary in South China for the *Groupe Chine*, an association of French exporters in China, picking up contracts and following them till completion. In 1932, he oversaw the purchase of 200 Hotchkiss machine guns by the First Army Corps[30] for USD 183,457, with a guarantee by the Guangzhou government and a collateral on the modern cement plant of Sai Tsun, opened in 1932.

On 22 February 1933, another contract for 260 *Brandt* mortars, 39,000 shells and ammunition worth gold-USD 624,999 was signed, with the last instalment made on 27 March 1934. In parallel, Henri Krebs, the head of the Augsburg house in Basel since 1921 and the representative in Guangzhou since 1931 of the Belgian *Fabrique d'Herstal*, also used *Banque de l'Indochine* as a financial lever, with loans of USD 150,000 in 1933 for the import of armaments.[31] All in all, the armament business varied depending on the Guangdong authorities and the rhythm of war, locally or northwards (to support the Nanking offensives against the guerrilla or the Japanese). The *Banque de l'Indochine*'s branch oversaw sales of armaments of USD 769,000 in 1932, 226,000 in the first half of 1933, and the fees earned on them made for half of the profits of the branch during the second half of 1933: "The arms business has gone up to FRF 6,826 million. The lion's share of this amount goes to the *Groupe Chine*, which has been, for the entire period, our branch's best client."[32]

Even though it faced competition from Bank of Kwangsi in Hong Kong for FOREX fees linked to the import of armaments (in 1934), the Guangzhou branch acquired a relevant portfolio of skills as a factor of "differentiation": "Good experience of the Guangzhou branch in the business of arms sales, with the support of the French Consul. Our branch has broken away from these affairs, which it has been successfully dealing with for the past three years and of profit."[33] This proved its efficiency: "The transfers of funds pertaining to the preceding contracts (Schneider, Hotchkiss, Brandt, etc.) were accomplished with regularity; on the whole, these contracts will very soon be completely settled."[34] It also fuelled cash into the silk business: "For us the arms business is a major source of revenue and it allows us, during normal times, to quickly cover our silk paper."[35]

Such expertise opened up several opportunities. Negotiations began in 1934 regarding a big contract (FRF 85 to 100 million): *Banque de l'Indochine* (in France and in Guangdong), as an active intermediary, and the *Groupe Chine* had to face a British coalition of HSBC and Jardine Matheson because its manager John Craven was also on the Board of Vickers. Six French firms, led by Brandt, were involved: Schneider (FRF 40 million), Hotchkiss (20 million), Renault (10 million), Brandt (10 million), Sauter-Harlé (4 million) and SOMUA (1 million). On the Chinese side were the government of Guangdong and Marshal Chan Chai Tong/Tchang Tchai Tong: "As long as Marshal Chan Chai Tong rules over the Guangdong, peace is assured in the city and in the provinces. His present situation is very strong."[36] Bank of Guangzhou (based in Hong Kong) acted as guarantor. After seven months of negotiations, the financial contract was signed in the summer 1934 by the head of the *Banque de l'Indochine*'s branch in Guangzhou, Jean Juge, and the Marshal's representatives. But its completion lasted only a few months due to the lack of money on the Chinese side. *Banque de l'Indochine* guaranteed the delivery of the military equipment against treasury bills from the Guangdong government (themselves pledged by taxes on tobacco and wine) and exchange bills on the bank's order, to be drawn in sixty months."[37]

Schneider, the big French manufacturer of heavy armaments,[38] was again involved in such a deal in July 1935, this time for three batteries of four canons, light canons, and ammunition. Payment instalments were scheduled for 1935–1938, once more based on taxes on wines and tobacco as collateral for promissory notes issued to cover the loan. *Banque de l'Indochine* acted as the agent for the transfer—with a 1 per cent fee, for its guarantee to the embarkation of the equipment in France, thus as some kind of comptroller for the completion of the operation.[39] Deliveries commenced in April 1936, cash was picked up by the Guangzhou branch on behalf of the *Groupe Chine*, just as new contracts were signed in March–May 1936 for more canons, 75-type batteries, mortars, shells, and so on. These orders amounted to around FRF 78 million in August 1936, with 33.7 million paid by the government against a value of 10.4 million for equipment already delivered—which could reinsure the bank despite the change of power in Guangzhou.[40]

During only the first half of 1936, the armament sales overseen by *Banque de l'Indochine* attained FRF 24 million of a total of 32 million: "Your arms deals have procured 24 million francs in sales [of credit paper]. The *Groupe Chine* and its directors have bought you, at most, $112 000, thus by procuring to the bank a sort of deposit guarantee, amounting to a total sale of 32 million francs."[41] The *Groupe Chine* itself took 11,254 paper pounds, and its directors the remaining: Bossut (from an industrial dynasty in the North of France) for an amount of 18,833 pounds, Ott for 13,290, and Marchad for USD 25,870. But the coup of August 1936 suspended the process, even if the new power eventually confirmed the contract, albeit imposing more "grey" payments and smaller fees: "At last the Guangzhouese authorities have recognized the *Groupe Chine*'s current contracts, but with lesser financial conditions, and consequently the failure to profit by the commissions to intermediaries."[42]

A final operation took place in March 1936, when *Banque de l'Indochine* provided the trading house of Feld & C° with a guarantee (£58,000) for the delivery of 10,000 *Mauser* guns ordered from the Belgian *Fonderie nationale* in the spring of 1938. It also managed the transfer of the first two instalments (USD 7,650) by the Kwangsi government—the other ones still pending in 1938. When the general crisis paralysed normal business in the Guangdong area, the sale of armaments became one of the key sources of revenue for the branch, under the account "interests and fees."[43]

B. Contributing to the modernisation of South China?

After *Banque de l'Indochine* had proved its talent in the field of armament contracts, it tried to extend its reach to the import of equipment. While China still faced political and military tensions, its actual economic development was gathering momentum, piece by piece. This explains the negotiations in 1935 between the Guangdong authorities and the Schneider group, in this case with its Czechoslovakian sister company, Skoda. It concerned the delivery of a big power plant for supplying energy to a paper mill, at a cost of HK$ 209,000 in 35 months. Guarantees were to be brought by *Zevnostenska Banka* and the *Anglo-Czekoslovenska Banka*, but Jean Laurent, head of the *Banque de l'Indochine*'s General Inspection and supervisor of its Asian activities, fought hard to introduce his bank into the pool, and succeeded in getting the *Banque de l'Indochine*'s Guangzhou branch a HK$ 86,000 loan to Skoda to help seal the contract: "Inspector General [Jean] Laurent finds it regrettable that the financing of this province's industrial equipment plan, pushed so actively by the local authorities, was ensured totally outside of us."[44]

Unfortunately, the project fell through. Skoda endeavoured to reach other agreements (for five sugar plants, etc.), while *Banque de l'Indochine* took part in a few other Czechoslovakian exports to Guangdong in the mid-1930s. The launch of the Three-Years Industrial Plan in 1934–1935 opened the door to new opportunities, but nothing much can be said regarding the Guangzhou banks' involvement from the archives available in Paris.

C. Financing fresh exports of wolfram ore

At the turn of the decade, the archives begin to refer to "wolfram" (or tungsten, a metal used for steel alloys after the advent of the Second Industrial Revolution and also for the production of light bulb filaments, X-ray tubes). The South China Trading C° (M.T.L. Laing) began exporting tungsten ore to the United States;[45] it owned a mine in Nananfu (Kiangsi, Yuet Wah Mining C°),[46] and collected the production of other mines for export to the United States—until its crash in October 1935. The *Banque de l'Indochine*'s branch granted it an advance on goods—the first was in 1931 (HK$ 8,000 on 78 wolfram sacks).[47] Another company, *Société commerciale asiatique*, also became an agent for such exports: its boss, Chan Yuk Lam, gave all its credit business to the *Banque de l'Indochine*'s branch. SCA had its headquarters in Guangzhou-Shameen, a branch in Hong Kong, and an agency in France (Jacques Labatut).[48] Thus, for years, it managed the remittances on four months' sight drawn by the firm on its agent in London (M.D. Ewart). It started discounting such bills from November 1937. Happily, as the depression worsened, the decline in silk exports was balanced somewhat by the rising demand for wolfram.

Notes

1 Marc Meuleau, *Des pionniers en Extrême-Orient. La the Banque de l'Indochine, 1875–1975*, Paris, Fayard, 1990. To be complemented by Yasuo Gonjo, *Banque coloniale ou banque d'affaires? La Banque de l'Indochine sous la IIIe République*, Paris, Comité pour l'histoire économique & financière de la France, 1993 (first published in Japanese, Tokyo, University of Tokyo Press, 1985).

2 *Crédit agricole* archives, *Banque de l'Indochine* fund, 323 DES 36/2, Letters and reports, second half of 1932, 12 January 1932.

3 *Banque de l'Indochine*, first half of 1931, 3 August 1931.

4 *Banque de l'Indochine*, first half of 1933.

5 See: Diana Lary, *Region and Nation: The Kwangsi Clique in Chinese Politics 1925–1937*, Cambridge University Press, "Cambridge Studies in Chinese History, Literature and Institutions", reissue, 2009.

6 *Crédit agricole* archives, *Banque de l'Indochine* fund, DES 13/4, Reports from the Guangzhou branch to the Paris headquarters, 16 November 1936.

7 *Ibidem*, 7 September 1938.

8 *Crédit agricole* archives, *Banque de l'Indochine* fund, special note n°21 from the Guangzhou branch to the Paris headquarters, 8 September 1937.

9 *Ibidem*, 1 October 1937.

10 *Crédit agricole* archives, *Banque de l'Indochine* fund, special note n°29 from the Guangzhou branch to the Paris headquarters, 10 October 1937.

11 *Crédit agricole* archives, *Banque de l'Indochine* fund, DES 13/4, Reports from the Guangzhou branch to the Paris headquarters, 1 September 1937.

12 DES 13/4, Reports from the Guangzhou branch to the Paris headquarters, 19 August 1937.

13 *Ibidem*, 24 February 1938.

14 *Ibidem*, 6 May 1939.

15 *Ibidem*, 31 May 1939.

16 *Ibidem*, 14 August 1939.

17 *Ibidem*, 31 May 1939.

18 Internal note of *Banque de l'Indochine*, 21 June 1939. *Ibidem*.

19 Confidential note to the Paris office, 16 December 1939.

20 *Crédit agricole* archives, *Banque de l'Indochine* fund, 323 DES 36/2, Letters and reports, 14 December 1930.

21 *Ibidem*, second half of 1933.

22 *Ibidem*, 14 December 1930.

23 *Ibidem*, "Political situation", first term 1933.

24 *Ibidem*, 14 December 1930.

25 *Ibidem*, second half of 1931, 6 February 1932.

26 *Ibidem*, 8 April 1932.

27 *Ibidem*, first half of 1932, 27 October 1932.
28 *Crédit agricole* archives, *Banque de l'Indochine* fund, DES 13/4, Reports from the Guang-zhou branch to the Paris headquarters, 21 February 1934.
29 *Ibidem*, 15 February 1932.
30 *Ibidem*, 19 September 1932.
31 *Ibidem*, 5 May 1933.
32 *Crédit agricole* archives, *Banque de l'Indochine* fund, 323 DES 36/2, Letters and reports, first half of 1933.
33 *Crédit agricole* archives, *Banque de l'Indochine* fund, DES 13/4, Letter from the Guangzhou branch to the Hong Kong branch, 27 April 1933.
34 DES 13/4, Reports from the Guangzhou branch to the Paris headquarters, 1 January 1934.
35 *Ibidem*, 27 April 1933.
36 *Ibidem*, 1 January 1934.
37 *Ibidem*, 21 June 1934.
38 See Tristan de la Broise & Félix Torres, *Schneider, l'histoire en force*, Paris, Jean-Pierre de Monza, 1996.
39 *Crédit agricole* archives, *Banque de l'Indochine* fund, DES 13/4, Reports from the Guang-zhou branch to the Paris headquarters, 15 July 1935.
40 *Ibidem*, 14 August 1936.
41 323 DES 36/2, Letters and reports, second half of 1936, 18 September 1936.
42 *Crédit agricole* archives, *Banque de l'Indochine* fund, DES 13/4, Reports from the Guang-zhou branch to the Paris headquarters, 16 November 1936.
43 323 DES 36/2, Letters and reports, first half of 1937, 18 October 1937.
44 DES 13/4, Reports from the Guangzhou branch to the Paris headquarters, 26 April 1935.
45 *Ibidem*, 5 January 1932.
46 *Ibidem*, 18 January 1933.
47 *Crédit agricole* archives, *Banque de l'Indochine* fund, 323 DES 36/2, Letters and reports, 21 March 1931.
48 *Ibidem*, second half of 1930, June 1931. *Crédit agricole* archives, *Banque de l'Indochine* fund, DES 13/4, Reports from the Guangzhou branch to the Paris headquarters, 22 August and 11 October 1934.

16 *Banque de l'Indochine* facing the crisis in Guangzhou in the 1930s

Whilst "positive" factors fostered the evolution and diversification of *Banque de l'Indochine*'s business and banking niche in Guangzhou despite the political and military uncertainties, the overall "negative" economic background ensured that trading houses continued to face harsh commercial and financial difficulties. This chapter will gauge the ability of the branch managers' portfolio of skills to resist the various factors and events of the crisis in south China and determine whether the branch provided at least balanced, if not good returns to its mother company.

The *Banque de l'Indochine*'s branch had to face credit crunches and the risk of insolvency. Its branch acted as a little bank abroad. Its size was far smaller than the Shanghai and Hong Kong outfits. It was comprised of two French managers, four Chinese or Annamite administrative employees, and four boys and coolies—supplemented by the comprador's team. As an "ambassador" of French business interests in Guangzhou, such a frail body had to make the most of its strategic "niche" but also to curtail its appetite for risks, avoid bad debts and maintain acceptable returns. At its scale, it had to contribute to the overall balance sheet of its mother house, whose gains came from the addition of numerous small fees, commissions and interest charges throughout its network. The Guangzhou branch could rely on three key assets: the support from the Paris head office, its managers, and its compradors.

1. The Guangzhou market hurt by the widespread economic crisis

At the turn of the decade, the *Banque de l'Indochine*'s branch had inherited from the twenties a few bad loans (on six failed clients), though all of them had been amortised on its balance sheet, with a few small amounts recovered in the 1930s by the sale of piled-up goods or the completion of pending bills of exchange. The sole debt still pending dated back to World War I, through the financing of a real estate company (China Land). Happily, despite harsher uncertainties, the modernisation of the city continued in the 1930s; the port was developed, the roadways extended: "In the city, the dark and infected alleys continue to be replaced by tar roads plied by buses. The entire physiognomy of this city is changing in front of our eyes, with its 'old China' character disappearing day by day."[1] And the real estate business strengthened.

The branch even succeeded in getting rid of its real estate asset: on 22 January 1932, it agreed to sell (for HK$ 430,000, less two "fees" paid to the city authorities as graft) a plot with 22 houses, an ancient theatre, and a garden to a Chinese investor (Cheng Tin Koo, from *Tai Li C°*). Thus, after the payment in October 1932, it could amortise its credit on the little firm which had developed this plot[2] and even use the surplus to garnish its provisions account for impaired debt.

Despite such a sound and steady base, the *Banque de l'Indochine*'s branch had to face the general depressive business mood: like any business city, Guangzhou was susceptible to the worldwide economic depression which hurt China through reduced exports and unstable credit.[3] Some French trading houses in Guangdong lost momentum and were on the brink of collapse. They suffered directly not only from bad business in the port-city but also from the effects of the crisis in other places. Thus, when the house Duffez fell in Shanghai, it left behind bills owed to its suppliers, some of whom were clients of the *Banque de l'Indochine*'s Guangzhou branch, which was itself bearing the weight of such unpaid bills to a tune of FRF 2,205 million. Local customers of *Banque de l'Indochine* in Guangzhou entangled in the Duffez liquidation were Hogg & C° (FRF 1,010), Boyer-Mazet, Gérin-Drevard, Central Produce C°, Wong Man Sang, Guangzhou Silk Trading (FRF 179,000), Cheong Ke.[4]

Lastly, trading houses had to impair losses on credits unpaid by their customers in France itself: for instance, several companies importing silk failed in Lyon and could not repay their debts, which led *Banque de l'Indochine* to call for the pledge of their supplier in Guangzhou, but the repayment generally lagged for months. In parallel, local houses, either Chinese or foreign, felt the effects of the crisis because their own customers had difficulties and could no longer assume their debts. Both events fuelled the uncertainty faced by bankers, who struggled to recover their endangered assets. Generally speaking, business dwindled throughout the 1930s. As an internationalised port-city, Guangzhou was pulled into the depression, which ended up hurting the banks and *Banque de l'Indochine*: "Profound depression reigning on our market."[5]

One event epitomised these concerns: in 1932, when the comprador of one major client of the *Banque de l'Indochine*'s branch fled because its customers were choked by the fall in silk prices,[6] the branch was itself embroiled in the turmoil, with credit on several houses brought by the comprador—amounting to FRF 202,000, offset by bills of exchange for 90,000 to be cashed: Remittances on a few French houses were pending on E. Bord in Aubenas (Ardèche); on G. Deval-Cozon frères in Lyon, themselves drawing this paper on Cotte Chavent Armandy; and on Morin Murit & Douare in Lyon (for HK$ 87,567 or FRF 202,000). Remittances on a few French houses were pending on E. Bord in Aubenas (Ardèche); on G. Deval-Cozon frères in Lyon, themselves drawing this paper on Cotte Chavent Armandy; and on Morin Murit & Douare in Lyon (for HK$ 87,567 or FRF 202,000).[7] Later on, the banking place was hurt when the Guangzhou branch of the Hong Kong based Bank of Guangzhou defaulted, overloaded with bad credit, despite the fact that its director was at the time chairman of the Bankers' Guild here. Fortunately, the *Banque de l'Indochine*'s branch had maintained only minor relations with its fellow member.

2. The silk business stricken by the crisis

The basic activity of financing the silk trade faced trying times. The market dwindled from November 1929, silk prices fell in Guangzhou in the last quarter of the year and several spinning plants closed down.[8] Overall, silk prices began to drift downward at the turn of 1930, falling 54 per cent in the course of the year. This depreciated the value of the stocks piled up by merchant houses, depriving banks of healthy pledges on its advances: by the yearend, they had to demand a reduction or supplementary guarantees:

> Several clients in unhealthy situation due to the over-stocking in the past year, when raw silk was quoting in New York at 4.90 dollars per pound while today it stands at 2.25 after a drop of 54 per cent. The present economic situation precludes any hope of a quick and steep rise in the price of raw materials.[9]

The branch recorded a decline of 41 per cent in assets and resources between the first half of 1929 and that of 1930. It also estimated the reduction of potential turnover of silk exports at HK$ 15 million, especially as silk stocks in Japan had risen considerably, which weighed on international prices:

> The crisis was especially keenly felt because it involved a semi-luxury item, silk, which is the main export article of our region and which dominates our activity. It was aggravated by the significant fall of the currency, which almost completely stopped all imports, but which still could not stop the fall of silk prices in the local currency.[10]

The significant fall of the Hong Kong dollars in the second half of 1930 could have eased Chinese silk exports against the Japanese, but the devaluation of the Japanese currency revived the international price wars and choked Chinese silk millers: "The Japanese abandoning of the *gold standard* had the immediate effect of lowering silk prices in New York, and the prices offered, despite the slump in the Guangzhou market were, over the last quarter, almost always lower by at least 5 percent than those asked for by the mills."[11] Inventories grew in the port-city, devaluing loan collaterals and thus weakening the credit circuit:

The majority of silk houses made bad business deals in 1931, and it would seem that only one, *Madier-Ribet*, managed to make a profit. The best ones, or more precisely the most prudent ones, covered their general expenses, but they make up an extremely small minority. Most of the Chinese houses who also went into spinning, suffered heavy losses and will find it very hard to recover.[12]

By the end of 1931, there were about 11,000 bales stocked as collaterals (see Table 16.1).

As early as 1930, clients who were already struggling had to extend their deadline for the repayment of their debts (Servanin, Cassa, Deyr, Guangzhou Raw Silk, etc.). Guangzhou Raw Silk had to be closed suddenly, following a fraudulent failure; it left behind unpaid bills, including HK$ 6,700 for the *Banque de l'Indochine*'s branch, with a final loss for it of 6,725, whilst City Bank faced a debt of 150,000 against overall liabilities of 600,000.[13] The case of Servanin encapsulated such delays of payment; a former manager of Madier-Ribet in Guangzhou, he had set up his own daughter house, *Comptoir franco-chinois*: "Servanin's $30,000 overdraft (advances on bills in pounds and losses through one of its clients, *Comptoir franco-chinois*) had to be repaid in three instalments; the collateralled goods had to be sold to clear the debt."[14]

> The realization, completed today, of the Central Produce Hong Kong's [a company with Japanese capital) unpaid overdrafts on France (Duffez at Lyon, L. Bancilhon, at Aubenas, Cros & Pommier at Aserjac) amounted to a total loss of HK$ 22,000. You dealt with a Chinese whom you hardly knew and from whom you came to know of the end of a fortuitous opportunity. You are very fortunate to have dealt with an honest man and that your losses are not greater.[15]

Table 16.1 Silk trade in Guangzhou in the 1930s

	Raw silk exported (bales of 480 catties)	Exports of waste silk (bales of 100 catties)	Exports of waste silk (in pieuls)	Raw silk exported (in pieuls)
Second half of 1929	33,479	28,215	54,854	54,958
First half of 1930	26,946	21,700	32,114	48,384
Second half of 1930	33,535	10,434		
First half of 1931	25,657	25,996	46,056	41,650
Second half of 1931	20,399	15,654		
First half of 1932	12,504	3,105		
May 1931–April 1932	27,129		25,489	
Second half of 1932	21,094	12,134		
First half of 1933	14,404/13,319	26,394		
May 1932–April 1933	28,074		13,914	
Second half of 1933	15,760			
First half of 1934	20,108			
May 1933–April 1934	28,641		42,825	
Second half of 1934				
May 1934–December 1934	26,241		25,953	

Source: *Crédit agricole* archives, *Banque de l'Indochine* fund, letters, reports and outcomes, date for each half-year

This case caused a loss of HK\$ 24,947 for the branch. A few bills drawn on French clients by trading houses resulted in losses for them and the bank, and generally the goods pledged as collateral had to be sold to get back some cash. That was the case in 1930 with Hoggwith a loss of 48,060 and *Comptoir franco-chinois*[16] with a loss of 13,129—a total of around 50,000: "Realization of the goods backing the unpaid overdrafts on Phocius Doulos, at Istanbul, Ipsilantis at Corfu, Apostalou at Karlovassi, and Gabriel Estève at Barcelona."[17] "The overdrafts on J. de Soulange, F. Duffez, F. Geoffray, discounted by your agency were not honored and the provisions which had guaranteed it have been absorbed"[18] with an operating loss of HK\$ 22 000 and a FOREX loss of 12,000. The package of bad debts was estimated at HK\$ 1 million at the end of 1930, after provisions extended by HK\$ 120,000. The portfolio of clients had to be reduced, but a bunch of pending overdrafts weighed on the *Banque de l'Indochine*'s debts and blocked fresh credits. But like any banker during any crisis, it strove hard and patiently to pick up a few of them.

When the silk markets crashed in Lyon and in the United States in February–May 1931, drastic instructions went out: maximal reduction of risks and purchase of remittances for only first-class houses,[19] that is, Madier-Ribet, T.E. Griffith, and Reiss-Massey: "Reiss-Massey is generally considered, along with Madier-Ribet and T.E. Griffith, as one of the best silk houses here and as prudent workers."[20] Even a big client like Gérin-Drevard faced dire situations[21] in 1930 and 1931 following hazardous speculations on prices in June–July 1931. *Banque de l'Indochine* had to bear a loss[22] of HK\$ 16,000, even if it got back "good debts" (pending remittances, successfully implemented on "well-off houses" in Lyon (FRF 4.5 million), London (£5,400) and New York (letters of credit on banks).

Following big losses in 1930, the partnership between Michel Drevard and Guillaume Gérin was broken, and the repayment of its debt had to be extended over the medium term. For example, Gérin-Drevard's old debt to the Guangzhou branch was repaid between July 1933 and February 1934, while the Hong Kong debt still had a few credits to pick up.[23] Even though Gérin-Drevard's good assets were picked up by a new boss, Joseph Baud—associated with Chung Tang, the very guarantor of the branch's comprador—Gérin-Drevard could not assume its liabilities because of deepening difficulties in the last quarter of 1931. Gérin-Drevard endured a huge debt to City Bank and had to sell its silk inventory, still leaving a debt of HK\$ 125,000, supplemented by a debt of 191,000 to Chinese merchants, whilst the *Banque de l'Indochine* itself had to pare down HK\$ 16,500 on Guangzhou—the Hong Kong branch bearing its own bad debt over Gérin-Drevard (HK\$ 10,055) since 1921.[24] This client even had to be liquidated.

Such disappointments brought on an era of prudence which turned out to be relevant as the Lyon market was completely shaken in 1931 by the collapse of big houses, both in the banking (for example, *Veuve Guérin*, a correspondent of Gérin-Drevard) and trading sectors (May): "The bad condition of the Lyon market, characterized by the closure of houses which were till now considered safe, such as *Veuve Guérin* and May, did not make our own situation worse"[25] (see Table 16.2).

The situation turned tighter with the worsening depression and the fall in silk prices (from HK$ 900 to 500 per *"pieul"*[26] from mid-1931 to mid-1932). The repercussions of the French crisis began to be felt more strongly in the mid-1930s. Thus, when the silk house G. Deval failed in Lyon in May 1933, even though *Banque de l'Indochine* bore no risks—Deval being a client of HSBC—it was concerned because a few of its own customers carried risks with it, for instance Reiss-Massey: it had exported about 100 bales from Guangzhou for this house, which remained unsold/unpaid for by its agent in Lyon. It also had unpaid remittances of bills amounting to FRF 86,600 in Lyon.[27]

The spinning and export houses struggled to keep some doors open abroad and dredged their markets for orders: Lyon, the United States or even India (in 1931 and 1932). In the latter case, the quality was lower, which required from the bank resiliency and reactivity to adapt to the flows, changes and fees.

> America was rarely a purchaser, and that too for insignificant quantities at rates generally far lower than those demanded by the Guangzhou merchants. Demand from Lyon was equally meager and the rates gradually fell from 780 per pieul to 520 (for 15/16 quality), despite all the efforts by Chinese traders whose stocks were generally made on a base of 900 per pieul and who tried all means to stop this decline. The fall in prices would have been even steeper had not Bombay begun to buy relatively large amounts of 20/22 quality. This allowed the few open mills to weave 20/22 instead of 13/15 or 14/1.[28]

Table 16.2 Breakdown of the remittances of bills managed by the *Banque de l'Indochine*'s branch (million FRF)

	Second half of 1932	First half of 1933
Madier-Ribet ("Madier-Ribet, SCA and Baud used our branch for all of their business".)	10	4
Société commerciale asiatique	5	3.75
Joseph Baud	3.5	
South Trading Company	2.5	1 by third for each
Griffith	1	
Ferguson	1	
Kuang Tung Silk Agency		0.5
Total:	25	10.5
of which:		
To France	FRF 9 million	6.5
To the UK	£55,000	£37,000
To the United States	$465,000	USD 45,000

Source: *Crédit agricole* archives, *Banque de l'Indochine* fund, 323 DES 36/2, Letters and reports, 28 February 1933, July 1933

A landmark of this crisis was the fall in the amount of bills of exchange (in francs and pounds) negotiated by the *Banque de l'Indochine*'s branch as remittances: FRF 23 million in the first half of 1931, 38 million in the second half, 16 million in the first half of 1932, before a rebound to 25 million in the second half (on France: 9 million). The whole of 1932 was marked by drastic cuts in orders from Lyon: "The demand from Lyon was very weak in the first half [1932] and almost nil in the second half [resulting] in year-end stocks of 10,000 bales."[29] The trend continued in 1933 and 1934:

> It is evident that our market could not but feel the effects of the general slump. When they were felt, the demand from Lyon was sudden and seemed to reflect a brutal optimism with no future. In the last half, we bought FRF 3,643,150 of silk paper instead of 4,6m from Madier-Ribet; 1,079m against 1,062m from the *Société commerciale asiatique* (diverse products).[30]

Moreover, the management's caution further constricted the part played by *Banque de l'Indochine*[31] in the silk business in Guangzhou (see Table 16.3).

In a nutshell, the crisis pared the branch's silk business and its opportunities for returns, either because the value of a bale had collapsed or due to the fall in the quantities being shipped out. Silk loans came to a standstill in the mid-1930s due to the over-prudence of the branch and the comprador and because the main firm active in Guangzhou, Madier-Ribet, often used less expensive bankers:

> The advances on silk, all well settled till now, were greatly reduced due to the following causes: the general sluggishness of the silk market (especially in Guangzhou) and the consequent fall in prices; the natural prudence of our comprador, heightened by the uncertainty regarding his situation after the loss of his guarantors; the prudence shown by your agents due to the overall situation and your instructions.[32]

Table 16.3 Silk exports from Guangzhou in 1930–1935

Export campaign	Total amount (thousand HK£)	To Europe	To the United States	To Asia (India)
1930/1931	49,593	14,265	32,327	3,001
1932 bales	33,420	6,237	12,430	14,757
1931/32	27,029	5,149	9,268	12,612
1933 bales	33,325	8,292	7,218	17,815
1932/1933	28,074	4,718	11,380	11,976
1933/1934	28,641	6,779	6,885	14,977
1934/1935				

Source: *Crédit agricole* archives, *Banque de l'Indochine* fund, 323 DES 36/2, letters and reports

3. Growing competition from Japanese trade houses

Competition from Japan in the international market grew because the quality of its silk was better than that of the Guangdong peasants who lacked technical education,[33] causing many spinning mills to either close down (from 112 in 1929, with 70,000 female workers, to 54 in 1937) or suspend their activities, thus cutting into trade banking opportunities (see Table 16.4). The *Banque de l'Indochine*'s branch struggled to pick up a few operations in the silk trade, but it was pushed aside for several main areas of this trade, regarding Indian and Japanese connections, for example, whereas the European and American ones had severely dwindled.

If we estimate the silk export at Guangzhou to be about 32,000 bales in an average year, we can say that in 1934, at least half was turned towards India and around ten to twelve thousand bales, bought directly by a Chinese consortium in Hong Kong, towards Tonkin. We have then more than 20,000 bales gone. What remains is to divide some four thousand bales between the various other banks. Also, we have to think of the part bought by Japan, which was naturally controlled by Japanese banks … . Competition had become so cutthroat that fruitful counterparties were required to be able to buy [commercial paper]. While the *Deutsch Asiatische Bank* received HK$ 213,000 every month, paid for the arms sold by Germany, and the Chartered Bank and HBSC shared between them the Vickers–Armstrong

Table 16.4 Advances on silk by the *Banque de l'Indochine* branch in Guangzhou in 1927–1935

	Total amount (thousands HK$)	Of which: amount managed through the comprador	Bales pledged as collateral	Average value per bale (HK$)	
				Comprador's business	Direct business
1927	2,402	1,624	4,079	233	107
1928	2,702	1,356	3,952	180	150
1929	3,737	1,909	5,810	253	231
1930	788	626	1,828	127	25
1931	1,452	437	3,322	88	188
1932	1,136	171,5	2,872	51	188
1933	347	116	1,404	50	24
1 January 1934	118				
30 June 1934	24				
1934	0	0	0	24	44
1 half of 1935	6	6	75	2	

Source: *Crédit agricole* archives, *Banque de l'Indochine* fund, annex to the special note n°17, 3 September 1935

and Ansaldo [armaments] deals, we have seen a significant decline in our own arms deals … While France persists in its desire to get from Nanking [the Chinese central power] the authorization for its arms imports in South China, there is little hope for improvement in 1935.[34]

4. The import trade shattered

The result of the fall in exports from the port-city was a shock to the general trade of imports. The overall purchasing power of the area had dwindled seriously and the fall of the Hong Kong dollar in the second half of 1930 reinforced that trend. A string of revenue opportunities was thus removed, cutting into the potential returns of the *Banque de l'Indochine*'s branch. But the boycott of Japanese goods from 1931 loosened the grip of the crisis, as it favoured imports from Europe, for wool yarn and the like. The South Trading C° was an active importer and used *Banque de l'Indochine* to finance its inventories (sometimes in the go-down of the bank itself), pending sales to Chinese distributors and merchants: "Advance on goods: $40,000 to South China C° guaranteed by glass, wool yarn, cotton yarn of $80,000, stored in our go-down and in those of the Hong Kong & Kowloon Wharf & Go-down C° at Hong Kong."[35]

But these put off picking them up since the outlets had dried up: "Traders found themselves incapable of taking delivery of the goods they had ordered. Importers found themselves stuck with large stocks, especially wool and cotton yarn."[36] Niche areas were anyway preserved (steel products imported by South Trading C°, chemicals, with credits to *Deutsche Farben Handelsgesellschaft*, etc.) to supply the local workshops: the *Handelsgesellchaft* "imports of chemical products put all banks in competition."[37]

5. The intensification of the crisis

The mid-1930s were a sad period as the crisis deepened. During the first half of 1934, armament sales were halted, advances on goods were all repaid and local advances fell (about $20,000 by the end of the second half). The first half

Table 16.5 Amount of negotiations of commercial remittances by the Guangzhou *Banque de l'Indochine* branch in 1932–1936 ($, £ or FRF, equivalent in FRF millions)

Second half of 1932	25	
First half of 1933	6.5–10	
Second half of 1933	10	
First half of 1934	4.6–5.5	
Second half of 1934	4.5	
First half of 1935	14	Madier-Ribet (7), *Société commerciale asiatique* (4), Griffith (1.8)
Second half of 1935	4.5	
First half of 1936	7.5	Madier-Ribet (1,7), *Société commerciale asiatique* (4.5)
Second half of 1936	9	Madier-Ribet (3), *Société commerciale asiatique* (5)

Table 16.6 Financial position of the *Banque de l'Indochine*'s branch in Guangzhou at the end of June 1931 (HK$)

Allocation by the Paris office or the Saigon branch (USD 1,444,000)	5,815,000
Deposits and creditor accounts at *Banque de l'Indochine*	900,000 from various clients
	57,000 from Chase
	377,000 from Bank of China
Total employed capital	9,700,000
Provisions on debtor accounts	740,000
Endangered assets (immobilisations, losses being impaired, thawed bad debts)	1,650,000
Sound pending remittances	1,975,000
Bills of exchange ("*effects* ACT")	300,000
Cash USD accounts at the central agency of the head office or at French & American Banking Corporation	2,000,000
Various deposits in banks in $ or £	5,450,000

Source: *Crédit agricole* archives, *Banque de l'Indochine* fund, 323 DES 36/2, Letters and reports, First half of 1931, 8 December 1931

of 1935 was a fiasco, with "an almost total suspension of the silk exports to Europe and America, while those to Indochina were financed by the Chinese. Moreover, there were no new armament deals with the *Groupe Chine*"[38] (see Table 16.5).

A wave of companies' defaults inundated the Guangzhou branch. The ongoing crisis eroded trade, repayments and trust, especially as the customers of banks active in Guangdong were exposed first to a liquidity crunch, then of solvency. The bankers tried to maintain their "relational banking" path to support their faithful clients, but they had finally to face losses. Classically, the account of provisions for impending credits had to be garnished, and a second stage was the amortisation of impaired debts, half after half, from the second one of 1930, when the first account reached HK$ 120,000, and the first amortised losses HK$ 53,000. A huge loss (HK$ 451,000) had to be amortised in three instalments[39] from 1931. The important Chinese client Yong suddenly fled, leaving a bad debt of FRF 25,000 (paper discounted by *Banque de l'Indochine*, on the way to the HBSC branch in Lyon), to be provisioned,[40] but it was mainly a debtor of Chartered Bank.

The South China Trading C°, a partner of the *Banque de l'Indochine*'s branch, was among the first major players to collapse, in October 1935. It could not repay the FOREX contracts which it had concluded with several banks: Chartered Bank (with an outstanding debt of HK$ 32,044), Yokohama Specie Bank (7,954), Sinese Bank (5,400) and Bank of East Asia (2,700). The eventual loss to *Banque de l'Indochine* (HK$ 5,252) resulted from "differences in FOREX contracts", supplemented by another pending debt to the Shanghai branch (SH$ 6,247). Provisions on debt accounts climbed to HK$ 740,000 in July 1931 against endangered assets of 1,650,000—to be compared with the branch's total capital of HK$ 9,700,000.[41]

The branch had to live through a sombre period as Guangzhou's commercial situation reached a critical state in 1934, even though the Kwangtung Bank supported a few houses. The overall opportunities for local credit through the comprador vanished.

Notes

1 *Crédit agricole* archives, *Banque de l'Indochine* fund, 323 DES 36/2, Letters and reports, second half of 1931, June 1931.
2 DES 13/4, Reports from the Guangzhou branch to the Paris headquarters, 25 January 1932 and 3 June 1932.
3 Tomoko Shiroyama, *China During the Great Depression: Market, State, and the World Economy, 1929–1937*, Cambridge, MA, Harvard University Asia Center, "Harvard East Asian monographs, 294", 2008.
4 *Crédit agricole* archives, *Banque de l'Indochine* fund, DES 13/4, Reports from the Guangzhou branch to the Paris headquarters, 14 January 1930.
5 *Ibidem*, 21 December 1933.
6 *Ibidem*, 5 May 1932.
7 *Ibidem*.
8 *Ibidem*, 18 April 1930.
9 *Crédit agricole* archives, *Banque de l'Indochine* fund, 323 DES 36/2, Letters and reports, 14 December 1930.
10 *Ibidem*, 14 December 1930.
11 *Ibidem*, second half of 1931, 6 February 1932.
12 *Ibidem*.
13 *Crédit agricole* archives, *Banque de l'Indochine* fund, DES 13/4, Reports from the Guangzhou branch to the Paris headquarters, 15 November 1930.
14 *Crédit agricole* archives, *Banque de l'Indochine* fund, 323 DES 36/2, Letters and reports, 9 September and 14 December 1930.
15 323 DES 36/2, Letters and reports, 14 December 1930.
16 *Ibidem*.
17 DES 13/4, Reports from the Guangzhou branch to the Paris headquarters, 15 November 1930.
18 *Ibidem*, 14 December 1930.
19 *Crédit agricole* archives, *Banque de l'Indochine* fund, 323 DES 36/2, Letters and reports, first half of 1931, 3 August 1931.
20 *Ibidem*.
21 *Crédit agricole* archives, *Banque de l'Indochine* fund, DES 13/4, Reports from the Guangzhou branch to the Paris headquarters, 26 January 1931.
22 323 DES 36/2, Letters and reports, second half of 1932, 12 January 1932.
23 DES 13/4, Reports from the Guangzhou branch to the Paris headquarters, 21 February 1934.
24 *Ibidem*, 5 October 1931.
25 *Crédit agricole* archives, *Banque de l'Indochine* fund, 323 DES 36/2, Letters and reports, second half of 1931, 6 February 1932.
26 A Chinese *pieul* weighed about 60 kg.
27 *Crédit agricole* archives, *Banque de l'Indochine* fund, DES 13/4, Reports from the Guangzhou branch to the Paris headquarters, 30 May 1933.
28 *Crédit agricole* archives, *Banque de l'Indochine* fund, 323 DES 36/2, Letters and reports, first half of 1932, 1 July 1932.
29 *Ibidem*, second half of 1932, 28 February 1933.
30 *Ibidem*, first half of 1933.

31 *Ibidem*, first half of 1934.
32 *Ibidem*.
33 *Ibidem*, second half of 1934.
34 *Ibidem*.
35 *Ibidem*, first half of 1932, 1 July 1932.
36 *Ibidem*.
37 *Ibidem*, second half of 1932, 28 February 1933.
38 *Ibidem*, first half of 1935, 22 November 1935.
39 The bad debtor was Cassa; a first instalment of 77,000 was amortised in summer 1931. *Ibidem*, 24 August 1931. Two other big debts, *Comptoirs franco-chinois* and Hogg, reached HK$ 53,000.
40 *Crédit agricole* archives, *Banque de l'Indochine* fund, 23 April and 24 October 1934; special notes "Failure of Yong & C", 3 and 24 January 1934.
41 *Crédit agricole* archives, *Banque de l'Indochine* fund, first half of 1931, 3 August 1931.

17 Positive reactions to the crisis in Guangzhou

The differentiation between banks has always relied on a better management of risks across crises and tensions. The *Banque de l'Indochine*'s branch had therefore to prove that it was able to resist the formidable challenges it faced.

1. Competition and risk management

Competition (for the connections between the Hong Kong and Guangzhou markets) was harsh in Guangzhou, as each branch struggled to draw a bigger part of the business fuelled by wholesale trading, and the houses did not miss stirring up such a competition. There were no "cartels", though bankers tried to respect some thresholds for their tariffs and interest rates.

Challenging its historical proximity to the leading firm of Madier-Ribet, *Banque de l'Indochine* established lower ceilings to its risks as early as the second half of 1930: it announced the purchase of the majority of its remittances of bills of exchange on the Lyon market because the management at Paris had guessed that good clients were fragile, like the Lyon bank's *Veuve Guérin & Fils*:

> Despite our desire to retain the maximum of remittances from Madier-Ribet, who are certainly the best silk merchants and the biggest exporters in Lyon, we have managed to buy only a small amount because about 30 percent of their paper is drawn D/P [documents against payment] on *Veuve Guérin & Fils*. We lost out on the bigger part of this paper due to the limit on our purchases imposed by you. Subsequently, we lost it completely when you forbade us to take D/A paper on Lyon. The other banks, who all take D/A [documents against acceptance] on *Veuve Guérin* only accept it on condition that they also get a more or less equivalent amount of DF/P paper on other good houses, so much so that about 60 percent of the Madiet-Ribet paper goes perforce to the competition.[1]

Moreover, *Banque de l'Indochine* could only compete for about two-fifths of the remittances offered by Madier-Ribet to the bankers as the other part was considered too risky. "Laffond, Madier-Ribet's representative in Guangzhou, had transferred almost the whole of his business to Chartered since about a year",[2] though Madier-Ribet itself remained faithful to the *Banque de l'Indochine* for its own parallel activities. Later, in 1934, the branch admitted once more that it had kept *Société commerciale asiatique* as its client, "but our conditions (on FOREX) had rarely been tight enough against those of [our] competitors to draw Madier-Ribet."[3]

> The only regrettable absence among our sellers of remittances in francs is Madier-Ribet who on its own accounted for FRF 839,371 in the first half of 1934 and 2,306,899 in the second half of 1933. We attribute it to the excellent relations maintained by its director with the Chartered Bank and especially to the significant diminution in this company's turnover.[4]

Risk management was the order of the day, especially as the depression played havoc with the already fragile balance sheets of several clients, bearing bad debts or faced by the extension of deadlines for repayments. But all in all, *Banque de l'Indochine* had joined the leaders on the market, National City Bank[5] and Yokohama Specie Bank: "We have here only two serious competitors, the National City Bank and the Yokohama Specie Bank: the former especially is redoubtable and is always the better buyer" of commercial paper to be recovered overseas.[6]

When the latter was boycotted by Chinese nationalist communities in 1931, the National City Bank and *Banque de l'Indochine* emerged as co-leaders in that niche, which the British banks managed only as an outpost of Hong Kong:

> The Japanese banks were severely handicapped by the boycott and did almost nothing over the past few months. The English banks are not serious competitors as they generally content themselves to quoting [credit with change] the price sent in the morning by their Hong Kong headquarters. The National City Bank is our most active competitor, but the major losses it had to bear in the course of 1931 seem to have made it more prudent.[7]

Japanese bankers worked with the British houses, reluctant to attend to *Banque de l'Indochine* and preferring Chartered. The branch succeeded in tackling the entire operations of a few big firms in 1931 and 1932 (Madier-Ribet, Baud, etc.) and to enhance its competitive edge: "You have successfully faced the competition of the other banks. You have retained for yourselves a large part of the negotiations on bank credit, and have handled all the affairs of Madier-Ribet, *Société commerciale asiatique* and South China Trading C°"[8] (see Table 17.1).

The branch's appetite for risk seems to reflect the central philosophy of *Banque de l'Indochine*: rather cautious, gauging the risks attentively—especially after its experience when it had faced, in the first half of the 1920s, intense competition from another French bank in Asia, *Banque industrielle de Chine*. But the latter finally collapsed, cementing the *Banque de l'Indochine*'s culture of risk throughout its operations in Asia. As soon as the crisis burst upon

Table 17.1 Breakdown of the 16 million in bills of exchange (francs and pounds) negotiated by the *Banque de l'Indochine*'s Guangzhou branch during the first half of 1932 (million FRF)

Madiet–Ribet	9
South China C°	2.5
Société commerciale asiatique	1.5
J. Baud	1
Others clients	2

Source: *Crédit agricole* archives, *Banque de l'Indochine* fund, 323 DES 36/2, Letters and reports, first half of 1932, 27 October 1932

them, it put the brakes on a whole range of operations. First of all, it froze its FOREX activities in the second half of 1930, making it reject fresh opportunities and end several contracts concluded in the second half of 1929 which ended in losses: "We have let pass business affairs for which our competitors were giving better rates by basing themselves on market trends which were often very uncertain. The second half of 1929 saw some profits on a large number of operations which, subsequently, turned contentious and led to big losses."[9]

Banque de l'Indochine also initiated an agreement among Guangzhou bankers to tighten the conditions of financing exports to Lyon: The bankers undertook:

> not to negotiate silk remittances on Europe except on D/P with a margin of guarantee of 25 per cent or against a letter of credit confirmed by a bank … This measure did not seem to meet any serious opposition from the buyers in Lyon as several of our clients [in Guangzhou] had already been informed of the opening of credit by their correspondents in Lyon.[10]

The amount of the advances on goods was drastically trimmed to avoid disappointments, from HK\$ 205,000 to 44,000 between 1st July 1933 and 15 February 1934: "Such deflation was rapid and proves by itself that our advances were sound",[11] argued the branch manager against his Paris direction: "We are of the opinion that, in the event you totally interdict all advances on goods, it would be preferable to close down the Guangzhou branch as soon as the arms deals are exhausted."[12]

2. Still a profitable branch?

Sailing the Chinese waters during the crisis could have meant running into reefs and squalls. But the branch was closely supervised from Shanghai and Paris (with weekly letters as mini-reports and instructions by return mail), and its managers displayed enough judgement to face the dangers. In the mid-1930s, merchant banking opportunities dried up, and the basis of the branch became fragile, forcing it to rely more on FOREX and armament operations:

> Our branch's profits come mainly from the remaining hedge contracts on the American currency and the income from arms deals. Both these sources are equally temporary and unhealthy. We believe that the time will come when, after having worked hard at reducing the unhealthy operations on our market, we will need to search, prudently but continuously, the commercial activities which could establish the Guangzhou branch on a healthy basis, if not completely devoid of all risk.[13]

Happily, one mainstream activity of the Guangzhou branch fuelled its return: arbitrages on FOREX, either directly or through brokers picking up operations in the port-city. For example, they brought in HK$ 132,312 as profit in the first half of 1936, allowing it to pay off the interests charged by its Paris headquarters for the permanent line of credit granted for its business and, moreover, to transfer some further cash.[14] Throughout the decade, the managers of the branch succeeded in reaping profits, except for the second half of 1934 due to the failure of FOREX operations in pounds (see Tables 17.2 and 17.3).

3. *Banque de l'Indochine* still more as a bank rooted in Guangzhou

The head of the *Banque de l'Indochine*'s branch had to prove his skills in fording a decade rife with risks and direct military and political threats—a decade which was worse even than the 1920s, when Guangzhou endured civil war and street battles, as the Sino-Japanese war spilt over into Guangdong. A succession of managers had to drastically check credit demands and closely follow their maturation and repayment.

All in all, after three decades of existence, the *Banque de l'Indochine*'s branch had acquired some stature on the Guangzhou marketplace. The competition from HBSC and Chartered Bank was less intense here than in Hong Kong, where they had a stranglehold. The branch managers had navigated the recessions, political and military tensions and client insolvency with relative success, which opened more doors among the community of foreign and Chinese businessmen. The port-city's own growth had gathered momentum, even though it remained a "niche" as compared to Shanghai and Hong Kong.

The *Banque de l'Indochine*'s stature was proven in August 1938 when the negotiations between bankers and the authorities regarding the control of FOREX and the management of foreign currencies on the "international" side of the money centre recognized the branch's French manager as "the representative of the Shameen banks"[15]. Whereas the big trading house of Madier-Ribet was the agent of *Messageries maritimes*, the shipping line joining France and China, the *Banque de l'Indochine*'s branch was chosen as the agent of *Air France* in February 1939.

Table 17.2 Results from operations by the *Banque de l'Indochine* branch in Guangzhou in the 1930s

In HK$	Average amount of use of funds	Gross returns	Net returns (after paying charges on resources: Paris and Saigon allocations, deposits, etc.)	Amortisation of impaired bad assets	Net profit (after deduction of operating costs)	Ratio of net profit (against resources)
Second half of 1929	15,690	600	390	131	218	2.778%
First half of 1930	9,434	327	206	120	37	0.777%
Second half of 1930				7	109	
First half of 1931				/	80	
Second half of 1931				60	122	3.458%
First half of 1932				/	169	
Second half of 1932				/	81	
First half of 1933			186	/	186	
Second half of 1933			100	/	100	
First half of 1934			91	25	91	
Second half of 1934					−11.4	
First half of 1935					34.5	
Second half of 1935					42	
First half of 1936					FRF 221 / 407	
Second half of 1936					FRF 1,964 / 482	
First half of 1937					FRF 3,206 / 401	
Second half of 1937					FRF 2,750 / 348	
First half of 1938					FRF 3,044 / 295	
Second half of 1938					FRF 3,267 / 190	
First half of 1939					FRF 2,137 / 371 / FRF 213	

Source: *Crédit agricole* archives, *Banque de l'Indochine* fund, letters, reports and outcomes, date for each half-year

Table 17.3 Data about specialised operations by the *Banque de l'Indochine* branch in Guangzhou in the 1930s

In thousands HK$	Purchase of bills of exchange (FRF) to be remitted and discounted in Europe	Purchase of bills of exchange (HK$) to be remitted and discounted (in Europe or elsewhere)	Purchase of bills of exchange (USD) to be remitted to the United States and discounted	Purchase of bills of exchange (HK$) to be remitted to the United States and discounted	Total amount of completed operations	Ratio of returns on operations	Revenues on interests and commissions	Ratio of net profit (against resources)
Second half of 1929	37,138	3,115	3,649	7,891	24,817	1.374	40	2.778%
First half of 1930	32,037	3,346	1,442	4,077	19,764	0.919	21	0.777%
Second half of 1930	14,343	1,795	975	671	11,818	1.262	14	
First half of 1931	11,999	1,947	739	518	10,334	1.471	0,6	
Second half of 1931	5,697	886	4,025	4,296	28,243	0.5258	31	
First half of 1932	8,929	1,415	2,565	633	16,823	1.0288	48	
Second half of 1932	8,737	1,478	673	1,983	6,438	1.8319	17	
First half of 1933	0,312			0,528	9,031			
Second half of 1933	0,288			0,162	7,395			
First half of 1934	0,169			0,068	7,459			

Source: *Crédit agricole* archives, *Banque de l'Indochine* fund, letters, reports and outcomes, date for each half-year

4. Success despite the crisis

Our concluding section will consider the evolution and the results of the *Banque de l'Indochine*'s branch in Guangzhou within the classic SWOT matrix (strengths, weaknesses, opportunities, threats).

A. Facing the demand for change

We have now to look at the extent of the changes in the *Banque de l'Indochine*'s activities in Guangzhou and to gauge its ability to adapt itself to the new conditions. Compared to the 1920s, the 1930s can be perceived as offering at the same time fewer and more *threats.* The political and military events were less dramatic than the revolutions, the civil war and banditry which blocked business in the mid-1920s. On the whole, public and military order was maintained by authoritative warlords, while active war had shifted northwards—till of course the Japanese offensive in 1937–1938. These reduced *threats* offered other *opportunities*: *Banque de l'Indochine* committed itself to co-organising the sale of arms to the local authorities and supplying them with guarantees and an efficient means of transferring payments.

Opportunities were also to be found in the growth of credit and transfers for the Wolfram business, with exports to the United States. But the silk trade remained its main activity and major source of income. One of the *strengths* and a key factor in the *Banque de l'Indochine*'s prosperity was the finance of trade for somewhat strong clients thanks to the connections between Guangzhou and Indochina, beyond the classical outlets in Lyon and New York. Another *strength* was the branch's embeddedness in the Chinese community, mainly through its compradors but also directly through major Chinese companies.

A final *strong position* was its market banking, with *Banque de l'Indochine* extending its skills in FOREX all over south-eastern China, the United States and Europe. In a few semesters, FOREX commissions and spreads provided it with ample revenues. These *strengths* came together to consolidate the *Banque de l'Indochine*'s position on the Guangzhou market and set it up as one of the leaders among foreign banks, along with City Bank, Chartered Bank and, in 1930–1931, Yokohama Specie Bank.

B. The crisis as a "stress test" for the Banque de l'Indochine *branch*

Though the war with Japan led to the closure of the connections to Japanese markets and firms, bankers were more troubled by the growing economic crisis. The depression was rife with *threats* because of the dire situation of the American and the European markets. Apart from the errors committed by a few firms active in Guangzhou which stretched their risks too far, the branch was subjected to the failures or difficulties of the clients of its clients, mainly in Lyon.

Its *strengths* were to be found in its several means of action. First, the reliability, honesty and resistance of its successive compradors and the quality of its successive seasoned managers were some of its key tools for success. "Good management" prevailed: the managers respected cardinal standards for risk management, masterminded with lucidity their appetite for risks, struck the right balance between supporting their faithful and big clients and avoiding extending overstretched loans to them. They showed banking wisdom in assessing *threats* and *opportunities*, for instance in covering bad debts and provisions, in cutting into ceilings for advances, in grappling with the FOREX operations—in contrast to some manager in the 1920s who had failed on several FOREX contracts.

The branch was also well connected with its relays in Hong Kong and Shanghai and received fresh operations, cash and also information. Last, a strict control from the General Inspection (in Asia, from Saigon) and from the Paris headquarters put pressure on the managers, who had frequently to justify their monthly choices. Such a range of *strengths* explains why Paris did not have to rescue the branch or prop up its balance sheet despite the intensity of the economic depression and the silk crisis.

5. The *Banque de l'Indochine*'s branch and Guangzhou port-city life

Our last point will grapple with the issue of the connection between an off-shoot of a French bank in far-off Asia and the very life of a growing port-city in Guangdong. The choice of settling in that "niche" was legitimised, first, by the development of Guangzhou as a regional "hub" with growing links to its hinterland by steamboats, railways (extended northwards) and roads. Merchants converged on the city, either on the petty market or for "big business" (silk, staples, sundry, etc.), which bolstered the warehouses (among them the *Banque de l'Indochine*'s go-downs), the harbour and the banks.

Second, connections with Hong Kong were strengthened via the railway to Kowloon, by the telephone line and by intense tramping feeding the international maritime centre. *Opportunities* for business were largely available. The import aspect faced difficulties due to the boycott of Japanese goods and because the purchasing power of the province was curtailed by the silk crisis. But it gained momentum thanks to the import of arms and the management of their payments.

Guangzhou's mission as a harbour for Chinese goods bound for overseas markets resisted the depression, and the port-city became more open to Pacific exchanges and Panama (towards New York) and still more connected with Suez and Europe, Marseille, Lyon and, afterwards, London. The immaterial exchanges of the port-city with the banking centres (New York, London, Lyon and Paris, Saigon, etc.) extended their stretch and volume. No more a "nimble economy", the "niche market" took profit from the emergence of Guangdong and of Chinese manufacturing and merchant houses to assert itself as an important stakeholder in the wave of modernisation, monetisation and "bankisation" of south-western China, serving as leverage to the valuation of *Banque de l'Indochine*'s strengths.

Although Guangzhou opened its doors to direct commerce with Tonkin for silk deliveries, fostering the insertion of the French Asian empire into the Chinese system in parallel with the Euro-Asian one, it also allowed *Banque de l'Indochine* to fuel its expansion outside Indochina and to complement the Hong Kong niche with a market and a banking centre which were quite different from its sisters. Guangzhou gradually extended its autonomy, favouring the two banking leaders there, City Bank and *Banque de l'Indochine*, who found it easier to compete there against their British rivals, HSBC and Chartered Bank, than in Hong Kong because they had seized the whole array of *opportunities* to broaden their *strengths*. For *Banque de l'Indochine* itself, it succeeded in enriching and consolidating its portfolio of skills, because it secured the stability, the solvency and the competitiveness of the branch, which resisted the local crisis and the general depression and confirmed that the "niche strategy", based on a deep embeddedness in the Guangzhou port-city, had been relevant.

We have last to talk about the usefulness of such a branch in a business outpost in south-east China. Obviously, its very role as a banking hub to support the silk trade toward Lyon and the development of its loans to big French firms taking part in the trade between Lyon (and London) and Guangdong justified its presence there. Thus more value was added to the French business community which now had an option instead of having to rely only on British banks, even if they were also stakeholders in the trade between Guangzhou and Lyon. The French banking activity there broadened directly or indirectly the French community of international interests in the trading business, maritime lines (*Messageries maritimes*) and even *Air France*.

Beyond pure business, the branch was inserted into the community of knowledge which consolidated the collection of economic intelligence by French businessmen, either in Asia (the connection Guangzhou–Hong Kong–Shanghai and the connection Guangzhou–Saigon) or abroad (Lyon/London/New York, etc.). In that sense, the branch also contributed to some form of French "economic patriotism". In fact, it also bolstered some French exports, mainly armaments, because the imports of sundry and general trade were often managed by British firms in Guangzhou, through their links with the Hong Kong harbour, and even a few small German ones.

Notes

1 *Crédit agricole* archives, *Banque de l'Indochine* fund, 323 DES 36/2, Letters and reports, second half of 1930, June 1931.
2 *Crédit agricole* archives, *Banque de l'Indochine* fund, DES 13/4, Reports from the Guangzhou branch to the Paris headquarters, 16 November 1933.
3 323 DES 36/2, Letters and reports, first half of 1934.
4 *Ibidem*, second half of 1934.
5 See Ayumu Sugawara, "American international banking in China before World War II: Beijing, Tianjin and Guangdong branches of international banking corporation", *Tōhoku Management & Accounting Research Group*, 2007, n°78, pp. 1–19. Peter Starr, *Citibank: A Century in Asia*, Singapore, Didier Millet & Citicorp, 2002.

6 *Crédit agricole* archives, *Banque de l'Indochine* fund, 323 DES 36/2, Letters and reports, 14 December 1930.
7 *Ibidem,* second half of 1931, 6 February 1932.
8 *Ibidem,* 8 April 1932.
9 *Ibidem,* Second half of 1930, June 1931.
10 *Ibidem,* second half of 1931, 6 February 1932.
11 *Ibidem,* second half of 1933.
12 *Ibidem.*
13 *Ibidem.*
14 *Banque de l'Indochine* archives, DES 13/4, Reports from the Guangzhou branch to the Paris headquarters, 1936.
15 *Ibidem,* 8 August 1938.

18 Classic business at stake in Guangzhou in the 1930s

Throughout the depression, "business as usual" went on, despite some disappointments and risks, but also thanks to small changes in market trends. Despite concerns about business, Guangzhou remained an attractive place for collecting deposits on bank accounts, for fuelling the day-to-day commodities market.

1. General considerations about Guangzhou exchanges

The diversification of the commerce in the Guangzhou marketplace remained low because silk drove its exchanges, and imports lagged far behind exports (see Tables 18.1–18.3).

As a regional port-city, Guangzhou depended heavily on the Hong Kong hub as an international, maritime, commercial and financial centre. And, whatever its colonial status, it acted as some kind of a "feeder" to the true capital of south-east China. This explains why all goods transhipped in Hong Kong were taken as Hong Kong exchanges, even if the contracts and orders had been generated in Guangdong (see Table 18.4).

2. The evolution of American outlets

Despite the worsening depression in the United States, trading houses active in Guangzhou tried to boost trans-Pacific trade via classic remittances borne by confirmed letters of credit on New York banks, for example: "Acceptation by the American company on irrevocable discounts on credit drawn by Gérin-Drevard on several clearing houses of New York."[1] In 1931–1932, they seized the opportunities offered by the boycott against Japanese goods and the depreciation of the British pound to push Chinese commodities and goods overseas. The South Trading Company, of American origin, was quoted as an active promoter of Guangdong products, not only for wolfram but also for general trade[2] (see Table 18.5).

Conversely, the South Trading Company and its boss Laing were granted credit to finance US exports to China, its steel and glass dealers and sundry goods merchants. But these loans had to be borne for longer periods than scheduled as the Chinese importers delayed recovering their goods, allowing them instead to pile up in Hong Kong before transferring them to Guangdong and selling them.

Table 18.1 Hints about Guangzhou trade in 1929–1931

In thousand taels	1929	1930	1930 (taking into account the fall of silver by 30%)	1931	1932
Imports from foreign countries	41,895	51,509	36,055		
Imports from China	56,086	75,630	52,941		
Exports from Guangzhou	85,607	69,070	48,349		

Table 18.2 Guangzhou trade: exports in 1930–1932 (in thousand *Haikwan taels*)

	1930	1931	1932
Total		62,000	38,000
Silk	45,089	37,365	14,240
Vegetable products	4,613	6,265	6,980
Animal products and hides	822	2,292	1,240
Textiles	611	1,362	
Mineral ores	2,759	2,498	1,060
Among which wolfram	2,358	2,058	

Source: *Crédit agricole* archives, *Banque de l'Indochine* fund, letters, reports and outcomes, 1930, 1931, 1932

All in all, this US firm[3] received HK $153,000 from *Banque de l'Indochine* in January 1933. The total amount touched $400,000 in the spring of 1933 (through remittances to be delivered and cashed in New York, with the risk borne till the completion of the operations), balanced by $85,000 in credit accounts.[4]

But crisis crept in: silk exports to the United States dwindled in the second half of 1930, and the slump was pervasive[5] in 1932–1933: "The American demand for silk fell by more than half compared to the previous half (4,735 raw silk bales instead of the 10,990 in the preceding half)". The *Banque de l'Indochine*'s remittances from Guangzhou to New York[6] fell from USD 1,063,000 to 155,000 between the first and the second halves of 1931. The big US house T.E. Griffith seemed on the verge of collapse in December 1931 with a total of FRF 344,000 in debts to *Banque de l'Indochine* on exchange contracts, on one side, and USD 78,210 of negotiable remittances on letters of credit, drawn on "high-rated"[7] American banks (Guaranty Trust, Chatham Phenix National Bank, Heidelbach Ickelheimer, Goldman Sachs, Bank of America, National Trust & Savings Association, Pacific National Bank, etc.). Happily, it managed to stay afloat and resumed its activities but working mainly with Chartered Bank:

> America bought very little on our market—only 4,735 bales from 1st January to 30 June [1933], about USD 650,000. The house of Madier-Ribet has practically stopped dealing with America, except through intermediaries,

Table 18.3 Guangzhou trade: Imports in 1930–1932 (in thousand *Haikwan taels*)

	1930	1931	1932
Total		56,000	47,000
Foodstuff			
Sugar	7,902	5,823	2,050
Oleaginous	5,644	4,604	2,670
Cereals, fruits, grains	4,192	5,930	8,510
Fish and sea products	2,260	2,284	2,000
Canned food	762	835	800
Commodities			
Chemicals	3,049	2,860	3,230
Coal	2,668	2,388	3,300
Metal and minerals	2,474	4,389	4,540
Stones, cement, glass, china		1,400	1,830
Equipment goods			
Piece goods	5,490	4,216/5,300	3,930
Cars	250	295	1,020
Machinery	710	270	2,930
Electric equipment	680	1,150	
Arms and ammunition	1,174	1,061	
Textiles			
Raw and spun cotton	1,067	1,130	
Wool and wool cloth	1,517	1,729	1,820
Miscellaneous			
Tobacco	1,070	807	630
Matches	361	293	
Paper and books	1,874	2,642	2,860

Source: *Crédit agricole* archives, *Banque de l'Indochine* fund, letters, reports and outcomes, 1930, 1931, 1932

Table 18.4 International trade of the Guangzhou port-city in 1930–1931 (in thousand *Haikwan taels*)

	Imports		Exports	
	1930	1931	1930	1931
Total	51,162	56,212	60,367	61,811
From or to Hong Kong	47,032	51,867	59,622	60,571
From or to Japan (with Formosa)	2,406	1,830	25,7	61,3
From or to the Dutch Indies	654	616	13	3,6
From or to Indochina	*651*	*1,329*	*75*	*66,3*
From or to France	*/*	*5,8*	*/*	*12*
From or to the United States	/	36,2	/	110,5
From or to Macao	297,6	376,1	631,3	893,9
From or to the British Indies	119,8	132,3	/	4,5
From or to UK	/	6,8	/	52,8
From or to Singapore	/	3	/	33,8

Source: *Crédit agricole* archives, *Banque de l'Indochine* fund, reports, letters and outcome, second half of 1931

Table 18.5 Main sellers of remittances in USD in 1930–1934 (companies trading from Guangzhou to the United States and transferring their risk to the Banque de l'Indochine)

	First half of 1930	Second half of 1930	First half of 1931	Second half of 1931	First half of 1932	Second half of 1932	First half of 1933	Second half of 1933	First half of 1934	Second half of 1934
Wing Tai Loong	679,595	68,942	49,350	64,326			23,632			
Guangzhou Silk Trading C°	217,810									
Madier-Ribet	103,415	3,940		524,372	116,080	216,207	14,774			
Gérin-Drevard	86,249	57,125								
J. Baud (successor to Gérin-Drevard)				37,121	9,309	107,412				
South China Trading C°	82,175	21,791	69,085		22,000	52,000				
Hogg	73,880									
General Silk Importing C°	56,181									
Guangzhou Raw Silk C°	35,472	3,940								
Wong Man Sang	34,671	326		18,819						
Guangzhou Mercantile & C°	24,522	20,683		11,324						
Mitsui Bussan Kaisha	20,338									
T.E. Griffith	13,033			107,263		18,046				
Société commerciale asiatique	8,801	27,763	5,106	10,953	1,334	18,547	5,440	39,150	14,760	16,800
J. Cassa	3,500									
N. Hashim	2,027	6,050								
South China Trading C°				36						
Wo Hing Silk Corp.				126,509		18,685				

(Continued)

Table 18.5 (Continued)

	First half of 1930	Second half of 1930	First half of 1931	Second half of 1931	First half of 1932	Second half of 1932	First half of 1933	Second half of 1933	First half of 1934	Second half of 1934
Ping Shick				92,432		11,536				
Reiss–Masset				15,793	124	5,440				
U. Spalinger				9,849						
Deacon				4,925	3,152	206				
Sang Wo Tai				3,394	350	1,863	1,750			
Guangzhou Overseas Trading C°					3,188					
China Overseas International Trading								6,000		
Dodwell						2,258				
H. Ferguson						2,500				
Jebsen						1,715				
Johnson						2,079				
H. Yong						2,077		5,176		
Total amount	1,441,669	210,261	125,541	1,063,090	155,617	460,581	45,596	50,326	14,760	16,800

Source: *Crédit agricole* archives, *Banque de l'Indochine* fund, letters, reports and outcomes, 1930 and 1931

L. Muguet, for USD 14,774. The sole house of Griffith, which confides the major part of its business to the Chartered Bank, has worked, encouraged as it was by the new branch of Gerli Inc. New York, which it succeeded in giving to J. Baud.[8]

In February 1936, John Ferguson & C° failed with pending credits of FRF 61,515 (cotton bales sold in Lyon) and USD 9,856 (waste silk sold to the American Spinning Company of Providence-Rhode Island).[9]

Faced by such concerns, *Banque de l'Indochine* hardened its stance in 1932 and imposed a package of services (transfer of remittances) and credit to increase its charges on the support of silk exports to the United States and to compensate for the risks: "As the drawings debtor on acceptor were not accepted by any bank and as all remittances on America were covered by credit lines, we have been able to renegotiate all of Madier-Ribet remittances" in New York (USD 524,000)[10]—even if the client did not anticipate the devaluation of the dollar. Bankers in Guangzhou and Hong Kong agreed to halt competition in favour of tough credit and remittance conditions for US operations:

> We thought that it was time to have our colleagues in the other Shameen banks agree to negotiate silk remittances on America only against a letter of credit given by a bank, and not solely against a letter of credit addressed only to the beneficiary (as for us, we only agree to do it this way with absolutely sure clients!). An identical agreement was reached between the Hong Kong banks, and its measures are now rigorously applied.[11]

Banque de l'Indochine focused its US connections on solid operations with reliable banks (Brown Brothers, Manufacturers Trust, etc.).

3. The evolution of the silk trade

Advances on silk bales remained important for the Guangzhou warehouses, and *Banque de l'Indochine* became more and more involved in this business, tackling bigger amounts of credit. The French house of Madier-Ribet, for long its client in the interwar period, was a leading company at that time.[12] It was active in Japan and Lyon with, for instance, FRF 2,300,000 million in negotiated bills of exchange and 2.9 million in pending orders, all on "very good houses of Lyon."[13] It also benefited from credit on goods: "The ceiling of our advance was reduced from HK\$ 1,015,000 to 965,000 on 7 January 1932, with a guarantee stabilised at 2,262 bales for HK\$ 1,452,000."[14]

This transnational firm was the main supplier of remittances to the *Banque de l'Indochine* branch, for half of such purchases in 1930 and an amount of about FRF 15 million. *Banque de l'Indochine* bought these bills of exchange in cash and later transferred them to Europe for recovery, earning fees and FOREX opportunities.[15] But its operations in FRF predominated and gave it a strong leadership (see Table 18.6).

Table 18.6 Main sellers of remittances in FRF (companies trading from Guangzhou to Lyon/Paris and transferring their risk to the *Banque de l'Indochine*) in 1930–1934

In thousand FRF	First half of 1930	First half of 1931	Second half of 1931	First half of 1932	First half of 1932	First half of 1933	Second half of 1933	First half of 1934	Second half of 1934
Madier-Ribet	15,178	8,534	3,964	5,947	4,639	3,643	2,307	839	
Gérin-Drevard	3,893	839	81						
J. Baud (successor to Gérin-Drevard)					107	108			
Reiss-Masset	2,942	1,766	607	923	886	125			
Guangzhou Mercantile C°	2,205			362				300	
T.E. Griffith	2,089	554	486	427	710	346	162	188	52
Wong Man Sang	1,916		168	218					
Varenne	960								
Wo Hing Silk Corporation	570	40					67		
Kwang Tung Silk					180	474	690	30	
Hogg	783				81				
Guangzhou Raw Silk C°	641								
Wing Tai Loong	219	203							
J. Cassa	155								
Société commerciale asiatique	76	64	310	413	1,062	1,079	1,199	1,065	765
Guangzhou Silk Trading C°	65				30				
China Overseas						9			
Guangzhou Overseas									
Jardine-Matheson	48								
South China Trading C°			78			61.5			
U. Spalinger				300	163	131	232	142	
Ping-Shick				247					
J. Ferguson				62	817	342	186		
Johnson				31	49				
J. Manners					12				
Total amount	32,037	11,999	5,700	8,929	8,737	6,319	4,942	2,564	817

Source: *Crédit agricole* archives, *Banque de l'Indochine* fund, letters and reports, 1930, 1931, 1932 (with divergent figures between the two sources), 1933, and 1934.

Another house, Gérin-Drevard, was also among the important customers, with bills on the United States being traded in London: "Purchases at Gérin-Drevard, who sell us bills on London, drawn on letters of credit against silk dispatches bound for America."[16] This supplemented current advances on silks in Guangzhou. It led the bunch of good customers, with a large credit on goods (HK$ 275,000 against silk bales valued at 325,000). The advance was reduced on 29 May 1930 to HK$ 204,000 against a pledge[17] of 210,000—before the firm was swallowed by the crisis at the end of 1930.

Although the connection with Lyon (and Paris) remained the key axis for the activities of the branch in merchant banking and despite the density of the connection with New York, *Banque de l'Indochine* also used London as a final destination for a bunch of remittances, even though the Guangzhou outfit lagged far behind the Hong Kong and Shanghai strongholds for the business with the British houses and banks. Anyway, it purchased remittances to its clients and recovered them in the City, picking up a few fees and commissions along the way (see Table 18.7).

Meanwhile a chain of credit was woven upstream: Madier-Ribet was itself giving loans to local Chinese houses and gathering momentum since the mid-1920s, thanks to the development of some modern capitalism in China. They brought their silk bales to Guangzhou and exported them, repaying the loans afterwards. Whereas the *Banque de l'Indochine*'s usual work involved bills of exchange and the management of remittances (Chinese merchants were also clients), it focused on advances on goods for them, no doubt to avoid taking excessive risks, despite the guarantee of the comprador for several operations (see Table 18.8).

This classic path reached a broader dimension at the start of the 1930s thanks to the growth of this type of credit to Chinese traders (see Table 18.9):

> These silk bales do not belong to Madier-Ribet. They were pledged to them by Chinese merchants to whom they give advances. Most often, for an advance, Chinese silk merchants prefer going to another silk merchant rather than a bank, most of which [banks], and especially we, refuse to deliver silk against a letter of guarantee at the time of dispatch. The European merchants who agree to these advances have their reasons: first, the difference between the rate of interest they charge their borrower and that taken by their bankers and second, the fact that they can often buy at higher rates the silks that have been pledged to them. These advantages [for trading houses] do not worry us. We have made sure to retain a 30 per cent, even 35 per cent margin for *Madier-Ribet*.[18]

In any case, the sizes of loans to local houses remained smaller than its operations with Madier-Ribet. But, for advances on goods and generally with the guarantee of the comprador, Chinese houses had become important clients of the branch (see Table 18.10).

Table 18.7 Main sellers of remittances in British pounds (companies trading from Guangzhou to the City and transferring their risk to the *Banque de l'Indochine*) in 1930–1934

	First half of 1930	Second half of 1930	First half of 1931	Second half of 1931	First half of 1932	Second half of 1932	First half of 1933	Second half of 1933	First half of 1934	Second half of 1934
Société commerciale asiatique	59,242	53,193	22,833	23,405	12,243	38,588	31,448	43,500	23,100	50,400
Gérin–Drevard	29,757	1,969	5,611							
J. Cassa	22,693									
C.H. Rolfe	13,550	605								
South China Trading C°	12,904	32,996	31,278	30,170	21,025	14,313	2,975	14,520	15	6,500
General Silk Importing C°	10,000									
Carlowitz &	5,125	984								
Guangzhou Silk Trading C°	5,000									
Jebsen	3,954					415				
T.E. Griffith	3,866									
U. Spalinger	3,431			0,487						
Madier-Ribet	3,106			6,084						
General Produce Exporting C°	2,189	425								
Melchers	1,827									
Guangzhou Overseas Trading C°	1,685					8	65			
Hogg	1,675									
N. Hasim	1,236	199								
R. Johnson	443									
Reuter Brockelmann	77		1,000							
Reiss-Masset				3,679						
Deacon				1,705						
China Overseas Trading C°					244	1,452	705			
U. Spalinger					160					
Guangzhou Hides								65		
H.Yong						352	2,034	1,155		
Lavadia							129			
J. Manners										4,500
Guangzhou United Manufacturers										52
Shainin									166	
Total amount	181,270	90,371	60,722	65,530	37,673	55,128	37,356	59,240	23,281	61,452

Table 18.8 Advances on goods by the *Banque de l'Indochine* branch in Guangzhou on 17 July 1930

	Amount (HK$)	Bales	Value of the pledged bales (with the margin for security varying in keeping with the quality of the client)
Hing Cheong Wo	200,000	500	260,000
Gérin-Drevard	138,000	300	156,000
Wing Tai Loong	40,000	100	52,000
Wing Wo	31,500	801	41,600
Hip Hing Loong	29,060	80	41,600
Comptoir franco-chinois	28,086	50	26,000
Tin Po Lun	18,000	45	23,400
Wo Shing Hing	11,500	29	15,080
Yue Hing Cheong	11,500	30	15,600
Hogg	8,275	15	9,600
Wong Man Sang	6,000	15	7,800

Source: *Crédit agricole* archives, *Banque de l'Indochine* fund, 323 DES 36/2, Letters and reports, December 1930

Table 18.9 Advances on goods by the *Banque de l'Indochine*'s branch (HK$): situation at the end of 1931 (note of 8 April 1932)

Madier-Ribet	1,015,000
Kwong Kun San	145,000 (against 370 bales)
Hau Tack Cheong	76,000 (220 bales)
Wo King	40,000 (100 bales)

Table 18.10 Advances granted through the intermediary of the comprador in 1932–1933 (HK$)

	At the end of 1932	At the end of 1933
Kwong Kun San	48,847	48,000
Wo King	43,759	33,000
Kwan Sing	16,282	
Kwong King		24,000
Ming Loong		21,000
Cheong Fat		15,000
Leung Cheuk Kee	6,360	6,250
Wo Lee	5,088	6,000
Total amount	48,847	153,250

Source: *Crédit agricole* archives, *Banque de l'Indochine* fund, 323 DES 36/2, Letters and reports, second half of 1932, 1933

The *Banque de l'Indochine*'s branch seized this window of opportunity to develop its knowledge in that field, with resolution but caution: "As we are relatively new to the silk market, we have consulted several silk merchants and also the director of Chartered, whose Guangzhou branch derives the lion's share of its revenue from silk loans and presently guarantees 3,000 bales."[19] The latter was expressed by the hardening of banking conditions, decided by the Shameen association of bankers in January 1932:

> The association of Shameen bankers has decided to accept on discount the remittances drawn on Europe, and conditional to the dispatch of silk, but only debtor to payer with a minimum guarantee margin of 25 per cent, against a bank letter of credit, as it is done for America. It is possible that the buyers of silk in Lyon will find it repugnant to accept these conditions, but, in the current state of the Lyon market, it is but natural for us to reduce as much as possible any risk to our clients.[20]

Such operations involved applying the drastic rules of guarantee used for US trade to the French ones. The bank also urged trading houses to get credit from their customers in Lyon to finance their purchases in China, instead of relying only on their bankers. *Banque de l'Indochine* continued to impose such restrictive measures even when its competitors welcomed a few disgruntled customers, like Massey-Reiss, who asked for HSBC's help for its French trade:[21] "The house of Reiss-Massey, to whom we refused some days back to fix change rates for the dispatch of silk, has just received from the house of Pila [in Lyon] a credit line of 200,000 francs, confirmed by HSBC". But it remained faithful to *Banque de l'Indochine* for its American business: "Reiss-Massey discount bills on Brown Brothers Harriman [New York], with FOREX contract; we have accepted the letters from this house."[22]

In fact, merchant traders used several banks to consolidate their resources or facilitate their exchanges and to put pressure on the fees and interests: "We had to fight against a competition which was always ready to pursue a policy of attrition regarding business deals which seem to us very interesting because of the reduced risks. Of our loyal clients, the house of Madiet-Ribet and the *Société commerciale asiatique* have entrusted to us the totality of their business."[23] It even happened that *Banque de l'Indochine* managed remittances on Lyon which ended at the HSBC branch there: "Presently, we have only three remittances from Reiss-Massey totalling 108,321 francs against thirty raw silk bales on four months at sight from debtor to payer negotiated on 13 January 1933, following authorization from HBSC Lyon."[24] Even Madier-Ribet, one of *Banque de l'Indochine*'s best customers, applied pressure by stirring up competition among its bankers.

Because the Paris management imposed a monthly ceiling of HK$ 500,000 as credit to that firm, it lost many major opportunities to British banks for remittances to France:

> These arrangements [a revolving credit of 1.5 million over three months, dated 19 November 1932] allow us to retain only a part of the affairs

of a house which should normally be this agency's main client. The house exports 5 to 600 bales per month which, at current rates, comes to between 1.250 and 1.5 million. We can conclude that 4 to 500,000 francs in remittances have slipped through our fingers and have gone to English banks, which would have handled them without the slightest difficulty.[25]

First, the branch manager succeeded in granting further credit by lodging bales in its go-down (or warehouse) as pledges against credit on warranted goods; second, it convinced the Paris management to allay its concerns regarding a relevant division of risks and to authorize an increase in the ceiling.

Financing the silk trade (either raw silk or waste silk scraps) thus remained a key banking activity, with exports to the United States, France and Zurich (Switzerland).[26] The branch was used to purchasing remittances in French francs on the Guangzhou and Hong Kong markets (against selling US dollars there).[27] Because of the crisis, a few bales destined for the United States had to be reoriented towards Lyon, and the houses connected to that city had themselves to extend the maturity of the loans to customers because the sales in France had longer deadlines. The French connection remained strong for a while anyway, with good clients like Madier-Ribet leading the bunch with an overall advance of HK$ 1,015,000 in December 1931, down to 680,000 in July 1932. The branch was also close to Gérin-Drevard, which became its first client for the transfer of bills to France in the second half of 1930. The branch also contracted with the US firm of T.E. Griffith for its European operations: it purchased its bills of exchange in Guangzhou to be paid in France, for instance on Ch. Rudolph and others in Lyon.[28]

4. A new silk connection: Indochina involved

After the breakthrough in silk exports to the United States in the 1920s, the 1930s saw new doors opening between Guangdong and French Indochina. While the colony exported huge amounts of rice to Hong Kong and South China, with a strong commitment of *Banque de l'Indochine* on both sides,[29] a trade axis emerged, with exports of raw silk and spun yarn to Tonkin (lacking an actual production of silkworms), with more than 6,000 bales in the first half of 1934, resold to petty Annamite craftsmen to be woven and dyed. But, paradoxically, although it was a key bank in Indochina and had strong connections in both Hong Kong and Guangzhou with the Chinese merchant community, it was short-circuited for the financing of such exchanges: a pool of Chinese businessmen assumed that function within its local networks and, probably thanks to Chinese banks, independent of any foreign bank. Another connection was set up by French houses, but they did not use credit as they were satisfied with the mere transmission of bills: "Silk dispatches in Indochina are made on short-term draws without opening of credit."[30]

Only through the overall effects of such exchanges could *Banque de l'Indochine* find some opportunities of development on both sides of the South China Sea and the Tonkin Gulf, as they couldn't but exert an effect on the prosperity of the clients of the bank and the overall growth of the silk business:

> The silk exports from Guangzhou to Tonkin will be large enough in 1934 to ensure a sizeable counterparty to the export of rice from Indochina to China. About 5,000 bales, the principal in firm orders 28/32, will come out in April–May—April being the last month of the 1933–34 campaign and May the first of the 1934/35 campaign. It seems that the number of bales going out since the beginning of the year towards Indochina is over 6,000. If we take an average value of HK$ 300 per bale, we arrive at a respectable total of 1,800,000, which is, at about 170, IC$ 1,058,000 ... A Chinese syndicate with large enough means will be formed in Hong Kong to finance a certain number of affairs, including silk export to Indochina. Purchases are made at Guangzhou by unknown intermediaries without any intervention from foreign banks. Both the silk and rice businesses slipped away from the *Banque de l'Indochine*, which took only a small part and had no control on Sino-Indochinese commerce.[31]

A landmark for this trend was the diversification of the French house active in Guangdong, Madier-Ribet, a key client of *Banque de l'Indochine*, which commenced exporting silk to Indochina, using correspondents there (Delignon in Annam, Denis in Tonkin). Whereas the majority of the silk was consumed locally, a small part was outsourced there for manufacturing before re-export to North China.

The rapid take-off of this trade (accounting for a quarter of all Guangzhou silk exports in the second half of 1934) opened doors for the intervention of banks, but it was only limited to operations of cash and bill transfers. The *Banque de l'Indochine*'s branch stole a march on its competitors HSBC and Chartered Bank,[32] either among the foreign traders, or among the four Chinese houses involved (Tchi Cheong, Yao Cheong, Kinh Ky, Ho Kwong Ky). Such exports to Indochina helped balance the shortage of exports to Europe (see Table 18.11):

> In April–May, several major purchases were made by Chinese houses for Indochina, and almost 5,000 bales were expedited towards Haiphong. All these purchases were firm orders, mainly 28/32 [good quality]. The demand from Indochina completely absorbed the first two harvests [of

Table 18.11 Silk dispatches from Guangdong during the export campaign of 1935/36 (HK$)

	To Europe	To Indochina
Madier-Ribet	3,509,000	51,000
Griffith	1,308,000	165,000

Source: *Crédit agricole* archives, *Banque de l'Indochine* fund, DES 13/4, Reports from the Guangzhou branch to the Paris headquarters, 7 August 1934

the 1933/34 campaign], estimated at 2,500 and 3,000 bales respectively. Around forty spinning mills [in the Guangdong] worked for these contracts, spinning all the firm orders.[33]

Because of the overall crisis, the connections with Indochina fostered interesting contracts for the *Banque de l'Indochine* branch in 1937, with large exports from Guangzhou by Madier-Ribet (to the houses of Delignon and *Denis Frères*, among the biggest French houses in Indochina) or by Griffith (to SFATE and Ogliastro),[34] perhaps because the purchasing power of the local bourgeoisie was maintained by its insertion into the French imperial system.

5. FOREX operations as a key activity

The Guangzhou branch still broadened its classic FOREX activities, along with what we would call today "proprietary trading" in order to value its assets in available treasury. It could use its returns in US dollars in reports for 1936 to compensate somewhat for the fluctuations in trade finance. The branch achieved several FOREX contracts with the US Lazard investment bank, exchanging its dollars against French francs, with nine operations in July 1936 (USD 900,000 against FRF 1.6 million), four in August (for USD 400,000). It also contracted with Chase in September (USD 250,000 against FRF four million), and, in October, with the French American & Banking Corporation (USD 200,000/FRF 4.3 million; then USD 100,000/FRF 2.2 million), Bankers Trust (USD 100,000/FRF 2.2 million; then USD 100,000/FRF 2.1 million). Like the other the *Banque de l'Indochine* outfits in China, the returns on FOREX business bolstered the overall financial stability of the Guangzhou branch.[35]

Along a different and less original path, the branch tackled commonplace FOREX arbitrage operations linked with its import–export financing, in the name of its customers, like Gérin-Drevard) or to accompany their operations in international trade, as it had to purchase currencies to cover its counterparties for exports: "Our market works only in one direction [towards export], and it is impossible to find here the counterparty of the paper purchased from exporters; therefore it is indispensable to pass via the Hong Kong dollar to get coverage."[36] But *Banque de l'Indochine* also practiced day-to-day small "speculations" on the spreads between the currencies available, either the international ones or the "Chinese" ones (HK$, Mexican $, etc.).

Such an activity was one basis of the art of its manager because he had to self-finance the general costs of his outfit, and the gains on FOREX were of great use for that: every half-year report thus insisted on them—even if the completion of the operations itself was mutualised with the Hong Kong branch since 1931. For instance, the year 1930 ended with an overall profit for the Guangzhou branch because of good returns on arbitrages: "You have been able to profit by the weakness of the metal-currency which persisted over the first half of 1930 and to obtain interesting results."[37] But the depreciation of the Hong Kong dollar in 1930 favoured the collection of Mexican dollars. The variation of values had negative effects (uncertainty) but offered also positive opportunities thanks to rapid arbitrages or penalties fixed on suspended contracts by clients reneging on their business: "Fortunately, your arbitrage benefits were influenced by lucrative arms deals and by exceptionally advantageous cancellations and penalizations of ailing FOREX contracts, made possible by the fall of the American currency."[38] The instability of prices also fuelled report operations: "We had to take into account the reports made either in Paris or Hong Kong (Pounds Sterling against USD) to profit from a high interest rate in London, that is Hong Kong so as to get the funds for financing our discount of remitted bills on America and our advances on silk or silver pieces."[39]

The clients of the branch bought or sold paper in US dollars along with their expectations—which the manager and his deputy (the sole direct actors for these FOREX operations) called "the speculative operations of our customers: Krebs, Pinguet, Ott, Tavadia, Otto, Lasalla, South China Trading, Madier-Ribet, Chow Mow Yip, Wo Hing, Fung Kok Lam, etc., all pledged, either by securities deposited at the branch, or by HK$ funds blocked as deposits",[40] with for instance, three contracts still pending in June 1933. Such commonplace FOREX trading came to the forefront in 1934 because it fostered the operations of the branch, deprived of classical commissions and fees on commercial exchanges,[41] but the volatility of markets[42] in the second half of 1934 led to a loss on the pound trading (HK$ 14,620) versus profits on the other currencies (30,890), which confirmed the importance of FOREX trading in that time of commercial crisis: fees, commissions and interests brought a net profit of only HK$ 26,629, against 16,270 for arbitrage (see Tables 8.12 and 8.13).

6. A diversified niche

Despite the difficulties imposed by military and political issues and the depression, the *Banque de l'Indochine*'s branch continued to put its resources to work, along with its skills, its capital and its opportunities.

A. The dependence on Paris allocations

Like the others branches overseas, the Guangzhou outlet had to raise profits from the capital allocated by the headquarters, that is, a three-partamount of FRF 30 million, £30,000 and USD 300,000. And like every bank, it had to balance its appetite for risks and profit with its need to respect the conditions offered to its customers. The Paris headquarters could not but entail the allocations to their branch because *Banque de l'Indochine* itself suffered from the depression. For instance, they put a halt to forward operations (*reports*) in US dollars "because of the tightening of the money markets."[43]

Due to this steady financial support, the Parisian management had to rely on trustworthy and competent managers in the Guangzhou branch. It would seem that its trust was rewarded with success. No one had to be recalled or dismissed, and the succession (Barrau, in 1930, Jean Juge, Jean R. Baylin; then Claude Fournier, till October 1935, the comptroller of the Shanghai branch)

Table 18.12 Forex operations completed by the *Banque de l'Indochine* branch in Guangzhou in 1930–1934

	Second half of 1930	First half of 1931	Second half of 1931	First half of 1933	Second half of 1933	First half of 1934
Forex operations (thousand HK$)						
In francs	3,099	2,274	1,866	3,231	2,004	1,999
In British pounds	5,403	3,525	2,332	2,599	2,303	1,300
In USD	2,147	1,002	6,250	10,173	3,201	1,633
Total	10,648	6,801	10,449	16,003	7,507	4,932
Returns on Forex (expressed through gold operations)	225,2	133	254	222	123	166
Net return on these gold operations	2.1176%	1.951%	2.4347%	1.3902	1.6444	3.365
Reports operations (thousand HK$)						
In Paris in £	/	$1,1667 £103	$6,074 £340			
In Paris in USD	312,5	$1,667 G$500	$6,074 G$1,500			
In Hong Kong in £	278	$199 £10	$1,716 £90			
In Hong Kong in USD (using the Hong Kong branch of the *Banque de l'Indochine*)	579	/	$3,930 G$1,003			

Source: *Crédit agricole* archives, *Banque de l'Indochine* fund, letters, reports and outcomes, 1931

Table 18.13 Results from arbitrage operations by the *Banque de l'Indochine*'s Guangzhou branch in the 1930s

In thousands HK$	Returns on arbitrage (in gold currencies)	Returns on arbitrage (in silver currencies)	Ratio of profit	Total amount of arbitrage operations
Second half of 1929	341	9		
First half of 1930	182	4		
Second half of 1930	149	2		
First half of 1931	152	0.6		
Second half of 1931	208	2		
First half of 1932	173	1		
Second half of 1932	128	0.4	1.8319%	6,438
First half of 1933	222	0.7	1.3902%	16,003
Second half of 1933	123	0.2	1.6444%	7,507
First half of 1934	166	0.9		
Second half of 1934	19	0.4		

Source: *Crédit agricole* archives, *Banque de l'Indochine* fund, letters, reports and outcomes, date for each half-year

followed a peaceful path, and Baylin, only an interim manager in Guangzhou, was promoted as the head of the Haiphong branch (14 October 1935).

B. The intermediation of the comprador

Another asset of the branch was classically its comprador. Its workforce was complemented by a kind of sub-bank managed by the latter. Mak Fook Cho (since 1927) had twelve employees in 1930: a deputy, two cashiers, two shroffs, an employee acting on the Chinese market, two boys, two coolies, a cook and a guard.[44] His expenses were covered by his HK$ 650 monthly allocation (850 after August 1930), but his return came from brokerage fees and commissions earned (HK$ 5,000 in 1929). In 1938, his team remained substantial with a shroff, a cashier (his nephew) and his deputy, a secretary (his step-brother), a second secretary, a go-down shroff, four coolies and a cook.

> A majority of his staff is freely lodged in a house neighbouring the go-down and the offices. He pays his shroffs directly, using the HK$ 750 allocated to him by the branch, whereas the other banks (HSBC, Chartered Bank, National City) pay their shroffs themselves ... His expenses amounted to $561, leaving 189 for the comprador himself.[45]

The comprador provided his guarantee to the advances to Chinese houses upstream. "Despite the difficult situation for the silk merchants, we have increased [at the bank's interest] these advances, either by reducing them, or by increasing our guarantees. All our Chinese advances are well covered."[46] The amount reached FRF 448,500 in May 1930, pledged by goods valued at 564,000 (eleven pending for HK$ 167,000 in July 1932), and Mak Fook Cho himself was pledged by Chinese tycoons (Chung Tang, then Lo Yuk Tong and Poon Hiu Cho, from September 1932). In 1931, he guaranteed advances on silk to Chinese merchants:"Advances of HK$ 257,000 to various Chinese merchants, guaranteed by 620 silk bales valued at 387,000 with the backing of our compra-dor."[47] Advances on silver were also granted:"Advances on money matters, HK$ 468,000, agreed by us for Chinese banks with the backing of our comprador and guaranteed by new Guangzhou silver pieces."[48]

But the branch had to put the brakes on the fragile Chinese prospects because its comprador lost two of his pledges, the first at the end of 1933 and the second in June 1934 when Chinese businessmen curtailed their risks due to the deepening general crisis. He could not therefore bring fresh opportuni-ties of business, but he kept his functions as an intermediary with the market, as an advisor, because he would check the proposals of Chinese business, without being involved in them directly:"Our comprador is a serious man, wise, very prudent, and has given us complete satisfaction. His risks have been reduced considerably. His role in the future will be much more as a verifying cashier than of a comprador guaranteeing himself long-term operations."[49]

We would prefer retaining Mak Foo Cho who has proved to be both honest and prudent, even with a small guarantee and as Chinese cashier in chief. Experience has shown that it is preferable to have an honesty tried by a long period of deflation with few real guarantees than to experiment with real guarantees which will not fare any better than the others through these adventurous times.[50]

He was replaced by Fung Cho Wan in March 1935 because his embedded-ness in the business community seemed far broader, with two successive func-tions as comprador from 1919, first in the Asia Banking Corporation (till 1924) and then at the P&O Banking Corporation in Shameen till its closure. He had been an employee of the comprador of the *Banque de l'Indochine*'s Hong Kong branch, then the first shroff at the HSBC branch in Guangzhou, before joining the Asia Banking Corporation. His guarantees consisted of several buildings owned in Hong Kong–Kowloon and four HSBC shares.[51] The comprador's busi-ness was guaranteed by a HK$ 60,000 mortgage on an estate in Kowloon valued at HK$ 62,000,500 shares of the Hong Kong Land Investment C° (43,000) and a cash deposit (15,000).[52] *Banque de l'Indochine* could thus rely clearly on his portfolio of skills and knowledge:"Fung Cho Wan is still comprador. He seems to me to be honest and prudent in business; he has his contacts and informs me regularly. He is less active in FOREX than the brokers Otto and Tavadis."[53]

C. Diversification at stake

All in all, the activities of the *Banque de l'Indochine* branch reflected the diver-sification and the growth of the functions of Guangzhou as an international

Table 18.14 Use of resources by the *Banque de l'Indochine*'s branch in Guangzhou in 1929–1934 (thousand HK$)

	Second half of 1929	First half of 1930	Second half of 1930	First half of 1931	Second half of 1931	First half of 1932	Second half of 1932	First half of 1933	Second half of 1933	First half of 1934	Second half of 1934
In gold assets											
Pending remittances in FRF	/	2,968	1,442	1,077	722	412	413,5	312	288	169	74
Pending remittances in £	12,147	1,142	597	500	571	262,5	218	302	242	142	132
Pending remittances in USD	/	2,563	2,086	691	1,679,5	1,223	899	528	162	68	23
Assets by the correspondents in the United States or elsewhere (USD)	108	138	57	627,5	56	55	132,5	135,5	142	70	9
Deposits (in gold value)	791			1,583	2,867	2,137	3,740	2,445			
Credit account in Paris (with a special account since 1933)				429	/	331	434	2,852	3,940	3,949	2,277
Special credit accounts at FABC New York								?	842	876	702
Total amount in gold-valued assets (the remnant of uses being in silver-valued assets in China)	13,242	6,902	4,291	5,015	6,214	4,651	6,038	5,068	4,453	5,412	5,417
Total amount of assets	15,690	9,434	6,766	6,959	8,909	8,129	9,198	9,031	7,394	7,459	7,265
Raw returns	7.654%	6.924%	6.748%	5.248%							
Advances on goods (flows)	2,890	1,494	1,700								
Their balance at the end of the half-year	1,175	539	133								
Advances on securities in HK$: balance at the end of the half-year	14	31	66								
Advances on securities in FRF: balance at the end of the half-year	175	246	76								

Sources: *Crédit agricole* archives, *Banque de l'Indochine* fund, half-yearly reports

port-city, evolving from a regional to an international trading hub. Remittances of bills of exchange and their discount remained the core of the branch's life. But it also activated a few local credits (in silver assets) and multiplied advances on goods as well as on securities. When the crisis intensified, the assets of the branch not only declined in volume, but the manager extended their liquidity, through deposits, to gain nimble returns in spite of the usual discount operations. And the "local" uses (in silver-valued assets) gained momentum because the international business was sometimes trimmed by the slump in transoceanic activities. Liquidity became the motto in 1933 and afterwards, with cash available either locally, in the Hong Kong branch or in Paris, while deposits in New York grew in size and drew more interest than in Hong Kong (see Table 18.14).

Notes

1 *Crédit agricole* archives, *Banque de l'Indochine* fund, DES 13/4, Reports from the Guangzhou branch to the Paris headquarters, 26 January 1931.
2 *Ibidem*, 5 January 1932.
3 *Ibidem*, 18 January 1933.
4 *Ibidem*, 30 May 1933.
5 *Crédit agricole* archives, *Banque de l'Indochine* fund, 323 DES 36/2, Letters and reports, first half of 1933.
6 *Ibidem*, 27 October 1932.
7 *Crédit agricole* archives, *Banque de l'Indochine* fund, DES 13/4, Reports from the Guangzhou branch to the Paris headquarters, 27 January 1932.
8 *Crédit agricole* archives, *Banque de l'Indochine* fund, 323 DES 36/2, Letters and reports, first half of 1933.
9 13/4, Reports from the Guangzhou branch to the Paris headquarters, 5 February 1936.
10 323 DES 36/2, Letters and reports, second half of 1931, 6 February 1932.
11 *Ibidem*, second half of 1931, 6 February 1932.
12 See Tse-Sio Tcheng (Zheng Zixiu), *Les relations de Lyon avec Chine*, Paris, L. Rodstein, 1937. Lillian M. Li, *China's Silk Trade: Traditional Industry in the Modern World, 1842–1937*, Cambridge, MA, Council on East Asian Studies, Harvard University, Series "Harvard East Asian Monographs, 97, xv", 1981.
13 *Crédit agricole* archives, *Banque de l'Indochine* fund, DES 13/4, Reports from the Guangzhou branch to the Paris headquarters, 13 July 1930.
14 *Ibidem*, 15 January 1932.
15 *Crédit agricole* archives, *Banque de l'Indochine* fund, 323 DES 36/2, Letters and reports, 14 December 1930.
16 *Ibidem*.
17 DES 13/4, Reports from the Guangzhou branch to the Paris headquarters, 18 April 1930.
18 *Ibidem*, 15 January 1932.
19 *Ibidem*.
20 *Ibidem*, 27 January 1932.
21 *Ibidem*.
22 *Ibidem*, 7 April 1932.
23 *Crédit agricole* archives, *Banque de l'Indochine* fund, 323 DES 36/2, Letters and reports, first half of 1933.
24 *Crédit agricole* archives, *Banque de l'Indochine* fund, DES 13/4, Reports from the Guangzhou branch to the Paris headquarters, 3 May 1933. See Claude Fivel-Démorel, "The Hong Kong & Shanghai bank in Lyon, 1881–1954. Busy, but too discreet", in Frank

King (ed.), *Eastern Banking*, London, Athlone, 1983, pp. 467–516. Louis Gueneau, *Lyon et le commerce de la soie*, Lyon, L. Bascou, 1932.

25 *Crédit agricole* archives, *Banque de l'Indochine* fund, DES 13/4, Reports from the Guangzhou branch to the Paris headquarters, 26 September 1935.

26 "Authorisation for a discount on FRF 500,000 from Griffith on Rudolph à Zurich", *Ibidem*, 7 June 1932.

27 *Ibidem*, 5 January 1933.

28 *Ibidem*, 7 March 1939.

29 See Hubert Bonin, "French banking in Hong Kong (1860s–1930s): Challenging British banks?", in H. Bonin (ed.), *French Banking and Entrepreneurialism in China and Hong Kong, from the 1850s to 1980s*, Abingdon, Routledge, "Banking, Money & International Finance", 2019, pp. 85–106.

30 *Crédit agricole* archives, *Banque de l'Indochine* fund, DES 13/4, Reports from the Guangzhou branch to the Paris headquarters, 3 May 1937.

31 *Ibidem*, 7 August 1934.

32 *Ibidem*, 3 May 1937.

33 *Crédit agricole* archives, *Banque de l'Indochine* fund, 323 DES 36/2, Letters and reports, first half of 1934.

34 *Ibidem*, first half of 1937, 18 October 1937.

35 *Crédit agricole* archives, *Banque de l'Indochine* fund, DES 13/4, Reports from the Guangzhou branch to the Paris headquarters, 4 August 1936.

36 *Crédit agricole* archives, *Banque de l'Indochine* fund, 323 DES 36/2, Letters and reports, 14 December 1930.

37 *Ibidem.*

38 *Ibidem*, first half of 1933, July 1933.

39 *Ibidem*, second half of 1931, February 1931.

40 *Ibidem*, first half of 1933.

41 *Ibidem.*

42 See Ming Chang, "Historical dimensions of the Hong Kong–Guangdong financial and monetary links: Three cases in politico-economic interactive dynamics, 1912–1935", paper for the HKMRJ banking and monetary history conference, April 2007.

43 *Crédit agricole* archives, *Banque de l'Indochine* fund, DES 13/4, Reports from the Guangzhou branch to the Paris headquarters, 21 December 1933.

44 *Ibidem*, 7 August 1930.

45 *Ibidem*, 24 February 1938.

46 *Ibidem*, 18 July 1930.

47 *Crédit agricole* archives, *Banque de l'Indochine* fund, 323 DES 36/2, Letters and reports, second half of 1931, 6 February 1932.

48 *Ibidem.*

49 *Crédit agricole* archives, *Banque de l'Indochine* fund, DES 13/4, Reports from the Guangzhou branch to the Paris headquarters, 18 May 1934.

50 *Ibidem*, first half of 1934.

51 *Crédit agricole* archives, *Banque de l'Indochine* fund, DES 13/4, Reports from the Guangzhou branch to the Paris headquarters, 28 March 1935.

52 *Ibidem*, first half of 1931, 8 December 1931.

53 *Banque de l'Indochine* archives, DES 13/4, Reports from the Guangzhou branch to the Paris headquarters, 24 February 1938.

19 Tianjin through issues of geopolitics (mid-1930s–mid-1940s)

Having told the history of the banking and business activities in the French settlement of Tianjin and in its overall zone of economic influence in the northeast area of China from the start of the twentieth century to the turn of the 1930s, the time has come to scrutinise the (dramatic) end of the story. Bankers had to cross times of hardships in Tianjin because the whole area was involved in geopolitical struggles. Little by little, that marketplace, which had been perceived as a far-fetched and second-level commercial objective, only to prop up emerging relationships with the business and financial activities of the Beijing capital, had become a useful bridgehead for French interests, first along the coasts and the river, second throughout the regions penetrated by roads and railways—for imports of equipment, durable goods, staples and high-end consuming goods or for locally produced exports, thus as a leverage to French global interests in China.[1] "By the 1930s, second only to Shanghai in the volume of foreign trade, Tianjin had become the largest centre of industry and commerce in north China"[2] (see Table 19.1).

The French concession itself, with its internal outlets (the army, the Catholic missions, a few lean layers of European bourgeois and employees, and then more and more Chinese civilian and military bigwigs, taking profit from the order, law and comfort provided by the city), offered opportunities for the distribution of consumer goods. It supplied, for instance, a credit for the import of French wine for the army in 1933: an amount of 3,100 hectoliters and FRF 500,000 was financed by *Banque de l'Indochine*;[3] the army in Shanghai got 800 hectolitres and the Tianjin corps the other part. The trade house Racine & C° was one key importer of wine carts for French troops in Tianjin at the turn of the 1930s.

A little *Bund*—far from the size of the Shanghai *Bund* but equipped with warehouses, business houses and bourgeois mansions—had somehow taken form in that "city port", with banks and trade houses gathering themselves along a few streets and quays. Tianjin had benefited too from the temporary completion of the Guo Ming Tang's China, when expectations of an era of growth and even prosperity had inspired by the structuring of "modern" markets, in cities, within the army, or through the industrial plants which the new regime and entrepreneurial bourgeoisies were favouring.

Table 19.1 Exports from Tianjin in 1936 (millions USD)

Total exports	110
Exports to Japan	24
Among which cotton	15
Exports besides Japan	86
Exports to UK and dominions	19
Exports to United States	44
Exports to France	3
Exports to Germany, Belgium, the Netherlands, Italy and Western Europe	20
France's portion among these exports besides Japan	3.5%
France's portion among these exports to Western Europe	15%

Source: *Banque de l'Indochine* correspondence, 21 March 1939, Historical archives of *Crédit agricole*, *Banque de l'Indochine* fund

Within the Tianjin settlement, *Banque de l'Indochine* had asserted itself as an "institution", which explains why its archives[4] can supply today much information about the economic life of the concession and of the whole city, whilst freshly opened archives from the *Consulat général de France* in Tianjin[5] have broadened our perception of the evolution of the French community there. But the apex reached at the turn of the 1930s left room for hard times: civil war, internecine struggles between Jiang Jieshi/Tchang Kai Chek's regime and the warlord fiefdoms, then the intrusion of Japanese officials and army in the Hebei, followed by the general war, caused a harsh crisis and perturbed the daily life of banking and trading houses. Several times, the very basis of business trust was therefore direly shaken; trust in paper money, in some banks—as there were 99 local banks in Tianjin in 1933 with only 30 million yuans in assets versus 320 million for the 29 modern banks also present on the marketplace—or in the local branches of big banks (Bank of China and Bank of Communications), as well as in some trade houses, was thus eroded,[6] leading to calls for rescue to the Shanghai marketplace from time to time to provide refinancing flows.

Throughout these years, within schemes of a new "Asian order"[7] in which Tianjin was a mere pawn, the fate of the Tianjin French community and even of its daily life were at stake: its very resiliency constituted a challenge, which this paper intends to reconstitute. We intend to provide glances of the businessmen and bankers' life in Tianjin amid concerning events which threatened first the course of trade and then everyday life and people's fate themselves. The very *raison d'être* of a European community of interests and business in a "city-port" was challenged because of the crisis of its hinterland and of the geopolitical and military events.

1. A troubled environment for business: Tianjin and Japanese inflows (1935–1937)

Whilst the French concession seemed to enjoy some peaceful and "business as usual" life, the Tianjin area became more and more confronted by the pressures of military tensions and Japanese discreet then massive progression. On one side, Tianjin businessmen had to take into account the dismantling of genuine administrative power between the Nankin/Nanjing regime and the warlords, whose tactics against the Nanjing government rekindled insecurity and weakened the Chinese ability to maintain durable control on the subregion. But a process toward stability prevailed when the authority of the generals supervising the area (Chang Tue Chung in Tianjin and Sung Cheh Yuan, governor of Hopeh-Chahar) was *de facto* reinforced in 1935–1937. But all stakeholders had to respect more and more the ascent of Japanese might in north-eastern China.

The *Banque de l'Indochine* branch could not escape the fate of northern China since Japanese troops first invaded it in 1933: the war commenced there[8] partly before the general one in 1937. Their incursions spurred huge moves of refugees, disturbed trade exchanges and the life of the Tianjin concessions. Japanese police and soldiers held their de facto rule on several areas, especially the trade ways, and they imposed their discreet grip on the economy. They helped Japanese company smuggling goods (wool and cotton fabrics, especially) into China,[9] thus robbing customs revenues from Chinese authorities and, more importantly for the bank, shrinking the activities of Chinese or European traders there, along with the outlets for credit. Tianjin became some kind of a challenged target, which created an atmosphere of distrust[10] throughout 1935 and 1936, even if traders and bankers maintained the momentum through such obstacles: "The 1936 year has been particularly favourable to the trade on piece goods."[11]

Because of the Japanese progress (and subversion, often from its own concession in Tianjin itself), little by little, all the French progress made for business and banking from the 1910s was halted in favour of the mere initial French purpose to serve the sole interests of the French concession. The French consul noticed that the import trade in Tianjin could not but lose ground and that in 1935 it reached the lowest level since 1917: insecurity of financial transactions, smuggling, organized commercial crime in the countryside, political uncertainties, and decline in purchasing power of the population all contributed to such a decline.[12]

The Tongku armistice between Japanese and Chinese authorities on 31 May 1933 had halted the north-eastern war, but it also opened doors to Japanese trading houses through the Koupeikou and Sigenkou passages of the Great Chinese Wall, almost to the outskirts of Beijing and Tianjin. Even a few Japanese troops were introduced to "keep order". Japanese business interests penetrated the regions more and more, even if officially they kept their administrative links with the Nankin/Nanjing regime.[13] Japanese goods ran there thanks to smuggling, short-circuiting Chinese customs. An actual strategy took shape to replace European imports by Japanese ones. Such moves led to the insensitive process of setting Japanese customs barriers all around the still Chinese north-eastern areas, with a customs office established in September 1935 in Tianjin for the whole Hopei-Chahar state and along the railway tracks. Railways became an issue: a project of a 450-km track joining Tianjin to Shijiazhuang was conceived in order to link Tianjin to this stretch of the Beijing–Wuhan, itself linked to the capital of Shansi, Taiyuanfou/Taiyuan.

Tianjin became a target for Japanese interests,[14] as Japan intended to reverse the move towards economic independence which the Washington treaty in 1922 had eased since it had allowed China to set up tariff barriers to protect its budding industries. The north-eastern Chinese market had therefore to join the "Asian area of co-prosperity" led by the Japanese. They multiplied bridgeheads in Tianjin, first acquiring the power plant located in the ex-German concession and gaining a foothold in *Énergie électrique de Tientsin*. They intended to get access to mining (iron and coal), to salt (for the soda industry, with Japan taking control of the Chinese plant in Tongku) and to tobacco activities. A subsidiary of the North China Development Company, an affiliate of the South-Manchuria Railway, was settled in Tianjin. Four spinning plants were opened which purchased cotton from local peasants and merchants. But the influence of European countries and companies still prevailed in Tianjin for a while.

2. Tianjin business during the Sino-Japanese war (1937–1941)

Ups and downs were the fate of the Tianjin business community throughout the years of localised war and of the progressive embeddedness of Japanese influence and power.

A. Tianjin taking profit from its position

Tianjin was caught between the Chinese and Japanese armies when the offensive of Nanking troops in north-eastern China was followed by a general offensive of the Japanese Army in July 1937. The latter lodged 20,000 soldiers[15] between Tianjin and Beijing in July 1937, but the Nippon treated with the generals supervising the area (Chang Tse Chung/Shang Zhen, the mayor of Tianjin, and Sung Cheh Yuan/Song Zheyuan, the governor of Hopeh-Chahar), and some kind of an "armed peace" preserved Tianjin from global fighting.[16] After the fall of Nanking in December 1937, Japan went on bullying the Chinese troops of the Wuhan regime, especially in May–June 1938. Tianjin should have escaped trouble, but communist guerrilla warfare arose in Shansi and Kiangsu, which often interrupted the functioning of the Tianjin–Pukow railway, and Tianjin was often isolated from Shanghai and Beijing. Then the destruction of dykes by the Chinese provoked flooding all over the Yellow River/Huang He in the summer. A provisional government, sponsored by Japan, was established in Beijing, which was to exert its authority over a few cities, among them Tianjin, and along the railway tracks:

> The occupied territories of China the Japanese were holding were the areas with the railways and the main roads and towns, while economically productive areas are more or less unconquered and Chinese ruled by a

varying mixture of old established local authorities, guerrilla soldiers and semi or full pledged bandits, some of whom still have some contact with the Chinese government in Wuhan.[17]

Generally speaking, confusion predominated,[18] with ups and downs amid the calm necessary for day-to-day business, through the various stages of the war.[19] "Guerrillas were rampant just outside of the cities and railway zones of northern China."[20] They gained ground in the first half of 1940 and disturbed agricultural production and commerce:

> The military operations recently undertaken aim, in what affects North China, less to widen the conquest than to strengthen it. A fast examination of the map shows that the vast plain of the Hopeh and the central valley of Shansi are, from a strategic point of view, commanded by a double mountainous bastion, Chungtiao in the southeast of Shansi, Taihang, in the southwest. All the Japanese columns sent to that plain against the guerrilla warfare had failed until now. Bands broke up in the attack to be then reconstituted and held the countryside, whereas the Japanese garrisons scattered in villages forbade farmers and city-dwellers any contact, any exchange, any provisioning ... The ground on which operations take place at the moment gave rise to ceaseless fights for two years ... The Japanese have just concentrated considerable strengths there by bringing in divisions which fought previously on Yangtze.[21]

Then some respite was felt in the first half of 1941 thanks to the non–aggression pact between the USSR and Japan, which imposed some kind of truce in Shansi.[22] Businessmen had thus to learn how to practice "business as usual" under Japanese occupation.[23] An awkward situation prevailed: a relative calm preserved a few regions in 1938–1939 (eastern Hopei, interior Mongolia). Cities had to get fresh supplies; the 600,000–700,000 Japanese troops and the civil servants accompanying them became an important outlet for goods. These factors explain a somewhat serious rebound of the exterior trade of Tianjin during the first months of 1938, all the more because, when the Japanese imposed strict controls on the Tsingtao exchanges, an important chunk of imports and exports of Shandong were reoriented toward Tianjin (see Table 19.2).

Table 19.2 Ships reaching Tianjin and Tsingtao harbours in 1937–1938

	Number of ships		*Total tonnage*	
	January– September 1937	January– September 1938	January– September 1937	January– September 1938
Tianjin	1,060	3,056	1,587,941	2,522,616
Tsingtao	1,052	772	2,500,642	1,252,659

Source: *Rapport-bilan. Situation économique et politique*, Second half 1938, *Banque de l'Indochine* correspondence, 17 January 1939, annex 3

The result was that, for a few months, Tianjin had become, since the start of 1938, the first Chinese harbour for exports, its transit representing 24 per cent of the total of China, against 23 per cent for Shanghai and 20 per cent for Canton. Its exports reached during this period 70 per cent of the amount of the corresponding period of 1937.[24] This trend was reinforced by a stiff drop of smuggling now that Japanese authorities controlled the whole area, even if Japanese generals sometimes short-circuited official orders. Benefiting with the cash operations fuelled by such trading and also from remittances still sent from overseas by Chinese diasporas, Tianjin appeared for a short while as a kind of island of compromise between the old Chinese order and the new Japanese order.

B. The concessions between autonomy and the Japanese order

The city itself had to respect a subtle balance. In a nutshell, Japan resented the predominance of British trade on the north-eastern exchanges and in Tianjin— not to speak of other areas—and its purpose was to encroach on such economic and financial power. The Japanese also grumbled over the principle of the British and French concessions because they were still "neutral" territories which could shelter Chinese people hostile to Japan—mainly "nationalists"— and express genuine economic and financial power of decision. Tianjin even remained in charge of the part of the silver reserve pledged by the Chinese Nanking regime for its note issuings which was placed under the control of the settlements (in parallel with the other deposit in the Beijing Legations).

The authorities of the concessions ended the recognition of Japan's authority over that silver, but hoarding was respected throughout the course of events.

> The question of the stocks of silver-metal, as a cover of the former Chinese bills, is the object at the moment of tightened discussions between the Japanese and the French–English consular authorities. The transaction suggested by Foreign Office, and which most probably has to succeed, by establishing the local French–English authorities as sequesters of funds, admits implicitly on behalf of the Japanese a right to inspect stocks, property of the Chinese national government, and authorizes *ipso facto* the managers of the (pro-Japanese) Federal Reserve Bank to include them in their guarantee of issue, at least as memory serves.[25]

The silver reserves, of a value of $45 million in 1928 had been deposited in the safes of the Tianjin branches of Bank of Communications and of Bank of China.

Just before the Munich agreement on November 1938, Japan would have been on the brink to take control of the settlements. Having abandoned the project, it established some kind of informal blockade. It built a network of barbed wire and control stations all along the road circling them, with only four entrances, where guards harassed transiting European and heavily checking

Chinese people, especially merchants or their transporters.[26] From July 1937, the controls drifted imperceptibly toward a blockade, to multiply obstacles to exchanges. In the meanwhile, the Japanese took over the salt tax office of Tianjin on 5 August 1937 (Changdu District of Salt Administration) and of its revenues. But the Japanese authorities still respected the function of this salt tax administration as a pledge to the old Western loans.[27]

Japanese power also increased substantially with the excise tax on imported goods (with collection just at the exit of the concessions)—which affected French wines and liquors to be sold in the province—and customs fees were raised too, for instance on tobacco, which impeded commerce.[28] In 1938–1939, Japanese people had to leave the concessions, to protect them from a specific identification, given the warmongering mindset; even Japanese banks (Yokohama Specie Bank, Chosen Bank) had to transfer their branches to provisional locations in the Japanese settlement as of January 1939.

Pressure and intimidation increased more and more on European managers and authorities and on the Chinese businessmen linked to them: "At any time, the Japanese command can forbid any traffic between the French–English concessions and outside or also limit the provisioning of the population which stays there, so as to hasten emigration. It thus holds in its hands the economic life of these two concessions."[29] They more or less admitted, therefore, to the Japanese say on daily life in the Tianjin area, even in the concessions. A genuine blockade was eventually fixed as of February–March 1939, with barriers all around the French settlement, for example,[30] and restrictions on trade (controls, export certificates on several goods) were then intensified.[31] The amounts of imports of flour and rice in Tianjin were taxed by Japanese authorities, through the Tianjin agencies of Japanese trade houses (*sogososha*), Mitsui Bussan Kaishua and Mitsubishi.[32] This led British authorities, as representatives of the foreign community in Tianjin and as the expression of the UK, to negotiate some terms of appeasement with Japan to delay hostilities and to recognise officially Japan's authority in the Tianjin area.

As a beacon for such compromise, Japanese guards were posted as a symbolic tutelage on the silver deposits of the (now faraway) Chinese central bank. A local British–Japanese treaty was signed in Tianjin on 21 June 1940 to implement Japan's control of the city and its concessions: Japan took profit from the defeat of France and from the desire of Great Britain to salvage part of its bases in China in order to impose drastic controls on the silver deposits, the general use of money and, moreover, information about commerce—with reports to civil servants and direct checking of goods transfers by police. "The silver coin and bullion now in the Bank of Communications in Tientsin shall remain in that bank under the joint seal of the British and Japanese Consuls-General in that city."[33]

French officials and businessmen vainly resented the shift in the balance of power obviously in favour of Japanese hegemony at the expense of British thalassocracy and United States might. Japan even succeeded in becoming the first supplier of China in 1938, ahead of the United States, with 23.49 per cent of its imports in 1938 instead of 15.77 per cent as in 1937, and with 15.76 per cent of its exports in 1938 instead of 10.05 per cent as in 1937.[34]

C. Confusion about currencies

In the event, negative factors put brakes on "business as usual", and uncertainties often prevailed:

> The future is full of uncertainties, and the experience of the last months recommends prudent reserve. As long as we will not have come to an end of the current hostilities, the marketplace of Tianjin can live only an abnormal existence. It is most probably necessary to expect a reduction in business because of the control of the foreign trade, and maybe also the pending exchange control.[35]

All these factors disturbed banking operations. A first cause stemmed from the 40 per cent fall of the Chinese "nationalist" dollar—itself dating back only to 1935 at the time of the Tchiang Kai Chek regime—in the second quarter of 1938. The multiplicity of currencies available in northern China reflected the lack of trust among cash holders and moreover the fragmentation of local and monetary power: about seven types of banknotes were circulating around Tianjin at the start of 1938 (see Table 19.3).

Table 19.3 Banknotes circulated in northern China in March 1938 (millions of dollars) (before the creation of the FRB$)

Central Bank of China notes	45
Bank of China notes issued in northern China with a special Tianjinn mention	250
Bank of Communications notes issued in northern China with a special Tianjin mention	80
Hopei Bank notes issued in Tianjin	50
Provincial notes issued in the Shansi province	40
Various banknotes	5
+ Yens issued by Bank of Korea	/

Source: *Note sur la situation monétaire en Chine du Nord,* by the head of the *Banque de l'Indochine* Tianjin branch Soliva for the *Consul général de France* in Tianjin, 21 March 1938, *Consulat général de France* archives, 62 9C3

The birth of a new central bank in the north-east, the Federal Reserve Bank, on 20 March 1938, on the side of the pro-Japan regime, fostered further trouble: Chinese northern dollars were to be exchanged by native banks and trade houses only against yens, not against "Shanghai dollars", of course, or "nationalist" dollars—even if the Korean yens were also used in the area along with the Japanese yens: "Connected with the dollar of Shanghai, the former dollar is exchangeable, with the aid of the latter, against currencies. So it remains the currency of banks and not of the Japanese foreign administrations. The former dollar does not serve to settle Japanese imports, loans; the new serves to pay the customs duties and the Japanese imports."[36] Some kind of a currency war arose, feeding volatility. Trust in northern Chinese currency (FRB$) had crumbled, all the more because foreign municipalities and banks had refused to accept it and because trust in the "nationalist" dollar (the Central China Currency or CNC$, or *fabi*, called "chunky dollar")[37] kept up momentum in 1938–1939, and it was used day to day by Chinese intermediaries despite Japanese pressures.

Northern China banks tried to sustain the value of the northern Chinese currency (FRB$) during the first quarter of 1938 in order to stabilise the market, but, as Japan refused to help them, a free currency market took shape after April 1938, especially in Tianjin, with a drift of the FRB$ value. In fact, the whole area practiced all together half a dozen currencies: the FRB dollar, the CNC dollar, discreetly the Shanghai dollar, the yen, the Korean yen, and also notes issued by big Chinese banks: Bank of China and Bank for Communications.[38] Checking the reliability of accounts was thus very difficult for businessmen and bankers: "The present situation is artificial and precarious",[39] all the more because inflation moved up from the middle of 1938 at the expense of the northern Chinese dollar and the yen as well, worrying the holders of FRB notes.[40]

Notes

1 See Jacques Weber (ed.), *La France en Chine, 1843–1940*, Nantes, Presses académiques de l'Ouest-Ouest Editions, Université de Nantes, 1997. Laurent Cesari & Denis Varaschin (eds.), *Les relations franco-chinoises au vingtième siècle et leurs antécédents*, Arras, Artois Presses Université, 2003.
2 Gail Hershatter, *op. cit.*, p. 10.
3 Historical archives of *Crédit agricole, Banque de l'Indochine* fund, *Banque de l'Indochine* correspondence, 14 August 1933.
4 We thank the *Archives historiques du Crédit agricole SA-CASA* and especially their head Roger Nougaret to have once more opened wide their records to our historical investigations.
5 We thank the *Archives diplomatiques* of the French *ministère des Affaires étrangères* to have eased our campaign of archive reading in their facilities in Nantes—and especially Ms Cras. See *Inventaire des archives du Consulat de France à Tientsin, 1861–1952*, 419 articles, *par André Bors, chargé de mission, sous la direction de Bruno Ricard, conservateur du Patrimoine, Nantes*, September 1999.
6 See Brett Sheehan, "Trust at a time of international crisis", in Brett Sheehan (ed.), *Trust in Troubled Times: Money, Banks and State–Society Relations in Republican Tianjin*, Cambridge, Cambridge University Press, 2003, pp. 152–176.
7 See Shigeru Akita & Nicholas White (eds.), *The International Order of Asia in the 1930s and 1950s*, Burlington, VT, London, Ashgate, 2009.
8 *Banque de l'Indochine*, correspondence between the Tianjin branch and the Paris headquarters of *Banque de l'Indochine*, 20 May 1933, Historical archives of *Crédit agricole, Banque de l'Indochine* fund.
9 *Banque de l'Indochine*, correspondence, 20 October 1935 and 21 September 1936.
10 Brett Sheehan, *Trust in Troubled Times: Money, Banks and State–Society Relations in Republican Tianjin*, Cambridge, MA, Harvard University Press, 2003.
11 *Banque de l'Indochine*, correspondence, 9 February 1937, Historical archives of *Crédit agricole, Banque de l'Indochine* fund.

12 Note of the French consul, 27 February 1936, *Consulat général de France* archives TT46. The amount of imports fell from 49,250 million gold unit dollars in 1934 to 46,620 (as a global estimate).

13 *Banque de l'Indochine* correspondence, 21 September 1936, Historical archives of *Crédit agricole, Banque de l'Indochine* fund.

14 *Rapport-bilan. Situation économique et politique*, second half of 1938, *Banque de l'Indochine* correspondence, 17 January 1939.

15 *Banque de l'Indochine* correspondence, 21 July 1937.

16 *Ibidem.*

17 *Semi-confidential Reuter, Economic XRay*, 12 September 1938, quoted by: Note from the Tianjin BIC branch's manager, *Consulat général de France* archives 9D/62.

18 Note *Situation économique et politique en Extrême-Orient*, BIC correspondence, 15 September 1938.

19 See James Hsiung & Steven Levine (eds.), *China's Bitter Victory: The War with Japan, 1937–1945*, Armonk, NY, M.E. Sharpe, 1992.

20 Note of the *Consul de France*, 1939, *Consulat général* archives 9D62.

21 *Rapport-bilan. Situation économique et politique*, first half of 1940, *Banque de l'Indochine* correspondence, 9 July 1940, pp. 1, 2.

22 *Ibidem*, first half of 1941, *Banque de l'Indochine* correspondence, 7 July 1941, p. 1.

23 Richard Banyai, *Money and Banking in China and South-East Asia During the Japanese Military Occupation, 1937–1945*, Taipei, Taiwan Enterprises Company, 1974.

24 Note *Situation économique et politique en Extrême-Orient, Banque de l'Indochine* correspondence, 15 September 1938.

25 *Rapport-bilan. Situation économique et politique*, second half of 1938, *Banque de l'Indochine* correspondence, 17 January 1939, p. 4. See also notice of 1939, *Consulat général* archives 9C161.

26 *Rapport-bilan. Situation économique et poltique*, second half of 1938, *Banque de l'Indochine* correspondence, 17 January 1939, p. 3.

27 Note from the *Consulat général de France in Tianjin*, 24 August 1937, *Consulat général* archives 9B1/58.

28 Note from the *Consulat général de France in Tianjin*, 19 September 1934, *Consulat général* archives, 9B2.

29 *Rapport-bilan. Situation économique et politique*, second half of 1938, *Banque de l'Indochine* correspondence, 17 January 1939, p. 4.

30 *Consulat général* archives, 9D62.

31 Letter, 25 February 1939, Consulat général archives, 9D62.

32 Notice in 1939, *Consulat général* archives, 9C61.

33 *Rapport-bilan. Situation économique et politique*, first half of 1940, *Banque de l'Indochine* correspondence, 9 July 1940, pp. 4–5.

34 *Banque de l'Indochine* yearly report, 24 May 1939.

35 *Rapport-bilan. Situation économique et politique*, second half of 1938, *Banque de l'Indochine* correspondence, 17 January 1939, p. 3.

36 Notice in 1938, *Consulat général archives*, 9D62.

37 *Ibidem.*

38 *Ibidem.*

39 Note in mid-1938, *Consulat général de France* archives, 629C3.

40 *Bulletin économique et politique*, March–April 1940, *Consulat général* archives, 9C1 61, Note *Agence de la Banque de l'Indochine à Tianjin*.

20 Geopolitics versus banking and business in Tianjin

Throughout any and all circumstances, "business as usual" had always been the motto for companies and banks. But against such dramatic geopolitical and even military events, the prospects of stability dwindled in Tianjin because of suchshocks. Despite the monetary and banking reforms launched by the Nankin/Nanjing government and the efforts by provincial and local authorities to design some relevant ways of financial management, uncertainties predominated. Bankers and businessmen of every origin had to struggle to avoid losses and to somehow draw some baskets of affairs and profits.

1. The ultimate apex of a micro–business world

Through these ordeals, the little French community struggled to preserve its activities and to contain business risks. But instability and incertitude prevailed, which caused high concerns about the resiliency of the firms and sometimes losses and about globally reduced trade and exchange operations.

A. The Mission still a key actor of the French concession

In the end of the 1930s, the "Sien Shien Mission" was still the other actor (along with the French army) of the French concession. Beyond its religious activities, it had preserved its commercial property and financial assets. Mainly in the 1920s, it had extended its real estate assets within the French concession but also in the other concessions and in the ex-concessions (Russian, Italian and German).[1] For example, in the ex-German settlement and at the limit of the British one, it owned a chapel, the *École des hautes études*, the Hoang Ho-Pai Ho Museum and laboratories, but its property fuelled revenues on rented fields, houses, warehouses or flats—for a total amount on the sole French concession of $52,000 in 1935. The branch managed a flow of day-to-day advances to the institution and lodged its cash deposits ($226,000 in November 1935, for instance).

Since World War I, it had played a role of some kind of a "holding financial company", using its reserves to invest in real property, business warehouses and merchant houses and in the equity itself of French companies active in the city port. If it had tried since the second turn of the 1930s to alleviate its financial portfolio comprising stakes in local companies which it had godfathered in the 1920s and had cut into a few of them, selling General Veneer Factory (a manu-facture of plywood) to the Chinese in 1936 and also *Huileries de Tientsin* (an oil plant) in 1934, it clung to others: General Dairy & Farm (with genuine farms in the outskirts), J. Gully (an import–export house created in 1931), Battegay or Arnoult (also two trade houses), *Énergie électrique de Tientsin* (with a fifth of the equity), and real estate developers, *Union immobilière de Tientsin* (created in 1925) or *Société foncière de Tientsin* (with O'Neill as manager). The Arnoult house had endured severe losses in 1929–1931, and its debt had then grown rapidly to $250,000 in January 1931, pledged by an amount of goods of 372,000.[2] Its amount happily fell to 37,000 taels in March 1935, and its situation became thus reasonable on the ledgers of its banker.

In 1938–1939, in a few cases, such commercial property activities benefited from a little boom which occurred throughout Tianjin when the depreciation of the northern Chinese dollar and the necessity to get rid of other hoarded currencies led some wealthy Chinese to invest their savings into real estate in Tianjin—in parallel with foreign currencies or goods to be piled up—but the main investments were achieved on the British concession because of the lack of available fields in the French concession.[3]

The *Banque de l'Indochine* branch tackled the treasury operations of the Mission, but this latter kept active accounts by other banks (*Banque belge pour l'étranger*, etc.) for cash deposits or equity accounts (American securities). For its "capitalist" (or "venture capital") activities, the Mission mobilised part of its renting revenues: loans or endorsing loans. It was thus placed at the heart of the business of the Tianjin concession.

B. The concession as a conservatoire of French entrepreneurship?

As in Shanghai, the French presence was active in utilities, thanks to *Compagnie des tramways et d'éclairage de Tientsin*, which used and distributed power (also in the Belgian concession and the Lao Si Kai territory, intimately linked to the French concession) delivered by *Énergie électrique de Tientsin*, and it was among the leading clients of the *Banque de l'Indochine* branch (see Table 20.1).

Table 20.1 Sales of electric power in Tianjin in 1937 (thousands kW)

	First half 1937	Second half 1937
Compagnie des tramways et d'éclairage de Tientsin (Chinese city)	12,755	11,211
Énergie électrique de Tientsin	3,322	3,503
British Municipal Council Electricity Department	6,675	6,654
	22,752	21,358

Source: Note *Situation économique et politique en Extrême-Orient*, *Banque de l'Indochine* correspondence, 15 September 1938

Trade houses—either French ones or other ones also co-financed by *Banque de l'Indochine*—struggled to get a chunk of Chinese exports and imports. *Banque de l'Indochine* noticed that the year 1936 had been very favourable to the "piece goods" trade, thus opening opportunities for loans to Chinese houses specialising in cotton and yarn commerce. North-eastern China[4] still exported camel hair, pork bristles, goat skins, cotton and eggs, and it imported artificial silk, cotton clothes, sugar, petrol oil, cigarette paper, among others. The breakdown of documentary credits granted by the *Banque de l'Indochine* branch helps to perceive the reality of trade as they stayed an efficient tool for financing Chinese exports through the Tianjin port. Trade houses could therefore benefit from such exchanges, along processes of shared economic intelligence (see Table 20.2).

Nonetheless, French traders could not actually contend with their German, US, then, more and more, Japanese competitors as they held broad markets shares in the main sectors of equipment goods and textile. They were "second-players", and one must avoid perceiving the French concession as a decisive "hub". For imports, French houses were dedicated to consuming goods earmarked for European customers, administrations and troops in the area, and they contributed to imports of durable goods only through metal equipment and cars. A few glimpses at the breakdown of imports in Tianjin confirm the "specialisation" which differentiated countries along their portfolio of productive skills and along the heritage of their industrial revolutions, as well as the weight of Japan in its Asian strongholds—which left to France a second-player role (see Table 20.3).

Table 20.2 Breakdown of *Banque de l'Indochine* branch operations on bills remitted against documentary credits in 1939

	As equivalent of nationalist Chinese dollars	Percentages
Vegetables		
Apricot kernels	50,318	11.07
Groundnuts	2,728	0.60
Animal products		
Pig intestines	162,264	37.72
Horse hair (for mattress)	36,748	8.09
Pork bristles	67,372	14.83
Hog casings	37,272	8.20
Fishskins	2,432	0.53
Egg albumen (and spray whole egg, hen yolk)	27,161	5.98
Furs (kidleg plates, dresses kidplates, weasel skins, fox skins, carpets, etc.)	67,854	14.94
Total	454,149	

Source: *Rapport-bilan. Situation économique et politique*, First half of 1939, *Banque de l'Indochine* correspondence, 15 July 1939

Table 20.3 Estimates of the origins of a few imports in Tianjin in 1935 (gold unit Chinese dollars)

Cotton cloth, cotton yarn, wool cloth	
Japan	2,552,397
United Kingdom	182,502
United States	13,348
France (0.37%)	10,685
Other countries	93,650
Total	2,852,684
Machines, tools, airspace and car equipment, railway and tramway equipment, cycles, various metal goods	
Japan	5,803,986
Germany	3,474,956
United Kingdom	1,964,349
United States	1,620,475
Belgium	749,200
France (5.047%)	727,076
Other countries	647,477
Total	14,404,789
Chemicals, drugs, dyestuffs, paints, varnish, etc.	
Japan	1,837,071
Germany	1,563,682
United Kingdom	321,527
United States	254,549
France (1.64%)	81,676
Other countries	380,084
Total	4,438,589
Wines, beer, liquors and waters	
France (36.93%)	155,675
Japan	143,191
United Kingdom	80,720
Other countries	45,965
Total	421,551

Source: Calculations from figures in "Note from Ch. Lépissier", *Consul de France à Tientsin*, to the Foreign Affairs minister, March 1936, *Consulat général de France* archives, 61

Strongly established since World War I, French business had developed its wholesale and retail activities and had reached a scope adapted to its local and provincial outlets: a dozen houses had thus succeeded in reaching World War II despite intensifying hardships (see Table 20.4).

A strong community of interests struggled and resisted hardships, relying on the *Consul général de France*,[5] also the chairman of the Municipality administrative commission; on the Tianjin section of the French Chamber of Commerce in China; on the *Mission de Shienshen* (and its business and property assets and affiliates); and on the branch of *Banque de l'Indochine*.[6] That latter was a key actor of the small banking marketplace which struggled to resist hardships in the 1930s–1940s amongits partners (among them *Banque franco-chinoise*), which constituted a little "Tientsin's Lombard Street"[7] along a micro-*Bund*[8] and more

Table 20.4 Main trading houses and merchants in Tianjin in the mid-1930s

Jacques Ulmann & C°	99 rue de France	Diamonds, clockware, books, goldsmith
Racine & C°	137 quai de France	Chemicals, dyeings, construction materials, etc.; insurance agency
Olivier-Chine	35 rue de Verdun	General import–export; insurance agency
Arnoult		Architecture, public works and construction, metal goods; car agency (*Citroën, Michelin*)
G. Colinet	6 rue Henry Bourgeois	Export and import house; insurance agency; shipping. *Renault* car agency. Colinet exported goat hides, lamb robes (both to Marseille) or walnut meats (to New Zealand) (*Consulat général* archives, 62/9D, 2 March 1939). It also exported furs, pork bristles, etc.
F. Leconte		Leconte exported straw braids to Australia, or imported rice from Indochina, etc. (*Consulat général* archives, 62/9D, 2 March 1939)
J. Gully & C°	54 rue Henry Bourgeois	Specialised in walnuts, walnut meats, egg products; insurance agency
La Mutuelle (J.-P. Ferrer)-*Union économique sino-française*		Foodstuff, wines and liquors
Émile Vernaudon		Wines and liquors, foodstuff
Victor Moyroux	41 rue de France	Wines and spirits, foodstuffs, etc.
Battegay		Export of pork bristles and furs

Source: *Livre d'or des maisons françaises établies à Tientsin*, Tianjin, Établissements artistiques-Feiyang Press, 1932

and more along Victoria Road, on both the British concession (HSBC, Chartered, *Banque belge pour l'étranger*—Yokohama Specie Bank had had to leave it) and the French concession (*Banque de l'Indochine*,[9] Commercial and Industrial Bank of China, Sino-Italian Bank), whilst sharing credits and fuelling a clearing inter-bank market. The French concession also welcomed an array of small Chinese banks (27 in 1940) acting as bridges between European and local business and between the Tianjin and the Shanghai marketplaces (through cash transfers).[10]

2. *Banque de l'Indochine* as a banking flagship amid foreign and Chinese competition

The *Banque de l'Indochine* branch kept its function as a leverage force in favour of French business. It worked at the time with a capital allocation of £60,000 (or Chinese dollars 300,000) and might reach a $1,670,000 draft credits limit.

But because of competition, of Japanese demands, and of uncertain times, it could bear draft credits for only USD 1 million[11] at the start of 1937. Even well-off French companies shared their operations among several banks: on January 1937, the leading Olivier house, for example, had been granted credits for $547,000, but *Banque de l'Indochine* got only $197,000 because of the division of risks with HSBC (150,000), City Bank (75,000) or *Banque belge pour l'étranger* (125,000).[12]

The regional tensions fostered hard times for the branch anyway because deposits were drawn back (from $1,550,000 to 670,000 between 15 September and 5 November 1938), and the branch endured a cash crisis when its treasury position became negative (from +361,000 on 15 September 1938 to −1,731,000 on 8 November and −1,220,000 on 15 November). It had to be refinanced by Bank of China (the recent central bank of the Nanking regime), which supplied an advance of $2,540,000 in the fall of 1938. The nationalist authorities fought to preserve a financial and economic life-as-usual in the areas in which they tried to assert control, in order to feed Chinese economy and thus entertain some positive perception, "popularity" or legitimacy despite the Japanese progress there. Still evading Japanese pressures, the *Banque de l'Indochine* branch kept grappling with a large array of currencies (see Table 20.5).

Commonplace operations were entertained in the wake of the years of greater prosperity. The *Banque de l'Indochine* branch traded on bills to be remitted in Europe in pounds, dollars or francs in places abroad to sustain exports, and it cashed exchange bills linked with imports. Promissory premises had been replaced by specially equipped offices in 1921, located on *rue de France*—today on 80 Jiefang Beilin[13] and still a kind of "finance street" in the city. Classically it complemented its operations with "reports" on currencies with its banking partners and kept trading a few bills transmitted by a few other branches (Beijing, Saigon).

The branch had taken profits from the rapid growth of the activities through Tianjin, which explains why more cash had been gotten from Paris to support them, acquiring thus its institutional legitimacy in the eyes of the head office. The funds provided to the branch were developed in the 1930s: they came from Paris as a permanent line for overdraft to be drawn on accounts in Paris (FRF 5 million in March 1933) and London (£30,000 in March 1933). But overdraft facilities were also opened at the *Banque de l'Indochine* branches of Saigon—always rich with availabilities, which brought deposits in Tianjin, for an amount of FRF 21.2 million in March 1933, for example—and of Shanghai—the hub of *Banque de l'Indochine* in China—and Hong Kong. But it acted from now on less and less with the support of the Shanghai branch and asserted somehow an independent mastership of banking for a few quarters.

Local loans provided it with its main returns through interests and commissions—and, in 1939, the comprador, Heng Chi Hao, pledged his own guarantee on the advances on promissory notes which he brought to the branch, with his counterparts of $781,880 (680,880 in real estate).[14] When foreign business

Table 20.5 Situation of the *Banque de l'Indochine* branch of Tianjin in 1939–1941 (thousands Chinese dollars)

	Resources in June 1939	Resources in December 1939	Average assets in January–June 1939	Average assets in July–December 1939	Average assets in July–December 1940	Average assets in January–June 1941	July–December 1941
In French francs	3,027	2,421	1,444	2,876	530	504	321
In sterling pounds	7,372	2,634	5,791	4,001	2,429	676	391
In US dollars	14,878	11,741	8,440	21,967	8,936	9,022	4,422
In nationalist Chinese dollars	4,711	5,720	3,949	6,309	4,874	5,056	2,113
Total	29,999	22,551	19,636	35,174	16,771	15,787	7,344

Source: *Rapport-bilan. Situation économique et politique*, first half of 1939, *Banque de l'Indochine* correspondence, 15 July 1939; second half of 1939, 18 January 1940; second half of 1940, January 1941; first half of 1941, 7 July 1941; second half of 1941, January 1942

declined, the comprador's operations were useful to feed the activities of the branch, through new advances on promissory notes: "During the [second] half-year [1941], we granted advances on promissory notes with the approval and the guarantee of the comprador. We were also handed, as additional guarantee, gold bars (kept in our safes) or piece goods, cotton yarns, stored in a go-down at our name"[15] (see Table 20.6).

Foreign exchange operations maintained their first-rank intensity because the *Banque de l'Indochine* branch sold francs against US dollars, sterlings or Shanghai dollars and in parallel also sold US dollars and sterlings against other currencies; it practiced report operations on US dollars and sterlings, and it managed interbank operations (for instance, with *Banque franco-chinoise*, the other French bank in Tianjin; with *Deutsch Asiatisch Bank*, National City Bank of New York, Chase Bank, Yokohama Specie Bank, *Banque belge pour l'étranger*, Bank of India and China, HSBC; and with Chinese banks, like Agricultural & Industrial Bank of China, China & South Sea Bank, Shanghai Commercial Bank or China State Bank), which all in all fostered cushions of spreads. Thanks to trade banking, FOREX or local (low-key) corporate banking, the profitability of the *Banque de l'Indochine* branch was safeguarded throughout these years of hardships, despite tensions and concerns (see Table 20.7).

3. *Banque de l'Indochine* practicing business in Tianjin, between hardships and stable clients

Against a background of instability, crisis, currency volatility, geopolitical and military tensions, it is hard to conceive that a few bankers and traders stuck to their "business as usual" issues and that the Tianjin marketplace was still fuelled by foreign exchanges.

A. Banking skills in risk management at stake

The shrinking market and mainly the growing incertitude throughout the networks of commerce explain the volatility of business. The management of risks, which had improved in the 1910s–1920s, was once more weakened, putting ceilings on the portfolio of competence. Overcoming bad debts, the *Banque de l'Indochine* branch succeeded in keeping its classic and somewhat faithful clientele. It could rely on the caution shown by its clients: "Very wisely, the French houses put themselves in night light [trying to remain discreet]. They decreased their overheads. They reduced their staff. They restricted their field of activity. Those who did not admit this discipline were hard struck", such as the Battegay trade house.[16] This important trading house, specialising in the exports of furs and pork bristles, had to be liquidated in February 1936, swallowing three-quarters of its capital, because of bad debts on its Chinese customers and essentially through operations on pork bristles with the Ta Yi Hang Tsang house, owned by the father of the comprador of Battegay.

Table 20.6 Interests and commissions earned by the *Banque de l'Indochine* branch in Tianjin in 1939–1941 (nationalist Chinese dollars)

	Second half of 1938	First half of 1939	Second half of 1939	First half of 1940	Second half of 1940	First half of 1941	Second half of 1941
On local loans	23,655	16,651	21,551	30,429	24480	53,452	41,813
Through operations with correspondents (National Provincial Bank in London, French American Banking Corporation in New York, and, far behind, the *Banque de l'Indochine* branch in Saigon)	78,519	22,957	/	1,895	3	19,941	19,712
Commissions	2,696	2,582	3,232	1,608	242	544	1,197
Provisions begin reintegrated	/	12,450	/	494	/	/	/
Total	107,436	54,868	25,092	34,796	27,991	88,334	75,382

Source: *Rapport-bilan. Situation économique et politique*, first half of 1939, *Banque de l'Indochine* correspondence, 15 July 1939; second half of 1939, 12 January 1940; second half of 1941, January 1942

Table 20.7 Returns of the *Banque de l'Indochine* branch in Tianjin in 1938–1941 (in "nationalist" Chinese dollars)

	First half 1938	Second half 1938	First half 1939	Second half 1939	Full year 1940	First half 1941	Second half 1941
Profits from arbitrage operations	901,000	180,000	476,000	1,496,000	1,632,000	257,000	94,000
Returns on interests and commissions on credit operations	65,000	98,000	41,000	15,000	66,000	55,000	69,000
Total of receipts	966,000	278,000	517,000	1,511,000	1,698,000	311,000	162,000
Overhead expenses	82,000	136,000	128,000	250,000	459,000	273,000	162000
Profits	884,000	142,000	389,000	1,261,000	1,239,000	39,000	70

Source: *Rapport-bilan. Situation économique et politique, Banque de l'Indochine* correspondence, first half of 1939, 15 July 1939; second half of 1939, 18 January 1940; first half of 1940, 9 July 1940; second half of 1940, January 1941; first half of 1941, 7 July 1941; second half of 1941, January 1942

By the fact of the lagging transmission of the causes, we see varied move-ments taking shape without knowing the motives, the rumours propa-gating more slowly and remaining for us, moreover, uncontrollable. We undergo this fact very brutally the reactions which affect Shanghai and the result of the ignorance where we are of their causes is that our market congeals: nobody operates, we wait …And when, afterward, the movement restarts, all the banks operate in the same way, and the counterparties are insignificant. So any position here is much more difficult to treat and much more dangerous because we are certain to act only in delay or even not to find the whole picture.[17]

Three banks (*Banque de l'Indochine* [itself with $282,000 in risks pending on the firm, leaving it finally with a bad debt of $59,000 in June 1939], HSBC, Commer-cial Bank) were involved in such losses (with liabilities totalling $400,000), and the warehouse inventories were revealed to be far lower than officially pledged:

We are one more time in the presence of one situation the risk of which was often cancelled but against which banks are more or less defenseless: an European house, closely linked to its comprador, or to a friendly Chinese firm, which supply, without known regular agreements, the funds which are necessary for it. The European house, which only banks can know and check, is in reality only a facade, while, in fact, its fate depends on the action of one or several Chinese characters whom the European banks ignore or on whom they can take no action … There is in China only a single [actual and structured] market, Shanghai. Tianjin is an important place where are treated a lot of affairs of exchange, it is not an exchange market. Our place, under this situation, is only the reflection of Shanghai.[18]

Should *Banque de l'Indochine* have imposed stricter demands on its clients, it would have lost momentum against its competitors and curtailed its market share:

Tianjin is especially an exporting place and almost the whole lot of the exported products require long and delicate manipulations in the ware-houses of the exporters, outside any effective control of banks. In the case of impossibility for us to continue to grant advances in trust without collat-eralised real guarantee, our role here will decrease. Our clientele is already of the most reduced, and this situation has in particular its repercussion on our foreign-exchange transactions for which we are almost always lacking clientele as counterparts. The English and American banks are obviously helped in this policy by the large number of houses of their nationality, which is not our case there.[19]

"At the slightest vague desire from us to surround us with more precautions than the local practices contain us, our customers would find immediately with our competitors the most liberal help."[20] No solidarity was anyway practiced onthe part of the French houses, which prompted competition among banks, and the Colinet house, for example, left the *Banque de l'Indochine* branch in 1933–1936 because it had found better conditions with five other banks.[21]

Customers had cut into their inventories, staff and overhead since the first half of the 1930s. In June 1939, the Catholic missions (*Procure des Lazaristes, Mission de Sienhsien, Procure des Franciscains*) were leading clients for their local operations, through exchange operations on French francs or advances pledged by US dollar deposits or securities—and they brought guarantees to several lines of credit in favour of trading houses.

Énergie électrique de Tientsin was an old client too; it was, for example, supplied with a credit to import equipment goods from Swiss Brown-Boveri (June 1939). It was followed by less known companies, which constituted the core of local business in Tianjin for local industry (*Tannerie franco-chinoise*, General Veneer Factory,[22] etc.). The control of the revenues of utilities companies was no longer guaranteed because of the regional military drift, and no more revenues from railway companies or elsewhere could be used as a pledge for loans. This enhanced the prospect of operations with the Tchengtai railway, which had kept a staff of French engineers and managers throughout the interwar period despite its sinisation because it had been built and managed (in Shihkiachwang) by the French in the 1900s. *Le Matériel technique* succeeded in selling fresh equipment (from French firms Daydé and *Comptoir sidérurgique de France*) in 1933 for FRF 20 million, then 29 million, and a package of credit was set up by the *Banque de l'Indochine* branch, even if the Paris office itself was involved for some millions,[23] against the deposit of part of the funds by the Chinese ministry on a Chinese account as a guarantee.

Instalments of promissory notes were issued by the Chinese ministry of railways, two paid on exchange of the equipment, the other guaranteed by three Chinese banks, themselves pledged by the trade house Sassoon. *Banque de l'Indochine* granted two credits (at 7 per cent plus commission): FRF 3.4 million as an irrevocable confirmed credit and bills of exchange for 4.154 million, with instalments to be paid through the monthly revenues of the railways. The project intended to draw a new railway in the Tsang Cheu from Shihkiachwang to Siao Fang; coal could be transported directly to the Tianjin harbour without transiting through Beijing.[24] The operation took shape effectively in 1934–1935.

Less pacific trade was also developed, when armaments were involved, owing to the fragmentation of military and political power at the turn of the 1930s. French firm Hotchkiss received an order from the Hei Lung Kiang government fora hundred machine guns;[25] *Banque de l'Indochine* brought its local guarantee ($80,000), while the Paris office opened a confirmed credit (USD 78,000). But the development of such business was obviously hindered by the military and political evolution of China and moreover by a disturbing position of the French state which refused to bring a public guarantee from credit insurance for the suppliers because it required that the Chinese 1902 loan be repaid in golden francs and not in current francs, which paralysed exports prospects. On its side, the group led by the businessman Pavlovski broadened its scope, and its subsidiary *Le Matériel technique* could propose anything to customers: eleven *Potez 25* planes with *Lorraine* engines were even sold to the Szechuen government in 1932, transported by boat to Haiphong, assembled there, but military troubles suspended the completion of the operation, co-financed by *Banque de l'Indochine* through confirmed credits.

B. Olivier still a close companion

Trading houses still attended the *Banque de l'Indochine* branch with intimacy and continuity. The Olivier affiliate in China was the most brilliant one, part of a "global" firm active in the whole Far East and extending its network to London and New York, thus fuelling broad remittances for *Banque de l'Indochine*. Supplied by little local dealers equipped with their go-downs, *Olivier-Chine* (based in Shanghai) was still the main French trade house active in the export of Chinese commodities through Tianjin to Europe and the United States: "Since in the middle of August [1939], *Olivier-Chine* does not pull more than checks in $FRB at the account Advances on drafts to be delivered to America; the account Europe in $CNC stopped playing since. A new credit of $200 000 FRB was granted to *Olivier-Chine*, following a telegram received on 24th January 1940."[26]

Its Tianjin branch was the second beneficiary of a global *Banque de l'Indochine* credit in China to the firm after that of Shanghai but ahead of that of Wuhan: "The revolving permanent credit permanent of 9,5 million francs in favour of this house was distributed by its direction in Shanghai: 3 million for Tianjin, 5m for Shanghai, 1m for Hong Kong."[27] Olivier had commercial points in Shanghai, Hong Kong, Harbin, Wuhan, Tsingtao, Ningpo and Tianjin and also on Java.

This trade house remained therefore a key customer of the *Banque de l'Indochine* branch of Tianjin throughout the 1930s, with large confirmed and irrevocable credits:

> It is a credit of pure trust which we grant to Olivier, and we are well aware of the danger of such facilities; but, should we operate differently, we ought to renounce this business and leave them to competitors. Neither Olivier house nor other ones would indeed accept to leave their goods piled up in the customs go-downs, bearing important charges, whereas these houses have an important commercial organisation including vast warehouses [where the bank cannot precisely determine the value of its pledge].[28]

Banque de l'Indochine's commitment to Olivier reached $89,000 in 1933 (48,000 in Europe; 41,000 in the United States), against 109,000 by HSBC and 68,000 by City Bank.[29] This heavy weight benefited from permanent or recurrent lines of credit at the *Banque de l'Indochine* branch. It called for advances on bills to be delivered (with an amount of FRB $113,745 (pledged by $142,131 in merchandise), for drafts and for exchange contracts (in francs or pounds against US dollars, but the operations with North America lost substance from the mid-1939), with also important remittances operations on the City. But in the mid-1940s, such remittances were put off at the expense of the branch, which endured bad debts in francs (602,000) and pounds (23,169) (see Table 20.8).

C. Narrow paths for business

Olivier was accompanied by far lesser known companies, which constituted the core of local business in Tianjin, either for local industrial (*Tannerie franco-chinoise*, General Veneer Factory,[30] etc.) or commercial operations, or for import trading, like the G. Colinet informal group (Daily Suppliers, *Renault* car imports, insurance agency, commodities exports), Gully & C°, Fernand Leconte or the E. Vernaudin houses.[31] The latter was, for instance, granted current advances in francs and sterling and credits earmarked to finance imports from French goods (pasta, *Guerlain* perfumes, *François Weiss* Bordeaux wines), tobacco (US Reynolds Tobacco or Hong Kong Oriental Tobacco-Ingenohl), chocolate and cocoa, and so on.[32] Foreign companies like Standard Vacuum Oil also gained access to *Banque de l'Indochine*'s services in direct.

But imports for the European customership collapsed in 1941, because of caps put on them by customs and exchange authorities: "For all the products unauthorized in the import, practically all those whom the European residents need, sales are made by taking on the previous stocks, moreover very wide, and on the secret entrances. Some substantial presents to the staff of the 'control' allow, where necessary, to soften the regulations ... For wines and liqueurs, the opportunities seem less big, and we envisage the moment when we shall have to content ourselves with Japanese beer and with saki. A short stay which I made in Shanghai at the beginning of the half-year allowed me to notice that the cost of living for the Europeans is hardly more half of the one who is at present practised in Tianjin. This difference ... can only grow, this especially as the German, excellent and relatively cheap, export products, cannot reach us

Table 20.8 Trade completed by *Olivier-Chine*'s branch in Tianjin at the end of the 1930s

Exports	To
Egg yolks and albumin	Europe
Furs	Marseille
Horse hairs	Lisbon, London
Walnut meats	Melbourne, New York
Fancy straw bread	New York
Imports	From
Cognac, chemicals, silk commodities	Europe

Source: Notice on 3 March 1939, *Consulat général* archives, 62/9C1

Table 20.9 Treasury operations in currencies by the *Banque de l'Indochine* branch in Tianjin in 1938–1941 (FRF thousands)

	Second half of 1938	First half of 1939	Second half of 1939	Second half of 1940	First half of 1941	Second half of 1941
Purchases of French francs (or sales as counterparts)	61,574	22,901	23,461	693,264	2,742,378	487,788
Purchases of sterling pounds (or sales as counterparts)	972,522	761,846	351,743	79,405	26,247	137
Purchases of USD (or sales as counterparts)	2,360	1,938	1,620	724,700	1,040,479	189,920
Purchases of nationalist Chinese dollars (or sales as counterparts)	35,309	32,477	17,396	7,649	931,530	240,078
Purchases of Shanghai dollars (or sales as counterparts)	9,641	12,325	15,494	2,425,219	1,719,046	3,379,222

Source: *Rapport-bilan. Situation économique et politique*, second half of 1939, *Banque de l'Indochine* correspondence, 12 January 1940; second half of 1940, January 1941; first half of 1941, 7 July 1941; second half of 1941, January 1942

any more."[33] Imports of 4,010 tons of rice were anyway allowed during the first half of 1941, from Indochina through the houses Daltotat, E. Gipperich and Fu Chung Trading C° (connected in Saigon with *Societé commerciale française de l'Indochine* for the first one and, for the two latter, Louis Dreyfus & C°).[34]

3. Managing treasuries as a challenge

All in all, the bankers succeeded in handling the difficulties or subtleties fostered by the volatility of the money markets, and they tackled the use of various currencies (Mexican dollars, taels, pounds). But they had to follow the suppression of the tael in 1933 in favour of the silver dollar,[35] which required delicate operations of conversion in May 1933. Such a move paved the way to the comprehensive monetary reform launched by the Chinese central government in 1935, which imposed the unification of bills and the conversion of all banking accounts and deposits.[36]

Locally, French institutions and authorities used the *Banque de l'Indochine* branch for their daily needs to get cash, to sell francs sent to them from Paris to finance their activities: the French Consulate and the treasurer of the local French troops were thus permanent clients. And an array of Chinese enterprises were direct clients (with or without the intermediary of the comprador) to finance their imports from the United States (like Yee Tsoong Tobacco Distributors or Asiatic Petroleum C°–North China, etc.). Despite the preservation of its capital of skills, networks and customers, the *Banque de l'Indochine* branch endured the overall difficulties of the Tianjin marketplace. Clues are to be found in the decline of treasury operations in currencies (see Table 20.9), which reflected the evolution of its turnover.

Notes

1 Note *Relations avec la Mission de Sien Shien, Banque de l'Indochine* correspondence, Archives of *Crédit agricole, Banque de l'Indochine* fund, 23 July 1936.
2 Correspondence, 20 January 1931 and 7 July 1931.
3 *Rapport-bilan. Situation économique et politique*, Second half of 1938, *Banque de l'Indochine* correspondence, 17 January 1939, annex 5.
4 BIC correspondence, 21 July 1937.
5 Charles Lépissier; Lucien Colin in 1939; J. Siguret.
6 With R. Soliva as manager, then S.A. Fuyet in November 1938.
7 R.T. Evans, "Tientsin's Lombard Street", *North China Star*, 12 August 1920, p. 11, *Consulat général* archives, 9C1.
8 See Marie-Claire Bergère, "The geography of finance in a semi-colonial metropolis: The Shanghai *Bund* (1842–1943)", in Herman Diedricks & David Reeder (eds.), *Cities of Finance*, Amsterdam, Koninklijke Nederlandse Akademie van Wetenschappen, 1996, pp. 303–317.
9 The *Banque de l'Indochine* branch was located on 73–75 avenue de France, which prolonged Victoria Road northwards.
10 *Consulat général* archives, 9D42. The *North China Star* was an American newspaper edited in the French concession in Tianjin.
11 *Banque de l'Indochine* correspondence, 27 January 1937.
12 *Ibidem.*
13 The building of the branch is still standing, and its houses the Fine Arts Museum of Tianjin in the Heping district. The office of HSBC was built a little later in 1925, on the same street, on 84 Jiefang North Road, whilst the Yokohama Specie Bank was built in 1926 at 80 Jiefan North Road. Both were therefore close to *Banque de l'Indochine* on 77 Jiefang North Road. Bank of Chosen stood on 101 Jiefang North Road and *Banque russo-asiatique* (since 1895) on 121 Jiefan North Road.
14 *Rapport-bilan. Situation économique et politique*, second half of 1939, *Banque de l'Indochine* correspondence, 12 January 1940, annex 9bis. This document indicates that Heng Chi Hao was still referred to as the comprador a few times in 1940, despite the name of Fa Chu Chai who took over this charge in 1933.
15 *Rapport-bilan. Situation économique et politique*, second half of 1941, *Banque de l'Indochine* correspondence, January 1942.
16 Note from the *Consul général de France*, 1936, *Consulat général* archives, TT46.
17 BIC correspondence, 5 February 1936.
18 *Ibidem.*
19 *Ibidem*, 4 March 1936.
20 *Ibidem*, 12 March 1936.
21 *Ibidem*, 4 March 1936.
22 General Veneer Factory-*Manufacture de bois contreplaqués* was located on 53 Lao Si Kai Road.
23 *Ibidem*, 19 September 1933.
24 *Ibidem*, 25 January 1934, 10 February 1934, 15 February 1934.
25 *Ibidem*, 23 July 1930.
26 Second half of 1939, *Banque de l'Indochine* correspondence, 18 January 1940, annex 8.

27 *Rapport-bilan. Situation économique et politique,* first half of 1940, *Banque de l'Indochine* correspondence, 9 July 1940, annex 2.
28 BIC correspondence, 13 June 1932.
29 *Ibidem,* 14 August 1933. On 27 January 1937, the shares of the global $547,000 credit became 197,000 for *Banque de l'Indochine,* 150,000 for HSBC, 125,000 for *Banque belge pour l'étranger* (the successor of *Banque sino-belge*), and 75,000 for City Bank.
30 General Veneer Factory-*Manufacture de bois contreplaqués* was located on 53 Lao Si Kai Road.
31 See *Questions financières. Dossier général,* around 1937–1939, *Consulat général* archives, 9A57.
32 *Rapport-bilan. Situation économique et politique,* first half of 1939, *Banque de l'Indochine* correspondence, 15 July 1939; second half of 1939, 12 January 1940.
33 *Rapport-bilan. Situation économique et politique,* first half of 1941, *Banque de l'Indochine* correspondence, 7 July 1941, p. 5.
34 *Ibidem,* annex 5.
35 *Ibidem,* 21 April 1933.
36 *Ibidem,* 5 November 1935.

21 The Tianjin marketplace struggling against ordeals (1939–1945)

Just before the period of Japanese rule, the fate of the *Banque de l'Indochine* branch in Tianjin was confronted with the dire issues of military, political, even national issues. But it still resisted, and the marketplace kept some momentum, even in favour of French business and banking, despite the war in Europe. Then, the Japanese power imposed new models of practicing business under the rule of military constraints. Remnants of exchanges subsisted in the event, but the Tianjin marketplace had lost its business model. French interests still survived as, officially, China was only conquered by its enemy and on its very territory and within the concession—to disappear soon—it kept de facto some ambiguous status, thus opening narrow doors for surviving.

1. Free trade at stake

A cause was the purpose of Japan to put brakes on free trade, with a control on foreign exchange emerging slowly in 1938 in order to avoid discontent from foreign countries, like France, which reacted by instituting a clearing system for Franco-Japanese trade. It created two FOREX markets in Tianjin: one with Japanese banks, another in the "Western market"—imposed on March 1939. It was strictly consolidated as of 26 June 1940, demanding authorisations by the Federal Reserve Bank for all foreign currencies—except for basic foodstuffs to be imported for populations and gasoline—in order to put the brakes on the import of equipment goods so as to favour the purchase of Japanese ones.[1] Japan's strategy was to draw from the interior increasing quantities of commodities and to barter against them, at proportions to be determined by the military victors, export goods from Japan to the exclusion of those from foreign trading nations—thus stirring an eviction effect at the expense of European trade houses in Tianjin.

Another obstacle appeared when Japan imposed its embargo on exports of cotton, jute, hemp, wool and raw hides, now earmarked for Japanese houses, which oriented the area towards the Manchurian way of life, from which European business had almost been excluded little by little. And sometimes the Japanese power went so far in 1938 as to commandeer cotton goods to compensate for the decline in value of the yen or of the new Beijing dollar—but finally such authoritarian moves (embargo and commandeering) prompted Chinese peasants to reduce crops and to avoid merchant circuits for fear of being stripped of their revenues: "Cotton producers had already curtailed production to circumvent the Japanese cotton monopoly."[2] Such attitudes across villages led to shrinking imports of European and also Japanese goods all around Tianjin and the other cities of the area (see Table 21.1).

As local producers (peasants or else) put brakes on their production or deliveries, imports overcame exports in 1938–1939, which discontented either the western Chinese regime or the Japanese de facto power, concerned by the drift of the value of their respective dollar.[3]

2. A dwindling marketplace at the start of the 1940s

Later on, in 1940, inflation triumphed due to the shortage of consuming goods and foodstuff and the smuggling within the Shanghai area—which had cut its traditional commercial links with Tianjin: "In the economic sense of the word, Shanghai and the South China became 'foreign countries' since the establishment, in North China, of $FRB and exchange control. The few relations which still remain are possible only by the preservation of the *fabi* and are brought to disappear gradually."[4]

As the military and geopolitical situation became relatively stabilised in the area, the FRB dollar gained substance against other currencies (the nationalist dollar, essentially, which lost credit in the area) for some quarters in late 1940 and early 1941, whilst US banks started repatriating US dollars to anticipate the rumoured risks of a US–Japan war. Such uncertainties and volatility were supplemented by the more and more tedious controls on exchanges by the Japanese and Beijing authorities, within the frame of clearing rules (called the "link system"): "The exporter can have 90 per cent of his currencies only in favour of an importer. This one, on his side, can benefit from a similar transfer only if he lets in products approved by the Federal Reserve Bank, that is until further notice cereal, textile fibers and metal."[5]

Table 21.1 Evolution of Tianjin trade in 1937–1938 (USD thousands)

	Imports		Exports	
	January–April 1937	*January–April 1938*	*January–April 1937*	*January–April 1938*
Trade with Japan	10,500	24,000	13,000	22,000
Trade with other powers	20,500	20,000	44,000	19,000
Total trade	31,000	44,000	57,000	41,000
Part of Japan	34%	55%	22%	53%

Source: Note *Situation économique et politique en Extrême-Orient, Banque de l'Indochine* correspondence, 15 September 1938

The market of the "link", that is quoted in $FRB, foreign currencies result-
ing from the export and used for the import of the only products approved
by the control, took such a development that it defines the course in $FRB
of the same currencies on the free market, where they record however, as
it is natural, a bonus which is at present of the order of 5 percent ... So
the considerable increase of the $FRB ... is exclusively understandable by
reasons of psychological order. It appeared to the carriers of $CNC—today
given up by the English export enterprises and the Consulate of Great
Britain itself—that the $FRB could not fail to appreciate, being given the
considerable diplomatic successes of Japan in the negotiations with Indochina, Siam and the USSR.[6]

Imports could only be processed against the consignment of foreign currencies
gained on exports. But more and more products were banned from imports
(luxury goods, mainly) to put ceilings on currency outflows.

Some relief was due in Tianjin to the autonomous statute of the concessions, which helped preserving part of "free market" for goods and currencies
exchanges. Bills could still be drawn in US dollars on American and German
buyers, and documentary credits granted by the Yokohama Specie Bank, and
transfers could be achieved in CNC or /and Shanghai dollars for operations
on opium, gold bars, diamonds, furs—that is, high-valued goods smuggled to
Shanghai: "The resistance of the foreign banks and the Chinese business circles
was able, thanks to the preservation of the concessions, to substitute a *de facto*
rigorous control, conceived German-style as a rather flexible regime, similar to
the one practiced in South America."[7]

But all in all, the Japanese grip over the Tianjin trade became more and more
heavy-handed: "The foreign trade of Tianjin fell in the hands of the Japanese,
because of the constitution of companies profiting from monopoly and obstacles were brought to foreign shipping."[8] And a mere 30 per cent of the trade
exchanges might be processed on a genuine free market.[9] A strict control of
exchanges was instituted since 1st March 1939, with FOREX operations to be
overtaken by the sole Yokohama Specie Bank.[10]

Caught in such hardships, the Tianjin marketplace lost momentum: "The
trade of the district was brought to a very bad pass through the introduction of
export trade and currency control."[11] Northwards, its outlets collapsed because
Manchukuo became a preserve of Japanese business within some kind of "a yen
zone": "North China imported formerly from Manchukuo ... foodstuffs and
raw materials. Manchukuo watches now to preserve its own interests: the weakness of its last harvests, embargos, the desire to channel its exports on countries with high exchange, broke secular links."[12] Southwards, another cause was
smuggling with Shanghai which often short-circuited the harbour, "through
the old trade routes of China."[13]

Third, because of the sharp rise in the cost of living within the concessions due to the collapse of the Chinese dollar, some of the poorest Chinese
inhabitants left them. Both French and British municipalities had to curtail
their budgets and in 1940 raised taxes and the tariffs of electricity, both having

negative effects on business.[14] Fourth, business was dealt a stiff blow by huge natural flooding in August 1939 at the scale of the whole northern China, and the Tianjin area endured dire months because of a convergent overflow by the tributaries of the Haiho.

The area suffered from thousands of deaths, starvation, poverty and decline in crops, which blocked transport and trade on natural commodities and consuming goods: "The flood extended over the Hopeh, the North of Honan, Shansi, the West of Shanting, the South of the Outer Mongolia, over several regions of Anhwei and Kangsu. In Shansi, one accounts 3,000 victims, 5,000 destroyed houses, 5,000 damaged. In the region Beijing-Tianjin, 50,000 inhabitants distributed in 150 villages are homeless. In the Shantung, the dikes of Wei-Ho and the Grand Canal were broken, the water submerging five districts and causing the exodus of farmers' Jinan by hundred one thousand ... The flood seriously struck the culture of cotton and the production of salt. It reduced in a considerable way the livelihood of the inhabitants. The autumn harvest for cereal was bad, when it was not completely destroyed. The top management of the Japanese garrison of Tianjin estimates the material losses undergone in the urban region of Tianjin to 400 million $FRB, among them 200 for the French and English concessions, 150 for the Japanese concession and 50 million for the Chinese city. Three million inhabitants suffered from the flood, 10,000 were flooded, 600,000 lost any means of existence; 120,000 houses were destroyed. In Tianjin, the water withdrew after one month only, following works which showed themselves effective but expensive. The only French municipality had to bear, because of the flood, a FRB$ 300,000-dollar load. The subscription opened in favour of the victims, in the concession, reaches at present FRB $170,000 ... The Japanese planned on their side a three million dollar credit for the restoration of the outside dike which protects Tianjin. In the absence of a common plan, where the expenses would fairly be distributed and completely justified, the authorities of the concessions can only take imaginary measures."[15]

Fifth, business was also affected when the German houses, which all in all were among the main clients of the Tianjin place, had to commence to fold up their Asian activities. Because the concessions were under a "neutral" statute, Chinese exports to Germany had first kept up momentum, thanks to the intermediation of the Yokohama Specie Bank for trade banking. Only French houses and banks had stopped trading with their German partners. Then British authorities blocked acceptances and remittances of bills in the City which involved German commerce, even through Japanese and American banks. Longer circuits had to be set up, which "transformed" such paper into "neutral" paper, processed in Asia by the Yokohama Specie Bank and relayed by western banks (City Bank, etc.) in Europe.

At the turn of 1941, due to the maritime war and exports through Man-chukuo and the USSR, instead of using Tianjin, German transit disappeared, depriving Tianjin of its main client and thus of currency liquidities: "The rough stop of the commercial transactions with Germany, following the Russian-Germanic hostilities, strikes hard the marketplace of Tianjin, the German firms handling the majority of business both in the import and in the export."[16]

Last, the American firms also commenced reducing their stake in the region:

> The holders of US dollars in account either in Tianjin, or in the United States, measured fast all the risks which they ran to be 'frozen', North China being an occupied territory by the Japanese, virtually the enemies of Washington. As besides the $FRB had rehabilitated itself, a very important repatriation of US dollars in $FRB intervened by the channel of the free market, and on certain days the panic took such proportions as we were able to give two percent in transfer of the US dollar by month.[17]

3. The French concession through dire ordeals

The European war had no direct effect on the life of the French concession by itself; its mood reflected resignation without positive expectations:

> The war in Europe did not bring a lot of visible change to the existence of Tianjin, which lives blocked and introverted for months. The mobilization affected until now only ten of our fellow countrymen, among them four reserve officers. The composition of the body of occupation has just been modified, on the other hand, rather seriously.[18]

But measures of economy led to the transfer of the headquarters of the French colonial troops from Tianjin to Shanghai (where the ambassador had been moved), and battalions (from the 16th *Régiment d'infanterie coloniale*) were seriously reduced in the whole north-eastern area (Beijing, Togku, Shan-Hai-Kan, and Tianjin), from 1,300 to 500 soldiers, part of them in Tianjin—the effects being a cut into the business and treasury facilities supplied by local houses and banks—and the same on the British side. The functions of French and British troops there had lost sense because Japanese troops oversaw the Beijing–Tianjin road and due to the general situation of the Chinese regimes.

Generally speaking, all these events converged to undermine the vitality of the Tianjin marketplace. Exports declined strongly in favour of imports, reversing the classic way of life of the harbour, mostly because cotton and wool (about half of previous exports) were bought/requisitioned (at low prices) by the Japanese army—which reinforced smuggling toward Shanghai—whilst the other com-modities lost about one-third of the traded amounts between 1938 and 1939.

Imports had to grow to compensate the reduction of rice and flour produc-tion in the close provinces, where peasants balked at being underpaid or obeyed the constraints imposed by communist guerrillas on sales to Japanese areas.

The Tianjin authorities had to import more and more flour and rice, which demanded larger amounts of currencies. "Tianjin is therefore losing its importance day after day."[19] The Chinese and European community tried to find new opportunities in speculation on "internal" changes, thanks to the volatile spreads between the nationalist dollar and the pro-Japanese one, with more or less transparent operations on call in Shanghai—and even Japanese fuelled that speculation with the "selfish speculation activities of civilian Japanese who smuggle yen notes into Shanghai and offer them for sale against Chinese dollars at the low prices they fetch there."[20] The "real" Tianjin economy dwindled throughout 1940–1941: "The economic life continues to disintegrate in North China, which has been the victim of an unprecedented flood and where the war has not stop existing since 1937. The future prospects justify no optimism."[21]

4. Tianjin through total war and the Japanese order (1941–1945)

We lack information about the business and banking life of the French community throughout the most notable events of World War II, because information did not circulate between the Consulate, the *Banque de l'Indochine* branch and their Paris counterparts. Our survey will therefore include only a few glances at the evolution of the little Tianjin marketplace. It joined in World War II directly when Japanese troops invaded the international concession on 8 December 1941, but the French settlement was prevented from turmoil because of the Vichy regime's "*de facto* alliance" with Japan—the Vichy government in France struggling to safeguard its control over Indochina. But the French authorities had to accept the control of the Chinese population by Japanese police and soldiers.

Then it was confronted with the agreement between the Nanking government and Japan about the retrocession of the settlements on 9 January 1943: France dragged feet but admitted it on 23 February 1943 and officially abandoned its historical concessions (Shanghai, Wuhan, Tianjin) on 5 June 1943, with the completion of the transfer being executed on 21 July 1943. Anyway, French authorities, civil servants and troops ultimately could not be repatriated to Europe (or to Indochina), and a meddling of "old times", of Nanking Chinese rule and of Japanese power lasted for a few quarters—till the thorough invasion of the French concession by the Japanese army on 10 March 1945—far later than that of Shanghai on 8 December 1941: an amazing French "island" had therefore lasted almost till the very end of World War II in Tianjin.

But business had dwindled to low levels because of the maritime war, the isolation, the lack of purchasing power or caution among potential customers. Threats to Tianjin business and trade pending in mid-1941 took form after the war broke out between Japan and the United States: deprived of US and German orders, northern China and the Tianjin marketplace would lose all means to finance, through the export of its commodities, its import of day-to-day goods such as cereals and raw materials.

Japan is not useful any more for the provisioning of Germany, with which it has just been cut following the German–Soviet conflict. Besides, its entry into war could follow that of the United States instead of causing it. In this hypothesis, deprived of its German and American buyers, North China would have no longer the currencies necessary for the payment of cereal and raw materials, which are essential to its daily life, and would be rather fast in a precarious situation. In such perspectives we would be able only to reduce at least the initiatives in the field of foreign trade, which also suffered from the economic regulations in force since the end of 1940.[22] We must fear that, if tensions between Tokyo and Washington still grow, the North becomes for a while a province of Japan without foreign trade, thus without operations which we can hold.[23]

Businessmen's mood was sagging in 1941. The Japanese controls had been reinforced since 1941, under the rule of the chief of the Japanese Special Military Mission in Tianjin, Lieutenant Colonel Tet Suo Yamashita. He acted "to block all old note accounts until further notice and exterminate [sic] transactions based on old notes" and "to discontinue Shanghai exchange business as well as every other inter-banking dealings except when special permit is given, and thus cooperate with Japanese authorities in order not to contradict policy of the Federal Reserve Bank of China", which required getting "permission of the chief of the Japanese Special Military Mission beforehand in case you place a new loan exceeding FRB\$ 100,000."[24]

Beyond the restrictions on free trade and the volatility and variety of currencies, one further negative aspect, effective from the turn of the 1940s, laid with the single use of "special yens" by Japanese banks to finance a range of imports by the administrations in the Japanese zones. "We are in front of a systematic obstruction, a carefully closed wall, which we cannot force, not possessing in Tianjin the only effective means: a bargaining chip."[25] *Banque de l'Indochine* suffered directly from that rule because rice imports from French Indochina had to use such a currency. Such imports had also to be fulfilled through Japanese ships which excluded European lines (and in that case, the French line *Messageries maritimes*, linking Indochina to Tianjin harbour).

French trade houses or intermediaries little by little were evicted from such orders, which curtailed downstream the activities of *Banque de l'Indochine* and of *Banque franco-chinoise*'s Tianjin branches. "The operations in special yens are reserved for the Japanese banks, in the case in point in Tianjin, Yokohama Specie Bank and Bank of Chosen. The role of the non-Japanese banks is reduced to that of agency asked to receive commercial documents and to make payments."[26] *Banque de l'Indochine*'s deposits and loans had been much lowered, its outstanding loans reached an ebb, and cash and liquidity prevailed (see Table 21.2).

5. From storytelling to assessment: Tianjin as a case study

Surely, our study about French business and banking in the Tianjin marketplace will not revolutionise the history of Chinese economy, nor will it compete

Table 21.2 The dwindling operations of *Banque de l'Indochine* in Tianjin in 1941–1944 (thousands FRB$)

	July 1941	31 August 1943	15 September 1944
Loans		459	125
Overdrafts		230	37
Total outstanding credits		1,657	482
Deposits at banks (Yokohama Specie Bank, Federal Reserve Bank of China, *Banque franco-chinoise*, HSBC)		941	560
Cash		90	249
Assets	7,344	2,888	1,854
Deposits collected		2,247	900

Source: *Consulat général* archives, 9C1

with Marie-Claire Bergère[27] or Frank King's[28] master books, but it will bring "capitalist" materials to the brilliant book by Pierre Singaravélou about *Tianjin Cosmopolis*.[29] It is focused on a small community of interests which had been embedded in the life of the Tianjin marketplace. Having established bridge-heads there in the 1910–1920s to pick up shares of an emerging customership, it had had to adapt to times of hardships: warfare all around, population moves, and misery in Tianjin city itself, two floods, the Japanese grip on security, business, exchange and banking, and so on. It might even seem improper to reconstitute the life of such a microcosm in light of such terrible events.

Business historians have got used to scrutinising the resiliency of businessmen during civil or general wars and hardships because micro-markets have ever been recreated and daily consumption always needs to be faced, which provides opportunities for sales. Our survey provides clues about French nimble entrepreneurship, which found business prospects among elites (for high-end consuming goods), either European or Chinese ones (even among warlords and the various go-between intermediaries or authorities which were set up more or less in dependence on the Japanese order in zones of military feuds and uncertain power). It also tried to get a share of the collection of commodities, those escaping the Japanese requirements and the smuggling flows towards Shanghai.

Moreover, the Tianjin harbour and railway hub kept its export function because demand pervaded abroad for commodities which the countryside was still able to deliver, whatsoever its submission to warfare, smuggling or racketeering from troops. Already a "niche" business place, the city and its concessions clung to their profile as a hub for "tiny markets", far from the dimension of Hong Kong, Shanghai, Guangzhou or Wuhan, where French bankers and businessmen were far more active and numerous but nonetheless actors in the small "Asian Mediterranean" analysed by François Gipouloux.[30]

About two handfuls of trading and banking houses went on practicing "business as usual", overseeing changes in currencies, in political regimes and witnessing "big history" in the making all around (the war in the Shansi, etc.).

Only at the very end did the French concession first lose its historical statute (in the summer 1943) and at last was invaded by Japanese troops. Tianjin and in particular the French concession asserted themselves as a little pole of resistance against overall hardships and against the curtailment of business (trade, credit, FOREX) and in the facilities linked to it (hotel accommodation, port activities, warehousing, transportation, insurance). What seems apparent is the preservation of a genuine purchasing power among these thin layers of bourgeoisies because either they had piled up profits during the years of prosperity, or they succeeded in reaping returns from the (sometimes speculative) trading activities of the 1930s–1940s.

The classic (however threatened) functions of the French community in the Tianjin port-city kept up momentum throughout the 1930s and even somewhat throughout World War II. What is striking is the resiliency of business despite the blows submitted by military events. The foothold of French business in north-east China succeeded in safeguarding its business services to business (firms active there, trade houses) and to consumer markets, as a "niche hub" for servicing the French community through imports and for trading on Chinese goods through export to Europe and the United States. The very resiliency of entrepreneurship against the hardships of the period helped to foster the community of interests which could thus last until the end of World War II. But if it had "resisted" harsh times, it could not have maintained its force of development and the extension of business: the function of Tianjin as a bridgehead to penetrate north-east China (and even to get connected with Manchuria) was put to a halt.

What is difficult to catch is the mood of this French community (about ten dozen people), of its Chinese companions in fortune and misfortune and of the whole European community there. How did they manage their new relationship with the Japanese circles, first through the localised war, then through total war and, lastly, through the occupation of the settlement? Without reaching the scope of Shanghai or Hong Kong, of course, Tianjin appears as an awkward community because German and American people were attending Japanese and later on "Allied" European (British and French) people during all these years in the name of "business as usual".

An amazing issue lies in the relationship with the Chinese themselves who, under Japanese rule, struggled to find out opportunities to keep trading alive, officially or underground, achieving tricky compromises with the authorities (at control or customs posts) and maintaining connections with Shanghai and the countryside despite the state of warfare, guerrilla or volatility in currencies. But overcoming such hardships was at stake, and Tianjin might be a landmark for the fate of marketplaces being swallowed up by the turmoil of history and warfare, fighting to safeguard their turnover and revenues. A further study should be dedicated to the story of the years of blinded expectations and demise in 1945–1955, in order to scrutinise how the French community, authorities and business dreamed of a "return to normal" and "business as usual" despite the civil war and the communist grip, before the ultimate collapse of Western and capitalist bridgeheads in Tianjin.[31]

Notes

1 *Rapport-bilan. Situation économique et politique*, first half of 1940, *Banque de l'Indochine* correspondence, 9 July 1940, p. 3.

2 Note from the *Consul de France* in 1939, *Consulat général* archives, 9D62.

3 *Rapport-bilan. Situation économique et politique*, first half of 1939, *Banque de l'Indochine* correspondence, 15 July 1939.

4 *Ibidem*, first half of 1940, *Banque de l'Indochine* correspondence, 9 July 1940, p. 3.

5 *Ibidem*, first half of 1941, *Banque de l'Indochine* correspondence, 7 July 1941, p. 2. First half of 1941, 7 July 1941, pp. 3–4.

6 *Rapport-bilan. Situation économique et politique*, first half of 1941, *Banque de l'Indochine* correspondence, 7 July 1941, pp. 3–4.

7 *Ibidem*, correspondence, p. 2.

8 *Banque de l'Indochine* yearly report, 24 May 1939.

9 Notice in 1938, *Consulat général* archives, 9D62.

10 Notice in 1939, *Consulat général* archives, 9D62. See "With effect from July 17, exporters must sell their foreign currency to FRB", *The Peking Chronicle*, 7 July 1939, p. 1, *Consulat général* archives, 9D62.

11 Notice in 1939, *Consulat général* archives, 9D62.

12 *Rapport-bilan. Situation économique et politique*, first half of 1940, *Banque de l'Indochine* correspondence, 9 July 1940, p. 2.

13 Notice in 1939, *Consulat général* archives, 9D62.

14 *Rapport-bilan. Situation économique et politique*, second half of 1939, *Banque de l'Indochine* correspondence, 18 January 1940.

15 *Ibidem*, p. 2.

16 *Rapport-bilan. Situation économique et politique*, first half of 1941, *Banque de l'Indochine* correspondence, 7 July 1941, p. 6.

17 *Ibidem*, p. 5.

18 *Rapport-bilan. Situation économique et politique*, second half of 1939, *Banque de l'Indochine* correspondence, 18 January 1940, p. 3.

19 *Ibidem*, p. 5.

20 Note from the *Banque de l'Indochine* Tianjin branch, 12 September 1938, *Consulat général* archives, 9D62.

21 Second half of 1939, *Banque de l'Indochine* correspondence, 18 January 1940, p. 6.

22 *Rapport-bilan. Situation économique et politique*, first half of 1941, *Banque de l'Indochine* correspondence, 7 July 1941, p. 1.

23 *Ibidem*, first half of 1941, *Banque de l'Indochine* correspondence, 7 July 1941, p. 6.

24 Notice on 17 December 1945, *Consulat général* archives, 9C1.

25 Letter from Consul Lucien Colin to French ambassador H. Cosne, 4 April 1943, *Consulat général archives*, 9C1, *Banques*, general file.

26 Telegram sent by Admiral Jean Decoux (Indochina governor) and transmitted to Tianjin consul by the French embassy, 2 March 1942, *Consulat général archives*, 9C1.

27 Marie-Claire Bergère, *L'âge d'or de la bourgeoisie chinoise, 1911–1937*, Paris, Flammarion, 1986. Marie-Claire Bergère, *The Golden Age of the Chinese Bourgeoisie*, Cambridge, Cambridge University Press, 1989. Marie-Claire Bergère, *Capitalismes et capitalistes en Chine, des origines à nos jours*, Paris, Perrin, 2007.

28 Frank King, *The History of the Hong Kong & Shanghai Banking Corporation. Volume 3: The Hong Kong Bank, 1918–1940*, Cambridge, Cambridge University Press, 1988.

29 Pierre Singaravélou, *Tianjin Cosmopolis. Une autre histoire de la mondialisation*, Paris, Seuil, "L'Univers historique", 2017.

30 François Gipouloux, *La Méditerranée asiatique. Villes portuaires et réseaux marchands en Chine, Japon et en Asie du Sud-Est*, XVIe–XXIe siècles, Paris, CNRS Éditions, 2009. François Gipouloux, *The Asian Mediterranean: Port Cities and Trading Networks in China, Japan, and Southeast Asia, 13th–21st Century*, Cheltenham, Elgar, 2011. François Gipouloux,

Gateways to Globalisation: Asia's International Trading and Finance Centres, Cheltenham, Elgar, 2011.

31 See Aron Shai, *The Fate of British and French Firms in China, 1949–1954: Imperialism Imprisoned*, Oxford, MacMillan, 1996. Robert Cliver, "Surviving socialism: Private industry and the transition to socialism in China, 1945–1958", *Cross-Currents: East Asian History and Culture Review* (Berkeley), 2015, n° 4, pp. 139–164. Sherman Cochran, "Capitalists choosing Communist China: The Liu family of Shanghai, 1948–1956", in Jeremy Brown & Paul Pickowicz (eds.), *Dilemmas of Victory: The Early Years of the People's Republic of China*, Cambridge, Harvard University Press, 2010.

22 French companies in Wuhan facing competition, crises and wars in the 1930s

Ever since the start of the century, *Banque de l'Indochine* and the French trading companies had battled to maintain a competitive presence along the Yangtze River and in the regions that supplied the flows of products transported along it, despite the military and political tensions and economic uncertainties. Unfortunately these efforts were prevented from bearing fruit in the 1930s: disappointment set in as the business climate deteriorated and then when geopolitical factors shattered the geo-economic hopes of the French business communities in the Hankeou/Wuhan market, in particular the war between China and Japan in which they found themselves trapped. The new manager appointed at the end of 1931 had to simultaneously familiarise himself with local business and establish himself as a determined anti-risk crusader, like his successor, De Courseulles, aided by several employees (including Vaucher, Bertrand and Schindler).

1. Crises cut off Wuhan's lifeblood

The Wuhan marketplace, an advance bastion of international trade in the region of the middle Yangtze, found itself weakened, slowly but surely, by various economic, military and political blows.

A. The effects of the global economic crisis on the Wuhan market

When the countries that were importers of Chinese products fell victim to the depression from the turn of the 1930s onwards, export flows gradually dried up.

> The crisis of under-consumption and the economic malaise prevailing in Europe have slowed demand for Chinese products. Demand from America, which appeared to be picking up, has dropped back to zero again following the fresh crisis at the beginning of June [1930]. Demand from Japan, which is heading for a very serious crisis, has also fallen. And all these countries, anticipating a renewed fall in silver, keep making offers [to purchase commodities] at sub-market rates,[1]

all this while the business climate among the Chinese was depressed, prompting a flight of capital from the market.

The banking and financial crisis dented the finances of all companies, be they buyers of these Asian products or Chinese or foreign importers importing capital goods, petroleum products and other goods into China from all over the world. Many of the companies operating in the Wuhan market faltered. For example, "the firm Vanderstegen & Crooks, a major client for transactions in USD, has had to suspend business in 1930. Fortunately Crooks is taking over the whole of the company and trying to revive it, but it is a tough task."[2]

B. The Wuhan marketplace once again the scene of military tensions

Little by little, the noose tightened on the Wuhan trading hub, with new rebellions in the north-west against the central government in Nanking, uprisings by the communist far left and then the Japanese offensive. The troubles resumed as early as 1930:

> Our market has been besieged, from a distance of 100 km or less, either by troops and organised armies of bandits calling themselves communists, or by rebel armies, and all communications with the producing regions of the interior have been virtually severed. Following the Northerners' declaration of war on Nanking/Nanjing, our port has so often been at risk of being overrun by armies that panic has broken out on several occasions, leading to account settlements, stock liquidation and currency shortages, which have put brakes to local trade. Telegraph communications have been cut by pillagers or rebel armies on several occasions, and wireless communications delayed by censorship.[3] or the last six months [second half of 1930] our region has been practically in the hands of communist armies which keep threatening our city, terrorising the province and ravaging the whole of the middle Yangtze valley.[4]

The situation gradually eased and peace prevailed even in Hupei and in Wuhan in the first half of 1934, providing some respite for the trading and banking houses. Then tensions mounted once again: the regions controlled by the communist armies in the north-west tightened their grip on the city of Wuhan from several dozen kilometres out. Meanwhile the burden of taxes and inspections resulted in a drop in production by smallholders and in commercial transactions, which put a damper on trade locally. Moreover, in the second half of 1930, with the "red" troops approaching:

> The city was saved only by the arrival of foreign naval forces sent as an emergency response: their presence kept the armies of pillagers [the "communist bandits"] at a respectable distance, as they were not keen to come into contact with the foreign artillery, the effects of which they had encountered on several occasions, both upstream and downstream of Wuhan.[5]

In 1933–1934, counteroffensives resulted in an expansion of the communist-held territories towards the north-west, but uncertainty still prevailed, often at the expense of trading activity.

In the south-east and in the north, rebel generals seized control of territories for which Wuhan served as the commercial outlet, including, in particular, Changsha. Meanwhile, to the west, Szechuan was controlled for a long time by an autonomous military power and the traditional flow of trade from there towards Wuhan slowed to a trickle, until the communist breakthrough in 1932. So the years 1930 and 1931 were marked by a plethora of small battles, the seizure and pillage of several towns, including some along the river, from where gunboats sometimes opened fire to protect commercial vessels. This kind of environment hardly encouraged the Chinese markets to remain open to imports of foreign goods: consumption and capital budgets started to shrink from the early 1930s onwards. Then, between 1933 and 1935, the generals' strongholds gradually rallied behind the Nanking regime. But they imposed their own taxes on top of those levied by Nanking, resulting in sizeable additional trade expenses.

The port-city itself remained officially under the control of the Nanking regime, but the state of order there was precarious: "April 1930. Visit by Chan Kai Shek to Wuhan. The concession has been invaded by Chinese troops [due to the cessation of extraterritoriality]. Pillage and murder are on the increase inland, and also martial law"[6] of a repressively arbitrary nature. Xenophobic rhetoric crystallised into attacks on foreigners, leading to day-to-day insecurity, while nationalist troops hurled abuse as they passed through. The calm that had prevailed in the city for a quarter of a century was shattered: the French concession was no longer a haven for commercial, cultural or human contact. "Foreigners are living in Wuhan as prisoners, not daring to venture outside of the former concessions and garden areas."[7] Fortunately, order was slowly restored in Wuhan itself (Wuhan, Wuchang, Hanyang) in 1934 and life returned to normal there.

Further obstacles added to the general woes, as the State stepped up its trade and currency supervision, with a large dose of State controls and a degree of arbitrariness: "The Nanking government, alarmed at the depreciation of the tael, keeps threatening the market with random measures such as duties on imports of silver, which have caused price fluctuations in Shanghai and panic buying and selling."[8] The more the budget deficit grew, the more taxes rose, adding to the levies imposed by the rebels or the communists and curbing trade. Monetary policy weakened companies for a time, due to high inflation which disrupted the process of replacing the tael with the Chinese dollar between 1933 and 1935.

Moreover, this State for a long time proved incapable of maintaining the road and rail transport networks:

> The seizure of transportation routes, shipping companies and railways for military purposes has pushed one after the other into bankruptcy. The

Peking–Wuhan line has next to no rolling stock left [for goods], the track is no longer maintained, and the few trains that travel on the usable parts have to proceed at reduced speed. On the Yangtze, the foreign shipping companies provide the only means of transport between the valley and Shanghai.[9]

The airline route that came into operation between Wuhan and Shanghai was not enough to compensate for these gaps. Although in 1934–1935 work was resumed, on the road network in particular, it was nowhere near enough. Indeed, worse still, it proved a hindrance to the port-city:

The extensions to the Lunghai railway line [in 1934] have been detrimental to our city: the one to Lien Yuen, where a new port has been created, has deprived it of business in goods heading down from Shensi and Honan, which used to go via the Peking–Wuhan line to come and be loaded up in our port and sent to the coast or to Haichow. Its western extension has in turn deprived it of the transit in goods, also from Honan, which used to be sent to the ports on the river Han before continuing downstream in junks as far as the Yangtze.[10]

On the other hand, the opening, at last, of the final section of the Guangzhou–Wuhan (Yueh Han Railway) in the second half of 1936 may have boosted trade.

Certainly, in the mid-1930s, the push by Chinese banks, of which there were seventeen in Wuhan in 1934, got the local economy moving again, basic trade in particular. In fact the surge of industrialisation itself, which had been so strong in the 1920s, was running out of steam: "Our city's position surrounded by provinces completely occupied by communists is too dangerous for the Chinese or foreigners to consider investing capital in our market",[11] not to mention the extra taxes imposed by the authorities. All but two (Chinese Factory Hin Chang, Asiatic Trading) of the tea factories had closed at the turn of the 1930s; the four Chinese cotton mills were operating at a loss, and the Japanese mill kept going until its closure in 1931—before this industry picked up in the second half of 1936. Supported by *France-Import*, the *Distillerie franco-chinoise* struggled to hold its own against the scores of small Chinese distilleries, especially as its sole client, the Hanyang naval dockyard, was financially in a bad way and closed its gates in 1932, leaving its supplier with a large unpaid bill.

Even Changsha and Ichang saw a slump in business. Only Chungking, far out to the west, seemed to fare well due to the calm that prevailed in Szechuan owing to the authority of two generals, but they imposed such high additional taxes that, in fact, few products made it into the Wuhan trading area in the early 1930s. Then it, too, went downhill in 1933: "This huge, magnificent province, whose natural products used to account for more than half of the trade handled by the port of Wuhan, is still caught in the throes of the civil war" between two generals. "This state of affairs has added significantly to the stagnation our market was already facing."[12]

Banque de l'Indochine calculated that the volume of exports of the main products (non-mining) plummeted from 2,316,414 piculs in the first half of 1930 to 1,027,891 in the first half of 1933, to 868,088 in the second half of 1933 and down as low as 299,660 in the first half of 1934, a slump of 86 per cent! "It really is a striking demonstration of how trade has collapsed in our market—striking particularly when, walking beside the Yangtze, one hears the accounts of the travellers of bygone days describing the city teeming with sampans which, in those days, crowded the now deserted shores"[13] (see Table 13.1).

Eventually the war between China and Japan in 1937–1938 placed the Yangtze and Wuhan at the centre of the fighting between the Nanking government troops and the Japanese army, until the Japanese occupied Shanghai and Nanking in November–December 1937, forcing Chiang Kai-shek to move his government to Wuhan for a year. Wuhan was sometimes hit by air raids. A mass of refugees flooded into the city.[14] The population of the French concession more than doubled from 15,000 to 35,000 in the first half of 1938. There was a great deal of fighting in the region between September and December 1938. So Wuhan's export trade contracted still further, from 1,156,731 quintals in 1936 to 876,639 in 1937.

2. A need for extreme prudence

Some client companies managed to maintain a flow of business, but the Paris head office of *Banque de l'Indochine* urged restraint in doing business with them: extreme prudence was the order of the day in a Paris market that was feeling the full force of a banking crisis that had claimed a number of large banks and was damaging the stability of some merchant banks. The important thing for *Banque de l'Indochine* was to avoid any risk of a liquidity crisis. All its branches had to make cutbacks to reduce their unreliable assets and to keep their heads above water in these dangerous times.

Table 22.1 Volume of exports handled by Wuhan in the 1930s (quintals)

First half of 1930	3,838,573
First half of 1934	495,704
Second half of 1934	939,417
First half of 1935	547,776
Second half of 1935	495,339
First half of 1936	411,350
Second half of 1936	745,381
Thereof destined for France	29,715
First half of 1937	577,719
Second half of 1937	298,920

Source: *Rapports-bilans* of the Wuhan branch of *Banque de l'Indochine*, *Crédit agricole* archives, *Banque de l'Indochine* fund

As early as December 1930, Paris sent instructions to suspend all "shipping credits granted for two or three days, when the goods are in the process of being loaded and we have some of the documents in our possession", like those issued to the large trading house Schnabel Gaumer & C°, a regular client. Yet "halting these will probably cause this firm to place the paper it used to keep for us with a rival bank, very likely HSBC. Indeed that latter is currently granting Schnabel Gaumer packing credits worth 100,000 taels and more."[15] The branch likewise had to curb the amounts owed on goods by Racine:

> I am working hard to collect this advance. I am not doing it willingly. I believe that Racine deserves this credit, and that this measure could jeopardise the good relations we have had with this firm, which will be reluctant to come back to us once the general environment improves and its business recovers to what it was before. The branch may well come to regret having offended this client. I cannot help recalling the trouble I had, when I arrived here, in attracting clients to our bank, since these clients were still aggrieved at the brutal, draconian measures we had taken, overhastily, in their regard in 1926–1927.[16]

The branch still had some business dealings with Racine (advances on goods in trust) but not of any significant size. Even its foremost client, *Olivier-Chine*, saw its current credit line cut from 100,000 to 50,000 taels on 20 April 1931 and its ceiling for advances on goods lowered to a maximum of 70,000 taels rather than 135,000. The French clientele faced testing times in 1933 when "Racine and *Crédit foncier d'Extrême-Orient* struggled in the face of the measures imposed by the Chinese authorities and tried to avoid the various taxes these authorities were trying to levy"[17] on their property assets.

Paris urged the branch not to contact Arnhold or Carlovitz which, though they were large firms, carried a high risk because of their large commitments. The branch continued doing regular, lower-risk business with them, such as "solid foreign exchange transactions with Arnhold New York": "Discounting of D/A [documents against acceptance] drawings with a single signature, effectively forming an advance on goods for 100 percent of the value of the security",[18] with the Bank of America of California–Los Angeles as the correspondent bank. Fraught discussions were held with longstanding debtors: "The agreement reached with the Kinhan Railway is enabling us to secure significant repayments of amounts owed."[19] The *Banque de l'Indochine* branch refused to issue advances to a considerable number of large clients, both foreign and Chinese, while HSBC and Chartered found themselves stuck with frozen debts and had to provide support for companies in crisis, though they were able to draw on funds procured by their robust Shanghai branch.

In 1930, the manager expressed his fears: "Firstly, we may end up having to cease all business from one day to the next, and secondly, in the last six months [first half of 1930], we have been living in a city in a state of almost constant panic. These two factors make it imperative that we pursue a policy of prudence and reduction of all risks, including foreign exchange risks."[20] They realised they needed to restrict business to short-term loans: "Of your current transactions, purchases of commercial remittances form the largest, but essentially the least profitable share, with an average return of 4 percent." And the client base contracted: "We are down to five or six sellers at most (Olivier, Schnabel Gaumer, Werner G. Smith, Chungking Import Chine, Crooks & Co.)."[21]

Liquidity was required, which is why priority was given to "arbitrage and discount revenues on foreign markets to compensate for the fall in income from foreign exchange transactions *per se*."[22] However, some secured overdrafts were maintained because otherwise the volume of business would contract by too much—hence, in 1934, for example, an "increase in advances on bills for forward delivery. They work like advances on current accounts secured by goods that come and go without details of the movements being provided."[23] But the head office demanded "a system of detailed checks on goods serving as security",[24] which would reinforce the bonds of trust between clients (P.H. Spire, Oriental Products Export, etc.) and their lender.

The downside to this prudence was that keen competitors took the opportunity to seize market share:

> The clients I had such trouble attracting when I arrived here have abandoned us again, as the lack of business is enabling them to make do with the facilities they find elsewhere while we won't grant them any and are more strict in our risk selection. The shortage of business means competition is tougher and it is no longer possible, by offering better rates, to acquire the [commercial] paper we could still take, without breaching our current policy.[25] The little [amount of commercial] paper on offer has been the subject of fierce competition. There have been cases where business has been carried out for 1/32 denier of profit [0.32 per cent], which had never previously happened here, and which constitutes an excessive risk relative to the profit and is incompatible with the situation of our market, where communications with Shanghai for hedging [of risks by compensation] are so unreliable [because of the telegraph network outages].[26]

However, the telegraph network, the branch's subscriptions to the financial news agency Reuters (in the second half of 1932) and the installation of a telephone line (in 1935) all enabled it, despite everything, to weather the commodity price swings and the fluctuations in foreign and Chinese currencies. Nevertheless, the inflation of the currency by the central power, followed even by the undermining of the relatively reliable tael, ended up fracturing the monetary basis of the nationalist State, leading to greater vigilance on the part of Chinese suppliers and more restrictions on their trade, which eroded trade in Wuhan even further.

3. Economic patriotism weakened

Considering the general environment, did anyone really believe that the *Banque de l'Indochine* branch could continue to embody French economic patriotism upriver from Shanghai?

A. French interests in decline

The branch manager could only lament the erosion of French positions in the Wuhan market and, more widely, throughout the regions served by the Yangtze.

> France effectively stopped being regarded as one of the active players in our port several years ago. Only *Olivier-Chine* is busy. The other French trading houses have to make do with 'grocery shopping' [trivial commerce]. Fortunately, the branch does not have to rely entirely on French trade to survive! Generally speaking, it seems that only the large foreign firms can manage to turn a profit in the current circumstances.[27]

The ambitions of economic patriotism were thwarted, since the Wuhan market continued to account for only a modest share of French imports, as shown by the figures for 1931, one of the last years in which there was still a significant amount of foreign trade from there, despite the slowdown that had already impacted output for some. Looking at some of the key products traded in Wuhan, French purchases accounted for only a minor share, though it had a decent share of the market for pork bristles (19.73 per cent), ramie (13.93 per cent), gall nuts (13.81 per cent) and antimony (10.31 per cent for unrefined and 1.03 per cent for babbitt). So it ranked as only a minor player here on the trading front, whereas its competitors were better placed for certain products, with the United States dominating the market for several products and the United Kingdom tending to be in second place. Between November 1932 and March 1933, France ranked only 13th out of the sources of imports into Wuhan (with 33,915 gold unit taels), far behind the United States (3,137,060), Japan (2,365,245), the Dutch Indies, Hong Kong, the United Kingdom (439,236) and Germany (354,414). At that time it only supplied metal products, tobacco, "paints and varnishes", as well as "fats and resins", not even wines and spirits—a market monopolised by Italy in Wuhan.

In short, the French market could manage its life without Wuhan! So it is not hard to understand why the trading firm Olivier, which operated across Asia, tried to make itself a platform for exports to the United States and several European countries. And the German firm Schnabel Gaumer also remained a key client for the branch, as did the American firm Werner G. Smith, for which *Banque de l'Indochine* was the second-line bank after National City Bank in 1934 (see Table 22.2).

An analysis of the second half of 1936 confirms the French market's small share of sales conducted via the Wuhan market, at 4 per cent of the total volume.

Table 22.2 France's share of foreign exports from Wuhan in 1931 (i.e., excluding sales from here to other parts of China)

	France	United Kingdom	Japan	United States	Germany	Italy	Belgium	Total (picals)
Cowhides	2,389	2,521	18,804	38	7,827	10,493	213	49,062
	4.87%	5.14%	38.33%	0.08%	15.95%	21.39%	0.43%	%
Buffalo hides	650	1279	777	0	2,367	43	544	10,837
	6%	11.8	7.17	0	21.84	0.40	5.01	%
Goat hides	104	0	14	20,186	1,469	0	775	22,864
	0.45%	0	0.06	88.29	6.42	0	3.39	%
Ramie	18,445	12,912	89,914	0	7,249	0	23,762	132,419
	13.93%	9.75	67.90	0	5.47	0	10.22	%
Gall nuts	4600	8376	4633	7038	4,265	623	1916	33,304
	13.81%	25.15	13.91	21.13	12.81	1.87	5.75	%
Cotton	0	704	5,977	377	571	0	0	7629
	0	9.23	78.35	4.94	7.48	0	0	%
Pork bristles	1,720	1,760	1,423	3,320	0	180	240	8717
	19.73%	20.19	16.32	38.09	0	2.06	2.75	%
Sesame	3,696	0	107,658	400,319	25,200	35,558	33,660	666,599
	0.55%	0	16.15	30.05	37.84	5.33	5.05	%
Wood oil	11,411	68,890	661	402,108	17,709	4145	2,374	562,187
	2.03%	12.25	0.12	71.53	3.15	0.74	0.81	%
Egg whites	655	10,940	0	3,929	1,523	95	1332	25,104
	2.61%	43.58	0	15.65	06.07	0.38	5.31	%
Egg yolks	1,792	18,318	158	4,123	17,135	0	6,873	63,277
	2.83%	28.95	0.25	6.52	27.08	0	10.86	%
Unrefined antimony	588	504	580	420	1,596	504	0	5704 tonnes
	10.31%	5.84	10.17	7.36	27.98	8.84	0	%
Antimony babbitt	5,040	14,432	1,596	8,694	11,424	924	1,344	45,714 tonnes
	11.03%	27.20	3.49	19.02	24.99	2.02	2.94	%

Source: Half-yearly rapports-bilans, Crédit agricole archives, Banque de l'Indochine fund

It was a big buyer, though, of unrefined antimony and agro-business products like pork bristles, intestines, buffalo hides and gall nuts (see Table 22.3).

B. A branch with close links to the French community

Fortunately, one reliable source of business was maintained for a time: the provision of banking services to the French community, although the consul himself had his personal account with *Banque belge pour l'étranger* (in 1934). In the first half of 1930, remittances of discount paper from the consulate and the navy amounted to 896,992 francs, allowing these two institutions to deal with their day-to-day purchases. Advances were also still being granted to the Municipality (with 25,000 taels outstanding in June 1930) and the *Cercle gaulois*, the French local bourgeois club.

"The activity on the franc account continues to benefit from the presence of the French warships in Wuhan, which regularly offer us their bills on the Ministry of the Navy. Competition from *Banque belge [pour l'étranger]* [on the discount market] means that, even when we do manage to secure them, these purchases are not that profitable. We have negotiated paper worth FRF 1,266,326 versus 896,992 in the first half", owing to the "large number of warships which have stayed put in our port due to the events of the summer."[28] Indeed, remittances of commercial paper on France advanced from FRF 1,266,326 in the second half of 1930 to FRF 2,387,718 in the first half of 1931, due to the needs of the army, the navy and the consulate, compensating for the lack of purchases of commercial paper on France (only FRF 168,393). In the second half of 1931, despite "fierce competition from *Banque belge pour l'étranger*", the branch secured bills from the navy and the consulate on the public treasury worth FRF 1,405,254.

Table 22.3 French market share by volume of exports from Wuhan in the second half of 1936 (%)

Cowhides	10.77
Buffalo hides	22.75
Ramie	16.44
Gall nuts	18.55
Pork bristles	22.35
Sesame seeds	6.35
Tea	1.34
Beans	4.37
Wood oil	2.2
Egg whites	7.46
Egg yolks	1.31
Intestines	42.72
Unrefined antimony	50
Antimony babbitt	2.09
Total	3.99

Source: *Crédit agricole* archives, *Banque de l'Indochine* fund

In the first half of 1935, the French Navy sold it bills for FRF 1.166 million and the military detachment 413,000; current account advances in dollars were granted to *Immeubles Racine* (30,000), to help with its stalled construction projects, to the French Municipality (20,000) and to the Apostolic Vicariate of Kaifend [or Dalian/Bianjing, in Henan] (180,000) backed by the Foreign Missions of Milan. The business with the Navy concerned the negotiation of remittances worth 637,000 in the first half of 1936, but "the ships are spending less and less time in Wuhan. Either they stay in Shanghai, or they dock in the ports of the upper river",[29] meaning they had less need to acquire supplies locally.

C. Olivier, still a special client of the Banque de l'Indochine branch

Constantly at the forefront of the trading efforts undertaken in the name of economic patriotism, the large firm Olivier kept its flag flying in the Wuhan marketplace. In November 1930 it needed a large advance on bills for forward delivery in the amount of 154,284 taels, in other words exceeding the cap of 140,000, of which "100,000 is for the financing of drawings on New York in connection with loans from American banks, and 40,000 for a usable tranche on Wuhan, including two advances on goods in trust, in other words actual unsecured overdrafts."[30]

The branch's proportion of the overall authorised credit issued by all the *Banque de l'Indochine* branches in China amounted to 113,863 taels in July 1930, with 40,421 utilised, thanks to a "close collaboration with its managing director and the trust he has shown us."[31] It had granted Olivier five advances on bills for forward delivery of 125,000 taels, two tranches of 20,000 taels for its business with Europe and 50,000 taels for its business with America. One advance on goods was intended "to enable it to keep a purchase option on stocks of hides belonging to its comprador, to whom it has advanced the sum it borrowed from us (24,140 taels)."[32]

Olivier-Chine used its advances (balance of 13,613 and 16,557 taels) "in full during these six months when it processed the products bought during the autumn campaign, which were shipped during the months of April, June and July",[33] with a limit of 90,000 taels on Paris and the United States. A sudden rise in remittances in francs was seen due to the abandonment of the British pound by exporters and, in the second half of 1931, the branch made FRF 650,256 worth of paper purchases, including 535,485 on *Olivier-Chine*. By contrast, purchases of dollar paper from Olivier, at 12,274, were sharply down on the first half of 1931 ($224,035). But the branch noted that Olivier's customers would be "much less lucrative" than those of its old clients Arnhold and Mitsui Bussan Kaisha because of the lower interest rates it had to grant them under pressure from the competition.

In the first half of 1932, in the market segment for export paper purchases, "*Olivier-Chine* was our main seller with FRF 1,865,000, $31,010 and £11,830 out of a total of FRF 1,985,891, $16,408 and £32,612 respectively."[34] "Our principal seller is still *Olivier-Chine* which, thanks to the efforts of its local manager, has been able to seal several deals involving pork bristles and salted hog casings. We have managed to win some of the company's business from *Banque belge [pour l'étranger]* in connection with the egg industry, which has close links with *Olivier-Chine.*"[35]

At the end of 1932, "your only seller of commercial paper is *Olivier-Chine*. Out of total remittances of 4.3 million francs, your purchases from this firm account for 3.8 millions".[36] The branch discounted sight bills from Olivier on the Chinese public treasury worth 1.8 million, "acquired despite stiff competition from *Banque belge*". But the firm itself was hit by the general downturn in trade:

> Despite the great number of export items it endeavours to handle, it has seen a considerable slowdown in its business [in 1932]. Clearly it must be hard for it to reconcile the ongoing fall in orders at head office with the exorbitant demands of its Chinese sellers. This state of affairs is inevitably leading the managing director of this firm to engage in currency speculation to try and turn a profit. He does not always succeed.[37]

The branch, in a sign of confidence, even allowed it to maintain an overdraft, with 35,000 taels outstanding in June 1933, while at the same time keeping up its purchases of paper in francs (totalling 420,000 in the second half of 1933). "Olivier, the only French export house in our market, seems to have benefited from an upturn in business over the last few months and has conducted a fruitful campaign of purchases on orders coming from its New York branch."[38]

In the first half of 1935, competition was so fierce between the banks that only three players were granted advances on bills for forward delivery: *Olivier-Chine*, which ended up with 70,000 taels outstanding on its two lines of 230,145 and 145,749 taels, well ahead of Schnabel Gaumer (20,000 taels outstanding on a line of 527,272) and Chungking Import Chine (20,000 taels out of a total of 71,753). Olivier was also the number one "drawer" of commercial paper negotiated by the *Banque de l'Indochine* branch, with FRF 762,262, £5,712 and USD 46,438 outstanding in June 1935—ahead of Werner Smith (USD 179,999), Arnhold (USD 91,119) and Schnabel Gaumer. In terms of paper negotiated in the United States only, Olivier (with FRF 591,073, £5,242 and $46,438 outstanding) surpassed Schnabel Gaumer (FRF 12,759, £18,914 and USD 28,919), Fuhrmeister (FRF 123,970), Nicea (FRF 28,919), Smith (USD 114,000), and Chungking Import (£4,224).[39]

Right until the end, Olivier stood firm in the face of the difficulties plaguing the region. In the first half of 1936, still, the branch noted "a surge in business with Olivier (FRF 1,356,000) and Schnabel (492,000)",[40] courtesy perhaps of a "resumption of exports of hides and pork bristles to the United States". "Our advances" to Olivier "serve to finance all its specified export-related activities (purchase of raw materials, processing, packaging, shipment etc.).[41] The bank took profit from the increase in trade destined for the United States, which was why two advance lines of USD 100,000 each were granted to Olivier. The branch spelled out the difference between this excellent client and the others: "The other clients [Chungking Export, Schnabel Gaumer, Nicea, Oriental Products Export] are quicker with their repayments because they only use our loans for settling their latest export charges: transportation, insurance, handling, invoice balances etc., previous activities having been financed either from their own capital or using advances obtained from other banks"[42] (see Table 22.4).

D. The downturn in business in francs

The downturn in business in francs and in credits designed to support "economic patriotism" was attributable to the lack of trade with France and the small number of French players. As far as the companies belonging to the French community were concerned, although Racine closed its export department and had no more advances outstanding in July 1930, "Schnabel Gaumer is obtaining shipping credits covering several days on goods currently being loaded, hence a debit balance of 22,661 taels. We can congratulate ourselves for not having abandoned this firm the moment it got into difficulties. Indeed we negotiated £50,402, FRF 60,000 and USD 10,428 with it."[43] Vanderstegen & Crooks was another loyal client (advance of 14,870 taels), but the withdrawal of Crooks led it to suspend advances due to a lack of confidence. On the whole, though, prudence prompted the branch to focus on "safe business transactions", which is why it halted advances on bills for forward delivery in the second half of 1930 (Racine, Borioni, Schnabel) in favour of advances on goods only (*Société française de distillerie* with 72,586 taels, Racine with an amount of 18,579) guaranteed by wood oil and goods stored in the French concession 25 metres from the branch.[44]

In the second half of 1931, "we were only able to work with two firms, Olivier (FRF 985,000) and Schnabel Gaumer (FRF 775,000), down by a factor of three on the previous half",[45] before business with Schnabel Gaumer in this market segment ceased in 1932. French viticulture received a boost in 1932 when the branch financed four bills of FRF 16,225 drawn on France Import by the wine merchant Mahler-Besse, of Bordeaux, for a special wine shipment. A new advance on goods was granted in 1932 to the local factory of *Société franco-chinoise de distillerie*, guaranteed by *Société française des distilleries*.

Table 22.4 Outstanding advances to client firms from *Banque de l'Indochine* in Wuhan in June 1936

Olivier			Schnabel Gaumer	Arnhold		Jardine Matheson	T.Y. Li		Chungkin Import
729,093	45,560	57,076	5275	113,301	16,327	169,128	19,068	12,575	19,879	2,150	30,126
FRF	USD	£	USD	£	FRF	USD	USD	USD	£	£

Source: *Crédit agricole* archives, *Banque de l'Indochine* fund

Overall, deals concluded in francs declined, falling to FRF 9,549,908 in the first half of 1933 compared to 34,785,443 in the first half of 1932 (due to a large contango transaction) and 14,232,921 in the second half of 1932— the sellers of francs being Wostrung (FRF 725,000), Olivier (265,000), Arnhold (205,000) and Schnabel Gaumer (45,000).[46] The branch manager gave this bitter assessment in July 1935: "Direct imports are non–existent, and transactions with the French colony remain negligible." Only a few clients came to the branch to withdraw francs for their day-to-day needs, such as, in 1935, *Deutsche Farben Industrie* (FRF 140,000), which imported chemical products from France, and Pearce & Harrick (77,000), while *Banque belge pour l'étranger* borrowed FRF 250,000 to finance its own clients.

Notes

 1 *Rapport-bilan*, first half of 1930, 20 July 1930, *Crédit agricole* archives, *Banque de l'Indochine* fund.
 2 Summary letters, *Crédit agricole* archives, *Banque de l'Indochine* fund, 439AH 535, 12 December 1930.
 3 *Rapport-bilan*, first half of 1930, 20 July 1930, *Crédit agricole* archives, *Banque de l'Indochine* fund.
 4 *Rapport-bilan*, second half of 1930, January 1931.
 5 *Ibidem*.
 6 *Rapport-bilan*, first half of 1930, 20 July 1930.
 7 *Ibidem*.
 8 *Ibidem*.
 9 *Ibidem*.
10 *Rapport-bilan*, second half of 1934, January 1935.
11 *Rapport-bilan*, first half of 1931, July 1931.
12 *Rapport-bilan*, first half of 1933, July 1933.
13 *Rapport-bilan*, first half of 1934, July 1934.
14 See Stephen MacKinnon, *Wuhan, 1938: War, Refugees, and the Making of Modern China*, Berkeley, University of California Press, 2008.
15 Summary letter, *Crédit agricole* archives, *Banque de l'Indochine* fund, 439AH 535, 12 December 1930.
16 Summary letter, 7 April 1931.
17 *Rapport-bilan* for the first half of 1933, July 1933.
18 Summary letter, 17 March 1931.
19 Summary letter, 6 October 1933.
20 *Rapport-bilan* for the first half of 1930, July 1930.
21 Summary letter, 22 November 1934.
22 Summary letter, 20 April 1934.
23 Summary letter, 10 April 1935.
24 Summary letter, 28 October 1936.
25 *Rapport-bilan*, second half of 1930, January 1931.
26 *Ibidem*.
27 *Ibidem*.
28 *Rapport-bilan*, second half of 1930, January 1931.
29 *Rapport-bilan* for the first half of 1936, July 1936.
30 Summary letter, 3 November 1930.
31 *Rapport-bilan*, first half of 1930, 20 July 1930.
32 *Ibidem*.

33 *Rapport-bilan* for the first half of 1931, July 1931.
34 *Rapport-bilan* for the first half of 1932, July 1932.
35 *Ibidem*.
36 Summary letter, 22 October 1932.
37 *Rapport-bilan*, second half of 1932, January 1933.
38 *Rapport-bilan*, second half of 1933, January 1934.
39 *Rapport-bilan*, first half of 1935, July 1935.
40 *Rapport-bilan*, first half of 1936, July 1936.
41 *Ibidem*.
42 *Ibidem*.
43 *Rapport-bilan*, first half of 1930, 20 July 1930.
44 *Rapport-bilan*, second half of 1930, January 1931.
45 *Rapport-bilan*, second half of 1931, January 1932.
46 *Rapport-bilan*, first half of 1933, July 1933.

23 The resilience of the *Banque de l'Indochine* branch in Wuhan (1930–1939)

Despite the unstable, even dangerous environment, *Banque de l'Indochine* could rely on its Wuhan branch to stand firm and even maintain a certain level of activity through these often trying times, not just with its core of loyal clients drawn mainly from the French communities, including the trading house Olivier.

1. The erosion of trade in the Wuhan marketplace (1930–1936)

The reports by the manager of *Banque de l'Indochine*'s Wuhan branch provide an account of an irreversible decline, punctuated by sudden tensions and moments of relief when the respites allowed business to resume, and of despair at the magnitude of the crisis.

A. A kind of final flourish?

The year 1930 got off to a promising start, with the branch announcing "good results" for the first half. This was:

> due to the foreign exchange income that we were able to earn on our paper purchases as a result of the fall in silver from 21 7/16 forward on 3d January to 15 7/8 forward on 30 June, a trend that was also reflected in paper purchase rates, which, for the four-month, slipped from 2.2 1/2 to 1.7 3/8, with some violent swings along the way. This income was only generated thanks firstly to the short positions we took at the actual time of the purchases, by quoting below parity with the hedging in Shanghai, and secondly to the efforts undertaken in the second half of 1929, when, entering the market again, our branch built up a pool of decent clients who, in the course of that half-year, often gave preference to us at equal rates, despite the fact they could have obtained the facilities elsewhere.[1]

In short, these were fairly speculative transactions. The bank successfully sold short just at the time when prices were heading down because of the start of the depression. While the loss in pounds on these foreign exchange transactions came to 20,483 taels, the profit on francs was 7,242 taels and on USD 198,775, giving a total profit of 94,895 taels. In addition some traditional discount transactions were recorded: "Our paper purchases were up significantly on the two previous six-month periods, despite the terms imposed on exporters. In terms of pounds, they amounted to 220,947 versus 149,274 in the first half of 1929 and 175,783 in the second half of 1929. Our paper purchases are up 67 percent compared to the first half of 1929."[2]

However, "our port's turnover has been 30 to 40 percent below what it was in the first half of 1929", the manager noted. He was determined to "maintain the low-risk policy that our market situation demanded": rigorous evaluation of outstanding amounts, loan ceilings, "time limits on advances in general and packing credits in particular, or even stopping them altogether". He admitted that: "For multiple reasons, we may end up having to cease business from one day to the next."[3] After all, for the Wuhan market there was no avoiding the fallout from the general economic crisis and the political and military crisis going on locally in the middle Yangtze.

B. The erosion of Wuhan's role in international trade

In the end it was not so much the precautionary measures that put a damper on business at the *Banque de l'Indochine* branch but more the erosion of trade over a period of months. Fear of pillagers and additional taxes, import deflation, the numerous obstacles to the collection of exportable products and currency instability were some of the factors behind the decline in business at many trading houses. In 1930, the manager spoke of the "stagnation in import business, which has been impacted by the civil wars".[4] "Numerous exporters were so hard pushed to guarantee their future shipments that, with communications with the interior being so unreliable, they no longer dared make offers in Europe unless they were certain that the goods were in place."[5]

The branch went so far as to suggest that "traders are thinking about an exodus to Shanghai, something that is already under way and will be difficult to halt. For the last three months of the second half, Wuhan and its trade were almost obliterated, first by the civil war and then by the resurgence of the global crisis".[6] "Wuhan has lost its supremacy as the centre of the tea trade to Shanghai; the hide and wood oil markets, two of our city's principal fields of business, are deserting it by the day, also in favour of Shanghai. Meanwhile the import trade, more than ever, remains the prerogative of the major distribution port, Wangpo."[7]

> Business is becoming extremely difficult for us as the firms in our market are increasingly tending to entrust their foreign exchange transactions to their parent companies in Shanghai rather than negotiating their paper themselves as they used to do. This phenomenon is also taking its toll on our sales of francs. Our main client, *Deutsche Farben Handelsgesellschaft*

Waibel & C°, has conducted virtually all its purchases of francs via its Shanghai division.[8]

Wuhan barely counted as a "market" any more, with inter-banking operations and the offsetting of debit and credit accounts, with liquidity in short supply, with the result that it depended increasingly on refinancing from Shanghai: "We are constantly obliged to speculate. As there is practically no hedging locally, we have to seal the deals in Shanghai, and messages from us take a long time to get through."[9] "Imports are handled in Shanghai and bills drawn on Wuhan from Shanghai are domiciled at the bank of the drawees. These are the banks with a large number of depositor clients who are benefiting from this business climate: the Chinese banks, HSBC and *Banque belge pour l'étranger*."[10] Even the French firm Racine closed its export department in Wuhan in 1934 and "does all its foreign exchange deals in Shanghai".[11]

"Now that our local risks have been virtually eliminated, thanks to the policy I have been pursuing since my arrival here and your recent instructions [from the head office], and no longer impact on our Interest & Commission account, [commercial] paper purchases are the most accurate measure of business activity at our branch." But "these have fallen to £103,307 (after conversion of francs and dollars), compared to £220,947 in the first half of 1930 and £175,783 in the second half of 1929."[12]

This erosion of the branch's core business continued in the first half of 1931: although, for "foreign exchange earnings, we can congratulate ourselves on always having entered the market at the right moment during the course of these six months, on having hedged our transactions for maximum profit and settled the small positions we thought we could take with anticipated profits", there was also a small risk to be noted, namely the fact that "the hedging can only be done in Shanghai with a morning-to-evening or full-day delay",[13] and in particular the fact that purchases of paper, at the equivalent of £105,426, were down 60 per cent in the first half of 1930. Risk limitation was the reason for the decrease in paper purchases in pounds to £45,733 from £175,607 in the second half of 1930.

C. A spirit of initiative to fend off the competition

Competition became even tougher, especially from National City Bank of New York and, in many cases, from Chartered, both of which picked up a lot of commercial paper, as was the case in 1933. However, the spirit of initiative was maintained at the *Banque de l'Indochine* branch, which was still keen to loosen its competitors' grip on a shrunken market: "Our personal connections with the managers of Standard Oil and Asiatic Petroleum Company have enabled us, when we were in a hurry [due to the under-utilisation of funds], to ask them, for the same rate, to have their weekly transfers handled by us",[14] which resulted in some foreign exchange commission in 1930. "We have tried to secure some new business, while keeping to the limits of your instructions, with the firms Arnhold, Fuhrmeiser, and especially *Société anonyme pour l'industrie des œufs* [egg industry company], formerly G.H. Roosen, a client poached from the *Banque belge pour l'étranger*'s monopoly."[15]

The branch maintained a small circle of clients for its sterling account, with purchases of "bills at usance" for £10,525, including Olivier (£5,300), Jardine Matheson (£1,950), *Société anonyme pour l'industrie des œufs* (£1,763), China Metal & Ore (£1,000), and Schnabel Gaumer (£481), while, for the dollar account, "our only export sellers were Schnabel Gaumer ($11,000), Arnhold (10,000) and Olivier (8,350)."[16] For its francs account, in the first half of 1933 it acquired paper from Olivier (FRF 414,000), the French Navy (FRF 854,000) and the French Army (FRF 324,000), while the main buyer, surprisingly, was the German firm *Deutsche Farben Handels Waibel* (FRF 2,376,000), probably because its exported Chinese goods in France and/or purchased them from French traders. In the second half of 1933, three sellers of francs called on its services: Chungking Import China (1,400,000), Schnabel Gaumer (FRF 582,000), and *Olivier-Chine* (FRF 420,000).

Foreign exchange deals and arbitrage transactions on commercial paper predominated, with the emphasis on looking after the short term, as well as seizing opportunities arising from rate variations: "Activity in our market, spurred on by speculation, has focused on the US currency. The growth in the volume of our business in USD is due to the need to settle our currency purchases as and when they occur so as to maintain or even improve our position."[17] But only "a very small number of sellers wanting to hedge their positions made use of our bank for settlement purposes. This is mainly due to the fact that the local branch of National City Bank has always been an excellent seller, operating for the Shanghai account at the market rate, without taking a profit".[18]

Fortunately, business with an American client increased in 1933: "We have generated significant revenues from Werner Smith & C°, [the offshoot of which] in Wuhan was headed by Li Jui. This firm specialising in the export of wood oil operates using credit lines opened by the parent company in Cleveland with top banks (Guaranty Trust). The negotiations involve [documents against payment] D/P sight remittances, which banks in our market are generally fighting over."[19] Werner Smith approached *Banque de l'Indochine* for an advance of USD 290,000 in 1935 because "it is probably the one in our market doing the most trade in wood oil."[20]

Some business in sterling was maintained, with a purchase of £128,500 in the first half of 1934, with Olivier (£97,000), Werner G. Smith (170,500), Arnhold (£25,000), the Catholic Mission of Milan (£38,000), T.Y. Ly (£45,000) and Crooks (65,000). Arbitrage generated some profit in the first half of 1935, including c$ 42,000 on the dollar and 5,500 on the franc: "The earnings on arbitrage are due ... to our gains on a long position in the dollar taken right at the beginning of the six-month period, which, for the sake of prudence, we were forced to close in the first half of April."[21]

It was fair to say that the *Banque de l'Indochine* branch's professionalism and financial approach enabled it to stand firm in the face of the economic fluctuations. Choosing its clients with care enabled it to avoid setbacks, which in turn preserved its liquid funds. Although, "overall, our total foreign currency transactions have fallen significantly", the branch noted a "slight improvement in our export business", thanks to the "return of clients which had almost given up doing business with our branch altogether"[22] (Arnhold, Crooks, Jardine-Matheson, France Import, *Deutsche Farben*, etc.), with these firms selling US dollars or sterling paper.

But the client base was shaky: in 1934, *Deutsche Farben* withdrew from its *Banque de l'Indochine* account and operated instead only in pounds, using the services of the British banks, while *SA des œufs* [Egg Company] did business solely with *Banque belge pour l'étranger*.[23] The contraction in business went so far as to cause a "real under-utilisation" of liquid funds, which led to placements with the Paris head office and with French American Banking Corporation in New York, to put this now surplus liquidity to work.

In 1935, monetary tightening and the lack of business took their toll on the branch, which talked of "pessimism" and "stagnation". "In the cities, silver has completely disappeared", resulting in "difficulties for the small Chinese banks, the disappearance of local foreign exchange business" and a "fall in earnings at the large banks due to the halt in arbitrage and the tendency for export business to be concentrated in Shanghai". In 1935, the Wuhan market handled only a seventh of the business it had handled in 1930. But foreign banks' refusal to close their doors resulted in continued "extravagant competition".[24]

2. A steady downturn between 1937 and 1939

The erosion of the Wuhan marketplace and slump in commercial activity in the French business community and at its bank branch were attributable to various factors. "Your local discounts and advances fell to $15,000 and your purchases of remittances practically ground to a halt at the end of the [second] half [1937]. Hence your business is in an almost complete state of stagnation."[25]

More serious still was the trend towards the use of Chinese institutions for banking and financial needs. As time went by and a proper central State was formed which equipped itself with the instruments of credit and currency management and generated a sense of confidence in the relative state of stability (though temporary), more and more credit transactions were handled by Chinese economic players, notably banks. This explains, in particular, their involvement in the management of international trade flows at the end of the 1930s: "The monopolisation of foreign exchange and foreign trade by government institutions has reduced your documentary paper purchases to almost zero."[26] The usable stock of currencies shrank, and public inspections became more stringent.

The Wuhan branch therefore had to resort to subterfuge to build up a buffer supply of currencies to support its business, using a kind of barter system among branches of *Banque de l'Indochine*. In 1938, this was seen in the "rise in your sterling purchases (£102,700) from the branch in Yunnan-Fu [Kunming, in the south, near the border with Indochina, in Yunnan], which obtained Chinese dollars from you, which it sold to the Central Bank of China in Yunnan-Fu". The branch then proceeded to "sell the pounds it obtained by doing this, as well as USD and HK£, to foreign importers in Wuhan (Jardine Matheson, for £410,000) which, being unable to transfer their funds to Shanghai, had to do their foreign exchange business locally."[27] The branch sold pounds to Hong Kong and Chinese dollars to Guangzhou to replenish its stocks of Hong Kong dollars, which it then sold on. So the quest for liquidity in foreign currencies led to collaboration among the three branches—Wuhan, Yunnan-Fu and Guangzhou—through a double cycle of beneficial arbitrage.

3. The resilience of the *Banque de l'Indochine* branch despite its faraway location

Far from Shanghai, 650 km upstream on the River Yangtze, the Wuhan branch was at the heart of *Banque de l'Indochine*'s activities in China. Supported by robust branches like Shanghai, Tianjin and Guantgzhou, it managed to survive some testing years of economic depression, monetary shocks, civil and international wars. In fact, despite all of this, it managed to keep its finances relatively stable and avoid a liquidity or solvency crisis. Admittedly, it benefited from the support of the head office, especially the Shanghai branch. But in a small way, it did count as a business and profit centre in its own right.

A. A mixed pool of funds

Initially it made use of ongoing financing provided by the Saigon branch—the heart of *Banque de l'Indochine*'s business in Asia—and the Shanghai branch, on top of the capital that the Paris head office had assigned it. Then it was able to draw on a small pool of deposits provided by clients, notably the trading houses, which deposited a portion of their current cash resources at the branch. In November 1931, for example, the branch's actual funds were put at USD 1,800,000; on top of that were deposits made by the Saigon branch (USD 2,075,000), local deposits and those of correspondent banks (USD 250,000). These contributions to liabilities helped feed its ongoing business activities and assets (see Tables 23.1 and 23.2).

B. A sensible balance between activities

In keeping with its prudent approach, the *Banque de l'Indochine* branch constantly tried to balance its short-term activities (discount business, handling of remittances of commercial bills) with higher-risk activities, notably overdrafts (advances on debit accounts). These stagnated in 1929–1932 before increasing noticeably in 1933–1934, from 1.4 to 2 million taels, and even 2.4 million taels, because the branch needed to support its valued clients like Olivier and remain competitive. It seems that this also enabled it to compensate for a dip in discount business, which dropped sharply in 1932 before picking up again in 1934. This low level of activity can be put down to restrictive measures and the effects of the global crisis (see Table 23.3).

It seems foreign exchange business remained as appealing as ever, as it entailed limited risks and a modest length of commitment, while at the same time generating decent profits (see Table 23.4).

Table 23.1 Wuhan branch funds in 1929–1934 (taels)

	First half 1929	Second half 1929	First half 1930	Second half 1930	First half 1931	Second half 1931
Total funds	3,224,293	3,435,810	3,603,795	4,702,057	3,894,645	3,730,317

	First half 1932	Second half 1932	First half 1933	Second half 1933	First half 1934	Second half 1934
Total funds	5,015,760	4,032,012	5,914,698	7,806,544	8,071,339	8,172,105

Source: Calculation basis changed in 1934, so comparisons cannot be exact

Table 23.2 Funds of the Wuhan branch of *Banque de l'Indochine* in 1935–1936 (local dollars)

	First half of 1935	Second half of 1935	First half of 1936	Second half of 1936
Gold resources	6,359,406	8,136,057	4,807,482	7,505,237
Of which capital account in USD, francs and £	2,607,842	2,908,738	3,311,535	3,302,832
Deposits in francs, no. 1 Saigon	2,994,240	3,341,514	3,831,549	3,264,704
Silver resources	2,233,752	227,972		
Silver resources; from 1936 in new Chinese dollars	187,573	183,146	231,224	286,619
Total resources	8,593,158	10,364,029	12,088,380	9,841,530
Average of foreign exchange order accounts (foreign currencies, currency buyers, foreign exchange sellers) = adds to funds	4,182,030	5,072,764	3,380,605	1,197,138

Source: Figures are not available for 1937. The others are taken from the half-yearly *rapports-bilans*

In the second half of the 1930s, flourishing foreign exchange and arbitrage business maintained the *Banque de l'Indochine* branch's ability to generate profits, despite the fact that numerous transactions were being handled in Shanghai, even by foreign trading houses and foreign banks in many cases, something which reduced the size of the clearing and hedging market in Wuhan (see Table 23.5).

In the second half of the 1930s, the branch demonstrated remarkable resilience. Despite the serious blows to trade in the Yangtze valley and the surrounding regions that supplied the Wuhan marketplace, the manager managed to maintain a decent flow of transactions, especially discount transactions, as the advances account had to be significantly scaled back in the interests of prudence (see Table 23.6).

Table 23.3 Business of the Wuhan branch of *Banque de l'Indochine* in 1929–1934 (taels)

	First half 1929	Second half 1929	First half 1930	Second half 1930	First half 1931	Second half 1931	First half 1932	Second half 1932	First half 1933	Second half 1933	First half 1934	Second half 1934
Advances and accounts receivable (average)	1,449,048	1,443,047	1,437,287	1,431,803	1,429,542	1,429,542	1,429,543	1,429,555	2,042,248	2,040,045	2,040,045	240,045
Remittances falling due (gold assets: FRF, £, $, in equivalent taels)	559,318	1,124,414	1,312,042	1,790,298	943,389	710,043	247,043	245,111	357,520	508,545	884,736	790,288

Source: Calculation basis changed in 1934, so comparisons cannot be exact

Table 23.4 Balance of the discount and arbitrage transactions of the Wuhan branch of *Banque de l'Indochine* in 1929–1934 (taels)

	First half 1929	Second half 1929	First half 1930	Second half 1930	First half 1931	Second half 1931	First half 1932	Second half 1932	First half 1933	Second half 1933	First half 1934	Second half 1934
Earnings on foreign exchange transactions: gold arbitrage	26,761	45,681	69,325	48,255	69,323	44,830	541,10	10,860	67,300	26,028	43,520	54,827
Of which £ account	21,102	28,956	44,217	66,685	6,560	13,309	2,790	13,127	-1,250	2,248	-11,665	-11,925
Of which $ account	2,136	12,763	107,163	22,353	47,345	24,690	-215,907	-53,855	1525,73	703,92	66,949	-52,959
Of which FRF account	3,523	3,962	7,018	3,923	15,418	6,831	2672,27	53,387	-84,386	42,282	34,375	119,721
Of which *Indochinese piastre* account								-1,799	363	165	1165	
Earnings on foreign exchange transactions: silver arbitrage	1,054	888	592	209	265	73	182	4,897	15,05	3,761	-98	2,961
Discount/arbitrage on foreign markets										60,019	55,523	132,280

C. A decline in profitability

The profitability of the Wuhan branch had already not been great at the end of the 1920s because of the series of crises affecting *Banque de l'Indochine*, which had to grapple with the start of the global depression and the ups and downs of Chinese political and military life. But profits receded sharply in the second half of 1930 and between the second half of 1931 and the first half of 1933. This recession-stricken period was a difficult time, since debit accounts proved hard to settle, as we have seen. In the second half of 1931, the causes of the deficit were many and varied: a jump in overheads from 25,140 taels on 31 October to 51,638 on 31 December, the cost of building repairs, two managers' salaries to be paid for a two-month period during the handover from one manager to the next, a fall in commercial paper purchases and a collapse in export revenues—this despite the arbitrage earnings.

A large fall in arbitrage earnings (15,900 taels as against an average of 49,500 in 1931) was the reason for the loss recorded in the first half of 1932. It was followed by a marked rebound in arbitrage on positions in US dollars in the first half of 1933, linked to dollar remittances falling due of USD 625,000 (2.23650 million taels): "Our earnings are due solely to the maintenance of our debit position in US dollars and to the fall in this currency."[28] During this period, revenues from discounts on foreign markets offset the dip in earnings on actual foreign exchange transactions. But it was thanks above all to rigorous management that profitability was restored in 1934 (see Table 23.7).

Paradoxically, in the second half of the 1930s, as the economic, political and military crisis took its toll on Wuhan, the *Banque de l'Indochine* branch managed to maintain its profitability. The explanation lies, as previously indicated, in the extremely rigorous way in which it was managed. Even translated into French francs, the branch maintained a small profit line: it may no longer have been contributing to the rise of French trade or of national economic patriotism, but its management expertise was something to be proud of (see Table 23.8).

Without claiming to be exhaustive, it is possible to do a rough calculation of the capital under management at the Wuhan branch in 1935–1936: the first half of 1936 was not good, but business in the other half-years generated a satisfactory minimum level of profitability for the bank (see Table 23.9).

4. The end of a chapter of banking and business history overseas

After the arrival of the Japanese army on 26 October 1938 and the withdrawal of the Chinese government to Chungking, for several quarters, trade in Wuhan

Table 23.5 Foreign exchange transactions of *Banque de l'Indochine* in Wuhan in 1935–1939 (local dollars)

	First half of 1935	*Second half of 1935*	*First half of 1936*	*Second half of 1936*	*Second half of 1938*	*First half of 1939*	*Second half of 1939*
Gold arbitrage	99,337	9,0843	27,035	24,401			
Of which							
In francs	62,811	44,547	13,200	12,100	2,722	−48,194	33,444
£	−2,532	−30,345	14,754	12,073	83,367	−32,254	−2,939
USD	39,058	76,641	−919	228	5,507	183,778	244,618
Shanghai dollars						76,242	−35,924
Silver arbitrage	1,447	5,470	186	/			
Arbitrage on foreign markets	46,640	36,559	18,602	37,620			

Table 23.6 Assets of the Wuhan branch of *Banque de l'Indochine* in the second half of the 1930s (taels)

	First half of 1935	*Second half of 1935*	*First half of 1936*	*Second half of 1936*	*Second half of 1938*	*First half of 1939*	*Second half of 1939*
Total assets	8,636,592	10,379,139	12,080,349	9,858,053	7,649,378	9,534,800	12,231,080
Gold assets							
French American Banking Corporation (unused cash deposit)	3,061,262						
Remittances falling due in francs	78,174	185,630	180,594	315,341			
Remittances falling due in £	265,702	466,127	539,132	430,820	30,344	/	/
Remittances falling due in USD	249,526	477,152	980,481	386,748			
Silver assets							
Interest-bearing advances	236,598	109,567	247,476	73,866	5,958	/	2,956
Silver assets	582,576	416,918	425,411	183,032			
Receivables in the process of liquidation					2,048,085	2,060,447	2,062,131
New advances on bills for forward delivery	974,918	1,526,740	1,987,181	1,488,935			
Interest collected on this item	2,738	2,564	7,625	2,299			

Source: *Rapports-bilans, Crédit agricole* archives, *Banque de l'Indochine* fund, 439AH

Table 23.7 Profitability of *Banque de l'Indochine*'s Wuhan branch in the first half of the 1930s (taels)

	First half 1929	Second half 1929	First half 1930	Second half 1930	First half 1931	Second half 1931	First half 1932	Second half 1932	First half 1933	First half 1933	First half 1933	First half 1934	Second half 1934
	In taels									*In Chinese dollars*			
Interests and commissions	4,595	3,934	3,504	6,222	12,566	-6,038	-2,061	4,616	6,935 taels	$35142	4,524	13,280	1,5186
Earnings on total transactions	32,410	50,503	73,421	54,268	82,154	38,865	52,231	20,373		96,900	94,332	112,225	265,254
Net profit	3,017	23,647	38,823	12,915	46,958	-12,773	13,779	-20,246		13,982	32,223	50,887	142,317
Recalculated at the new rates							19,854	-29,173-					
Real earnings before transfer of a portion of the arbitrage earnings in USD to Paris (excluding interest on capital)					29,250	-29,597				253,324 (transfer of 218,182)	221,400 (transfer of 189,217)	98,192 (transfer of 272,000)	
Additional profit: collection of coupon on French municipal bonds 6% 1934 deposited in New York										21,160	60,019		

Table 23.8 Profits of *Banque de l'Indochine*'s Wuhan branch in 1935–1939 (local dollars)

	First half 1935	Second half 1935	First half 1936	Second half 1936	First half 1937	Second half 1937	First half 1938	Second half 1938	First half 1939	Second half 1939
Interests and commissions	13,412	14,848	35,309	18,639				3062	82	848
Gross earnings	157,942	147,720	81,132	80,660				104,338	179,654	171,463
Overheads	54,366	54,785	646,95	74,583				87,047	90,092	140,753
Net profit	103,576	92,667	16,437	6,077	17,982	9,938	86,646	17,291	89,562	30710
Net profit in francs	569,668	424,619	77,103		120,478	82,484	529,790	106,444		

Source: *Rapports-bilans, Crédit agricole* archives, *Banque de l'Indochine* fund, 439AH

Table 23.9 Return on capital employed at the Wuhan branch of *Banque de l'Indochine* in 1935–1936

	First half of 1935	Second half of 1935	First half of 1936	Second half of 1936
Capital employed in silver	2,151,228	1,986,208		
Annual net return	0.98784%	1.9488%		
Capital employed in gold	6,013,348	7,920,915	9,615,551	7,633,623
Annual net gold return	4.902%	3.2412%	1.512%	1.027%
Half-year real total net return on capital supplied by head office	1.797%	1.2403%	Negative	0.784%
Real annual net return	3.594%	2.4806%	Negative	1.57%
New advances on bills for forward delivery	974,918	1,526,740	1987,181	14,889,35
Interest collected on this item	2,738	2,564	7,625	2,299

Source: *Rapports-bilans, Crédit agricole* archives, *Banque de l'Indochine* fund, 439AH

was conducted under the control of the Japanese authorities. Free trade ceased to exist, and there was a heavy military presence in these regions. Then Japan's entry into World War II in December 1941 wiped out any prospect, for the representatives of enemy nations, of being able to continue to pursue any kind of business in occupied China.

The story ends for this book at the beginning of 1939, when negative effects piled up due to various factors: "The monopolisation of foreign exchange and foreign trade by the government institutions, then the military operations and the occupation of Wuhan by the Japanese inevitably resulted in your business coming to an almost complete standstill."[29] *Banque de l'Indochine* even referred to "the cessation of your commercial activities" due to a lack of clients, since "your only seller of paper was the National Navy (FRF 2.4 millions)".[30]

In the first half of 1939, alarm bells sounded with the closure of the Yangtze to imports and exports. The *Banque de l'Indochine* branch complained of "arbitrary measures by the Japanese restricting the free movement of people and of the Chinese national currency". "All export activity has halted and import activity is monopolised, without exception, by Japan."[31]

The "definitive withdrawal of the French and British gunboats and the withdrawal of the garrison from the French concession" were to prove even more serious: "Our isolation from the outside world is only getting worse."[32] Even the renowned gunboat *Doudart de Lagrée* made its way down the river in early 1940, as *Banque de l'Indochine* noticed. This ship had been based rub off:

in Shanghai, Nanking, Kiukiang and Wuhan, and later operated essentially in the Chongqing region as the situation deteriorated and the Japanese took control. It was driven out of Shanghai by the Japanese on 7 February 1938, and had to retreat to Nanking. The *Doudart de Lagrée* was in the port of the French concession in Wuhan when war was declared on 3 September 1939. It stayed there until 3 December, when it cast off for Shanghai. It arrived there a week later and was disarmed [having been in China since July 1909].[33]

"The departure of the detachment of the colonial infantry and of the station ship [local soldiers] has deprived us of our last fairly regular source of purchases."[34]

The *Banque de l'Indochine* branch reduced its cash balance as far as possible in case of seizure by the Japanese. Nevertheless, it maintained its credit position in dollars. It was because of these precautions that its account at the London branch of *Banque de l'Indochine* ballooned from USD 3,414,076 in June 1938 and USD 1,340,005 in December 1938 to USD 8,269,300 in June 1939.

It was no longer possible to conduct foreign forward transactions. It now took longer for postal deliveries to get through because they were subject to Japanese checks. European and Chinese merchants began their withdrawal from the market, but some foreign exchange transactions continued all the same, based on speculation on a fall in the local dollar and a turnaround in the local market when it emerged that Japan would not be drawn into the world war. All at sudden this news sparked a speculative flurry on gold, which drained clients' cash supplies, resulting in a mini-crisis at the *Banque de l'Indochine* branch as these clients withdrew their current deposits.

Notes

 1 *Rapport-bilan,* Wuhan branch, *Crédit agricole* archives, *Banque de l'Indochine* fund, 439AH 1930, first half of 1930, 20 July 1930.
 2 *Rapport-bilan,* 20 July 1930.
 3 *Rapport-bilan,* first half of 1930, 20 July 1930.
 4 *Ibidem.*
 5 *Ibidem.*
 6 *Rapport-bilan* for the second half of 1930, January 1931.
 7 *Ibidem.*
 8 *Rapport-bilan,* first half of 1933, July 1933.
 9 *Rapport-bilan* for the second half of 1930, January 1931.
10 *Rapport-bilan* for the first half of 1931, July 1931.
11 *Rapport-bilan* for the first half of 1934, July 1934.
12 *Rapport-bilan* for the second half of 1930, January 1931.
13 *Rapport-bilan* for the first half of 1931, July 1931.
14 *Rapport-bilan* for the first half of 1930, July 1930.
15 *Rapport-bilan* for the first half of 1932, July 1932.
16 *Rapport-bilan* for the second half of 1932, January 1933.
17 *Rapport-bilan* for the second half of 1933, January 1934.
18 *Ibidem.*
19 *Ibidem.*
20 *Rapport-bilan* for the first half of 1935, July 1935.

21 *Ibidem.*
22 *Rapport-bilan* for the first half of 1933, July 1933.
23 *Rapport-bilan* for the first half of 1934, July 1934.
24 *Rapport-bilan* for the second half of 1935, January 1936.
25 Summary letter, 3 May 1938.
26 Summary letter, 24 October 1938.
27 *Ibidem.*
28 *Rapport-bilan,* first half of 1933, July 1933.
29 Summary letter, 8 March 1939.
30 *Ibidem.*
31 *Rapport-bilan,* second half of 1939, January 1940.
32 *Ibidem.*
33 [Wikipedia]. See Hervé Barbier, *Les canonnières françaises du Yang-Tsé. De Shanghai à Chongqing (1900–1941)*, Paris, Les Indes savantes, 2004. Bernard Estival, *Les canonnières de Chine, 1900–1945*, Nantes, Marines Éditions, 2001.
34 *Rapport-bilan,* second half of 1939, January 1940.

Part V

From conclusions to broader issues

24 The Asian scope of French business and banking (1890s–1940s)

Three conclusive chapters will assess the overall contribution of the Chinese concessions to the enhancement of French business and banking, in Wuhan, Guangzhou and Tianjin—pending a future book dedicated to the Shanghai *Bund*. The French communities of interest involved in Far Eastern trade were expected by the French state, industrialists and business communities of the French port-cities committed to overseas trade to support French production, services and financial investments in the bridgeheads established in several concessions (Tianjin, Shanghai, Guangzhou, Wuhan, Yunnanfu) or colony (Hong Kong). The successive banks active in the area (*Comptoir national d'escompte de Paris, Banque de l'Indochine, Banque russo-chinoise, Banque industrielle de Chine* etc.) were meant to serve as conduits of French outflows and inflows. But, under the pressure of competition and the need of finding new sources of operations and profits, the need for the mutualisation of their means and amortisation of capital employed (ROCE), they became more and more embedded in the business life of these port-cities. They began to assume a mixed profile, spurring the interests of the "local" business communities in France at the "global" level of the Chinese economy and weaving networks among "local" trading houses in China to fuel their "global" development.

The main issue is did French banks promote French companies in the Chinese port-cities, or did they act more as globalised business partners? How did they manage to tackle the interests of French firms in the host country and its port-cities and become positive intermediaries in favour of Chinese business firms? We wished to determine how far the interests of *Banque de l'Indochine* as a firm tended to establish a balance between both demands—those of economic patriotism and those of local embeddedness—along what is called today a "multi-domestic strategy". Such an approach allowed us to design the connections established between the business communities of the port-cities and the building of autonomous strategies to prospect these markets. Our text will, of course, gauge the formation of a new "culture of risk management" in such "imperial" offshoots, thus fostering a reshaping of the overall corporate culture of the firm.

As we used direct archival records, we intend that this case study on *Banque de l'Indochine* broadens the scope set out by Frank King regarding HSBC and

Banque industrielle de Chine,[1] the studies by some Japanese colleagues on the role played by the Yokohama Specie Bank, the book retracing Citibank's history in China, books about Asian or Pacific banking,[2] and the pioneering collective book about *Asian Imperial Banking History*.[3]

1. The emergence of a French banking strategy in China

Throughout South-East Asian and Chinese commercial flows, the British and Japanese banks prevailed by scale and strength over those of the French. Nevertheless, the latter continued to try to loosen the hold of their competitors, to play a greater part in the Asian money market and to follow the development of trade, whether local or in joining the Pacific hubs or those linking Asia and Europe. Three axes of action can be defined: supporting trade between the Far East and Europe; propping up the half-political/half-financial penetration in China, especially against the United Kingdom—a penetration which was to strengthen the size and range of the Paris financial hub; and taking part in the trade between China and North America.

The competitiveness of French banks was tested in every commercial and money market all along the Chinese coast which had been opened to Western traders and bankers, where they could broaden the scope of their portfolio of skills through the acquisition of the specific commercial and financial know-how required for dealing with Chinese customers, Asian traders or European firms active there. This process demanded the consolidation of their ability to master the particular risks created by extending their reach in such new business areas against a background of stiff competition, with foreign firms scrambling to get footholds in the north Chinese and Hebei markets.[4]

In fact, French banks active in Asia had not targeted China as a priority because they had to first nurture the business fostered by the development of French firms in Indochina from the 1860s–1880s after the two-stage conquest of the peninsula. The Indochinese commercial business itself opened the doors to the Hong Kong market (for rice exports). But French traders gradually penetrated deeper into Chinese markets to get high-valued materials (silk)[5] and to establish bridgeheads for the export of consumer goods (textiles, machines, etc.), particularly through Hong Kong and the Guangzhou coast. Banks accompanied the move with the opening of branches.

A second area, the centre-west, joined Haiphong harbour via the newly completed Yunnan railway[6] and led French businessmen to hope that it would become a key outlet, able to short-circuit British predominance on the Yangze basin,[7] all the more because of the amplification of commercial relations with the East owing to the opening of the Suez Canal[8] in 1869.

A "Chinese strategy" took shape in the 1890s within French diplomatic[9] and business circles. They longed for a powerful banking arm there, able to counter the weight and influence of British trading firms in China[10] and especially the banking hegemony exerted by the Hong Kong & Shanghai Bank (HSBC)[11] and Chartered Bank. Several banks drew up schemes for their Asian deployment, but a spirit of cooperation prevailed in favour of building a single entity capable of challenging the British leaders and their competitors from Japan (Yokohama Specie Bank,[12] in charge of financing foreign trade) and Germany (*Deutsch-Asiatisch Bank*, linked to *Deutsche Bank*).[13] In fact, several countries lagging behind British influence had also thought of promoting a single banking firm which would represent the interests of its country in China and its environs: *Deutsch-Asiatisch Bank*, the Russian-Chinese Bank (with a few French interests), *Banque sino-belge* and *Banque belge pour l'étranger* from Brussels are examples of such a strategy to promote national interests abroad in this Asian area along geo-economics.

A first stage of the process had been animated by a bank created as early as 1848, *Comptoir d'escompte de Paris*. It defined a strategy which melded national growth with support for traders, especially at the import–export hubs and ports in order to stimulate the spirit of enterprise after the conclusion of the free trade treaties.[14] It decided to settle in Shanghai as early as 1860 and set up about ten branches in the Eastern countries: in Yokohama (1867), Hong Kong, Calcutta, Bombay, Madras and Pondicherry, and Cochinchina. *Comptoir d'escompte de Paris* was "the French Bank" in the Orient, especially when it strengthened its Chinese settlement in 1886/1887 with the opening of branches in Tianjin, Fou Tcheou and Wuhan. But the bank faced a major crisis in Paris in 1889 and collapsed, and its successor, *Comptoir national d'escompte de Paris* (CNEP), focused its activities in Egypt, India and Australia.

The French State was thus committed to luring bankers in to succeed to *Comptoir d'escompte de Paris* along the Sea of China: it asked *Banque de l'Indochine*,[15] which had been the issuing and commercial bank of southern and central Indochina (Cochinchina and Annam) since 1875 and of northern Indochina (Tonkin) from 1888, to change its geo-economic scope. In November 1897, it balanced the renewal of its issuing concession in Indochina for thirty years against the deployment of the bank in China and in South-East Asia through the opening of branches. *Banque de l'Indochine* had to bear the French flag at key commercial markets, in Hong Kong, Guangzhou and Shanghai of course, but also in northern China.

After *Banque de Paris & des Pays-Bas*, *Crédit industriel & commercial*, *Comptoir d'escompte de Paris* and the *Haute Banque* (the Parisian merchant banks) had godfathered the creation of *Banque de l'Indochine* in 1875, other big Paris deposit banks (*Société générale* in 1887 and *Crédit lyonnais* in 1896) joined the equity and its board, relying on their daughter or sister banks to represent the French business community in China.

They saw that the Far East French colonies required an autonomous banking institution which would be the vanguard and representative of French High Finance in Asia, gathering major affairs and transmitting them to its Parisian partners, to which it procured a flow of profitable operations, like the credit issued through acceptances or FOREX operations. Multiplying banking institutions in Asia would weaken the French position there in the face of the British who knew how to mix diplomacy and finance and found strong colonial banks like HSBC or Chartered.[16]

Meanwhile, CNEP had been weakened by the resignation of its German and Swiss managers in Asia who joined British or German banks there, by the crash of 1889, and by the economic, monetary (with the acute depreciation of silver) and military (Sino-Japanese war) turmoil in the Far East during the first half of the 1890s. It decided therefore to close its branch in Yokohama in 1893 and those of Tianjin and Fou Tcheou in 1899. For some time, the whole banking strategy in China had to be borne by *Banque de l'Indochine*, which inherited CNEP's Hong Kong branch[17] in 1894, settled in Shanghai in July 1898 and in Singapore in 1905.[18]

Geopolitical events dictated such a move because China was forced into granting a series of newer, harsh concessions to "the Powers", having to lease more harbours, to dedicate more tax revenues to the Boxers indemnity as pledges against bonds and even to accept the presence of troops to guarantee the completion of the agreements—even as Chinese nationalists denounced them as "unequal agreements". The balance of power was not in favour of China, and the installation of *Banque de l'Indochine* in the northern cities was in fact part of this "imperialist" system linking geopolitical pressure and business penetration[19]—part of the strategy of "*impérialisme à la française*" and promoting "*la France impériale*"[20] beyond mere colonial deployment.

At the same time, some French groups of interests in Asia started being promoted by another bank, *Banque russo-chinoise*,[21] which, in 1896, associated some banks from Paris, with two-thirds of the capital subscribed in France, Belgium and Russia—especially *Banque internationale de Saint-Petersbourg*—in order to get a share in the development of Manchuria and northern China. This development was stimulated by the opening of the Trans-Siberian and Trans-Manchurian railway, for the construction of which *Banque russo-chinoise* constituted *Compagnie des chemins de fer de l'Est chinois* in 1896 (Eastern Chinese Railway).

But the purpose was larger as *Banque russo-chinoise* intended to become the spearhead of the penetration of French and Russian interests in the Chinese regions located north of the Yang Ze Kiang. It acquired CNEP's Wuhan and Tianjin branches in 1895 and settled in Beijing in order to be close to the financial authorities, especially for loans intended for the payment of the war indemnity to Japan and of other loans and treasury advances: it led the negotiations for the financing of the Shansi railway in 1902–1903 and negotiated its FRF 40 million bonds on the Paris stock market.

However, *Banque russo-chinoise* soon escaped French influence as its German and Russian managers seemed to favour only Russian interests and did not promote French banks' business with the Chinese government. In fact, the latter called British and German banks when it looked for subscriptions to the last portion of the indemnity it had to pay to the Powers in 1905, for their having to intervene during the Boxers war. This choice aroused strong discontent amongst the French authorities. *Banque russo-chinoise* ended up competing against *Banque de l'Indochine* in Southern China and opened a branch in Hong Kong in 1904. This managerial dissent, coupled with the inability of Russian interests to exert strong pressure on China after Russia's military defeat to Japan in 1905, excluded *Banque russo-chinoise* from playing any part in the great French financial strategy in China. Moreover, when *Banque russo-chinoise* was merged with the Russian *Banque du Nord* to create the *Banque russo-asiatique*[22] in 1910, it rejoined the sphere of influence of French banks and its successor devoted itself mainly to its Russian and Manchurian business and, in spite of the desires of its managers in China, did not project itself significantly southwards.

This development emphasised the *Banque de l'Indochine*'s mission of a double strategy of reinforcement of its commercial implantation in South China and of breakthroughs in the centre and north. An agreement with the French state on 16 May 1900 confirmed this move. It included a change to its statutes in order to adapt them to the practices in Chinese markets and an increase in its capital. The bank thus opened branches in Wuhan and Guangzhou in 1902, in Tianjin in February 1907 and in Beijing in April 1907. This program was soon crowned with success, as these branches, equipped with the comprador system, using an intermediary with the Chinese community, gathered a wide clientele of local traders and bankers for short-term advances on commodities (opium, raw cotton, raw silk, tea), industrial products (cotton and silk fabric, raw materials like tungsten),[23] gold and silver.

Banque de l'Indochine limited its operations to short-term loans, currency exchange operations and participation in the issuing of securities subscribed abroad. It refused to get involved in the construction of a branch network in the Chinese provinces and in the direct financing of local business, then considered as entailing high risks and financial immobilisations, even though the granting of credit to trading houses and even to local bankers does imply the indirect financing of indigenous merchants.

Chinese affairs provided *Banque de l'Indochine* with 27 per cent of its total operations in 1905 and 33 per cent[24] in 1910, with advances to local customers; European firms like the utility *Compagnie française de tramways & d'éclairage électrique de Shanghai*; public works companies, real estate developers, like the Franco-Belgian *Crédit foncier d'Extrême-Orient* or (in Wuhan) Racine; the transfer of public monies between Indochina and metropolitan France; currency exchange operations; and the trading of remittances and bills, particularly in Shanghai, which had become "the heart of the circuits of *Banque de l'Indochine*, the centre of its network."[25] Beyond its clientele of European firms it had acquired, and thanks to the reform of its statutes in 1900 which allowed it to be engaged in loans lacking the usual collaterals and credentials, it developed an outstanding capacity for risk assessment of credit operations with Asian bankers and large merchants.

> By their knowledge of Chinese affairs and their know-how in FOREX techniques that allowed them to rapidly transfer the millions subscribed by French savings or the redemptions of the Chinese government, the agents of *Banque de l'Indochine* brought an organisation and a range of abilities

that were necessary to the success of large affairs. We may affirm that never before had "the French Bank" so deserved its nickname overseas.[26]

This assumes what Michel Bruguière called "flag imperialism", even though a partnership between French and Belgian businessmen (*Banque d'outre-mer, Banque sino-belge*, linked to *Société générale de Belgique*) was maintained for some Chinese financial and railway businesses.

2. From imperialism to economic patriotism

This background served as a basis for implementing a concrete strategy for the deployment of banking activities to promote French enterprises in China. It consisted of going well beyond the issues of a simple "imperialism"[27] and the relationships of geopolitical and financial dependence as, ultimately, it could find only a few opportunities for any real business or orders for French firms. The financing of the Beijing–Wuhan railroad in the 1890s was accompanied by massive orders for the Belgian industry.[28] And so experts suggested that the bank orient itself resolutely towards directly promoting French capitalism and driving a wedge between the competing banking, commercial and industrial powers.

This book has determined the *Banque de l'Indochine*'s and eventually its French colleagues' field of intervention as regarding the promotion of French national interests. Economic patriotism[29] grew at the turn of the century: letting the market self-regulate would leave the field open to foreign competitors and hinder French firms from developing their internationalisation and share of global money flows at a time when protectionism added to the difficulties of entering foreign markets. A strategy of economic patriotism would entail the mobilisation of all national forces towards the growth of commercial power and the development of exportable products by showing a heightened reactivity and aggression.

Economic nationalism did not consist in any policy of "folding", sheltered by protectionism, which was toned down in the years 1890–1910, or in the famous "imperial folding" around the colonial "preserves". It consisted in stimulating the spirit of enterprise within companies so that they could be more aggressive in the markets, which were beginning to turn into "open economies"[30] such as China and Latin America. The involvement of the political powers (renegotiating the concession in Indochina and asking the bank to deploy in Chinese port-cities) and diplomatic powers (asking consulates to collect information and support the expatriate members of the French business communities in these cities) also formed a part of this economic patriotism.

These issues covered a still larger dimension: the fact that a major portion of Franco-Chinese trade consisted of imports from China, especially the silk trade. Consequently, banks needed to enter into the heart of these East–West commercial flows and prevent their rivals from making hay. It must be noted that HSBC had even established a subsidiary at Lyon, the French silk capital, in open defiance of French bankers. This meant convincing the French merchant houses that were active in China to patronise *Banque de l'Indochine* and to remain loyal to it in order to benefit from its services (FOREX, supply of means of payment, management of international flows of payments) and loans (seasonal credit, documentary credit, warrants) for their imports from China.

3. Managing trade between Indochina and China

The first intervention, in Asia itself, was in the trade financing market between Indochina and China, mainly in the export of Indochinese rice to Hong Kong (which had increased sharply) and, on a lesser scale, in the import of specific Chinese consumer goods for the local population (including the Chinese community). Here too one had to loosen the grip of the two British banks in South-East Asia (HSBC, Chartered Bank), which had long financed intra-Asian trade (see Table 24.1).

Banque de l'Indochine had to work from its Hong Kong base, as we pondered it in our first volume about the history of French business and banking in China.[31] It linked its information network with its Indochinese subsidiaries to its presence within the Chinese business community in Hong Kong. It had to try to capture an increasing share of banking operations induced by the trade between Indochina and China, mainly for imports but also, more and more, for exports. In fact, Chinese business houses began to export regular consumer goods adapted to the local lifestyle, thus opening a niche for *Banque de l'Indochine*. The important role played by the trade between Indochina and China is well reflected by the volume of trade passing through the port of Canton at the beginning of the 1930s: the development of French economic patriotism helped the French colonial space in South-East Asia (see Table 24.2).

The *Banque de l'Indochine*'s branch in Hong Kong joined the fray of French interests in South-East Asia along two main commercial axes: the first connecting Indochina to Hong Kong and the second, Guangzhou and south-west China to Hong Kong. The Hong Kong branch became a hub for favouring the relationship between Hong Kong and Indochina when this latter emerged as a somewhat prosperous country, able to export commodities.[32] Its very first mission was to serve traders in Indochina who, *Banque de l'Indochine* argued, lacked the Hong Kong branch's information and competence capital and convinced

Table 24.1 Trade between China and Indochina (thousand francs)

	Imports by Indochina	Exports from Indochina	Total
In 1906	12,982	10,750	23,732
In 1907	15,073	37,697	52,769

Source: Charles Augier & Angel Marvaud, *La politique douanière de la France dans ses rapports avec celle des autres États*, Paris, Félix Alcan, 1911, p. 337

Table 24.2 International trade of the Guangzhou port-city (thousand *Haikwan taels*)

	Imports		Exports	
	1930	1931	1930	1931
Total	51.162	56.212	60.367	61.811
From or to Hong Kong	47.032	51.867	59.622	60.571
From or to Japan (with Formosa)	2.406	1.830	25.7	61.3
From or to the Dutch Indies	654	616	13	3.6
From or to Indochina	*651*	*1.329*	*75*	*66.3*
From or to France	*/*	*5.8*	*/*	*12*
From or to the United States	/	36.2	/	110.5
From or to Macao	297.6	376.1	631.3	893.9
From or to the British Indies	119.8	132.3	/	4.5
From or to UK	/	6.8	/	52.8
From or to Singapore	/	3	/	33.8

Source: The *Banque de l'Indochine* archives, reports, letters and outcome, second half of 1931

them in the 1890s to use the branch instead of trying to manage their surplus funds in Hong Kong through their own investments:

> Up to now, for their shipments of goods [of the Chinese traders in Haiphong] to Hong Kong and those which they received, exporters and importers agreed to clearing their operations, and the balance was sold to Hong Kong in cash. This caused them difficulties, delays, and thus losses in interest. I showed them the advantages of using *Banque de l'Indochine* for these operations, and they understood very well.[33]

Generally speaking, Hong Kong became a key hub for Indochinese exports, especially as rice plants in Saigon-Cholon were in the hands of Chinese manufacturers and traders (see Table 24.3).

Indochinese traders exported huge amounts of rice to China, generally through Hong Kong, though some of the cargoes were delivered to the coast ports without transiting through Hong Kong. Saigon emerged as the key port exporting rice to Hong Kong (541,000 tonnes in 1890), while Haïphong asserted itself as new source of trade as soon as it was equipped with a modern port (in the 1890s) and rice cultivation continued in Tonkin: with rice exports to Hong Kong growing to reach 60,000 tonnes in 1892. Indochina remained the main supplier to the Hong Kong market in the 1920s–1930s. Chinese merchants purchased rice in Saigon, Bangkok and Burma and sold it to Hong Kong traders, who selected, mixed, and stored them, before selling them to export houses (to China, Japan or elsewhere), thus opening opportunities to several stages of credit financing in which *Banque de l'Indochine* took a small part in Hong Kong—its main involvement being in Indochina (see Table 24.4).

Table 24.3 Share of Saigon exports as part of exports
to Hong Kong in 1905–1924 (%)[34]

1905	20
1907	25
1907	50
1909	15
1911–1913	25–30
1919–1921	35
1923–1924	60

Table 24.4 Rice flows at Hong Kong hub in April–October 1930
(piculs)[35]

Source	Quantity	Percentage
Imports to Hong Kong	5,570,000	
From Indochina	2,855,000	51.3
From Siam	2,216,000	39.8
From Burma	474,000	8.5
Exports from Hong Kong	4,488,000	
North China	784,000	
Middle China	152,000	
South China	2,646,000	
Macao	152,000	
Philippines	90,000	
Japan	347,000	
South America	77,000	
United States	37,000	

A special line (with two ships) joined Indochina and Hong Kong in the first decade of the twentieth century; it was managed from its inception in 1907 by *Compagnie française des Indes & de l'Extrême-Orient*, itself created in 1903 by the Combarieu family.[36] A special shipping line between Haiphong and Hong Kong was adjudicated in 1910 (to East Asiatic shipping),[37] but the Tonkin Shipping Company (from 1893) and the (German-Danish) Jebsen Shipping Company, with an affiliate in Hong Kong since 1895, shared the major part of such regional shipping flows. Hong Kong banks were used to finance loans to Saigon traders exporting rice to Hong Kong (and often to Japan), and *Banque de l'Indochine* joined HSBC and Bank of China in this business. Gradually, it enlarged its market share. Chinese rice merchants in Saigon-Cholon gathered packs of documentary credits on Hong Kong, and the payments by Hong Kong importers fuelled the dispersal of cash, which was used there (see Table 24.5).

Meanwhile, the coal trade opened doors to important credits: *Charbonnages du Tonkin*, a Franco-British colliery company, sold coal in Hong Kong and became a client of the *Banque de l'Indochine*'s branch there from the start. Houses in Hong Kong were financed by the latter to trade in Tonkin coal. But

Table 24.5 Rice export from Indochina in 1929–1939 (tons)

	Total	To Hong Kong	Hong Kong's share of the total amount (%)	To China (either through Hong Kong or directly)	To metropolitan France
1929	1,256,887	379,454	30.2	64,490	188,044
1930	1,058,410	310,991	29.4	190,320	203,610
1931	961,206	330,823	34.4	48,682	292,044
1932	1,191,649	451,217	37.9	63,351	408,271
1933	1,220,988	492,177	10.3	1,831	533,958
1934	1275,539	343,313	26.9	100,491	698,738
1935	1,718,013	437,372	25.5	369,938	348,563
1936	1,711,775	161,074	9.4	6,933	995,277
1937	1,548,358	290,182	17.7	102,878	674,487
1938	1,077,637	140,173	13.0	17,940	562,944
1939	1,680,822	162,212	9.7	78,148	461,035

Table 24.6 Indochina's commercial partners[38] in 1924 (FRF million)

From/to	Import to Indochina	Export from Indochina
Metropolitan France	712	346
Hong Kong	247	743
China	129	121
Singapore	49	153
Dutch Indies	62	74
British Indies	62	?
Philippines	?	124

the large dimensions of this trade explain why companies preferred HBSC as their banker in Hong Kong instead of *Banque de l'Indochine*, which complained about such an attitude.[39]

Trade on goods was also financed by the *Banque de l'Indochine*'s branch, especially as some of its clients in Indochina intensified their operations with Hong Kong: the *Union commerciale indochinoise et africaine* (UCIA) opened an office in Hong Kong in 1907 for import–export wholesale trading. A comprehensive assessment of such flows seems impossible, but the Hong Kong branch showed its usefulness and efficiency on several occasions—for example, when the French Descours & Cabaud trade house (from Lyon) sent tyres to the Europe Asia Trading company in Indochina with a discount from *Banque de l'Indochine* in Hong Kong.[40]

The trading house Optorg—diversifying from its age-old activities in Russia—moved to Hong Kong and Shanghai in 1923 and began the import and trade of goods (mainly wool cloth, but also spirits, champagne and pharmaceuticals) which it delivered against promissory notes.[41] *Banque de l'Indochine*-Hong Kong became its leverage in Asia. It collected its remittances in Hong Kong, fuelled exchange contracts (FRF 982,000 in 1931) and carried a large portfolio of bills drawn on Chinese clients ($82,000 on I.P. Hang Fong in 1931) for goods stored in the name of the bank pending sales.[42] But generally speaking, imports from Hong Kong were inferior to exports from Indochina to Hong Kong. This explains the amount of cash to be used as treasury deposits or short-term investments on the Hong Kong markets or even to purchase bills of exchange to be remitted in London or Paris by the circuit of *Banque de l'Indochine* in these marketplaces (see Table 24.6).

Notes

1 Frank King, "Sino-French *Banque industrielle de Chine* between 1900 and 1922", in Peter Hertner (ed.), *Finance and Modernization: A Transnational and Transcontinental Perspective for the Nineteenth and Twentieth Centuries*, Farnham, Ashgate, 2008.

2 Shizuya Nishimura, Toshio Suzuki & Ranald Michie (eds.), *The Origins of International Banking in Asia: The Nineteenth and Twentieth Centuries*, Oxford, Oxford University Press, 2012. Olive Checkland, Shizuya Nishimura & Norio Tamaki (eds.), *Pacific Banking (1859–1959): East Meets West*, London, Macmillan; New York, St. Martin's Press, 1994. Frank King (ed.), *Eastern Banking*, London, Athlone, 1983.

3 Hubert Bonin, Nuno Valerio & Kazuhiko Yago (eds.), *Asian Imperial Banking History*, London, Pickering & Chatto, Routledge, 2015.

4 See Albert Feuerwerker, *The Foreign Establishment in China in the Early Twentieth Century*, Ann Arbor, Center for Chinese Studies, University of Michigan, 1976.

5 Louis Gueneau, *Lyon et le commerce de la soie*, Lyon, L. Bascou, 1932. John Laffey, "Les racines de l'impérialisme français en Extrême-Orient. À propos des thèses de J.F. Cady", *Revue d'histoire moderne & contemporaine*, April–June 1969, pp. 282–299. John Cady, *The Roots of French Imperialism in Eastern Asia*, New York & Ithaca, Cornell University Press, 1954 and 1967. John Cady, *Southeast Asia—Its Historical Development*, New York, McGraw-Hill, 1964. John Laffey, *French Imperialism and the Lyon Mission to China*, New York & Ithaca, Cornell University, 1966. Claude Fivel-Démorel, "The Hong Kong & Shanghai bank in Lyon, 1881–1954: Busy, but too discreet", in Frank King (ed.), *Eastern Banking*, London, Athlone, 1983, pp. 467–516. Henri Brenier, *La mission lyonnaise d'exploration commerciale en Chine, 1895–1897*, Lyon, Alexandre Rey, 1898.

6 Michel Bruguière, "Le chemin de fer du Yunnan. Paul Doumer et la politique d'intervention française en Chine (1889–1902)", first published in 1963 in *Revue d'histoire diplomatique*; republished in Michel Bruguière, *Pour une renaissance de l'histoire financière, XVIIIe–XXe siècles*, Paris, Comité pour l'histoire économique & financière de la France, 1992, p. 84.

7 Evan Watts Edwards, "British policy in China, 1913–1914: Rivalry with France in the Yangtze valley", *Journal of Oriental Studies*, 1977, n°40, pp. 20–36. E.W. Edwards, "The origins of British financial cooperation with France in China, 1903–1906", *English Historical Review*, April 1971, n°86, pp. 285–317.

8 Hubert Bonin, *History of the Suez Canal Company, 1858–1960: Between Controversy and Utility*, Geneva, Droz, 2010. Hubert Bonin, "Suez canal", in John Zumerchik & Steven Danver (eds.), *Seas and Waterways of the World: An Encyclopedia of History, Uses, and Issues (2 volumes)*, Santa Barbara, CA, ABC-CLIO, 2009, pp. 257–270.

9 Nicole Tixier, "La Chine dans la stratégie impériale: le rôle du Quai d'Orsay et de ses agents", in Hubert Bonin, Catherine Hodeir & Jean-François Klein (eds.), *L'esprit économique impérial (1830–1970). Groupes de pression & réseaux du patronat colonial en France & dans l'empire*, Paris, Publications de la SFHOM, 2008, pp. 65–84. And about the origins of the role of the consuls: Jean Fredet, *Quand la Chine s'ouvrait. Charles de Montigny consul de France*, Paris, Société de l'histoire des colonies françaises & Larose, 1953.

10 See Jürgen Osterhammel, "British business in China, 1860s–1950s", in Richard Peter Treadwell Davenport & Geoffrey Jones (eds.), *British Business in Asia Since 1860,* Cambridge, Cambridge University Press, 1989, pp. 189–227. Robert Bickers, *Britain in China: Community, Culture and Colonialism, 1900–1949*, Manchester & New York, Manchester University Press, 1999.

11 Frank King, *The History of the Hong Kong and Shanghai Banking Corporation. Volume 1: The Hong Kong Bank in Late Imperial China, 1864–1902: On an Even Kneel*, Cambridge, Cambridge University Press, 1987. Geoffrey Jones, *British Multinational Banking, 1830–1990*, Oxford, Clarendon Press, 1993.

12 Kanji Ishii, "Japanese foreign trade and the Yokohama Specie Bank, 1880–1913", in Olive Checkland, Shizuya Nishimura & Norio Tamaki (eds.), *Pacific Banking, 1859–1959: East Meets West*, London, Macmillan; New York, St. Martin's Press, 1994, pp. 1–23.

13 Motoaki Akagawa, "German banks in East Asia: The Deutsche bank (1870–1875) and the Deutsch-Asiatische bank (1889–1913)", *Keio Business Review*, The Society of Business and Commerce, Keio University, 2009, volume 45, n°1, pp. 1–20.

14 Hubert Bonin, "Le Comptoir national d'escompte de Paris, une banque impériale (1848–1940)", *Revue française d'histoire d'outre-mer*, 1991, volume 78, n°293, pp. 477–497.

15 Marc Meuleau, *Des pionniers en Extrême-Orient. Histoire de la Banque de l'Indochine (1875–1975)*, Paris, Fayard, 1990. Let me specify that, without this very book, this text would have considerably suffered from a lack of materials, which explains my gratefulness towards Marc Meuleau, and also Yasuo Gonjo, *The History of the Banque de l'Indochine (1875–1939): French Imperialism in the Far East*, Tokyo University Press, 1985, thesis in Japanese, translated into French and published in 1993 by the *publisher Comité pour l'histoire économique & financière de la France*, Paris.

16 Marc Meuleau, *op. cit.*, p. 145.

17 Hubert Bonin, "French banking in Hong Kong: From the 1860s to the 1950s", in Shizuya Nishimura, Toshio Suzuki & Ranald Michie (eds.), *The Origins of International Banking in Asia: The Nineteenth and Twentieth Centuries*, Oxford, Oxford University Press, 2012, pp. 124–144. H. Bonin, *French Banking and Entrepreneurialism in China and Hong Kong, from the 1850s to 1980s*, Abingdon, Routledge, "Banking, Money & International Finance", 2019.

18 Hubert Bonin, "The French banks in the Pacific area (1860–1945)", in Olive Checkland, Shizuya Nishimura & Norio Tamaki (eds.), *Pacific Banking (1859–1959): East Meets West*, London, Macmillan; New York, St. Martin's Press, 1994, pp. 61–74.

19 See Frank King, "Extra-regional banks and investment in China", in Rondo Cameron & Valery Bovykin (eds.), *International Banking, 1870–1914*, Oxford, Oxford University Press, 1991.

20 Jean Bouvier, René Girault & Jacques Thobie, *L'impérialisme à la française, 1914–1940*, Paris, La Découverte, 1986.

21 Rosemary Quested, *The Russo-Chinese Bank*, Birmingham, "Slavonic monographs, n°2", 1977. Kazuhiko Yago, "The Russo-Chinese bank (1896–1910): An international bank in Russia and Asia", in Shizuya Nishimura, Toshio Suzuki & Ranald Michie (eds.), *The Origins of International Banking in Asia: The Nineteenth & Twentieth Centuries*, Oxford, Oxford University Press, 2012, pp. 145–165.

22 See Hubert Bonin, *La Société générale en Russie (Histoire des activités financières et bancaires de la Société générale en Russie dans les années 1880–1917)*, Paris, La collection historique de la Société générale, 1994 and 2005. H. Bonin, "Chapter XVIII. Le paradoxe d'une banque de plus en plus russe: de l'impérialisme français à l'impérialisme russe?", in *La Société générale en 1890–1914*, Geneva, Droz, 2018.

23 See L. Fabel, "Le tungstène: minerai le plus important de la Chine", *Bulletin de l'Université L'Aurore 3*, 1943, n°4.

24 See Marc Meuleau, *op. cit.*, p. 238.

25 *Ibidem.*

26 *Ibidem.*
27 David Kenneth Fieldhouse, *The Economics of Empire, 1830–1914,* Ithaca, Cornwell University Press, 1973. David Kenneth Fieldhouse, *The Theory of Capitalist Imperialism,* London, Longman, 1967. David Kenneth Fieldhouse, "'Imperialism': An historiographical revision", *Economic History Review,* 1961, n°14, pp. 187–209. Richard Koerner & Helmut Dan Schmidt, *Imperialism: The Story and Significance of a Political Word, 1940–1960,* Cambridge, Cambridge University Press, 1964. Jean-François Cady, *The Roots of French Imperialism in Eastern Asia, op. cit.* John Laffey, "Les racines de l'impérialisme français en Extrême-Orient", *op. cit.*
28 Ginette Kurgan-Van Hentenryk, *Léopold II et les groupes financiers belges en Chine,* Brussels, Palais des Académies, 1972. Ginette Kurgan-Van Hentenryk, "Un aspect de l'exportation des capitaux en Chine: les entreprises franco-belges, 1896–1914", in Maurice Lévy-Leboyer (ed.), *La position internationale de la France: Aspects économiques et financiers, XIXe–XXe siècles,* Paris, Éditions de l'École des hautes études en sciences sociales, 1977.
29 See Ben Clift & Cornelia Woll, "The revival of economic patriotism. Part 2: The genealogy of economic patriotism", in Glenn Morgan & Richard Whitley (eds.), *Capitalisms & Capitalism in the Twenty-First Century,* Oxford, Oxford University Press, 2012, pp. 70–89.
30 See Hubert Bonin, "Les vertus de l'économie ouverte?", in Bertrand Blancheton & Hubert Bonin (eds.), *La croissance en économie ouverte (XVIIIe–XXIe siècles). Hommages à Jean-Charles Asselain,* Brussels, Peter Lang, 2009, pp. 13–42.
31 Hubert Bonin, *French Economic Patriotism and Banking in China and Hong Kong (1890–1990),* Abingdon, Routledge, "Banking, Money & International Finance", 2019.
32 Patrice Morlat, *Indochine années vingt: le balcon de la France sur le Pacifique. Une page de l'histoire, de France en Extrême-Orient, 1918–1928,* Paris, Les Indes savantes, 2001. See also Pierre Brocheux & Daniel Hémery, *Indochine, la colonisation ambiguë, 1858–1954,* Paris, La Découverte, 1994 (reedition 2001). Irène Nordlund, "Rice production in colonial Vietnam, 1900–1930", in Irène Nordlund (*et alii,* eds.), *Rice Societies: Asian Problems and Prospects,* London, Curzon Press, 1986.
33 Letter from the *Banque de l'Indochine* Saigon director, 4 March 1889, in Marc Meuleau, *op. cit.,* p. 130.
34 Paul Caron, "Le riz", *L'Illustration économique et financière,* special issue *L'Indochine,* 1925, n°15, pp. 40–41.
35 Report on the rice market in Hong Kong, 25 May 1931.
36 Letter from the branch manager, 5 May 1907.
37 Bert Becker dedicated several texts to such a maritime history. See "The Haiphong boycotts of 1907 and 1909–10: Business interactions in the Haiphong–Hong Kong rice shipping trade", in *Modern Asian Studies,* Cambridge, Cambridge University Press, 2019, pp. 1–40. "France and the Gulf of Tonkin region: Shipping markets and political interventions in South China in the 1890s", *Cross-Currents: East Asian History and Culture Review,* November 2015, volume 4, n°2, pp. 560–600.
38 Patrice Morlat, *op. cit.,* p. 3.
39 *Ibidem,* 29 December 1925, about *Charbonnages du Tonkin,* which left its funds by HSBC because its suppliers had accounts in this bank.
40 *Ibidem,* 26 March 1924.
41 *Ibidem,* 20 November 1924.
42 *Ibidem,* 23 February 1931.

25 French bankers and economic patriotism in the Chinese port-cities (1890s–1930s)

The promotion of French economic patriotism followed several tacks which impelled businessmen and bankers to become embedded in the Chinese concessions and to prospect opportunities first for exports and then, and more and more, for materials and goods to import from China—either in France or elsewhere, because French trade houses (like Olivier) had to become "transnational" to resist competition from their British, Belgian or German rivals, whilst Japanese firms conducted their own intra-Asian strategy.

1. A growing concern: supporting French exports to China

A form of economic patriotism would consist in promoting French produce in China, and the banks should play a pivotal role, in the manner of their Anglo-Saxon rivals![1] Chinese imports are ten times bigger than our exports ... . Our exports to China are spread over a rather large number of articles, most of which are of insignificant value in themselves. Only the silk cloth and ribbons merit being mentioned as they attain to some respectable figure. After them come the wines, cotton and wool cloth, watches and jewelry, machines, etc.[2] It is true that French firms kept captive markets within the concessions: regular equipment for the troops stationed there and meeting the daily requirements of expatriates working in the administration, service and commercial enterprises or Catholic missions. They brought in modest though regular inflows (especially for the medium–high range consumer goods: wines and spirits; clothing, jewellery, perfumes; stationery, books, etc.).

At the same time, Chinese outlets were yet to be conquered. But the country was not inclined favourably towards French products, which did not seem to have any competitive advantages. In fact, the United Kingdom, Germany, Japan and even Belgium—if we think of the Beijin–Wuhan railroad[3]—had already established themselves solidly (railroads, arms, harbour facilities), while the United States began making inroads in the 1910s–1820s. Capital goods played only a small part of French manufactured products exported to China. It was then that the triptych "diplomacy-industry-bank", as defined by historian Jacques Thobie[4] and used by Jean Bouvier and René Girault, was deployed in this geographic region—just as it had been earlier during the Ottoman Empire, followed by Central and Eastern Europe and sometimes in Latin America.

French diplomats (at the embassy but more often from the consulates, who were cultured and often dynamic), were constantly mobilised from Paris[5] to collect information on the development and modernisation plans of cities (orders for transportation facilities, electricity production), harbour development plans (orders for public works), new arms for the army, etc., in a foreshadowing of economic intelligence gathering. French Chambers of Commerce in city-ports and industrial federations at home and abroad completed these information gathering networks, while the managers of the bank subsidiaries in China often acted as intermediaries at the heart of local business communities.

A. Capital goods at stake

In a movement of cooperation among enterprises, the French business community explored the markets for electrotechnology (small power stations, often for tramways or lighting), for harbour and automobile equipment, for building sites as part of real estate development, for factory equipment (sugar factory, flourmill etc.). The Fives-Lille equipment manufacturing company exported three 115,000-HP electric turbines to the Sungari power station in Manchukuo in the 1930s. If we focus on the north-eastern area, in the mid-1920s, *Banque de l'Indochine* partnered a French group which wanted to bag public orders for telecommunications equipment. The group was known as *Société française des téléphones interurbains* (SFTI). It had installed the networks in Tianjin, Harbin and Mukden (in Manchuria). It had moved its headquarters from Harbin to Tianjin in 1925 because, from being an Anglo-Russian company, it had turned into a French one in September 1924, even though it kept links with the British Far Eastern company, a supplier to the Chinese Eastern Railway. Its purpose was to expand its activities from Manchuria to the broader north-eastern areas of China. It won the contract for the telephone and wireless link between Tianjin and Shanghai for the Tianjin–Pukow railway (Chinese Eastern Railway).

Though it issued a loan to finance this investment, it needed bank credits to finance its purchases in Europe and the United States (copper, equipment), in Manchuria (wood poles) and its day-to-day operations in China as a representative of French telecommunications firms, with advances[6] of G$ 148,000, £11,000 and taels 10,000 in 1926. Such an opportunity seemed relevant to *Banque de l'Indochine*.[7] It was modestly involved in a major agreement among European, Chinese banks and SFTI in the summer of 1926 to provide big advances pledged against seven years of revenues from the network to be set up, but *Banque de l'Indochine* provided it with advances pending the first instalment of credit—with the equipment pledged in a warehouse. Part of the equipment was ordered in France from *Câbles de Lyon* and part in the UK from Siemens UK.[8] Another contract was made in 1927: the Far Eastern Bank financed (through a G$ 175,000 documentary credit and a global G$ 400,000 advance) the telecommunications equipment at Mukden (exchange centre and 3,000 automatic units).[9]

The group enlarged its scope and its subsidiary, *Le Matériel technique*, could offer almost anything to customers, as we analysed it beforehand: eleven *Potez 25* planes with *Lorraine* engines were sold to the Szechuen government in 1932. Though transported by boat to Haiphong and assembled there, military troubles suspended the completion of the operation, which was co-financed by *Banque de l'Indochine* through confirmed credits. It also considered the prospect of operations with the Tchengtai railway, which had kept some French engineers and managers throughout the interwar period despite its sinisation, because it had been built and managed (in Shihkiachwang) by Frenchmen in the 1900s. *Le Matériel technique* succeeded in selling new equipment (from French firms Daydé and *Comptoir sidérurgique de France*) in 1933 for FRF 20 million and later FRF 29 million. A credit package was set up by the *Banque de l'Indochine*'s branch, even though the Paris office itself was involved in some millions,[10] against the deposit of part of the funds by the Chinese ministry in a Chinese account as a guarantee.[11] The operation took shape in 1934–1935.

Anyway, the fragmentation of Chinese power and networks of influence resulted in massive graft: for example, the telephone contract required G$ 237,000 against a total amount of G$ 859,000. French economic patriotism had to take into account the local practices, even the "bad" ones caused by the regional power of "cliques", as has been referred to beforehand.

> No state operation could be concluded in China without considerable 'squeezes' given to help in getting the contracts signed. This explains why big German firms (Siemens, Carlovitz, Arnhold, Karber) had won the monopoly of large industrial firms in the country before the war. Far from changing, the system has been greatly amplified by the colossal appetite of the present politicians who are primarily interested in concluding such operations. Large orders for planes, trucks, railway equipment, etc. are brokered only via such a system. We have to accept such constraints and shut out eyes if we wish to work in this country.[12]

We do not have any systematic reviews of this development in the export of manufactured goods, only glimpses from the archives. Still, we can clearly detect a collective entrepreneurial dynamism which nevertheless remained modest in size in the face of Japanese investments in textiles and clothing, especially in the cotton industry, and within the Shanghai economic space. Because of these limits, the French economic offensive could not open major outlets for structured finance or supplier credit operations which could have greatly benefited *Banque de l'Indochine* and the Parisian interbanking pools upstream. These were all only individual cases succeeding one another, far from the "economic system" that was established between France and the USSR in 1960–1980, for example.[13]

B. Armaments at stake

Several chapters pointed out that a less pacific trade in armaments was also developed owing to the fragmentation of military and political power. In the 1920s, several branches of *Banque de l'Indochine* and its Parisian headquarters served as levers for processing arms orders from warlords who, either in agreement with the central government which entrusted them with the mission of building regional arsenals, or autonomously, had acquired from Europe armoured vehicles, artillery, munitions and even airplanes. This Chinese rearmament drive also benefited French firms from time to time.

In 1929, *Banque de l'Indochine* (from Guangzhou) became involved in the sale of armaments by French (and Belgian) companies: as the orders from the Guangdong authorities grew in size, so did FOREX activities and cash transfers (repayment in Europe of the receipts paid by Chinese clients), offering good returns through commissions. On one side, the bank practiced normal banking: the import of airplane engines for the Guangdong air force in 1930 resulted in a fat bill of exchange (FRF 833,000) to be discounted. Similarly, when the house of Pinguet acted as an intermediary for selling armaments to the local warlord, another bill of exchange (£16,000) drawn on the Reuter-Brockmann house was discounted by the bank, with a collateral in cash for 75 per cent.[14] Another service concerned the provision of FOREX facilities, as it was the case in 1931 for an order of armaments, thanks to the *Banque de l'Indochine*'s FOREX capabilities.[15] The total amount overseen by the bank in the first half of 1932 attained USD 760,000.[16]

For the major orders, *Banque de l'Indochine* assumed no risk at all, except the "risk of execution"[17]: for example, in 1932, the two brokers handling armaments deliveries, Ott and Krebs, had to fuel cash upstream on a current account in Europe as an actual guarantee.[18] The bank partnered larger operations in 1932: the sale of armaments by the French firms Schneider and Hotchkiss (and also consultancy to the Belgian firm, *Fabrique d'Herstal*). E. Ott, a Swiss heading the Industrial Export C°, acted as an intermediary in South China for the *Groupe Chine*, an association of French exporters into China, picking up contracts and following them until completion. In 1932, he oversaw the purchase of 200 *Hotchkiss* machine guns by the First Army Corps[19] for USD 183,457, with a guarantee by the Canton government and collateral on the modern cement plant of Sai Tsun, opened in 1932.

On 22 February 1933, another contract for 260 *Brandt* mortars, 39,000 shells and ammunition worth gold-USD 624,999 was signed, with the last instalment made on 27 March 1934. In parallel, Henri Krebs, the head of the Augsburg house in Basel since 1921, and the representative in Canton of *Fabrique d'Herstal* from 1931, also used *Banque de l'Indochine* as a financial lever, with loans of USD 150,000 in 1933 for the import of armaments.[20] All in all, the armament business varied depending on the Guangdong authorities and the rhythm of war, locally or to the north (in support of the Nanking offensives against the guerrillas or the Japanese). The *Banque de l'Indochine*'s branch oversaw sales of armaments of USD 769,000 in 1932, and USD 226,000 in the first half of 1933. The fees earned on them made for half of the profits of the branch during the second half of 1933. "The arms business has gone up to FRF 6,826 million. The lion's share of this amount goes to the *Groupe Chine*, which has been, for the entire period, our branch's best client."[21]

Even though it faced competition from the Bank of Kwangsi in Hong Kong for FOREX fees linked to the import of armaments (in 1934), the Guangzhou branch acquired a relevant portfolio of skills as a factor of "differentiation" and profit, thus proving its efficiency: "The transfer of funds pertaining to the preceding contracts (Schneider, Hotchkiss, Brandt, etc.) were accomplished with regularity. On the whole, these contracts will very soon be completely settled."[22] This fuelled the flow of cash into the silk business: "For us the arms business is a major source of revenue and it allows us, during normal times, to quickly cover our silk paper."[23] Such expertise opened up several opportunities. Negotiations began in 1934 regarding a big contract (FRF 85–100 million): *Banque de l'Indochine* (in France and in Guangdong) as an active intermediary and the *Groupe Chine* (a coalition of French firms) had to face a British coalition of HSBC and Jardine Matheson[24] because its manager, John Craven, was also on the Board of Vickers.

As we studied it, six French firms, led by Brandt, were involved: Schneider (FRF 40 million), Hotchkiss (20 million), Renault (10 million), Brandt (10 million), Sauter-Harlé (4 million), and SOMUA (1 million). On the Chinese side the government of Guangdong and Marshal Chan Chai Tong/Tchang Tchai Tong, with Bank of Guangzhou (a Chinese bank based in Hong Kong) as guarantor, were present. After seven months of negotiations, the financial contract was signed in summer 1934 by the head of the *Banque de l'Indochine*'s branch in Canton, Jean Juge, and the Marshal's representatives. But it lasted only a few months due to the lack of money on the Chinese side. The bank guaranteed the delivery of military equipment against treasury bills from the Guangdong government (themselves pledged by taxes on tobacco and wine) and exchange bills on the bank's order, to be drawn in 60 months.[25]

Schneider, the big French manufacturer of heavy armaments,[26] was again involved in such a deal in July 1935, this time for three batteries of four canons, light canons and ammunition. Payment instalments were scheduled for 1935–1938, once again based on taxes on wines and tobacco as collateral for promissory notes issued to cover the loan. *Banque de l'Indochine* acted as the agent for the transfer—with a 1 per cent fee, for its guarantee for the embarkation of the equipment in France, thus as a kind of comptroller for the completion of the operation.[27] Deliveries commenced in April 1936, and cash was picked up by the Guangzhou branch on behalf of the *Groupe Chine*, just as new contracts were signed in March–May 1936 for more canons, 75-type batteries, mortars, shells, etc. These orders amounted to around FRF 78 million in August 1936, with 33.7 million paid by the government against a value of 10.4 million for equipment already delivered—which could reinsure the bank despite a change of power in Guangzhou.[28]

During only the first half of 1936, the armament sales overseen by *Banque de l'Indochine* attained FRF 24 million of a total of 32 million. The coup of August 1936 suspended the process, but the new power eventually confirmed the contract, albeit imposing "greyer" payments and smaller fees. A final operation took place in 1936, when *Banque de l'Indochine* provided the trading house of Feld & C° with a guarantee (£58,000) for the delivery of 10,000 *Mauser* guns ordered from the Belgian *Fonderie nationale* in the spring of 1938. It also managed the transfer of the first two instalments ($ USD 7,650) by the Guangxi government—the other ones still pending in 1938. When the general crisis paralysed normal business in the Guangdong area, the sale of armaments became one of the key sources of revenue for the branch, under the account "interests & fees."[29]

After *Banque de l'Indochine* had proved its talent in the field of armament contracts, it tried to extend its reach to the import of equipment. While China still faced political and military tensions, its actual economic development was gradually gathering momentum. This explains the negotiations of 1935 between the Guangdong authorities and the Schneider group, in this case with its Czechoslovakian sister company, Skoda. It concerned the delivery of a big power plant for supplying energy to a paper mill at a cost of HK$ 209,000 in 35 months. Guarantees were to be brought by *Zevnostenska Banka* and *Anglo-Czekoslovenska Banka*, but Jean Laurent, head of the *Banque de l'Indochine*'s General Inspection and supervisor of its Asian activities, fought hard to introduce his bank into the pool and succeeded in getting the *Banque de l'Indochine*'s Canton branch a HK$ 86,000 loan to Skoda to help seal the contract. Unfortunately, the project fell through. Skoda endeavoured to reach other agreements (for five sugar plants, etc.), while *Banque de l'Indochine* took part in a few other Czechoslovakian exports to Guangdong in the mid-1930s. The launch of the Three-Year Industrial Plan in 1934/1935 opened the doors to new opportunities, but nothing much can be had from the archives available in Paris regarding the Canton banks' involvement.

Meanwhile, in Tianjin, the Hei Lung Kiang government placed an order for a hundred machine guns with the French firm Hotchkiss,[30] and *Banque de l'Indochine* brought its local guarantee (USD 80,000) while the Paris office opened a confirmed credit (USD 78,000). But the development of such business was hindered by military and political developments in China and the disturbing stand taken by the French government, which refused to give a public guarantee for credit insurance to the suppliers because it required that the Chinese loan of 1902 be repaid in gold francs and not in current francs. This paralysed exports.

2. The French government supporting the import of Chinese products

The book tackled the issue of one of the aims of the French government from the turn of the twentieth century: an increasing share of the imports from

China was to be financed by French banks, especially *Banque de l'Indochine* as a key tool to fuel such commercial flows.

A. Banque de l'Indochine *as the banker for the silk trade*

The silk trade was at the core of these East–West flows. A business community grew between the subsidiaries or branches of Lyon silk trading houses in Guangdong and Hong Kong. An entire credit chain was formed: from the collection points along the riverbanks to storage in the port-city, between Canton and Hong Kong and between Asia and Europe, with flurries of bills of exchange, discount and warranty, followed by documentary credit and FOREX operations, often with a clearing stage in the city (through the *Banque de l'Indochine*'s London branch) and banking facilities in French ports, and at Lyon by the mainland *Banque de l'Indochine* itself—with an entire chain of commissions and interest revenues. It is clear that henceforth HSBC's power had been successfully contained in these markets: fed by liquidity from its Paris headquarters or the seasonal availability from its Hong Kong and Shanghai subsidiaries, *Banque de l'Indochine* became a key player in the silk trade. Thus, a growing share of the profits it generated entered the coffers of a bank flying the French flag.

It asserted itself as a leveraging force at the service of the silk trade between China and France. Apart from Lebanon and Japan, China had become a key supplier of raw silk, mainly because it was cheaper and because French silk production had been badly hit by disease. French trading houses had settled in Canton because the port was the outlet for silk producers from several districts. Together, they tackled a huge amount of silk trade[31], with the total estimated at 25 million francs in 1905. Two leaders, R. Chauvin and E. Pasquet, competed mainly with the British Jardine Matheson and with the German-Danish Arnhold Karberg. They were joined by some rapidly growing competitors (*Générale des soies*, Gérin & Drevard, *Meurer frères*, Boyer Mazet, Albert & Wullschleger, Th. Varenne, etc.).

Warehouses lodged silk, either with merchant intermediaries or at the *Banque de l'Indochine*'s own go-down in Guangzhou, well separated from other goods for fear of infection. The bank offered a classic range of credit and first loans pledged against silk balls or cloth piled in the go-downs. The trading houses thus welcomed the introduction of its local branch which saved them from having to use Hong Kong brokers (with an 1/8 per cent commission) and banks, as well as sending a constant stream of telegrams, which led to significant cost cuttings.

The *Banque de l'Indochine*'s branch was inserted into the chain of trade and credit linking Guangzhou to Europe: transportation, inventories in Marseille and Lyon, and pending sales to French merchants and (spilling and weaving) industrialists. This fuelled the remittance of bills of exchange, with the risk on credit (documentary credits) and foreign exchange (FOREX), which was granted autonomy from the Hong Kong branch in April 1910. The branch thus accomplished the mission entrusted to it: French trading houses and the

Lyon market could now avail themselves of an efficient platform to get information, connections, credit, FOREX, international clearing, and cash transfers. No doubt they could have found similar facilities elsewhere too, in Hong Kong and from British banks, but the fighting spirit and the growing skills of the branch undoubtedly facilitated their modus operandi in the region and contributed to the French competitive edge. This led to a partial transfer of activity from Hong Kong to Guangzhou, reinforcing the rise of the latter as a key silk port-city.

In the 1920s, the *Banque de l'Indochine*'s branch increased its commitment to silk trade banking. Taking full advantage of the rebirth of commerce and its own portfolio of skills and connections, it turned itself into a major player in the port-city's silk trade. Over the first quarter of 1923, it financed three-quarters of all silk balls sent to Lyon.[32] In France, artificial silk (rayon) began replacing natural silk in the mid-1920s, forcing merchant houses to redefine their business model. They had to demand higher-quality raw silks to be delivered to high-class weavers and luxury houses in Lyon. The Guangdong constituency and its traditional spinning mills had to redeploy, causing more trouble: Chinese bankers became wary of their credits to such customers and sifted them carefully.[33]

Another point was the *Banque de l'Indochine*'s focus on French houses because, during the 1921–1924 crisis, British houses had depended heavily on advances from British banks, which afterwards demanded that they remain loyal and not go to their French competitors.[34] The *Banque de l'Indochine*'s competitive edge rested in its permanent funds (allocated by its mother company and sometimes by sister branches, mainly that of Saigon or Shanghai) which allowed it to grant increasing amounts as loans on silk balls, which in turn allowed its merchant clients to repay their suppliers without long deadlines. It was a traditional clientele with a renewed profile because a few houses withdrew or even disappeared. Apart from a bunch of small and medium-sized merchants, the leaders provided banks with large amounts of business. They included Canton Silk & C°, South China Trading C°, Madier-Ribet, *Comptoir franco-chinois*, Central Produce & C°, Hogg & C°, J. Cassa, Gérin-Drevard and Boyer-Mazet (whose building was adjacent to that of *Banque de l'Indochine*).

B. Banque de l'Indochine *as a companion to French trading houses*

Banque de l'Indochine began to partner with an ever increasing number of French trading houses in every port-city's concession, houses which were scrambling to get a share of Chinese exports. In Tianjin, where the French presence was scarce because of the might of British and American competitors, there were about 34 French trading houses against a total of 625 in the mid-1920s. The only major company active there was the international wholesale commission trader Olivier, with bases in Paris, London and Milan and offices and warehouses in Tianjin and Wuhan—but no history or archives are presently available in France.

Even though *Olivier-Chine* faced a constant financial crunch, the branches financed its Tianjin and Wuhan activities from the 1920s. It required guarantees on inventories stored in a special go-down dedicated to goods pledged against its "packing credits", that is, advances on merchandise transiting through the warehouses. Despite Olivier's failure in March 1922, it restarted its operations and remained a faithful customer to *Banque de l'Indochine* in Tianjin and Wuhan. It exported basic goods (wool, walnuts) as well as high-value "exotic" goods: goat beards, horsetails, bristles (pork hair), animal casings, stumps (drawings on special paper), carpets, furs, straw braids, egg albumine and the like, often sold in NewYork.

Despite the constant support from *Banque de l'Indochine* in Paris (its house banker) and in Tianjin and Wuhan, the complaint was that Olivier also used other banks to finance its exports—for example, the current overdraft advances were shared: 43 per cent for *Banque de l'Indochine*, 42 per cent for HSBC, and 12 per cent for *Banque industrielle de Chine*. But it favoured a sound division of risks: the bank could not bear by itself the whole amount of "packing credits" which Olivier needed in Wuhan in the 1920s–1930s. And it remained the key banker with two-thirds of the 1.5 million taels borrowed by Olivier through packing credits in 1924–1925.

Olivier remained a key customer of the *Banque de l'Indochine*'s branches throughout the 1930s, with large confirmed and irrevocable credits:

> It is a credit of pure trust which we grant to Olivier, and we are well aware of the danger of such facilities. But, should we operate differently, we would have to renounce this business and leave it to our competitors. Neither the house of Olivier nor the others would accept leaving their goods piled up in customs go-downs costing high rates when they own massive commercial assets including vast warehouses.[35]

At the same time, banks could not precisely determine the value of its pledge in these warehouses. The *Banque de l'Indochine*'s commitments to Olivier reached USD 89,000 in 1933 (USD 48,000 on Europe; 41,000 on the United States), against USD 109,000 by HSBC and 68,000 by City Bank.[36] On 27 January 1937, the shares of the global USD 547,000 credit were 197,000 for the *Banque de l'Indochine*, 150,000 for HSBC, 125,000 for *Banque belge pour l'étranger*, and 75,000 for City Bank.

> Tianjin is mainly an exporting hub and almost all the exported goods need long and delicate manipulations in the exporters' warehouses, outside any kind of proper monitoring by banks. If we stopped opening overdrafts in trust without actual collateral guarantee, our part would dwindle there. Our clientele is already very small and this situation has a notable effect on our FOREX operations which lack counterparts. In contrast to us, British and American banks are helped in this policy by the large number of houses from their own countries.[37]

3. Regaining decisive roles
for financing international trade

Having said that, promoting such forms of economic patriotism could be rather disappointing and vain: in fact, Franco–Chinese trade remained rather modest as several figures indicate on an overall scale or about each main port-city (see Table 25.1). And France's role in Tianjin or Wuhan remained small as many chapters of this book have scrutinised and related in its dedicated tables of figures (see Table 25.2).

Whatever the levers of its growth, especially in the silk trade, the prosperity of the commercial banking network built by *Banque de l'Indochine* in China could no longer depend solely on these activities—it needed to diversify. Franco–Chinese trade could no longer remain the only basis for growth: a second base was built when *Banque de l'Indochine* entered the trade between China and other countries such as the United States. The first target was international trade itself—whether with stakeholder French firms (the priority) or with foreign firms as clients. Foreign banks could no longer be allowed to have a free hand, especially the British entities. The monovalent strategy of economic

Table 25.1 France's major Asian commercial partners in 1913 (million francs)

	Exports	*Imports*
Indochina	104	108
China	**48**	**298**
Japan	32	175
British Indies	82	466
China's share of total French trade	0.6%	0.3%
Total French trade	8,091	9,836

Table 25.2 Exports from Tianjin in 1936 (million $)

Total exports	110
Exports to Japan	24
of which cotton	15
Exports other than Japan	86
Exports to UK & dominions	19
Exports to United States	44
Exports to France	3
Exports to Germany, Belgium, the Netherlands, Italy and Western Europe	20
France's share of the exports excluding to Japan	3.5%
France's share of exports to Western Europe	15%

Source: Correspondence by *Banque de l'Indochine*, 21 March 1939

patriotism needed to be replaced by an autonomous economic model as practiced by *Banque de l'Indochine*:[38] serving the interests of both French firms and its own. The French bank deployed within multiple business communities and along multiple commercial axes.

A. Participating in intercontinental FOREX and payment flows

As several chapters of the book have underlined, the first challenge was managing FOREX and payment transfers. As the London money market was the hub of global compensation, French banks had to use their bases there to control a growing part of the trade between Asia and Europe which often passed via the London money market,[39] the hub of global clearing operations. Thus they had to strengthen their presence in London, Hong Kong and Shanghai. In the Far East, French and British banks were both competitors and co-operators as they had to share payment, FOREX and refinancing means via complementary bodies and axes of flow[40] which simplified the flow of goods, commodities and money involving the branches of *Banque de l'Indochine* because each port-city relied on networks of correspondents for clearing operations and FOREX.

B. New scope for silk trading: Guangzhou on two international legs

The chapters about the Guangzhou port-city epitomized the commitment of trade houses and bankers to renew permanently their involvement in international flows of commerce: if they stuck to their mission of supporting French economic patriotism, they also considered that the reinforcement of French capitalism and world influence were two instruments to broaden the scope of that economic patriotism—which helps in understanding that the book often delved into "connected history".

The resurgence of the silk trade was based on new connections. While European outlets retained their momentum, the US market opened up a whole new dimension for Chinese exports when the US economy began to mature from the start of the twentieth century, with the growth of the luxury industry centred around New York. During the 1923 season, silk exports from Canton to the United States attained 47,342 units as against 18,298 to Europe and Lyon.[41] One of the *Banque de l'Indochine*'s best clients, the General Silk Importing C° shared its silk exports equally between Lyon and New York in 1928. An approximate balance was reached in the years 1926 and 1928 when 23,239 and 18,005 balls, respectively, left Canton for the United States, and 20,316 and 17,625 for Europe. Between May 1926 and December 1927, Gérin-Drevard, the biggest French firm there, sold 3,096 balls to Lyon and 5,895 to the United States, Arnhold 909 and 4,320, and the entire business, 45,634 and 55,792, respectively (see Table 25.3).

French banks had to evolve in parallel: as an offshoot of French interests along the Pearl Rivers, it could not but join the growing China–US connections, where the port-city was strongly involved, thus changing its scope from

Table 25.3 Guangzhou from merely a Chinese-European port-city to a trans-Pacific hub in 1928–1929

	Towards Lyon		Towards United States		Towards Italy
	May 1928–April 1929	May–December 1929	May 1928–April 1929	May–December 1929	May 1928–April 1929
Export of raw silk balls	21,773	15,079	26,972	34,061	
Silk waste products	21,084		21,825		6,817

Source: Report from the *Banque de l'Indochine*'s Canton manager for the first and second terms of 1929

Asia–Europe to Asia–US business. But such developments required its insertion into a new "financial system" with FOREX operations no longer linked to the French franc and the British pound (through the Hong Kong dollar or the Chinese-Mexican silver dollar) but to the US dollar. Far from the stature of Shanghai and Hong Kong, Guangzhou had to diversify its banking modus operandi. Massive FOREX contracts had to be set up, with maturities up to one year or more. Apart from volumes and maturities, the *Banque de l'Indochine* branch could not act on its own because of its lack of correspondents in New York—and it faced stiff competition from National City Bank, which even managed to lure French houses with better interest conditions.

French trans-Atlantic interests moved rapidly forward in the immediate postwar period and led, in 1919, to the foundation of the French American Banking Corporation, a federated initiative by two US banks and CNEP; which were involved in non-European international operations,. This affiliate became the correspondent of *Banque de l'Indochine*'s Guangzhou branch[42] in 1920—with a security deposit of $500,000 made by *Banque de l'Indochine*–Paris in the name of its Canton offshoot.

Trading houses exporting to the United States could now transfer their letters of credit and trading documents (for documentary credit) and rely on that platform to clear the banking operations with their US counterparts. The bills ("silk paper") arrived in New York and were paid for in cash or, pending their repayment, were rediscounted locally for a few months (three to four). Acceptance operations complemented the process,[43] with a final profit margin of about 0.5 per cent.

In the first half of 1928, the branch purchased commercial paper from the United States worth $2,063 million, for French (Madier-Ribet, Gérin-Drevard, etc.), British (Arnhold, T.E. Griffith, Mac Neary, etc.) and Japanese (*Mitsui Bussan Kaisha*) houses. Operations completed in US dollars by the branch rose significantly: from the first (4,538 million) and second (5,874 million) halves of 1928 to the first half of 1929 (8,529 million): it "walked on two legs"—Lyon and New York. A precise breakdown of the silk credit activities of the branch for the first half of 1925 shows the *Banque de l'Indochine*'s involvement on both international markets, financing about a fifth of Guangzhou's total silk exports.

The evolution of the branch thus epitomised the port-city's three-fold dimension, with operations with France, London and New York, and the whole range of FOREX and clearing markets in their wake. The branch even commenced purchasing credit papers on London and New York issued in Guangzhou by trading houses, whether they were its customers or not: it wagered on pure FOREX operations, without any direct link to its own clients' operations.

Notes

1 See, as a case study, Clarence Davis, "Financing imperialism: British and American bankers as vectors of imperial expansion in China, 1908–1920", *Business History Review*, 1982, volume 56, n°2, pp. 236–264.
2 Charles Augier & Angel Marvaud, *La politique douanière de la France dans ses rapports avec celle des autres États*, Paris, Félix Alcan, 1911, p. 337.
3 See Robert Lee, "French finance and railway construction in Northern China, 1895–1905", in Ralf Roth & Günter Dinhobl (eds.), *Across the Borders: Financing the World's Railways in the Nineteenth and Twentieth Centuries*, London, Ashgate, 2008, pp. 241–254. Robert Lee, *France and the Exploitation of China, 1885–1901: A Study in Economic Imperialism*, Hong Kong, Oxford University Press, 1989.
4 Jacques Thobie, *La France impériale, 1880–1914*, Paris, Mégrelis, 1982. Jacques Thobie, *La France, l'Europe et l'Est méditerranéen depuis deux siècles. Économie, finance, diplomatie*, Istanbul, Isis, 2007. Jacques Thobie, *Intérêts et impérialisme français dans l'Empire ottoman (1895–1914)*, Paris, Publications de la Sorbonne-Imprimerie nationale, 1977.
5 See Nicole Tixier, "La Chine dans la stratégie impériale: le rôle du Quai d'Orsay et de ses agents", in Hubert Bonin, Catherine Hodeir & Jean-François Klein (eds.), *L'esprit économique impérial (1830–1970). Groupes de pression & réseaux du patronat colonial en France & dans l'empire*, Paris, Publications de la SFHOM, 2008, pp. 65–84.
6 Letter from a *Banque de l'Indochine* manager, June 1926.
7 *Ibidem*, 15 July 1926.
8 *Ibidem*, 26 August 1926.
9 *Ibidem*, 27 October 1927. But *Banque de l'Indochine* was not directly involved.
10 *Ibidem*, 19 September 1933.
11 *Ibidem*, 25 January 1934, 10 February 1934, 15 February 1934.
12 *Ibidem*, 9 February 1927.
13 Hubert Bonin, "Business interests versus geopolitics: The case of the Siberian pipeline in the 1980s", *Business History*, March 2007, volume 49, n°2, pp. 235–254. Hubert Bonin, "L'émergence de la coopération industrielle, bancaire et commerciale franco-soviétique dans les années 1960", in Maurice Vaïsse (ed.), *De Gaulle et la Russie*, Paris, CNRS Éditions, 2006, pp. 229–252.
14 *Ibidem*, 14 December 1930.
15 *Ibidem*, second half of 1931, 8 April 1932.
16 *Ibidem*, first half of 1932, 27 October 1932.
17 Historical archives of *Crédit agricole*, fund *Banque de l'Indochine*, DES 13/4, Reports from the Canton branch to the Paris headquarters, 21 February 1934.
18 *Ibidem*, 15 February 1932.
19 *Ibidem*, 19 September 1932.
20 *Ibidem*, 5 May 1933.
21 Historical archives of *Crédit agricole*, fund *Banque de l'Indochine*, 323 DES 36/2, Letters and reports, first half of 1933.
22 Historical archives of *Crédit agricole*, fund *Banque de l'Indochine*, DES 13/4, Reports from the Canton branch to the Paris headquarters, 1 January 1934.
23 *Ibidem*, 27 April 1933.

24 About this *hong* (trading house), see Maggie Keswick (ed.), *The Thistle and the Jade: Jardine Matheson*, London, Octopus, 1982.
25 Historical archives of *Crédit agricole*, fund *Banque de l'Indochine*, DES 13/4, Reports from the Canton branch to the Paris headquarters, 21 June 1934.
26 See Tristan de la Broise & Félix Torres, *Schneider, l'histoire en force*, Paris, Jean-Pierre de Monza, 1996.
27 Historical archives of *Crédit agricole*, fund *Banque de l'Indochine*, DES 13/4, Reports from the Canton branch to the Paris headquarters, 15 July 1935.
28 *Ibidem*, 14 August 1936.
29 Historical archives of *Crédit agricole*, fund *Banque de l'Indochine*, 323 DES 36/2, Letters and reports, first half of 1937, 18 October 1937.
30 *Ibidem*, 23 July 1930.
31 Louis Gueneau, *Lyon et le commerce de la soie*, Lyon, L. Bascou, 1932.
32 The manager of the *Banque de l'Indochine*'s branch to Paris headquarters, 3 December 1923.
33 *Ibidem*, 22 December 1927.
34 Report by the manager of the *Banque de l'Indochine* branch in Tianjin, second term 1927.
35 *Ibidem*, 13 June 1932.
36 *Ibidem*, 14 August 1933.
37 *Ibidem*, 4 March 1936.
38 Hubert Bonin, "Les banquiers français en Chine (1860–1950): Shanghai et Hong Kong, relais d'un impérialisme bancaire ou plates-formes d'outre-mers multiformes?" *op. cit.*
39 See Philip Cottrell, "Connections and new opportunities: London as an international financial centre, 1914–1958", in Cassis Youssef & Bussière Éric (eds.), *London and Paris as International Financial Centres in the Twentieth Century*, Oxford, Oxford University Press, 2005, pp. 153–182. Hubert Bonin, "The challenged competitiveness of the Paris banking and finance markets, 1914–1958", *ibidem*, pp. 183–204. Youssef Cassis, *Capitals of Capital. A History of International Financial Centers, 1780–2005*, Cambridge, Cambridge University Press, 2006. Youssef Cassis, "Les places de Londres et de Paris au début du xxᵉ siècle. Quelques réflexions comparatives", in Olivier Feiertag & Isabelle Lespinet-Moret (eds.), *L'économie faite homme. Hommage à Alain Plessis*, Geneva, Droz, 2010, pp. 487–501. Hubert Bonin, *La Société générale en Grande-Bretagne (1871–1996)*, Paris, La collection historique de la Société générale, 1996.
40 Evan Watts Edwards, "The origins of British financial co-operation with France in China, 1906–1961", *English Historical Review*, 1971, volume LXXXVI, pp. 285–317. Evan Watts Edwards, "British policy in China, 1913–1914. Rivalry with France in the Yangtze Valley", *Journal of Oriental Studies*, 1977, n°40, pp. 20–36. Evan Watts Edwards, *British Diplomacy and Finance in China, 1855–1914*, Oxford, Clarendon Press, 1987.
41 Report by the manager of the *Banque de l'Indochine* branch in Tianjin, 3 December 1923.
42 The manager of the *Banque de l'Indochine*'s branch to Paris headquarters, 23 April 1920.
43 "Acceptance by an American company of remittances on irrevocable confirmed credit drawn by Gérin Drevard on a few banks of the New York clearing houses", *Ibidem*, 26 January 1931.

26 Was the strategy of economic patriotism successful?

From an imperial bank to an international bank?

The aims of "economic patriotism" set at the turn of the twentieth century and retained by the French commercial and industrial business communities in Paris and every port-city were not achieved. French industrial and commercial influence was not strong enough (after World War I) to fight against the "economic war machines" of the British, Japanese, Americans or even Germans, even if French entrepreneurialism had been so many times reactivated by business communities with the support of State administrations, as has been shown previously.[1] Chinese interest in French products proved limited, with no decisive relative advantages. In fact, French firms seemed to have targeted other geo-economic regions such as Central Europe, their colonial empire and the United States.

Nevertheless, a part of the objective was well and truly achieved. A succession of large orders for capital goods and arms concretely benefited French industrial exports. More importantly, a "French system" or cluster took shape in south-west China which helped take advantage of the silk trade. The most decisive aspect was the insertion of French banks—mainly *Banque de l'Indochine* but also its partners and correspondents in France and London and, for the CNEP, in the United States—in the internationalised Chinese commercial system. By flexing its Asian arm, *Banque de l'Indochine* and the Parisian market succeeded in nibbling some market share at the heart of payment, FOREX and finance flows between China and Europe on one hand and between China and the United States on the other.

Such a process led to a rebalancing of the *Banque de l'Indochine*'s activities. It was an "imperial bank" at the heart of the colonial system in Indochina, and an internationalised bank, acting within the core exchanges of China with Europe and North America. It contributed significantly in changing its strategic nature and business model and considerably broadening its portfolio of globalised skills. Through the diversification of its geographical basis in Asia and particularly in China and thanks to the enrichment of its "tool box" and its portfolio of skills, the bank decidedly and positively met the expectations of the state, the experts of Asian economics and the chambers of commerce, as well as the business communities involved in overseas trade.

1. Internationalised economic patriotism

Banque de l'Indochine therefore seized on one of the banners of French economic patriotism in a few important port-cities in China—even if the results might seem tiny in terms of the overall economic competitiveness of the French economy and its balance of exchanges. And the strict definition of "economic patriotism" had to be broadened: in parallel with the bilateral exchanges of trade and bills between France (and Indochina) and China, the bank helpfully fostered the very "internationalisation" of French banking, trade and economy, on an Asian-European level and more and more, too, on an Asian-American level. Moreover, its partner, French-American Banking Corporation, was a beacon of such involvement in trans-Pacific exchanges. More than the competitiveness of the mainland platform, what was at stake, in fact, was the competitiveness of French firms and banks on a globalised field, which could not but entice arguments about the meaning of economic patriotism for a country involved in an "open economy".

This book evolved therefore from a mere history of French business and banking history in China (Shanghai excepted) to an actual slice of "connected history". Networks of exchanges, of correspondents, of clearing operations, and of FOREX were more and more densified, along some kind of a "double life" by each French stakeholder of this "proto-globalised" economy. Bankers supported French businessmen, trade houses, mining or utilities companies, sales of armaments or equipment goods; but French traders themselves could not confine their activity to Franco-French interests, importing only China goods from France or exporting Chinese products to France—all the more because a few foreign houses also prospected the French market, like Schnabel Gaumer, selling huge amounts of goods from Wuhan to France, whilst HSBC could finance imports of silk in France through its own branch in Lyon. Their turnover had to grow alongside that of their competitors in order to resist their terrible competition, often helped by British thalassocracy, shipping companies, powerful banks (HSBC, Chartered Bank).

In the meanwhile, French trade houses also entertained networks of commerce with Western Europe and even, like *Olivier-Chine*, with the United States. French banks, particularly *Banque de l'Indochine* and also French American Banking Corporation or others, sometimes relying on their London offshoot (like Paribas[2] or *Société générale*),[3] took part in the financing of Chinese international trade. Connected banking history therefore takes advantage of these interconnected firms, house traders, clearing and FOREX marketplaces and port-cities.

2. French communities of interests involved in emerging China

Sure, the 1920s–1930s were years of internecine political and military struggle in China, even of civil wars. The book has described the uncertainties that such tensions caused for trading, transporting and banking. Sometimes, the French concessions were even thrown into Big History, as the neighbouring Chinese city was crossed by troops, transformed into street-battlefields or as the rivers and ports were submitted to racketeering, plundering, overtaxing. Resiliency became a key word for bankers and businessmen, fighting to regain momentum in the process of collecting goods to be traded and financed.

But they were also indirectly involved in a long-term trend to build a "new China", already maturing from the 1900s–1910s along the term of "awakening",[4] perhaps as an imitation of the *Meiji* turn in Japan, mixing self-centred development and internationalisation.[5] They themselves promoted steamboats and shipping companies on the rivers, warehouses on the ports, even plants (cotton, spirits, in Wuhan, etc.). They intensified the use of "modern" forms of credit and of international currencies in order to sustain the growth or the successive restarts of growth of the Chinese economy, thus fostering money in the backyards of rural areas.

Moreover they became indirect stakeholders of the construction of Republican China ("Rising China")[6] by the Kuo Min Dang, from Sun Yat Sen to a few dojuns/warlords thankful for modernity in their fiefdom and to the state of Tchiang Kai Shek. Such commitment of French communities of interests was reinforced for a while by the new Franco-Chinese treaty on 22 December 1928 (in force on 1st February 1929), which took into account the Chinese autonomy regarding customs tariffs, in contrast to the 1858 ("unequal") treaty.[7]

Whilst wars went on here and there—and even during the war against Japan[8]—for instance around Wuhan,[9] little by little an economic strategy was defined to set up an administration and public finances, despite bad practices of kleptocracy. Even the managers of *Banque de l'Indochine* branches had to recognize such efforts, despite their denunciation of taxes, currency changes, inflation and the like. "State-building in modern China"[10] could not but establish new networks of railways,[11] roads, airports, telegraph and telephone, as leverages to the restart of trade and to cutting into general costs. The cementing of an informal coalition between the State power and capitalist bourgeoisies ought to contribute to fresh mindsets favouring entrepreneurship, accumulation of capital and so on—all themes already deeply studied by specialists of Chinese history, as a new and far broader stage of "the golden age of the Chinese bourgeoisie."[12]

3. Business in China confronted with alternate history

This raises the issue of "counterfactual (or uchronic) history",[13] or alternate history: would the French offshoots in the concessions—even after the loss of extraterritoriality—have joined the fray of a strong demultiplied and durable trend of growth and become important cogwheels of this economic and capitalist "making up" of big economic powers by China? As nobody could have imagined the conquest of China by Japan, World War II or the Maoist victory and revolution, one may still imagine the fate of French business and banking in a "modern and strong China" in the 1940s–1950s.

Whether the new Power had persevered in its attempts to design some kind of mixed economy—along the provisional New Economic Policy[14] in the USSR in the 1920s—as imagined by Liu Shaoqi for a while, one could dream of French entrepreneurialism to have succeeded to keep some room for manœuvre in a few marketplaces, depending on the degree of openness to foreign markets, of course. That could have allowed French efforts and investments (extended branches, with more staff, warehouses) to get amortised and their risks to be rewarded.

Even the communist power preserved for a while in the 1950s some pockets of capitalism, trade bourgeoisies, foreign banking branches, as Sherman Cochran somewhat related through a few case studies.[15] In Tianjin, for example, as elsewhere, the period between communist takeover and the "Five Anti" campaign of 1952 were often portrayed as a honeymoon of patriotic "United Front" cooperation between the CCP and China's capitalists. The Communist Party aggressively courted particular "patriotic" capitalist representatives and simultaneously implemented policies supposedly favourable to the inclusion of private business within the structures of the new China. Sherman Cochran stated that the party dispatched Liu Shaoqi, second only to Mao in the party hierarchy, for a month-long stay in Tianjin in the spring of 1949 to see if he could make the party's new urban policies work. In a series of talks with local officials, labour representatives and business leaders, Liu managed to perform a shotgun wedding between socialism and capitalism. He chastised local party officials, reined in labour and buttered up capitalists.

After this shotgun wedding, the party promoted Tianjin as the model of how to apply moderate policies to business. For example, the party passed out propaganda to local businesspeople in Chengdu in south-west China pointing to Tianjin as a successful case of cooperation between patriotic capitalists and the Chinese Communist Party. But we must be conscious that, even during this honeymoon period, the party was able to impose its will on private industry, leaving little freedom for actual capitalist manœuvre. The party constructed a web of controls on work methods, production goals, finance, markets and disposition of company resources that eliminated any possibility for autonomous capitalist activity.

This one-sided marriage looked happy in public and allowed private enterprises to make money but simultaneously quickly subordinated capitalist enterprises and their workers to party goals in a process of "partification" and therefore of subordination of economic life.[16] In a similar manner, Kenneth Lieberthal saw the period in Tianjin prior to 1952 as one of providing a foundation that made later campaigns possible,[17] all the more that one issue could have been the geo-economic position in China at the scale of East Asia.[18]

As for the French ex-concession community of business, no data are at present available, and Aron Shai dedicated only a single chapter about French interests in his pioneering book.[19] Would we dream of "alternate history", therefore, where French banks would have to invest into the new native economy: their economic patriotism would have demanded to support Chinese companies despite the development of Chinese banks—as was already the case in the

1930s, despite the frailty of many of them. They would have reinvented the functions of the compradors, transformed into high-level managers in charge of the department for foreign affairs—and the Hong Kong branches (among them that of *Banque de l'Indochine*) or subsidiaries would become rich with Asian managers in the 1950s–1970s.

But such kind of history cannot at all allow any blindness about such a deadlock in analysis. A provisional (on the long-term history) balance of autarchy and international connections (with the USSR and with South-East Asia) took shape in the 1950s.[20] All in all, the fate of foreign business in China's port-cities was condemned: Chinese State entrepreneurialism and economic patriotism replaced business entrepreneurialism borne by (in that case French) economic patriotism abroad, and the geo-economic background completely changed.

French economic patriotism had now onwards to be patient till the rebirth of relations between France and China,[21] before the jump into the globalised Chinese economy by French firms and banks,[22] within a new wave of "awakening" of China opening the gates to a co-leadership of the world economy.[23] From the 1980s, for instance, the concept of "concessions" was replaced by that of "special economic zones" in order to attract investors and labour,[24] and new commercial networks were engineered as a consequence in order to actualize the former ones.[25]

4. Portfolios of skills and capital of competence

Last but not least, this book has proved the very resiliency of French business stakeholders on emerging and then fast-developing Chinese port-cities (either river ones or maritime ones). Far from their roots in the metropolis, deprived of the energetic support of the authorities as was the case for their counterparts in the colonial empire, managers and clerks succeeded (mainly) to overcome hardships, civil wars, fluctuations of currencies, economic crisis and the like to maintain their basis and network of branches, either bank offshoots or trade factories and warehouses.

A. Management history at stake

A commonplace explanation lies with the management structures. The business model was a dual one, with a necessary decentralisation of management because of distances and circumstances on one side and rigorous and permanent controls on the other. General inspectors crossing the branches network, almost daily correspondence with the Paris head office, frequent reports on the overall, economic, commercial and banking situation, dire assessments of accounting ledgers every semester: managers were closely scrutinised, enriched with advice and instructions and the like. In these times of the first globalisation or of proto-globalisation, the expansion of banks and trade houses benefited from the building of "firm management", as part of "institutional history of management."[26] Although depending on postal exchanges, written documents, files, reports and accounting ledgers, later on using telephone too in complement to telegraph, living on the rhythm of maritime lines (often *Messageries maritimes*, for French people, or Peninsular & Oriental, mainly), companies anyway wove endless connections to get and dispatch information. They had in mind, of course, the need to reduce the cost of the exchanges of commercial paper or of foreign exchange operations, and they were also pieces of the "machinery" managing transaction costs but with a special profile, that of being actors in a "merchant empire."[27]

The key explanation is to be found in the recurrent adaptability of the *Banque de l'Indochine* firm and of its commercial partners. Its array of strategic targets on the level of corporate banking and of geographic expansion in China and Hong Kong, along actual "geopolitics of banking", helped them to resist British, Belgian, Japanese, German and then also North American competitors. The flexibility of this strategy fuelled initiatives to adapt to the changes in the production and trade of goods and to detect opportunities of new outlets for the consumption of equipment goods (even armaments).

They provide therefore case studies of the capability of the firm[28] to follow the moves of its background—thus avoiding collapse, even if the book has showed that a few banks (*Banque industrielle de Chine, Banque russo-asiatique*) had to cease their operations and that some trade houses failed here and there. The need for endless adaptation was imposed on managers at times when the Chinese economy grew up and diversified itself rapidly (in the 1890s–1930s), even if it would be more reliable to talk about Chinese "economies" because of the variety of capitalism in the agricultural, commercial and logistic areas. Here, too, our book might foster case studies about this "adaptation of the firm."[29]

Such schemes of resilient management couldn't but exert pressure on the portfolio of skills of *Banque de l'Indochine* and of its commercial partners in China (and Hong Kong). Sure, they inspired themselves from their "core competences"[30] of the firm, but they had to take in consideration the Chinese core mindsets (different in every large area), the uses in money exchanges and accounting, sometimes the "bad practices" in frauds, the inner competition within local communities of business and the like. They had, of course, to move along the institutional and military changes, to respect the sources of power, to mix with the bad practices of kleptocracy (racketeering or over taxation by local authorities, "cliques", piracy along rivers, etc.). Specific skills had thus to be engineered through processes of managerial decentralisation.

B. A capital of cultural connections

The last points will be fostered by these very considerations. The distance from the head office, the specificity of local practices and connections (*guanxi*), the permanent "revolutions" in Chinese national or regional power all had to be balanced by practices of "economic intelligence". Managers were often meeting in their local communities of business and banking, at the Chambers of commerce, at the "clubs" (like the *Club gaulois* in Guangzhou). They had dinners within their national communities to deepen connexions of socialisation.[31] They argued permanently with commercial partners to share information about trade flows and opportunities, risk management, risky houses and such issues. This was indeed the true life of every marketplace, either in France or in China: enriching the capital of knowledge[32] helped cement the immaterial capital of managerial skills—and this book provides a large range of case studies thereabout.

Classically, bankers and traders struggled to detect and isolate "the black lemons",[33] that is, houses which tried to circumvent information to hide their bad practices and unbalanced or swindled financial balance sheets, favouring asymmetry of information. Of course, while sharing information with them, they fought as competitors on the field of commercial seduction and of the promotion of their "better" conditions. But all in all those stakeholders of Chinese marketplaces and port-cities did share the same concern, that is, to deepen their "embeddedness", an issue long recognised as a key leverage force to sustain the development of banks and companies when they risk acting far from their core positions.[34] Along the same way of acting in colonial empires or far-flung Pacific, Latin-American or Central Asian markets, bankers and merchants had to structure, entertain, and renew their "business culture"[35] thanks to such embedded branches in the foreign concessions and in their surroundings.

About that topic, the eminent role often played by the compradors has been underlined in almost each chapter of the book. With just a daring essay, we could pretend that the success (or failure) of the managers of *Banque de l'Indochine* branches (or those of HSBC, *Banque belge pour l'étranger, Deutsch Asiatisch Bank* or Chartered Bank) depended on their ability to establish bridges between their capital of knowledge about the regional developments of local productive systems (silk, agro-business goods, mining minerals, etc.) and to become stakeholders (within their specialties and their range of intervention, far different from that of indigenous Chinese trade houses and lenders, then also banks) of some kind of "clusters" which took shape during that half-century—and this demanded the adaptation of these segments of the "knowledge economy" to "regional developments."[36]

In any case, we have to admit that one topic is missing in that very book: the issue of French *guanxi*, that is, the cementing of the communities of French businessmen and bankers either abroad or back in the French marketplaces.[37] Except for a few data supplied by some correspondence sent by the managers of the branch of *Banque de l'Indochine* and mostly the analysis of some consuls whenever their reports are still available in the Foreign Affairs archives, we cannot actually deeply perceive the mindsets of these business communities—what were their weekly modus vivendi and relationships?

Did these managers create strong personal connections beyond their daily jobs? Did the bosses at trade houses (Madier-Ribet, Monbaron, Gérin-Drevard, Olivier, Racine, Boyer-Mazet, Meurer frères, Romagoux, Gaussin or others) entertain close relations, in keeping with the model of those deeply analysed by

British historians about the Hong Kong or the Shanghai port-cities? Moreover, did they weave some *guanxi*-style community in Lyon or Paris, for instance, for the family or management teams active in the metropolis or, when back there, after the first part of their career abroad?

I am quite aware that these human and sociological aspects of social network analysis[38] will be missed from this book and demand further investigations. Entrepreneurial networks[39] have ever cemented business cultures[40] in marketplaces and within local clusters,[41] and we can presume that such "French-overseas" and "Franco-Chinese" mindsets and practices took shape little by little from the 1890s to the 1940s in the French concessions and their fields of activity.

5. Issues of business and connected history

Once more, as the end of this conclusive chapter helps us understand, business history, institutional management history and banking history are intimately linked, with another dimension, that of "connected history" because of the internationalised paths followed by *Banque de l'Indochine* and its competitors or partners. This very book can be perceived on that level of "connected history", as another sign or proof (if required) that French capitalism, companies and banks acted on a worldwide level, that the "worldwide history of France"[42] took the profits of "growth within open economy"[43].

In that field, *Banque de l'Indochine* provides a relevant case study: epitomizing the "imperial economic spirit" in Indochina,[44] it succeeded in asserting itself as a leverage force on several Chinese marketplaces and in Honk Kong[45] and in challenging the British thalassocracy there. And moreover it can foster arguments about the "geo-economics" of banking[46] as a springboard to broaden the scope of the history of geopolitics; this book intends to foster further considerations and arguments about rivalries and altogether about cooperation among trade, maritime and banking companies involved in the process of "modernising" and "awakening" Chinese regions connected with river and maritime port-cities.

Sure, the dimension of commercial flows and banking operations is by noway comparable to the figures of present times. But French entrepreneurialism did seize many opportunities, in the maritime or river port-cities, to promote French economic patriotism and thus to foster competition against the European bigwigs, then also against Japan and the USA. Such narrative history is therefore to be used as a springboard to argue about the resilience of French capitalism overseas, and to fuel considerations about the stages of growth and of localisation of French connected economic history.

Notes

1 Hubert Bonin, *French Banking and Entrepreneurialism in China and Hong Kong, from the 1850s to 1980s*, Abingdon, Routledge, "Banking, Money & International Finance", 2019.
2 Éric Bussière, *Paribas, l'Europe et le monde, 1872–1992*, Anvers, Fonds Mercator, 1992.

3   Hubert Bonin, *La Société générale en Grande-Bretagne (1871–1996)*, Paris, "Historical series of Société générale", 1996. Hubert Bonin, "La stratégie de déploiement international de la Société générale (des années 1870 aux années 1970)", in Olivier Feiertag & Isabelle Lespinet-Moret (eds.), *L'économie faite homme. Hommage à Alain Plessis*, Geneva, Droz, "Publications d'histoire économique & sociale internationale", 2010, pp. 303–324.

4   Arthur Judson Brown, *New Forces in Old China: An Unwelcome but Inevitable Awakening*, New York, F.H. Revell, 1904. James Cantlie, *Sun Yat Sen and the Awakening of China*, New York, F.H. Revell, 1912. Michael Godley, "Socialism with Chinese characteristics: Sun Yat-Sen and the international development of China", *Australian Journal of Chinese Affairs*, July 1987, n°18, pp. 109–125. Aage Krarup-Nielsen, *The Dragon Awakes*, London, J. Lane, 1928.

5   See Sun Yat-Sen, *The International Development of China*, London, G.P. Putnam's Sons, 1922.

6   William Burbidge, *Rising China: A Brief History of China and a Bibliographical Sketch of Generalissime and Madame Chiang Kai-Shek*, London, J. Crowther, 1943. Xavier Paulès, *La République de Chine. Histoire générale de la Chine (1912–1949)*, Paris, Les Belles Lettres, « Histoire. Histoire générale de la Chine », 2019.

7   Note of the French ambassador in China, archives of the ministry for Foreign Affairs, 9/B/2, 26 April 1929.

8   William Kirby, "The Chinese-war economy: Mobilisation, control, and planning in nationalist China", in Steven Levine & James Hsiung (eds.), *China's Bitter Victory: The War with Japan, 1937–1945*, New York, M.E. Sharpe, 1992, pp. 185–212. Diana Lary, "One province' experience of war: Guangxi, 1937–1945", in Stephen McKinnon, Diana Lary & Ezra Vogel (eds.), *China at War: Regions of China, 1937–1945*, Stanford, Stanford University Press, 2007.

9   See Stephen MacKinnon, *Wuhan, 1938: War, Refugees, and the Making of Modern China*, Berkeley, University of California Press, 2008.

10 Robert Bodeski, *State-Building in Modern China: The Kuomintang in the Prewar Period*, Berkeley, Center for Chinese Studies, University of California, 1981.

11 Louis Richard Edmonds, "The legacy of Sun Yat Sen's railway plans", *China Quarterly*, September 1987, n111, pp. 421–443. Ralph William Heunemann, *The Dragon and the Iron Horse: The Economics of Railroads in China, 1876–1937*, Cambridge, MA, Harvard University Press, "Council on East Asian studies", 1984.

12 See Marie-Claire Bergère, *The Golden Age of the Chinese Bourgeoisie, 1911–1937*, Cambridge, Cambridge University Press, "Studies in modern capitalism", 1989. Marie-Claire Bergère, "The Chinese bourgeoisie", in Denis Crispin Twitchett & John King Fairbank (eds.), *The Cambridge History of China*, Volume 12, *Republican China*, Cambridge, Cambridge University Press, 1983.

13 See Quentin Deluermoz & Pierre Singaravélou, "Explorer le champ des possibles. Approches contrefactuelles et futurs non advenus en histoire", *Revue d'histoire moderne & contemporaine*, 2012, n°59–3, pp. 70–95. Pierre Singaravélou & Quentin Deluermoz (eds.), *Pour une histoire des possibles. Analyses contrefactuelles et futurs non advenus du passé*, Paris, Seuil, 2016.

14 Alan Ball, *Russia's Last Capitalists: The Nepmen, 1921–1929*, Berkeley, University of California Press, 1990.

15 Sherman Cochran, "Capitalists choosing communist China: The Liu family of Shanghai, 1948–1956", in Jeremy Brown & Paul Pickowicz (eds.), *Dilemmas of Victory: The Early Years of the People's Republic of China*, Cambridge, Harvard University Press, 2010, pp. 359–385.

16 Sherman Cochran (dir.), *The Capitalist Dilemma in China's Communist Revolution*, Ithaca, East Asia Program, Cornell University, Project MUSE, "CornellEast Asia Series", 2014, University of Hawaï Press, 2015.

17 Kenneth Lieberthal, *Revolution and Tradition in Tientsin, 1949–1952*, Stanford, Stanford University Press, 1980.
18 See Toru Kubo, "China's economic development and the international order of Asia, 1930s–1950s", in Shigeru Akita & Nicholas White (eds.), *The International Order of Asia in the 1930s and 1950s*, London, Ashgate, 2010, pp. 233–253.
19 Aron Shai, *The Fate of British and French Firms in China, 1949–1954: Imperialism Imprisoned*, Oxford, Macmillan, 1996.
20 Toru Kubo, "China's economic development and the international order of Asia, 1930s–1950s", in Shigeru Akita & Nicholas White (eds.), *The International Order of Asia in the 1930s and 1950s*, Farnham, Ashgate, "Modern economic and social history", 2010, pp. 233–254.
21 Bernard Krouck, *De Gaulle et la Chine. La politique française à l'égard de la République populaire de Chine, 1958–1969*, Paris, Les Indes savantes, 2012. Thierry Robin, *Les relations économiques et financières entre la France et la Chine (1945–1973)*, Geneva, Droz, "Publications d'histoire économique & sociale", 2013.
22 See Félix Torres, *Le chemin partagé: Une histoire d'EDF en Chine (1983–2011)*, Paris, François Bourin, 2011. Chambre de commerce & d'industrie en Chine, *Le temps de la Chine. La France au défi du plus grand marché du monde*, Paris, Félix Torres Éditeur, 2013.
23 See Regina Abrami, William Kirby & Warren McFarlan, *Can China Lead? Reaching the Limits of Power and Growth*, Boston, Harvard Business Review Press, 2014.
24 Christopher Miller, "Chapter 12: From foreign concessions to special economic zones: Decolonization and foreign investment in twentieth-century Asia", in Leslie James & Elisabeth Leake (eds.), *Decolonization and the Cold War: Negotiating Independence*, London, Bloomsbury Academic, "New Approaches to International History", 2015.
25 Shinya Sugiyama & Linda Grove (eds.), *Commercial Networks in Modern Asia*, Richmond, Surrey, Curzon Press, 2001.
26 *Cf.* Douglass North, "Institutions", *Journal of Economic Perspectives*, 1990, volume 5, n°12, pp. 97–112. Mark Casson, "Institutional economics and business history: A way forward?", in Mark Casson & Mary Rose (eds.), *Institutions and the Evolution of Modern Business*, special issue, *Business History*, October 1997, volume 39, n°4, London, Frank Cass, pp. 151–175. Jean-Michel Plane, *Théorie des organisations*, Paris, Dunod, 2003 (2nd edition). Marcelo Bucheli & Daniel Wadhwani, "The future of the past in management and organisation studies", in Marcelo Bucheli & Daniel Wadhwani (eds.), *Organizations in the Time: History, Theory, Methods*, New York, Oxford University Press, 2014, pp. 3–32. Michael Rowlinson, John Hassard & Stephanie Decker, "Research strategies for organizational history: A dialogue between historical theory and organizational theory", *Academic of Management Review*, 2014, volume 39, n°3, pp. 250–274. Mathias Kipping & Behlül Üsdiken, "History in organization and management theory: More than meets the eye", *The Academy of Management Annals*, 2014, volume 8, n°1, pp. 535–588. Alun Munslow, "Managing the past", in Patricia Genoe McLaren, Albert Mills & Terrance Weatherbee (eds.), *The Routledge Companion to Management & Organizational History*, Abingdon, Routledge, "Business & Economics", 2015, pp. 12–142. Stephanie Decker, "Paradigms lost: Integrating history and organization studies", *Management & Organizational History*, 2016, volume 11, n°4, pp.364–379.
27 Douglass North, "Institutions, transactions costs, and the rise of merchant empires", in James Tracy (ed.), *The Political Economy of Merchant Empires*, Cambridge, Cambridge University Press, 1991.
28 Richard Langlois & Paul Robertson, *Firms, Markets, and Economic Change: A Dynamic Theory of Business Institutions*, Abingdon, Routledge, 1995. Alfred Chandler, "Organizational capabilities and the economic history of the industrial enterprise", *Journal of Economic Perspectives*, Summer 1992, n°6, pp. 79–100.
29 See Charles Baden Fuller & Henk Volberda, "Strategic renewal: How large complex organizations prepare to the future", *International Studies of Management & Organisation*,

1997, volume 27, n°2, pp. 95–120. Olivier Germain, "Charles Baden Fuller: A contre-courant stratégique: expérimentation, régénération, coévolution", in Thomas Loilier & Albéric Tellier (eds.), *Les grands auteurs en stratégie*, Colombelles, EMS Management & Société, 2007, pp. 359–377.

30 See Coimbatore Krishnarao Prahalad & Gary Hamel, "The core competence of the corporation", *Harvard Business Review*, May–June 1990, pp. 79–90.

31 Richard Drummond Whitley, "Societies, firms and markets: The social structuring of business systems", in Richard Whitley (ed.), *European Business Systems: Firms, Markets in Their National Context*, London, Sage, 1992.

32 Bart Noteboom (ed.), *Knowledge and Learning in the Firm*, Abingdon, Edward Elgar, 2006.

33 See Garrett Hardin, "The tragedy of the commons", *Science*, 1968, n°162, pp. 1243–1248 (the founding article). George Akerlof, "The market for lemons: Qualitative uncertainty and the market mechanism", *Quarterly Journal of Economics*, 1970, volume 84, pp. 488–500. David Feeny, Fikret Berkes, Bonnie McCay & James Acheson, "The tragedy of commons: Twenty-two years later", *Human Ecology*, 1990, n°18, pp. 1–19.

34 Mark Granovetter, "Economic action and social structure: The problem of embedded-ness", *American Journal of Sociology*, 1985, volume 91, n°3, pp. 481–510. Isabelle Huault, "Embeddedness et théorie de l'entreprise. Autour des travaux de Mark Granovetter", *Annales des Mines. Gérer et comprendre*, June 1998, pp. 73–86. Bruce Edmonds, "Captur-ing social embeddedness: A constructivist approach", *Adaptive Behavior*, 1999, volume 7, pp. 323–348. Greta Krippner, "The elusive market: Embeddedness and the paradigm of economic sociology", *Theory & Society*, 2001, volume 30, n°6, pp. 775–810.

35 Kenneth Lipartito, "Business culture: The embeddedness of business", in Geoffrey Jones & Jonathan Zeitlin (eds.), *The Oxford Handbook of Business History*, New York, 2007; Oxford, Oxford University Press, 2008, pp. 605–610.

36 Bjorn Asheim, Philip Cooke & Ron Martin (eds.), *Clusters and Regional Development: Critical Reflections and Explorations*, London, Routledge, 2008. Matthew Jackson, *Social and Economic Networks*, Princeton, Princeton University Press, 2008. Philip Cooke & Andrea Piccaluga (eds.), *Regional Development in the Knowledge Economy*, London, Rout-ledge, 2008.

37 See: Richard Drummond Whitley, "Societies, firms and markets: The social structuring of business systems", in Richard Whitley (ed.), *European Business Systems: Firms, Markets in their National Context*, London, Sage, 1992.

38 John Scott, *Social Network Analysis. A Handbook*, Beverly Hills & London, Sage, 2000 (1st edition, 1995). Matthew Jackson, *Social and Economic Networks*, Princeton, Princeton University Press, 2008.

39 Mark Casson, "Entrepreneurial networks: A theoretical perspective", in Michael Moss, Anthony Slaven & Clara Eugenia Nunez (eds.), *Entrepreneurial Networks and Business Culture*, Seville, Fundacion Fomento de la historian economica, Publicaciones de la Uni-versidad de Sevilla, 1998, pp. 13–28.

40 Kenneth Lipartito, *op. cit.*, pp. 605–610.

41 See Bjorn Asheim, Philip Cooke & Ron Martin (eds.), *Clusters and Regional Development: Critical Reflections and Explorations*, Abingdon, Routledge, 2008.

42 Patrick Boucheron (*et alii*, eds.), *Histoire mondiale de la France*, Paris, Seuil, 2017 (1st edition).

43 Hubert Bonin, "Les vertus de l'économie ouverte?", in Bertrand Blancheton & Hubert Bonin (eds.), *La croissance en économie ouverte (XVIII°–XXI° siècles). Hommages à Jean-Charles Asselain*, Brussels, Peter Lang, 2009, pp. 13–42.

44 Hubert Bonin & Nuno Valerio (eds.), *Colonial & Imperial Banking History*, Abingdon, Routledge, "Banking, Money & International Finance", 2016 (reedited in paperback in 2018).

45 Hubert Bonin, Nuno Valerio & Kazuhiko Yago (eds.), *Asian Imperial Banking History*, Abingdon, Routledge, "Banking, Money & International Finance", 2015. Hubert Bonin,

"French banking in Hong Kong: From the 1860s to the 1950s", in Shizuya Nishimura, Toshio Suzuki & Ranald Michie (eds.), *The Origins of International Banking in Asia: The Nineteenth & Twentieth Centuries*, Oxford, Oxford University Press, 2012, pp. 124–144.

46 Hubert Bonin, "Geo-economics and banking", in Joseph Mark Munoz (ed.), *Advances in Geoeconomics*, Cheltenham, UK; Northampton, US, Edward Elgar, 2017, pp. 217–226. Hubert Bonin, "Banks and geopolitics: Issues of finance connections", in Joseph Mark Munoz (ed.), *Handbook in the Geopolitics of Business*, Cheltenham, UK; Northampton, US, Edward Elgar, 2013, pp. 125–138.

Name index

Abrami, Regina 333
Agawaka, Motoaki 308
Akiter, Shiyern 233
Ardan 23
Arnhold, Jakob 19, 119
Ashein, Bjorn 334
Audap, R. J. 24
Augier, Charles 322

Ball, Alan 332
Banyiai, Richard 234
Barbier Hervé 293
Barrau 202, 218
Bastid, Marianne 24, 34
Baumann 21
Baylin, Jean 218
Becker, Bert 309
Bergère, Marie-Claire 23, 34, 85, 250, 259,
    261, 332
Bertrand 263
Bickers, Robert 11, 34
Blake, Robert 52
Bodeski, Robert 332
Bondeuf 63
Bonin, Hubert xx, 4, 5, 12, 23, 51, 104,
    126, 114, 224, 307, 308, 322, 323,
    331, 332
Borodine, Mikhaël 132
Bouchard 66
Boucheron, Patrick 334
Bouvier, Jean 308, 310
Brandt 63
Branotel 141
Brenier, Henri 307
Brion, René 23
Brocheux, Pierre 309
Brown, Arthur Jodson 332
Brugh, A. 141
Bruguière, Michel 11, 85, 302, 307
Brunterch, Anne xiv, 23
Bucheli, Marcelo 333
Bussière, Éric 331

Cady, Jean-François 309
Cady, John 307
Carlowitz 21, 48, 57, 119
Carlson, Ellsworth 34
Caron, Paul 309
Cassis, Youssef 323
Casson, Mark 334
Césari, Laurent 34
Chain Tong, Chan 173, 174, 178
Chai Sum, Li 87
Chandler, Alfred 333
Chang Kei, Tchou 264
Charlot, E. 108
Charvet 106, 116
Chassagne, Serge 5, 25
Chauvin, R. 19
Checkland, Olive 307
Cheong, Ke 95
Chesneaux, Jean 34
Chih Fu, Tzu 109
Chung, Chang Tue 227, 228
Chung, Tong Fong 84
Clift, Ben 309
Clive, Robert 262
Cochran, Sherman 34, 262, 327, 332
Colin, Lucien 261
Cosnett 261
Cottrell, Philip 323
Cras 233
Craven, John 314
Crisp, Olga 51

Davis, Clarence 44, 322
Dean, Britten 51
De Broc 142
Decker, Stephanie 333
De Courseulles 263
Decoux, Jean 261
Dehoux-Dutilleux 116
Delaunay 54
Deluermoz, Quentin 332
Demaretz, André 84

De Sercey 174
Deu-Fillon, Anne XIV
Drevard, Michel 89

Edmonds, Louis Richard 332
Edward, Evan Watts 11, 23, 51,
    307, 323
Estival, Bernard 293
Evans, R.T. 250
Eynard, G. 143
Ezras 140

Fairbank, John King 63
Feuerwerker, Albert 11, 307
Fieldhouse, David Kenneth 308
Fivel-Démorel, Claude 24, 223, 307
Fook Lam, Li 87
Foo Yao, Chen 66, 84, 95, 221
Forbes, William 116
Fournier, Claude 218
Fredet, Jean 307
Fuller, Charles Baden 333

Gérin, H. Guillaume 84
German, Olivier 333
Gestreaux 156
Gipouloux, François 24, 51, 261
Girault, René 310
Godley, Michael 332
Gonjo, Yasuo 23, 62, 180, 308
Göring, Louis 62, 123
Goubault, G. 43, 142
Grenard 102
Grosjean, Adolphe 57, 124
Grove, Linda 34
Gueneau, Louis 11, 24, 307, 323
Guérin, Veuve 20
Gung, Tse Kai lee 156

Hamaide, Éric 24
Hang Choi, Sze Henry 24
Hao, Yen-P'ing 308
Hei Lung Kiang 314
Heineberg 156
Heng Chi Hao 240
Hen Tang, Tzu 109
Herstatter, Gael 29, 35, 116, 233
Hervy 63
Ho Kieng 132
Hong Thai, Pham 83
Ho, Pui-Yin 104
Hou Chi Ming 34
Hsiang, Ling Chi 109
Hsiang, Liu 132
Hsiung, James 234
Hsu, Joseph 33
Huei, Wang Sing 131

Hung Chang, Li 109
Hy San, Lee 84

Ishii, Kanji 51, 84, 308

Jackson, Matthews 334
Jiang Jieshi/Tchian Kai Chek 173, 226, 265, 326
Jones, Geoffrey 11, 23, 52, 85, 308
Jones, Stephanie 52
Juge, Jean 178, 218, 314

Karberg, Peter 19
Kelly, John 51
Keswick, Maggie 52, 323
Ki Cheung, Wong 87
King, Frank 11, 12, 63, 73, 126, 259, 261,
    307, 308
Kio Ming, Cheng 83
Kipping, Matthias 333
Kirby, William 332
Klein, O. 156
Koerner, Richard 309
Kou, Cheng Tin 183
Krebs, Henri 313
Kronck, Bernard 333
Kubo, Toro 333
Kou Wu, Yung 130
Kurgan-Van Hentenryk, Ginette 51,
    63, 309
Kwang, Kun San 212
Kwung, Chan 79, 80, 85

Labatut 180
Laffey, John 307
Laffond 194
Lam, Chan Yuk 180
Langlois, Richard 333
Lanxin, Xian 34
Lary, Diana 180
Laurent, Jean 179
Le Carduner, Émile 102
Lecomte 53
Lee, Robert 51, 104, 322
Lehman 54, 63
Leong, Shan Ding 84
Li Chai Shum 86
Lieberthal, Kenneth 327, 332
Li 41
Li, Lillian 24, 102, 223
Ling, Chan So 114
Ling General 79
Ling, Wai Tsuk 84
Linsun, Cheng 44
Lipartito, Kenneth 334
Liu 40, 138
Liu, Man-Houng 24
Lordereau 143

Macmillan, Allister 102
Maillard, A. 143
Mak Fook Cho 96, 220
Man Bun, Kwan 44
Man Sang, Wong 89, 95
Marchat, Philippe 72
McKinnon, Stephen 276, 332
Médard 108
Ménouville, Corinne (de) 35
Merlin, Martial 83
Meuleau, Marc 12, 23, 62, 180, 308
Miffret, A. 65, 66, 69
Miller, Christopher 333
Ming, Chang 104
Morlat, Patrice 309
Munslow, Alyn 333
Murphey, Rhoads 63

Nishimura, Shizuya 307
Nordlund, Irene 309
North, Douglass 333

O'Malley 132
O'Neil, Jean 63, 107, 116, 236
Osterhammel, Jürgen 11, 23, 308
Ott, E. 313

Panoff, J. K. 57, 59, 66, 119, 122, 138
Pazsquet, E. 19
Peirlot 156
Pénot, Pascal xiv
Pernotte, André-Joseph 54, 63, 112, 117, 125
Plane, Jean-Michel 333
Poisat, Ch. 8
Poon Hiu Cho 213
Poullet-Osier, G. 24
Prahalad, Coimbatore 334

Quang 41
Quested Rosemary 308

Rawski, Thomas 117
Rayner, Charles 21
Réau, Joseph 53, 63, 72
Rihal, Dorothée 63
Robin, Thierry 333
Rougeau 83
Rowe, William 51
Rowlinson, Michael 333
Ruicheng 68
Ruyters 141

Samarcq, Louis 116
Sassoons 140, 246
Schindler 263
Scott, John 334
Shai, Aron 262, 327, 333
Sheehan, Brett 34, 233
Shen She, Tang 131, 132
Shinonaga, Nobutaka 51, 117
Simon, Philippe 176
Singaravélou, Pierre 11, 26, 34, 43, 332
Sing Seng, Liu 60
Sophers 140
Starr, Peter 85, 202
Sugawara, Ayumu 85, 102
Sugiyama, Shinya 333
Sun Fo 83
Sun Yat Sen 83, 332

Tai Loong, Wing 89, 95
Tamaki, Norio 52, 75
Tang, Chung 186, 222
Tcheng, Chuen Liu 120
Tcheng, Tse-Sio 102, 223
Thang, Leong Dinh 18
Thesmar, J. 24, 102
Thobie, Jacques 23, 306, 322
Tixier, Nicole 11, 23, 24, 72, 307, 322
Tong, Lo Yuk 221
Torres, Félix 333
Trouillet 124
Tsou, Nicolas 109

Varaschin, Denis 34
Varenne, Th. 78
Vaucher 263

Warner, Torsten 51
Weber, Jacques 233
Wei 40
White, Nicholas 233
Whitley, Richard 334
William, Edward 24
Wu, Peifu 130, 131, 133

Yago, Kasuhiko 308
Yamashita, Tet Suo 258
Yang, Sen 130, 133
Yong 191
Yuan, Shi Kai 68, 79, 130
Yuan, Sung Cheh 227, 228
Yung Cieng, Ye 109

Subject index

American interests 7, 92, 93, 94, 95, 105, 108, 109, 144, 153, 154, 155, 161, 162, 187, 202, 203, 214, 215, 280, 281, 282, 320, 321

armaments imports 111, 176–179, 190, 246, 247, 313–315

Banque industrielle de Chine (then *Banque franco-chinoise*) 72, 81, 82, 105, 106, 109, 112, 113, 124, 125, 126, 134, 140, 143, 158, 195, 242, 259, 297, 298

Belgian interests and *Banque belge pour l'étranger* 7, 10, 15, 31, 33, 59, 60, 65, 105, 133, 146, 157, 162, 177, 240, 242, 272, 276, 282, 302, 318, 330

Boyer-Mazet trade house 21, 78, 89, 90, 95, 183, 330

British interests 7, 18, 32, 61, 62, 146, 211, 163, 178, 254, 270

Catholic Missions 33, 65, 80, 106, 107, 235, 236, 246, 281

Chartered Bank 7, 8, 15, 30, 50, 97, 98, 105, 134, 146, 147, 156, 162, 189, 191, 194, 195, 197, 205, 209, 214, 216, 220, 280, 325, 330

Chinese emerging capitalism (trade and banking) 22, 31, 32, 39, 42, 60, 89, 90, 96, 110, 171, 179, 211, 212, 227, 242, 266, 326, 327

Chinese equipment and consuming goods imports 15, 49, 143, 144, 157, 158, 179, 190, 205, 206, 237, 246, 247, 248, 311, 312

Chinese exports of mining ores 156, 157, 166, 179, 180, 267, 270, 272

Chinese goods exports 15, 31, 47, 48, 59, 69, 70, 108, 145, 155, 156, 157, 166, 205, 226, 237, 267, 270, 271, 272, 282, 315, 319

City Bank, and International Banking Corporation 20, 65, 81, 86, 97, 98, 105, 112, 133, 144, 145, 148, 153, 162, 185, 186, 195, 242, 247, 255, 270, 281, 318

Civil wars' effects 27, 36, 37, 67, 68, 77, 79, 80, 83, 84, 113, 120, 121, 129, 130, 131, 132, 133, 173, 174, 264, 265

Comprador's functions 18, 22, 40, 41, 60, 84, 88, 89, 94, 96, 102, 109, 114, 137, 138, 175, 183, 188, 211, 220, 221, 301, 328

Comptoir national d'escompte de Paris (CNEP) 8, 9, 15, 16, 94, 98, 297, 299, 300

currencies markets 29, 36, 57, 81, 93, 94, 97, 107, 119, 120, 140, 141, 174, 175, 184, 187, 217, 218, 230, 232, 233, 241, 249, 250, 252, 253, 256, 272, 275, 280, 281, 282, 288, 320

Deutsch-Asiatische Bank 7, 15, 23, 31, 50, 84, 105, 148, 162, 241, 299, 330

economic crisis 67, 82, 83, 121, 122, 125, 129, 139, 161, 162, 182–184, 190, 191, 263, 279, 282, 287

foreign exchange operations (FOREX) 20, 21, 37, 38, 56, 57, 58, 62, 67, 71, 93, 94, 95, 103, 107, 120, 122, 123, 124, 140, 141, 146, 147, 175, 176, 177, 186, 196, 197, 204, 214, 217, 218, 242, 272, 281, 286, 288, 299, 301, 313, 316, 318, 320, 321, 322, 325

French American Banking Corporation 94, 98, 140, 191, 217, 219, 220, 282, 325

French concession's civil and military life 27, 28, 33, 34, 53, 54, 78, 142, 143, 225, 238, 239, 256, 257, 260, 273, 292

French economic patriotism 6, 7, 8, 9, 10, 15, 43, 45, 55, 68, 69, 71, 98, 105,

142, 144, 236, 237, 246, 270, 275, 280, 297–300, 302, 310, 311, 319, 324–328

Gérin-Drevard trade house 20, 78, 82, 84, 89, 94, 95, 183, 186, 202, 207, 210, 211, 212, 213, 215, 217, 316, 317, 330
German interests 7, 19, 21, 37, 57, 61, 67, 96, 109, 111, 118, 119, 133, 138, 157, 255, 256, 270, 276, 279, 280, 312, 312
Grosjean trade house 66, 120, 124, 138
Guangxi and cluster embeddedness 11, 40, 197, 227, 238, 239, 297, 329, 330

Hong Kong marketplace 7, 20, 97, 98, 147, 173, 176, 190, 197, 204, 303–305
HSBC 7, 8, 15, 16, 20, 22, 23, 30, 31, 40, 50, 65, 67, 69, 72, 81, 86, 92, 97, 98, 105, 109, 125, 133, 134, 145, 146, 152, 156, 162, 163, 178, 187, 189, 191, 197, 214, 216, 220, 221, 240, 245, 268, 297, 298, 302, 303, 305–307, 314, 318, 325, 330

Indochinese connections 8, 202, 215, 216, 217, 303–307
industrial issues 10, 30, 39, 59, 66, 110, 156, 157
international commercial paper exchanges 20, 56, 57, 82, 146, 147, 148, 150, 152, 153, 158, 190, 191, 196, 204, 207, 210, 214, 237, 240, 268, 269, 280, 316

Japanese interests 50, 94, 154, 158, 160, 189, 195, 226, 227, 253
Japanese wars' effects 174, 175, 228–233, 252–256, 264, 265, 288–292
Jardine Matheson 19, 30, 57, 89, 90, 95, 108, 130, 178, 210, 275, 281, 282, 283, 314, 316

Lyon marketplace 19, 20, 88, 89, 90, 91, 95, 183–188, 194, 196, 202, 211, 316, 317, 331

Madier-Ribet trade house 89, 90, 93, 94, 95, 185, 186, 187, 188, 190, 194, 195, 196, 205, 206, 207, 209, 210, 211, 212, 214, 216, 317
management of *Banque de l'Indochine* branches 54, 55, 56, 72, 92, 119, 120, 123, 134, 135, 138, 139, 153, 154, 163, 194–196, 215, 218, 219, 242, 243, 267–269, 283, 284, 328

nationalist and social crisis 86, 87, 131, 132, 175

Olivier trade house 48, 57, 65, 69, 107, 108, 127, 125, 143, 144, 145, 146, 150, 153, 154, 155, 157, 159, 160, 163, 166, 239, 240, 247, 248, 268, 270, 273, 274, 275, 276, 281, 310, 317, 318, 330
open economy, proto-globalisation, and connected history 101, 102, 155, 201, 252, 254, 297, 317, 318, 319, 331

Paris banking and financial place 5, 8
Pearl Rivers cluster 16–18, 21, 22, 77, 78, 86, 96, 98, 100, 172, 197, 201, 202, 223

Racine trade house 48, 65, 66, 69, 107, 108, 120, 135, 143, 144, 145, 146, 159, 239, 268, 275, 301, 330
railways and trade 7, 9, 16, 22, 27, 31, 46, 105, 110, 121, 127, 128, 131, 161, 173, 174, 175, 227, 266, 300, 302, 313
Russian-Chinese Bank (*Banque russo-chinoise*), then Russian-Asiatic Banks 7, 9, 10, 30, 49, 50, 72, 105, 111, 112, 120, 126, 143, 150, 300, 301
Russian interests 7, 9, 16, 39, 48, 49, 111, 112, 132, 301

Shanghai marketplace 17, 38, 47, 59, 67, 107, 150, 197, 279, 283
shipping and trade 15, 18, 22, 118, 172, 202
silk trade 7, 10, 15, 18, 20, 86, 87, 88, 89, 90, 91, 92, 93, 94, 96, 171, 175, 184–188, 205, 207, 209, 214, 215, 216, 217, 316, 317, 320, 321
SWOT management applied analysis 17, 97, 98, 200, 201

tea trade 48, 49, 62, 155, 161, 266
T. E. Griffith (American trade house) 212, 215, 216
Tianjin cluster 26, 29, 30, 32, 33, 34, 237–239, 259, 260

World World I's effects 6, 21, 118–125

Yangze Kiang river cluster 9, 16, 46, 47, 71, 127, 128, 129, 160, 263, 264, 283
Yokohama Specie Bank 7, 50, 81, 86, 97, 158, 174, 195, 231, 242, 255, 258, 259, 299

Printed in the United States
by Baker & Taylor Publisher Services